7/06

FAR

Prais

Path of Honor

"A stubborn, likable heroine."   —Kristen Britain

"An appealing magical fantasy tale featuring a stubborn, independent heroine."   —Baryon Online

"Well plotted and exhibiting superior characterization, it is definitely a worthy sequel that *Path of Fate* readers will want to read."   —*Booklist*

Path of Fate

"Plausible, engrossing characters, a well-designed world, and a well-realized plot."   —*Booklist*

"I thoroughly enjoyed *Path of Fate* by the talented Diana Pharaoh Francis and look forward to more of the adventures of Reisil and her goshawk, Saljane."
          —Kristen Britain, bestselling author of *Green Rider*

"This is an entertaining book—at times compelling—from one of fantasy's promising new voices."
          —David B. Coe, award-winning author of
          Seeds of Betrayal

"In this delightful debut, Diana Pharaoh Francis caught me with a compelling story, intrigued me with the magic of her *ahalad-kaaslane*, and swept me away with her masterful feel for the natural world."
          —Carol Berg, critically acclaimed author of
          Daughter of Ancients

PATH OF BLOOD

Diana Pharaoh Francis

RoC
A ROC BOOK

ROC
Published by New American Library, a division of
Penguin Group (USA) Inc., 375 Hudson Street,
New York, New York 10014, USA
Penguin Group (Canada), 90 Eglinton Avenue East, Suite 700, Toronto,
Ontario M4P 2Y3, Canada (a division of Pearson Penguin Canada Inc.)
Penguin Books Ltd., 80 Strand, London WC2R 0RL, England
Penguin Ireland, 25 St. Stephen's Green, Dublin 2,
Ireland (a division of Penguin Books Ltd.)
Penguin Group (Australia), 250 Camberwell Road, Camberwell, Victoria 3124,
Australia (a division of Pearson Australia Group Pty. Ltd.)
Penguin Books India Pvt. Ltd., 11 Community Centre, Panchsheel Park,
New Delhi - 110 017, India
Penguin Group (NZ), cnr Airborne and Rosedale Roads, Albany,
Auckland 1310, New Zealand (a division of Pearson New Zealand Ltd.)
Penguin Books (South Africa) (Pty.) Ltd., 24 Sturdee Avenue,
Rosebank, Johannesburg 2196, South Africa

Penguin Books Ltd., Registered Offices:
80 Strand, London WC2R 0RL, England

First published by Roc, an imprint of New American Library,
a division of Penguin Group (USA) Inc.

First Printing, May 2006
10 9 8 7 6 5 4 3 2 1

ROC REGISTERED TRADEMARK—MARCA REGISTRADA

Printed in the United States of America

PUBLISHER'S NOTE
This is a work of fiction. Names, characters, places, and incidents either are
the product of the author's imagination or are used fictitiously, and any resem-
blance to actual persons, living or dead, business establishments, events, or
locales is entirely coincidental.

The publisher does not have any control over and does not assume any
responsibility for author or third-party Web sites or their content.

If you purchased this book without a cover you should be aware that this
book is stolen property. It was reported as "unsold and destroyed" to the
publisher and neither the author nor the publisher has received any payment
for this "stripped book."

For Tony, for all you do

ACKNOWLEDGMENTS

Path of Blood is the end of a trilogy. It has been a lot of fun to write in this world and about these characters. It seems appropriate to look back to all those who helped me in so many ways to write this book—who gave me time, space, encouragement, medical treatment, help with research, second and third pairs of eyes, advice, friendship, and plain old love. So let me first thank Tony, Quentin, and Sydney. Likewise Bill and Vi Pharaoh, David and Linda Francis, Megan Glasscock, Sharman Horwood, Elizabeth Covington, Lucienne Diver, Gerald Dorros, Gus Varnavus, Pat Grantham, Carol Berg, Fighter Guy and the Roundtable, Kevin Kvalvik, Mindy Klasky, Lyn McConchie, Kristen Britain, David Coe, Jennifer Stevenson, M. Joan Harvey, the entire Cox clan, Jack Kirkley, Alan Pollack, Ray Lundgren, Tiffany Yates, Debbie Sporich, and Kathryn LaFerriere.

I'd like especially to thank Jennifer Heddle and Liz Scheier. Jen bought these books and had faith that I could pull them off. Liz adopted me after Jen left and has been a great editor and very enthusiastic about my books.

And last, and most important of all, thank you to all of you who have bought my books and read them. You are my heroes. I couldn't do this without you. Don't forget to visit me at www.sff.net/people/di-francis. Thanks to you, there will be more books coming.

I know there are some whose names I've forgotten here, and for that I apologize. I wish I had a better memory.

Chapter 1

Tapit wasn't dead.

Reisil drove her sweat-drenched gelding across the scree, her heart thundering in her chest. She felt a sickening lurch as the rocky slope began to roll away beneath them. Ahead, Yohuac's horse—formerly Tapit's—bounded onto firm ground and galloped into the trees.

Indigo twisted, his haunches sliding as he scrabbled over the tumbling rocks. He neighed: a desperate, braying sound. Reisil leaned forward, catching at the rolling scree with a net of magic. She gasped at the pain, the magic flowing through her. She grinned fiercely as the rocks firmed into a stony carpet. Indigo lunged to safety with a groan. Reisil reined him in and swung around.

Tapit appeared from behind an outcropping. Quickly, Reisil let the magical net unravel. The freed rocks thundered down the escarpment between them. In the same heartbeat, Reisil reached out to Saljane.

~Where are you?

The image of a glittering snow-covered peak whirled across Reisil's mind's eye, followed by a pastiche of blue sky, trees, and Baku's reptilian shape.

~With Baku. Mysane Kosk is not far. Saljane paused. *He comes?*

The fear in Saljane's mindvoice stung Reisil like a nettle. It was the only thing the goshawk feared: Tapit and his *ilgas* and losing her tie to her *ahalad-kaaslane*.

Reisil glared across the churning stones. The wizard wore his hood down around his shoulders. His features were sharp and austere beneath his bristle of dark hair. She felt his dour gaze on her like a coal-hot brand.

Her hands tightened on her reins. Indigo snorted and took a step back.

~He's here.

Saljane clutched at Reisil's mind with iron talons.

~Watch well, she urged, her voice sounding wire-thin.

~I will, beloved.

Reisil held her magic ready. Her skin prickled. She darted a glance about herself. She couldn't let him drop an *ilgas* on her. If he did, she would be helpless. Infinitely worse, she'd be cut off from Saljane. The prospect was unbearable. Never again would she let Tapit do that to her. Her fist knotted. How much she would love to drive it down his throat! But she didn't dare try. Not now. Too much was at stake, and she was too weak.

She eyed the scree. It wouldn't hold him long. Tapit was relentless. But his horse was as tired as Indigo, and it appeared the wizard had outstripped his companions. That might give Reisil the advantage she needed.

"Don't stop running now. I was looking forward to a better fight than this," Tapit taunted through the dusty haze left behind by the slide.

"You haven't caught me yet. And don't forget I destroyed your stronghold," Reisil retorted.

"The stronghold still stands, and only a handful of us lost. We are eager for your return."

His gloating words sent a tremor through Reisil. The stronghold still stood? It wasn't possible. She'd seen . . .

She'd seen the entry valley cave in when she'd driven a spear of pure power deep into the mountain's core. She'd seen rubble falling over the small group of defenders as the ground leaped and buckled. The stronghold had been crushed. Hadn't it? But then again, she'd thought she'd killed Tapit, too. Fear slithered like a snake in her gut. She was counting on having crippled the wizards so that she wouldn't have to deal with them plus the sorcerers and the Regent's army.

"You're a liar!" she shouted back, refusing to let him see her doubt.

"You shall see for yourself soon enough. You should not have run away. You belong to us. As does the property you took with you."

"Never. I am *ahalad-kaaslane*. I'll not let you take us again. And if I haven't destroyed the stronghold, I'll come back and do it. That much I *can* promise you."

"Ah, yes. *Ahalad-kaaslane*." He said it the way one would speak of a rat infestation. "Where is your bird? That was our mistake. To be one of us, you must be rid of your pet."

"To be one of you?" Reisil repeated, her mouth dropping open.

"Of course."

Reisil's teeth cracked together as she snapped her mouth shut. She shook her head in disbelief. "After all of you I've killed? You're howling mad."

"We know how to muzzle your bite. You will be made to heel."

He sounded so sure, so smug. Anger flamed in Reisil, and power crackled around her fingers. She would never succumb to them again. Her lip curled and she pulled her arm back, feeling the magic surging through her. But reason caught her. She balled her fist, forcing the power down with effort. "How do you think you'll catch me? I know about the *ilgas*. I won't walk into that trap again."

Tapit smiled. It was the first time Reisil could ever remember seeing such an expression cross his basalt features. Fear screwed through the marrow of her bones.

"Not *that* trap, no."

Reisil recoiled, then felt a small smile begin. He loved the hunt, the struggle. *Don't stop running now. . . .* He wanted her to sweat, to fear, to fight. He relished it. So much so that he wasn't going to even try to use his power against her in a head-on battle. That wasn't sporting. He wanted to match wits, to finesse her, to draw this hunt out. And she was happy to oblige. It gained her time.

And she'd begin right now.

~Baku?

The coal-drake's awareness bubbled in her mind. His presence was muted, as if he had to push through a dense, fibrous mist to reach her. The effects of the magic leaching from Mysane Kosk. It was the reason he hadn't been able to speak with their friends who camped near the destroyed city. He couldn't tell Juhrnus they were coming, or ask for help. But it also meant that Tapit would have a harder time tracking them. The wizard had the ability to sniff out their magic footprint, but soon it would be smothered by the tide of magic rolling out of Mysane Kosk. It was the reason Reisil had sent Baku and Saljane ahead: to hide them from Tapit and to warn those gathered at Mysane Kosk that she was coming.

~I have an idea, but I need your help. Can you do it? she sent to Baku, picturing for him what she wanted him to do.

The coal-drake did not respond immediately. Reisil got the impression he was considering whether he *wanted* to help her. She held her breath. He had every right to resent her. If only she had learned faster, if only she could have rescued him from the wizards sooner. But she hadn't known what to do, and instead she'd been forced to watch silently as Kvepi Debess tortured Baku. Sometimes she had even helped. It had been the only way to discover the key to unlocking the prison spells. It wasn't until later that she could tell Baku, and by then their delicate trust was ruined.

~Can you do it? she pressed gently.

When his answer came, he sounded hollow.

~It will be difficult. The magic thickens here. . . . I will try.

~Hurry.

Reisil waited, watching not Tapit, but his leggy roan mare. The horse tossed her head, ears twitching. Then suddenly she leaped into the air, twisting and bucking. The wizard gave a startled yell and fell onto the scree. The hillside began to roll again. The mare came down and bolted, disappearing over the ridge. Tapit tumbled down the slope like a bundle of rags.

~She won't soon trust him again, came Baku's smug voice.

~Well-done, Reisil said, following Yohuac's trail into the trees. By the time Tapit could bespell the mare to stop, he'd have a good walk to retrieve her. It gave them a little breathing room.

"A very little," Reisil muttered.

Yohuac was waiting just inside the trees. He smiled crookedly at her scowl. His scalp gleamed white through the stubble of his hair. Scars showed livid on his head and neck. There were plenty more hidden by his clothing.

"You shouldn't have waited."

He shrugged.

Reisil blew out a tense breath. "Come on then. We've still got a long way to go."

She took the lead, angling down a steep ravine and following it up across a ridge. Clouds thickened above, and as evening approached, a heavy, solid rain began to fall. She looked back at Yohuac. He had begun to list to the right, his hands clamped around the pommel, his shoulders bowed. He couldn't keep on much longer. Reisil swallowed her frustration. He was doing all he could. The wizards had nearly killed him. It was a lot that he could sit a horse at all. She scanned the wood slope, angling up along the ridge. They would have to stop and rest, and hope Tapit didn't overtake them in the night.

As darkness fell, the two found a traveler's pine and took shelter under its sweeping boughs, staking the horses out in a nearby clearing.

Reisil dug a hole and built a tiny fire. She set a pot over it and made a hearty soup of roots and dried meat, crumbling stale acorn cakes into it. "I can't wait to eat some real bread," Reisil said to Yohuac, who sat shivering beneath both their blankets. "And hot kohv. With nussa spice."

"The bread I would like. But you may keep your kohv," he said, accepting the cup of soup and wrapping both his hands around it.

"That's right. You like that other stuff—what do you call it?"

"Xochil. It has . . . character."

"Mmm. I don't much care if my kohv has character."

"Your kohv is like— It's like the sun without heat, without flame. Xochil lights fire to the soul."

"Sounds unsettling."

"Someday you will try it and see."

Reisil finished eating and scooted over next to him, curling close against his side. He put an arm around her shoulders and snugged the blankets around her. Soon their shared warmth permeated them both. Yohuac's hands began to wander over her, absently at first, and then earnestly. Reisil caught them.

"You need to rest. You are still not well."

Yohuac's dark eyes shone like polished onyx. "I am well enough for this." He bent and kissed her. Reisil kissed him back. She pushed aside his clothing, grappling him close against her, his heart beating rapidly beneath her fingers. There was an urgency to their lovemaking. They hadn't lain together since Tapit had sent them fleeing; neither knew when they'd have the chance again.

Time was running out.

Reisil nestled against Yohuac's side, their legs tangled together. His chest rose and fell in a slow rhythm. She stared up at the branches overhead. Time was running out, and she had no solution to Mysane Kosk.

She'd thought about nothing else since escaping the wizards, and she still had no ideas.

She sighed and sat up, pulling her clothes on. She crawled out from under the drooping branches of the great pine, needing to be out under the sky. The rain had settled into a soft drizzle. Mist wound through the trees. The pungent scents of pine, hemlock, and cedar filled her nose as she drew a cleansing breath. She closed her eyes, listening to the patter of the rain on the trees, the rush of the wind through the treetops, and the trickle of water across the ground.

She wondered where Tapit was. Her stomach tightened and she scanned the tree line. Nothing. She turned and climbed up the slope to the top of the ridge. There was nothing to see. The mist filled the hollows and valleys in softly glowing gauze. Gray hid the moon and stars. She sat down on a boulder, unmindful of the rain soaking her clothes.

She didn't know how long she sat before Yohuac appeared out of the drizzling wet like a ghost. He settled beside her, not touching. She was glad of that.

"What good am I if I can't figure out what to do?" she demanded suddenly, the sudden sharpness shattering the rhythmic peace of the rain. She flushed hotly and clamped her lips together. But the words were coming now and she couldn't stop them. "It all seems impossible. Like a lock without a key." Reisil dug her fingers through her hair. "The Lady told me I have judgment, that I'm capable of making the right choices for Kodu Riik. But the Lady was wrong. I don't know how to stop the plague or the spell the wizards cast. And now Tapit is chewing at our heels."

"You will find a way. I am certain."

"And if I don't? Kvepi Debess said that I wasn't really a healer. That I was better at destroying. Battlemagics, he said. What if that's true? Right now Kodu Riik and Mysane Kosk need healing. What if I can't do it?"

"Then all will be remade. Nothing we care about will remain."

"That's helpful. Got any other advice?"

"It is what it is."

Reisil chewed the inside of her cheek, tasting blood. The pain felt like punishment, one that she deserved. She'd been keeping a terrible secret. She didn't want to confess it, but she forced the words past her constricted throat.

"It might be my fault," she said tightly. "I know, I *know,* like I know my own name, that I am supposed to save the *nokulas.* The Lady said to protect *all Her people,* and She meant the *nokulas* too." She paused, tasting the bitterness of her feelings. "But . . . *I do not want to.* They took the Iisand, they took Sodur—"

She broke off and swallowed. How much of what Sodur had done to her had been because he was turning into a *nokula*? Would he have turned the *ahalad-kaaslane* against her if the *nokulas* hadn't infected him? She curled her hands into fists. She hated them. Almost as much as she hated the wizards. "They've slaughtered entire villages. I've seen it. They're vicious. They like to torture people, and they don't care about who they used to be. They'd just as soon kill us all as not. They aren't really ours anymore. They don't belong in Kodu Riik." She spit the last words with a venom that came from the deepest part of her soul.

"You wish to see them exterminated."

"Of course not!" Reisil said quickly. And was astonished to find it was true. Somewhere deep inside burned the hope that they could be returned to themselves. That she could have Sodur back. Finding the plague-healers had fanned the flames of that hope. But either way . . . she was supposed to save them. The Lady had given her no choice. Being *ahalad-kaaslane* meant obeying the Lady, even when She had abandoned Kodu Riik. Even if it meant watching her friends die to help save the monsters that wanted to kill them. Reisil's lip curled in silent fury.

Yohuac began coughing beside her, and she suddenly became aware how wet he was. She jumped to her feet, frowning.

"You shouldn't be out in the rain. Why aren't you asleep?"

He reached out and curled a long, damp tendril of her hair around his fingers. Reisil leaned into his touch. "I sleep better with you."

"I don't think I'm going to sleep well for a long time to come," Reisil said. She stood. "Come on. You need to get dry."

Under the traveler's pine, she rekindled the fire and made more soup. While it cooked, she and Yohuac dressed in dry clothing from their packs. The soup bubbled and sizzled as drops spattered into the fire. Reisil rescued the pot and served them both and sat opposite Yohuac to avoid temptation. When each had scraped the bottom of the bowl, Reisil turned her attention back to Yohuac. Weariness made his shoulders droop and dulled his eyes. Worse were the scars that marked him from head to foot. She was responsible for some of those. And there would be more to come. She gathered herself.

Throughout the five weeks since their escape from the wizards, she'd been content to drift from moment to moment, speaking little, thinking even less. It had been a time of healing, a chance to rebuild their strength. But Tapit's arrival had shattered their idyll, and it was time to get back to work.

"Tell me about your magic. What can you do?"

Yohuac's body twitched, his expression shuttering. He sat straight, his legs crossed, fingers laced tightly.

"Understand that I was never supposed to *use* magic," he said harshly. "I was meant to be a vessel— to win the *pahtia* and become *Ilhuicatl*'s son-in-the-flesh. In the following year of celebration, every woman in Cemanahuatl would come to my bed. On each I would get a child. Even barren women. In this way, the nahuallis thought to revive the magic in our people."

Reisil nodded, unnerved by a sudden avalanche of jealousy. He'd told her this once before. But then he didn't mean anything to her. Now . . . her toes curled inside her boots.

"Are you saying that you don't know what you can do?" Reisil asked, frowning.

He lifted his shoulders in a jerky shrug.

"You've never tried anything at all?"

He looked away, his face wooden.

"Yohuac?"

"It's useless. I can do nothing."

Reisil leaned forward, touching his arm with her fingers. He flinched. "You *have* tried something, haven't you? I need to know. You're a piece of this puzzle, and I have to know what you are if I'm going to succeed."

He swallowed, his throat jerking, and then nodded. "As you wish. But be warned. . . ."

And then he lifted his hand, holding it out, palm down. After a moment, small clumps of dirt danced into the air and began to rotate slowly. Their speed increased, drawing up more dirt, twigs, and needles. Soon a small tornado whirled beneath Yohuac's hand. It began to widen. Reisil could feel the tug of coiling wind. The fire flamed higher and then guttered as the funnel pulled harder. Pressure built against Reisil's lungs, and she fought for breath. Dark spots clouded her vision as flying debris stung her face and hands.

"Yohuac, stop!"

He looked up at her, his mouth a stiff line. Blood trickled down his cheeks and forehead where he'd been struck by a chunk of wood. He jerked his head, fear flickering in his eyes. Reisil's stomach twisted. He *couldn't* stop. By the Lady, *he couldn't stop!*

She rolled up onto her knees, her heart pounding in her ears. Her head ached as if it were being squeezed in a vise, and she wheezed as she tried to breathe. She reached for her magic. It filled her raw channels in a flood of pain. She ignored it, feeling the ground beneath her knees beginning to shudder as the great pine that sheltered them began to uproot itself.

She released her magic slowly, in loose, gauzy strands. They wound around Yohuac and the maelstrom, wrapping them in a smothering ball like sticky silk. Reisil bore down carefully. Her magic swelled and pushed against her fragile control. Reisil trembled as she fought to hold the flow steady. Yohuac thrashed against the wild tide of his own raging power. It ricocheted violently within the cocoon Reisil wove. Its whirling edges tore the strands. As fast as she repaired them, they were torn again.

She could see his panic—felt its echo pounding its fists inside her. Yohuac's eyes bulged as he fought with silent desperation. Sweat ran down Reisil's forehead and stung her eyes. Her chest ached and her jaw hung open as she gasped for air. Dirt and needles filled her mouth. She coughed. Her magic roared as her concentration slipped. Frantically she grappled at it. She let it flow faster, knowing neither she nor Yohuac could last much longer before they both exploded in flames. The sticky strands whipped from her hands in thick ropes. Soon she could no longer see him behind the wrap of magic. She tightened. Slowly she could feel the maelstrom beginning to subside as she pushed against it.

Reisil felt something *give*, like a stubborn lock turning. Relief rushed over her. She let go of the cocoon, her magic draining away. Debris pattered down onto the ground, dust hazing the air. Yohuac keeled over on his side, panting heavily. Reisil sucked in a deep breath and then another, feeling her spinning head beginning to steady. She crawled over to Yohuac, pulling the blanket over his clammy length.

"So you can move the earth. I thought that was just in bed," she rasped, resting her forehead on his shoulder. She wrinkled her nose, smelling her own stink of sweat and fear.

He slid his arms around her. "You should see what I can do with wind."

Reisil closed her eyes. Yohuac had far more power than she'd ever dreamed. No wonder the wizards wanted him back. *He is what he was bred to be. The seed of the nahualli magic. And they didn't bother to train him. Idiots. And being this close to Mysane Kosk isn't helping.*

"I'll show you how to control it."

She was surprised when he pushed her away. "No. I am not meant to use this power, only to carry it. It is forbidden."

Reisil's eyes narrowed. "You have to. I can't do this alone."

"Don't forget the nahualli—Nurema. Baku has his own powers as well. And your friends. They are very resourceful."

Reisil bit back her reply. He looked haggard. His skin was scraped raw. She would work on convincing him later. "They'll have to be."

Reisil clambered to her feet, banking the fire. "You rest. I'll keep first watch."

"Don't forget to wake me. You need to rest as much as I." Yohuac waited until she nodded agreement before closing his eyes and dropping instantly into a heavy sleep. Reisil donned her green cloak and crawled out from under the tree. She took up a position in the shadow of a narrow ledge.

The mist grew thicker, even as the rain pelted harder. Soon it was difficult to see more than a few yards. Nor could she hear anything but the rushing wind and the rattling water.

Her eyes grew heavy and she knuckled them, watching the mist slide in and out of the trees. And then she went cold, her skin prickling.

She wasn't alone.

She stiffened, blinking the rain from her lashes as a monstrous shape shivered into being before her.

It was the color of moonlit water, with silver eyes that curved like a bowl. Its face was heavy-boned, with jutting jaws and dagger teeth. Its body was muscular, fluid and sleek—like a mountain lion. Its fingers moved like tentacles and were tipped with thick, tearing claws. Its feet were bony and long, with talons that curved like scythes and bit gouges in the dirt. A long tail twitched slowly back and forth behind it.

Reisil stared up at it in frozen horror, too stunned to defend herself.

Nothing remained of the man he'd been. Its expression was alien, its body monstrous. But there was something about the tilt of its head, the way it turned sideways to look at her, like a bird.

"Sodur," she whispered past the hard lump lodged in her throat. "By the Lady, it's you."

Chapter 2

The world spun around Reisil. She smelled the tang of wet bark and pine—the fresh-washed scent of the mountains. Impinging on it was a cold, flat odor that made her skin crawl and lungs ache. Roaring filled her ears like the sound of stampeding horses. Behind her, the rock shelf dug unforgiving into her back as she shoved away from the *nokula*. She scrabbled for a weapon, finding a sharp-edged stone. This was not Sodur. Could not be Sodur.

The *nokula* stood an arm's length away, the rain beading on its silvery hide. It watched her. She shifted, making no attempt to move. She didn't want to get any closer to those knife-filled jaws than she had to.

~You are hunted.

Reisil shuddered and jerked away, yelping as her head bounced off the stone shelf. Needles splintered through her skull, and she was grateful for the pain.

"Don't," she said, holding up the rock, though she hardly knew what she might do with it. "Stay out of my head."

~We must speak. I have little time left. Reisil's gorge rose, and she swallowed noisily.

"Who are you?" she asked, though the cadence of his words and the brusque edge to his tone were as familiar to her as her own hands.

The *nokula* smiled. Or Reisil thought it was a smile. Perhaps it was a snarl. They were likely the same. Its voice sounded amused and predatory.

~You have already guessed.

Unbidden, an image rose in her mind. It was a bittersweet memory, from before Sodur's betrayal, before he made everyone think she was the worm in their apple. He was showing her around the Lady's Temple for the first time. He had led her beneath the trees, their leaves sifting together softly in the breeze, the air smelling softly of wisteria and roses. His back had been to her as he recited the history of the Temple.

As the memory rolled through her mind, Reisil's teeth clicked together and her skin went clammy. She was seeing it exactly as she remembered, from *her* perspective. Fear uncoiled in her chest. Somehow he'd plucked it from her mind. Furiously she slammed her mental barriers shut, ejecting him forcefully from her thoughts.

A faintly startled expression crossed his face.

Reisil's chin jutted. "Stay. Out. Of. My. Head."

He opened his mouth. His rounded tongue lolled out, slithering in the air. Nonsensical breathy sounds issued forth.

For a moment Reisil wanted to laugh. Then a tide of fury and bitterness rose up in her. He was manipulating her again. Making her do things his way. Did it never stop?

She took a breath, counting to ten. She let it out with a whoosh and glared at him resentfully. He knew more about Mysane Kosk and his fellow *nokulas* than she did. She didn't have a choice.

~Fine. What do you want?

~You must not go to Mysane Kosk.

~Why not?

Sodur made a guttural sound and swiped suddenly at his head with a heavy paw. Sparkling ridges rose where his claws scraped painful, deep furrows into his flesh. If it could be called flesh. Reisil gasped and drew back against the rock.

~You are hunted, he repeated, his voice sounding tinny and frayed.

~Tell me something I don't know.

~Not just the wizards. They . . . we *. . . want you.*

He cuffed at himself again and hunched lower to the ground. Reisil watched in fascination as he twisted his head as if to escape some sort of painful sound. Suddenly an unearthly wail rose out of the night. Reisil found herself raising the rock above her head. The sound went on and on. An earthquake began deep in her gut, moving outward and growing more powerful with every breath. The rock dropped from her limp fingers.

Then a wordless screech broke across Reisil's mind, shattering the howl into pieces. Reisil slammed closed her mental barriers.

~Dear heart, thank you.

~It is really Sodur?

~He hasn't been Sodur for a long time.

Before she could answer, another shape emerged out of the misty trees. It was half again as large as Sodur. It reminded her of Baku, with elegant ripples of muscle and a long, reptilian body. It radiated tension and threat. Reisil swallowed jerkily. Could it be? How could Lume have turned into something so big? And yet she didn't doubt it was Sodur's *ahalad-kaaslane* turned *nokula*. Somehow the lynx had become this hulking brute.

She felt the scritch of claws against her mental walls and stared in repulsion. Lume too?

The beast bared his fangs at her and pressed close to Sodur, who nudged him with his shoulder in affectionate acknowledgment. Lume regarded Reisil, dipping his head in something like an apology. Reisil lowered her mental walls uneasily.

~They didn't plan for us, Sodur said, stroking Lume in a loving way that struck Reisil as somehow reassuring. Maybe something of Sodur yet remained. Maybe he could still be recovered.

~We have resisted the call to come to Mysane Kosk, he continued, oblivious to the whisper of thought. *But*

the pull is strong. Soon we must go. He whipped his head from side to side as if to dislodge a swarm of biting flies. *This must be quick. Everything I say, everything I think, the rest know. We share a mind; they would silence me—*

He recoiled suddenly, collapsing on the ground and twitching spasmodically. He emitted an aching cry that sounded like a soul-riven *rashani* and made Reisil's intestines contract. He flailed and clawed furrows into his neck and face. Lume nuzzled close, and his touch seemed to lend Sodur the strength to resist the invisible onslaught. He rolled to his feet, staring at Reisil with that unnerving, lidless gaze. There were chunks of silvery flesh clotted in his claws. The gashes gaped bloodless like wounds on a corpse.

~I still don't understand what you want.

He gave a frustrated sigh. It sounded so . . . human . . . that Reisil stared askance.

~Imagine a school of fish, the way it turns and moves as if of a single mind. So are nokulas. The individual cannot resist. His mind conforms, like sand under the lash of the wind and sea.

~But you are here even though the rest don't want you to talk to me?

The Sodur nodded in that oddly human fashion.

~Lume and I have resisted. And some others. Ahaladkaaslane mostly. But the others are very strong.

He was referring to the wizards who had been caught up in the spell they cast at Mysane Kosk. Reisil shuddered.

~You must not go to Mysane Kosk. You must go far away.

~Why?

~They know you have come to destroy Mysane Kosk. They will stop you. They mean to . . . convert . . . you. It requires only that you be drawn inside the circle surrounding Mysane Kosk. You will become nokula. There will be no hope for Kodu Riik. Get away where they cannot find you! And do not fool yourself. This

is no illness that can be cured or reversed. The change is irrevocable. You can neither save us, nor can you be saved if you are changed.

She eyed Sodur closely, ice spiraling down her spine and boring into her stomach. Here was a danger she hadn't considered. Bright Lady, what could she do? She could defend herself with magic, but could she fight them off without killing them? Or worse, without destroying Mysane Kosk, and Kodu Riik with it? Could she fight them off at all? They were made of magic. And the change was eternal. There was no reversing it. The spark of hope she'd nurtured for Sodur and the Iisand guttered and went out. She shoved the pain of that final loss away, focusing on the problem at hand. The entire cadre of wizards who'd created the spell had become *nokula*. She couldn't begin to guess how powerful they were. Reisil licked her lips, taking a slow breath, fear clamping her throat. But she couldn't run. Kodu Riik would still be destroyed, not to mention the rest of the world—and Cemanahuatl.

Sodur picked this out of her racing mind. She felt his urgency shoving at her with physical force. She pushed back.

"Do not try that again," she said, her voice like metal.

~You must go! If you stay—if you are caught—you will destroy Kodu Riik!

His frantic words lashed her mind, and black streaks sizzled across her vision at their intensity. She doubled over, bracing herself against the rock shelf and locking her knees against the agonized clench of her body.

"To leave means the same." It was all she could do to force the words out. "The only hope is to continue. If I don't save Mysane Kosk then Kodu Riik dies too." Her body shuddered and spasmed as agony burrowed into her mind, chewing nerves and shredding bone.

~No! They will not allow it! They will take you!

The battering on her mind redoubled. Reisil sobbed and fell to the ground.

Sudden fury erupted in her mind. A tearing beak and slashing talons. Saljane. The goshawk ripped at Sodur's hold on Reisil's mind. He gave a high-pitched yelp and reeled backward. Lume crouched, a growl sounding loud in his throat. Into the battlefield of Reisil's mind bounded his animal presence. He howled and launched himself at Saljane, following Reisil's mental tie to the goshawk. But Reisil had defeated a harder foe in Baku. Freed of Sodur's onslaught, she snatched Lume and flung him forty paces to crash against the thick bole of an ancient hemlock.

There was a crackling sound like bones snapping, but Reisil couldn't care. He vanished from her mind. Breathing heavily, she quickly reconstructed the blockade protecting her mind, holding fast to Saljane's fierce strength.

Lume lay in a limp heap at the base of the tree. Sodur had not moved, had not made a sound. He might as well have been made of stone. Reisil could not read the expression on his face. And she would not open her mind again to hear his words.

When he continued motionless, watching her, she gritted her teeth and strode over to Lume, driven by her healer nature and the memory of the lynx. As she neared, the great beast's skin began to wriggle and twitch. Knobby shapes thrust angularly outward, distorting the silvery expanse of his hide. Reisil halted, fear curling through her. It looked as if something inside was trying to escape. Then as abruptly as they began, the movements ceased. Long moments trickled past, marked only by the sough of the wind and the drip of the rain.

Suddenly Lume gave a loud *chuff* and rolled lightly to his feet, his brilliant silver eyes hard, his head ducked low. Reisil lunged away, her magic balled ready in her hands. But faster than a thought, Sodur rushed between, one taloned claw splayed over his

companion's face, the other held up curved and ready
as he watched Reisil.

Reisil and Sodur stared at each other, held in place
by threat and— Memories of Sodur skipped across Reisil's mind. His kindness when she'd refused the bond
with Saljane, his strength when she struggled to find
out who she was, his guidance when she felt so lost.
It hadn't been all lies.

"You were wrong before and you're wrong now. If
you want to help, convince your new friends to stay
out of my way. You, too."

Sodur's head tilted, but he remained a menacing
statue. He would stay frozen, she realized slowly. Until
he could speak to her again. She clung more tightly
to Saljane.

~Speak.

~I can no longer resist them. They will have all I know.

Reisil didn't answer for a long moment, realization
dawning. A slight sigh escaped her.

*~You want me to kill you, to keep them from taking
you. They have enough of you to keep you from doing
it yourself.*

~Yes.

There was a desperate wealth of hope in the word.
Reisil could see the logic. Sodur knew so much about
the *ahalad-kaaslane,* about her, and about Kodu Riik.
That knowledge could only help the *nokulas.* She shook
her head, pulling her magic in and sending it back to
where it belonged. She sagged as it drained away.

~No.

He snarled. Reisil found herself smiling at his fury,
her cheeks feeling cramped and stiff.

~They already have other ahalad-kaaslane—*who
knows how many? They have the Iisand—I'm assum-
ing he's already gone to them, right?* Reisil nodded at
Sodur's faint affirmative. *And you have said they can
read your mind. Likely the real damage is done. But
there's a chance you'll still be able to help me. I don't
think they can make you or any other* ahalad-kaaslane
forget your vows to the Lady and this land.

She squared her shoulders.

"It's a chance. You have to take it. I know—I *know*—the Lady wants me to save Mysane Kosk. And the *nokulas*. Tell them that. Tell them if the spell the wizards cast to create the *nokulas* isn't stopped, it will destroy Kodu Riik. It will destroy the entire world. Maybe if they know that, they'll give me time to find a way. But no matter what, it's time you stopped sabotaging me and do something helpful."

~They will not risk letting you go free. You are too dangerous. Again pressure rose in her mind, hammering at her. *Go!*

She slammed her mental walls shut for the last time. She shook her head. "I'm going to Mysane Kosk. You do what you have to do."

With that she turned and strode away in measured steps. Not running, though every minute she half expected to be knocked to the ground. Her mouth was dry and she felt cold. She slipped through the mist between the trees. When she thought she was out of sight, she glanced over her shoulder and then jeered at herself. They could be right beside her for all she knew. She couldn't see them unless they wanted to her to.

Could she?

Her steps faltered. Reisil stopped, turning. She refocused her eyes, looking about her with spellsight. The world glowed in muted pastel shades of life—the foundation of magic. But nothing else. So either they remained behind, or they were invisible still.

Reisil spun around and hurried through the darkness. She and Yohuac had to leave now. And they'd not stop again until they reached Mysane Kosk.

~Saljane! Take Baku. Go to Mysane Kosk. Go now, fast as you can. Warn the others. I'm coming and bringing the wizards and nokulas *with me.*

For a moment Reisil thought of Tapit and smiled. Her blood roared and her hands trembled. But it wasn't fear. She felt more like a mother bear protecting her cubs. And she was done running.

Chapter 3

The morning dawned cold and wet over Mysane Kosk and the stockade settlement that Mctyein, Kebonsat, and Juhrnus had named Honor. Mist filled the valley like a bowl of milk. Eight hulking shapes humped out of the ghostly gloom. A cacaphony sounded from its blanketing depths: whacking hammers and axes, grating saws, creaking wagons, barking dogs, and anxious shouts.

Kebonsat stood in the unnamed seventh stockade, which consisted of hardly more than palisade walls. There weren't even gates yet. He frowned at the eighth, which looked like it had been eaten away by maggots, leaving only skeletal timbers poking up through the mist. Eight stockades, only six of them completed. And there were plans for more, as time allowed. If time allowed. It still wasn't going to be enough. Wooden walls and earthworks weren't going to slow the Regent's army much. Without weapons, the defenders were toothless.

"Will it all get done in time?"

Kebonsat started, glancing over at Metyein, who had climbed up to stand beside him. His hair was damp and curling. Beneath his cloak, he wore serviceable clothing made of blue wool and leather. Kebonsat's eyes narrowed. Metyein was not wearing his newly-minted pin of office marking him as Lord Marshal of Honor.

"In time for what, exactly? The Regent to come

calling? The plague? Mysane Kosk to swallow us?" he asked sardonically. He pulled up his hood as the rain began again, tangled in a bitterness that never let go. "When the plague hits here, we'll have more room than we want."

Metyein said nothing, his face pulled into sharp lines of worry.

"We should think about a quarantine station—a way to protect ourselves from infected newcomers," Kebonsat said. It wasn't the first time he'd made the argument, and already Metyein was shaking his head.

"We can't. Everyone is welcome here. And we can't afford to split our defenses."

"The people aren't going to be so generous when their families start getting sick. We'll likely have a revolt. It's going to get very ugly."

"We can't protect something that far away from our center. Even if we had enough weapons."

There was no good argument for that, and so Kebonsat remained silent. He brooded down at the thinning mist, beginning to see the scuttling shapes of working men like beatles exploding from a nest.

"At least we have shelter and crops in the ground," Metyein said in the voice of someone trying to look at the bright side of things.

Kebonsat relented. They *had* done a lot. More than he'd expected. Metyein had turned out to be a decisive and organized leader. Thanks to him, they had walls, planted fields, firewood, and hunters bringing in meat. "With Dannen Relvi's shipments, I imagine we'll not starve," he said, meaning it to be a compliment. But it sounded more like an accusation. The never-resolved fears of how to defend against Aare's army nagged at him. "But you know as well as I that it won't mean a thing unless we can make some weapons. Something better than cudgels and arrows. We won't hold a siege long with those."

"We don't have a choice," Metyein snapped. "Every bit of metal we find has to go to protecting our people and stock. Otherwise there won't even be a siege, just a bloodbath." He grimaced. "My horse has given his shoes to the cause. There's not a metal fork or spoon to be had, and the miners have been sleeping with their shovels."

Kebonsat sighed, admitting defeat. For now. Metyein was right. They both were. Priorities.

"How are the tunnels coming?" he asked briskly, forcibly turning his mind from his worries about weapons and plague.

"We had several collapses last night. Right now, the only two with a through drift are Lion and Eagle. How we can have so much rain here and the rest of Kodu Riik be so dry, I cannot understand. Once we get some decent weather, we'll be able to shore up the tunnels easily enough." He paused. "I wish—" He broke off, flicking a glance at Kebonsat.

"You wish Reisil would get here and we'd know what we were going to do," Kebonsat finished.

"Yes, but—" Metyein paced away restlessly.

"But what?"

"What happens when Reisiltark gets here? What happens if she wants to destroy Mysane Kosk? All our preparations are designed to protect the place. What do we do?"

"We follow Reisil," Kebonsat said firmly.

"How can you be sure her way is right? Everyone is looking to us to make the right choices." He shook his head, his lips pinching together. "How can we be sure?"

"I am sure of Reisil. No one can match her honor or sense of duty."

"They said that about Upsakes."

Kebonsat scowled, opening his mouth to make a cutting reply.

Metyein held up a restraining hand. "I'm sorry. That is not what I believe. Reisiltark saved my life. I trust her completely. But I cannot help but fear—what if Yohuac was right? What if the wizards killed Saljane, and Reisiltark went mad?"

"Reisil will not fail us. She doesn't know how." Kebonsat gazed heavily at Metyein. He liked what he saw. The younger man had a good mind, and despite a history of dilettantish dueling, he was steady under pressure. "And the Regent won't find us easy prey."

When the network of tunnels was completed, they'd have multiple access points between the stockades, allowing them to share food, water, and fighters. It would also allow for evacuation should a stockade fall. Kebonsat and Metyein had situated the stockades to maximize the killing fields between them, required that there be a well dug inside each, and made sure all the interior buildings were masked entirely with nonflammable mud and sod. They'd also planned a series of escape routes into the mountains. If things got dire, they'd get the children, Emelovi, and the other women out. Kebonsat was well satisfied with their defensive plan, but it would serve them little if they couldn't fight back. They needed metal for weapons. And Reisil. She was the only one who could fight off the Scallacians. Even the witch Nurema admitted as much.

"Reisil will not fail us," Kebonsat repeated. "But we need to help her. Dannen Relvi has been nothing short of miraculous in getting us food and supplies, but I wish he'd send weapons."

"Or metal. We've got more blacksmiths than we can use right now." Metyein gave a little shrug. "But metal is scarce in Kodu Riik. Most of it the crown took for the war. And since then, with the plague and *nokulas,* most mines haven't been producing much."

"If only we could get into Patverseme . . ."

"Don't even think about it. It would be suicide, with the blockade. And I need you. I can't train or lead an army alone."

"What army? We don't even have pitchforks. Men with sticks," Kebonsat said in bitter frustration, pounding his fist against his thigh.

Metyein sighed, looking troubled. "There is one possibility. . . ."

"Where?"

Metyein rubbed a hand over his mouth. At last he spoke. "Bro-heyek. A lot of rich mines up there. My father often complained that the Thevul was witholding his metal harvests, though there was never time or men to go clear up there to force the issue. Thevul Bro-heyek was never fond of the Iisand; he's got reason to care even less for Aare. He might help."

There was something queer about Metyein's voice, as if he'd eaten something he wasn't sure he liked.

"What else?"

"The Thevul is Soka's father."

"Ah. I see."

The small hope that had begun to flicker with Metyein's first words curled up like burnt paper. No man should betray his son as Soka's father had. As a boy, Soka had been made a hostage to the Kodu Riikian court to keep the marauding Thevul leashed, and keep his noble neighbors safe. When the Thevul ignored the threats to his son and continued his raids, the Iisand had ordered Soka's eye put out, sending it as a warning to the Thevul. A map of the Bro-heyek lands had been scarred onto Soka's empty eyelid as a warning to other nobles who wanted to challenge the Iisand's authority.

"Will he go?" Kebonsat asked. And if he did, would he negotiate for them? Or take the opportunity to get retribution?

Metyein's lips pulled into a humorless grin. "A year ago I would have said no. But since Aare captured him . . . He was never a coward, but now he's . . . reckless. I think he would definitely . . . *like* . . . to see his father again. If only to get his eye back."

"Which may get us nothing." Kebonsat didn't know what he'd feel in Soka's position. He liked the other man, though *reckless* didn't begin to address Soka's recent behavior. He was acerbic and rude. His honesty was tactless, and applied with the force of an assassin's dagger. He was quick to offer violence to insult, and he'd become formidable with a sword since Metyein had begun instructing him. Yet despite his faults,

Soka's loyalty to Metyein and Emelovi was absolutely undiluted. "It's worth a try. He should leave right away."

"I know. But don't bet your sister's virtue he'll succeed. The Thevul is known to be inflexible, and Soka has never been diplomatic."

"And for what do I need diplomacy?"

The subject of their conversation climbed up the ladder behind them and leaped gracefully onto the platform. His long hair clung to his head. His features were dagger-fine. He sported a close-cropped beard, and his single eye was a brilliant blue topaz. The other was covered by a scarlet eye patch. A detailed map of the Bro-heyek lands was picked out in gold threads on its surface—a gesture of insolence. He was dressed similarly to Metyein, though he was splashed liberally with mud. There was a weal along his right cheekbone. Blood seeped down to stain his collar.

"What happened?" Metyein asked, pointing to the wound.

Soka touched his fingers to his face and looked at the blood on his fingers. He shrugged. "Tree branch probably."

"You were in a hurry," Kebonsat said, his voice questioning.

Soka slapped his shoulder and grinned. "I wasn't running from some pretty woman's husband. Not this time, at any rate. Merely a race for a small wager, which I won. The two of you look sorry as half-drowned cats. What can I do?"

Kebonsat met Metyein's gaze fleetingly. "We want you to go home."

The smile froze on Soka's face. "Home?"

Kebonsat nodded. "Bro-heyek may have the metal we need for weapons."

Soka was still a moment. Then his lips parted in a hungry smile that chilled Kebonsat to the marrow. "I'll go. It's getting boring here anyhow."

Metyein exchanged a worried glance with Kebonsat, and then wrapped his arm around Soka's shoulder. In a falsely jovial voice, he said, "You do your house credit. You should leave tomorrow or the day after. You can't go empty-handed. . . ."

Kebonsat followed the other two men down the ladder, jumping the last couple of feet, his boots squelching in the mud. All around them boiled stern-faced people. They were soaked to the skin, going about their business with grim concentration—hammering together the two-story row of buildings nestled against the interior of the stockade, swinging quarterstaves in preparation for war, fletching headless arrows, fixing carts, digging a well. Others were fetching and carrying, trundling dirt from the tunnels, hauling wood for the buildings. There wasn't a lazy soul in sight. Everyone knew what was coming: the plague, winter, and the Regent. Not necessarily in that order. There was little time to prepare for any of them. *If the plague comes first, we won't have to worry about winter or the Regent.* Kebonsat quashed the thought and followed after Metyein and Soka. At least there was a hope for metal to make weapons. As thin a chance as it was, it was more than they'd had an hour ago.

"So put plague victims in Fox and move Emelovi and the regular hospital to Hawk?" Kebonsat repeated thoughtfully, running his fingers over the map before raking his hand through his hair and kicking out his feet to the fire. Across the table, Metyein dabbed a pen into an inkwell and scratched some additions to an already long list. "Puts the plague at our heart—that's a big risk."

Metyein reached for more ink. "It puts the least stress on our defenses, while giving us something of a quarantine space. And it'll help keep up morale when it comes down to it. People are going to want to know their families are cared for. It tells everyone that we're not walking away from the weak and the helpless, the way Aare's done in Koduteel."

"There's a good chance we won't be able to evacuate Fox when the blight circle expands," Kebonsat warned.

"If it keeps going at its current rate, we won't have to worry about it for a year and a half." Metyein set aside the pen and reached for his mug of kohv. "By then I doubt it will matter much. We'll either have won or lost and we won't be needing the stockades any longer."

"Fair enough. What are you planning to do with the bodies? We won't be able to have mass pyres once we're under siege."

"You mean besides dumping them into the blight and letting the *nokulas* deal with them?" Metyein smoothed a finger around the rim of his mug. "I'd do it, too, if I didn't worry they'd come alive and turn into more of the beasts. It had also occurred to me to load the dead in the trebuchets and lob them at Aare's army, but it is a bit uncivilized."

"A bit," Kebonsat said dryly. "Their families might find it unseemly."

Metyein sighed and rolled his head around his neck to loosen the muscles. "Don't tell Soka. He'd be only too delighted I'd sunk so low in my thinking."

"Strutting like a proud papa," agreed Kebonsat with a sardonic smile.

Metyein grinned. "Anyhow, I figure to dig a tunnel out toward those ravines above the river. We won't be able to burn the bodies without calling attention to ourselves, but they'll be far enough away to keep us out of danger. If we dump the midden waste there as well, it'll keep the animals away. Worse comes to worst, we fill the tunnel with the dead and collapse it back bit by bit and pray we don't have more corpses than tunnel."

Kebonsat nodded, closing his eyes. He felt a hundred years old. "What else?"

"We're going to set up a tannery in stockade eight—what are we calling it? Salamander? We need leather. It'll stink, but we've got the hides coming in now. In winter, we may not have the supply, but we'll have plenty of need. And I've approved putting the sheep and goats back in Hawk. We'll want milk and cheese come winter, and meat into a siege; they'll be best protected there. We'll get the weavers going in Hawk too, now that we're using Fox for quarantine. Won't have to move them until our first victim, so no hurry. I hope.

"I've assigned a whole host of clerks to inventory supplies and needs. I'll not see people freeze when snow flies, and there's not going to be any hoarding either. If folks don't want to contribute what they've brought, they can march back out of here." Metyein yawned, rubbing a finger down a list. "Oh, and I've decided to send woodchoppers north. They'll fell whatever they can into the river and we'll fish the logs out. When Aare comes, I don't want to have depleted all the firewood close to hand."

"That's risky. Aare could just as well use the timber."

"Risk worth taking. We'll know they're coming long before they get here. We'll cut what we can and fire the rest. Or get Nurema to destroy it. Let's see, what else? We're still using Wolf and Raven for cooking, but we're going to have to start spreading that out for efficiency. Disrupts the workday too much to have everyone hiking across the valley for food, and we don't want them tracking through the fields. Plus apparently a few folks have found time to pick fights. Keeping them from grouping up might help."

"You've been busy since supper," Kebonsat said. "Maybe we'll get this anthill organized yet."

"But I've saved the best for last."

Kebonsat lifted his brow. "What's that?"

Just then from outside came the scuffling of boots and the sounds of yipping. Kebonsat and Metyein stood as the plank doors were unceremoniously shoved open. In walked three *ahalad-kaaslane* looking both angry and nervous. And well they might be, Kebonsat thought, his eyes narrowing as he folded his arms across his chest. They'd turned on Reisil, then joined her cause. They had lost the power of the Lady, and they had little credibility amongst the Kodu Riikian people. At least with Juhrnus, Metyein, and Soka, who were in charge of this sprawling compound. *And you,* he told himself. *Don't forget yourself in that list.* Except Kebonsat was Patversemese. He didn't belong here, fighting in a Kodu Riikian civil war. But he had no other place to go. And no where else he *wanted* to go.

"*Ahalad-kaaslane,*" Metyein said. "What brings you here?"

There was a bare hint of reproval in his voice that they ought to be elsewhere, ought to be doing something useful. Kebonsat saw the earnest young woman on the left wince. She had short brown hair and a round face. Her gaze flickered over him and then shifted to Metyein, her cheeks flushing rusty red beneath a spattering of freckles. Her *ahalad-kaaslane* was a tall, buff-colored mountain cat. Its talons curled into the hickory floor, splintering the wood.

A short man, coming only to Kebonsat's shoulder, with thinning copper hair and rough, pocked skin stood on her right. His *ahalad-kaaslane* was one of the northern wild dogs, its stature halfway between a wolf and a fox. The animal had yellow eyes and a ridge of frost-tipped fur running from ears to the tip of its tail. Otherwise it was the blue-gray color of smoke. Beside him was another man, this one older than the others, though probably not more than thirty-five years old. His gaze was as sharp as a hunting knife. He stared at Metyein and Kebonsat from beneath bushy black brows. He wore a full beard streaked with gray, and his teeth were stained brown. His *ahalad-kaaslane* was a weirmart that clung to his neck beneath his loose fall of hair. Kebonsat frowned at the minklike animal. Upsakes had been paired with one of those. And Upsakes had been a traitor.

"We would like to see Vertina Emelovi," declared the gray-bearded man abruptly.

Metyein lifted one of his brows. "Would you, now? Why?"

The pock-faced man flushed and glowered. "We don't have to explain ourselves to you. We are *ahalad-kaaslane.*"

"Yes, that you are," Metyein said, perching on the edge of the table and turning a gimlet eye on the three of them. "Why are you talking to me then?"

"We tried. Her guards sent us to you." The woman spoke this time, sounding uncertain and strained. "They said . . . they said you had to approve first."

"I see." Metyein said nothing more.

An uncomfortable silence fell. The three *ahalad-kaaslane* shifted awkwardly, and the wild dog whined. Kebonsat couldn't help but feel a reluctant sympathy. Certainly the *ahalad-kaaslane* had not behaved well to Reisil. But they'd been misled by Sodur, and now they had lost the power of the Lady and the confidence of their people.

"If you wish, I will carry a message to the Vertina," Metyein said at last, more gently, when none of them seemed inclined to speak. Kebonsat could tell his friend was torn between resentment for what they'd done to Reisil, and a lifetime of ingrained respect for the *ahalad-kaaslane.*

The visitors exchanged unhappy glances, and at last the pock-faced man spoke in a subdued tone. "We wish to ask— That is, we hope that she might allow us to aid in the defense of Honor until Reisiltark can offer her guidance. We know now she is the Lady's voice and wish to serve Kodu Riik as she directs."

Metyein didn't speak. He'd gone gray. Kebonsat's knees sagged. *Oh, dear Ellini!* What kind of fool was he? He'd been so focused on building the stockades, on their defenses. The obvious, the inevitable, had been staring him in the face and he'd not seen it. Not wanted to see it. His stomach turned over and he closed his eyes, feeling as if the floor were moving beneath him.

They'd come to see Emelovi. To ask her to let them serve. He scraped his fingers through his hair, digging them hard into his scalp. Because they naturally thought she ruled here, that she was a pretender to the throne in opposition to her brother. Otherwise she would be at his side.

Nothing could be farther from the truth. It was the last thing Emelovi wanted. The last thing she'd dream of.

Kebonsat had lured Emelovi away from Koduteel with the promise of finding her missing father, even though he'd known her father had been made a *nokula* and was lost to her forever. At the time he'd justified lying to her by telling himself he was keeping her safe from her brother. Aare had tried to force her to bed one of the Scallacian sorcerers under the threat of killing her. Kebonsat *couldn't,* with any honor at all, have let her stay there.

He closed his eyes, struck to the core. *Honor.* No matter how good his intentions, he'd *lied* to her. And now she could never go back, never convince her brother she hadn't had a part in this, that she didn't want to rule. And she would want to. She was loyal to a fault. When she discovered Kebonsat's duplicity, she would hate him.

Kebonsat swallowed convulsively, starting as the door suddenly swung open. He watched with glazed eyes as Emelovi entered, her steps faltering as she realized Metyein and Kebonsat were not alone.

The three *ahalad-kaaslane* bowed eagerly to Emelovi. She nodded and smiled uncertainly, her eyes softening as they settled on Kebonsat. He cringed, guilt gnawing at his bowels.

The bearded *ahalad-kaaslane*'s face was determined. He squared his shoulders, speaking quickly and respectfully. "Vertina, we wish to have a place in your army, in reclaiming Kodu Riik from your traitorous brother and fighting off the Scallacians. He has severed ties with the Lady, abandoning his duty to this land and murdering the *ahalad-kaaslane*. We offer our service to you. Let us help you take the throne and return Kodu Riik to the light of the Lady."

Kebonsat held himself rigid, watching in pained si-

lence as comprehension struck. Emelovi's body twitched.
She darted a quick glance at Metyein and Kebonsat and
then back to the waiting *ahalad-kaaslane*. Her mouth
opened and then closed, the color draining from her
face.

"You are mistaken. We will hold the throne for my
father's return," she said in a strangled voice. She
swayed and Metyein leaped to guide her to a chair.

"The Vertina is unwell. Please excuse her. I will
speak with you as soon as I may." He looked pointedly at the door and then to the disconcerted *ahalad-
kaaslane*.

They exchanged glances, hesitating. Then the woman
spoke, even as Kebonsat stepped in front of Emelovi,
blocking her from their sight.

"Please, we wish only to help, to serve Kodu Riik,"
she said, her hands twisting together. Her mountain
cat made an anxious growling sound and clawed at
the floor. She set a calming hand on the animal's head,
her fingers trembling.

"Aren't you *ahalad-kaaslane*? What approval can
you possibly need to do anything you want to do?"
Kebonsat demanded in sudden fury. The question
drew blood. The woman looked away, biting her lip.
Kebonsat no longer felt sympathy. He couldn't. Not
with Emelovi devastated behind him. Metyein laid a
hand on his arm.

"We will consult with the Vertina and apprise you
of her wishes," he said. When the pock-faced *ahalad-
kaaslane* began to expostulate, Metyein raised one
brow, his voice turning glacial. "I am sure you do not
mean to impose on the Vertina when she is ill."

"Of course not," the bearded man said. "We will
wait patiently." He turned to leave and then paused.
"It is our hope to begin serving as soon as may be."

"Of course," Metyein said blandly, and the three
departed, dismissed.

Metyein turned and met Kebonsat's gaze over Emelovi's bowed head. She stared at her fingers knotted
together in her lap. Her breath came fast and light in

the silence of the room. Neither man spoke. At last she looked up, her face waxy.

"You must find my father." Her voice was scratchy and desperate as she lurched to her feet, eyes fastened on Kebonsat. "Only he can stop this. If he returns to Koduteel, Aare will have to stop, and I— Please, please, you *must* find him. Otherwise I must return and beg forgiveness for my treachery."

Kebonsat felt himself nodding as he took her chilled hands in his. His lips felt stiff as iron as he lied. "Of course we'll find him."

Chapter 4

"You're making me tired with all that fidgeting. Since you cannot sit still, shall we take the afternoon and tour Honor? We can collect Soka on the way."

Kebonsat didn't have to be asked twice. He jumped to his feet, snatching up his cloak. He ignored Metyein's grin. "Soka? What do we want him for? He'll make targets of us all with the men he's cuckolded," Kebonsat said. "We'll be lucky to get fifty paces without getting an arrow in the chest."

"True enough, but he's a sewer for gossip and sordid rumor. We may as well learn what he knows while we can."

"Very well. But he gives even the horses the flux with that sharp tongue of his. Does he never stop talking?"

"I believe that is something only the ladies know for sure," Metyein said, donning his cloak. A heavy silver pin was stuck through the collar.

Kebonsat flicked a glance at the pin. "I'm glad to see you didn't lose it."

Metyein pulled his gloves on with deliberate care. "I'd as soon wear it on my cods."

Kebonsat grinned. "A poor sense of gratitude for such an honor."

"You can have it."

"Not me, my friend. I am Patversemese. Or I was, before all this." He made a circular motion in the air with his hand. "The moment the Regent took me prisoner, I was disinherited and disowned. Now I am a man without a country. Either way, I am no leader for this army to follow. Accept it gracefully. You are the only choice. I am here merely to advise."

Metyein snorted, fingering the pin. It was shaped like a gryphon, two stalks of wheat in its beak, a sword clutched in its claws. Rubies flashed in the eyes, while sapphires and ebony sparkled in the hilt of the sword and topaz gleamed in the wheat. "You're better qualified. You have been in the field; I have not. You have led men into battle; I have not. You have been besieged; I have not. You ought to be wearing this Lady-cursed bauble, not I."

"At least you're aware of your limitations. Makes you a better Lord Marshal than most. And you've studied under one of the best."

"My father. Who has been Lord Marshal since before my birth. Who will be leading the army against us. He'll be six steps ahead of me. And they'll have metal weapons and shields, and plenty of them."

Kebonsat shrugged. "Your father also has the Regent. He's a liability. If he thinks your father's off on the wrong track, he'll step in. And he's likely to make emotional and stupid choices. And don't forget your father has to deal with the sorcerers."

"Aare knows enough to let my father do his work. And the sorcerers want this place as much as Aare. They won't turn on him until the day is won."

Kebonsat adjusted the sword on his hip and banked the coals of the fire. "Your Regent isn't one to keep his hands to himself, not when he's so hungry for victory. And with any luck, Juhrnus's sorceress will be our fox in the henhouse."

"I would feel a whole lot better if Reisiltark were here."

"We have Nurema."

Metyein's eyebrows arched.

Kebonsat conceded, "I don't trust her either. I don't know that I *can't* trust her, but . . ." He shrugged. "She's a mystery and could very well be playing a game all her own. On the other hand, there's no gain-saying that she *does* have power and she's the only one on our side who does, except Reisil," he said, swinging open the door.

Metyein stepped out into the muddy street. "I hope she shows up soon."

Won't do any good if she hasn't learned to use her power. Kebonsat didn't say it. Metyein had enough to stew about. But Reisil had gone to the wizards to find out how to use her magic. Had she succeeded? Or was she even now their prisoner? Or worse?

They found Soka emerging from one of the drill arenas. His shirt was open to his waist and he was soaked to his skin. His long, foxy hair hung loose in wet draggles around his face. Silver and ivory beads were woven into braids behind his ear, and more were strung around his neck. He was panting, and there were two long tears in his shirt, one over his chest and the other in his left sleeve. A new bruise was spreading over his left cheek beneath his eye patch.

"I hope your opponent looks worse than you," Kebonsat said.

Soka's grin was feral. "Considerably so."

"You have certainly come a long way since I began tutoring you," said Metyein with a gesture toward Soka's sword, nicked and scarred by hard use.

"Women adore a man who can use his sword well." He leered, another ivory bead caught between his teeth, the ends filled with lead.

Metyein's gaze hardened as he caught sight of it. "Someday you're going to trip and crack that thing open. Stupid way to die."

Soka's smile only widened as he stepped into the weapons shack to towel himself off and change his shirt. He wiped down his sword carefully before sheathing it and then pulled on his coat, hat, and gloves. "There are worse ways." His expression darkened. "Much worse." Then he shook himself, the bead lumping between his lip and jaw. "What brings you?"

"Taking stock of things. Care to join us?"

Soka's stomach chose that moment to gurgle loudly. He patted it. "If we can eat on the way."

"Your wish is our command," said Metyein dryly.

They retrieved their horses and rode out along the muddy streets and then to Wolf, where the midday meal was under way. Kebonsat allowed Soka and Metyein to take the lead. They were greeted with friendly calls as they entered the crude hall. Few spoke to Kebonsat, giving him only reserved nods as he trailed his gregarious companions silently through the long line. He filled his bowl with the hearty game stew that was the perpetual menu in the valley and grabbed a loaf of chewy brown bread.

"When all this is over, I will be grateful for a haunch of roast beef, succulent puddings, pot pies, pastries, candied fruits, gravies, cakes, roast fowl, glazed suckling pig—"

"Enough!" Metyein interrupted Soka's gluttonous ramblings. "You oughtn't torture your friends so. And anyway . . ." He trailed off, his lips clamping tight for a moment, and then he speared a hunk of venison and pushed it into his mouth.

"Anyway?" Soka prompted, one eyebrow raised.

Metyein flashed his friend a cutting look, but did not answer.

"Rats got your tongue?" Soka pressed, disregarding the dangerous glint in Metyein's eyes and the red flagging his cheeks.

"*Anyway,* we probably won't survive to enjoy such delicacies," Kebonsat drawled, soaking a hunk of bread in his stew and stuffing it in his mouth.

Soka sat up, eyes wide with feigned innocence. "You don't say?"

"You're a demon-spawned bastard," Metyein said, shaking his head.

"Demon-spawned certainly. But we know the demon who is my father, so really, that's a ridiculous accusation."

Metyein chuckled and met Kebonsat's gaze with a resigned look. "At least he's done blathering on about food."

"Until the next time," Kebonsat agreed.

Metyein waved his hand. "Oh, no, my friend. Soka's off on his own adventure. We'll be free of his foolishness for a bit."

"All the more reason to give you the full benefit of my companionship before I depart into the hinterlands, back to my father's lair, as it were. Who knows if either of us will survive the encounter?"

"Do *try*. We need that metal," Kebonsat admonished.

"You only ever think of metal. One wonders if parts of you are made of it . . ." Soka said, his eyes wandering suggestively. "Still, if the ever-watchful Hag has anything to say for it, I will get what we need. She has been most accomodating in escaping Aare. In the meantime, we should all have dreams. I'm dreaming of baked apples with honey and cinnamon, crepes, stuffed salmon, kohv with nussa, pumpkin soup with walnuts and scarlet cherries—"

Metyein groaned and banged his knife down on the table with a loud clatter.

"Have you thought about what to do with the *ahalad-kaaslane?*" Kebonsat inserted quickly.

"Aside from locking them in a deep, dark cellar and losing the key?" Metyein sighed, pushing back his plate. "That isn't fair. They want to help. They are at loose ends without the Lady to guide them, and they know they treated Reisiltark badly. They are truly faithful to Kodu Riik."

"Their support will be needed after this is over."

"*Emelovi* will need their support." Metyein looked at Kebonsat, unblinking.

Kebonsat felt as if Metyein had thrust a spear through his gut. He couldn't speak.

"The *ahalad-kaaslane* were right. She's got a rightful claim on the throne. People are coming here because they choose to follow her. There're no other heirs, no other choices."

"That's not entirely true," Soka murmured, glancing over his shoulder. "There are other heirs. The three little ones who were sent to safety when the Iisand began to change. We haven't thought of them. Aare will have."

Kebonsat stiffened, the hairs on his body prickling. "You don't think he would—" But he would. The new Regent wanted the throne. Craved it bad enough to kill whoever might stand in his way, even his young siblings. And now that Emelovi had challenged him, he would move to cut off any other opposition. Emelovi couldn't afford to lose anyone else. He stared at his white-knuckled fingers clenching his knife and fork.

"We can't spare anyone."

"Not entirely true," Soka drawled. "You have that pesky *ahalad-kaaslane* problem."

Hope caught in Kebonsat's chest. He straightened, his gaze locking with Metyein's. "Not a bad idea."

Metyein nodded thoughtfully. "They would be grateful for the trust. It would allow them to prove themselves to Emelovi, and to the people."

"And if they succeed, it will flay at Aare's rock-sac like a swarm of hungry termites," Soka observed crudely. "It might distract him."

Before Kebonsat could answer, a clarion rang down the valley, echoing from the surrounding mountain peaks.

For the space of one long breath, every soul in the room sat frozen.

The dining hall erupted. Benches were overturned and trenchers and cups went flying as men leaped for the doors. They slapped for the hilts of their swords, their faces twisted in expressions of fear and fury.

Kebonsat boiled out of the hall with the others, his mind cold. The clarion warned of strangers at the gates. Aare could not have brought his army to their doors without the scouts sending an alert. Raiders, then? A *nokula* attack? Or . . . An eel slithered into Kebonsat's stomach. Wizards.

Before he could do more than turn to find Metyein in the crush, another volley of notes sang across the valley. *All clear.* Relieved laughter broke out amongst the milling crowd. The sound was too loud, with a forced edge.

"Care to wager it's Juhrnus causing this rumpus? Our fair boy returned at last?" Soka asked.

"Let's go see," Metyein said, untying his horse from its hitching post.

They rode out of the stockade and up the rutted, muddy track that served as the main avenue for the valley. Heavy logwagons had cut deep gouges into the road that now filled with water, making their progress treacherous. But the fields on either side were planted to the verge and there was no room to ride alongside the river of mud.

By the time they had struggled up the length of the valley into the rising hills beyond, they were each splattered with mud to their chins, and none in a good humor for it. Juhrnus looked little better. He rode at the head of a long column of wagons and people, most on foot or driving pony carts. He was filthy, wearing a bushy beard matted with mud and twigs and leaves. Beneath the beard his face was gaunt. He broke into a smile at the sight of the trio, lifting his arm in a tired wave.

"Bright day! You are a sight, my friends." He snatched his hat from his head and rubbed the damp from his forehead. "Mind, I'd rather you were a soft bed and a mug of hot wine, but you'll do."

They greeted him loudly, thumping his shoulders. Kebonsat cast a sharp eye at Juhrnus's retinue.

"What have you brought? Metals?"

Juhrnus shook his head, reaching absently under his cloak to stroke the head of a green-and-yellow-striped sisalik. It had a black, fleshy tongue and yellow eyes that gleamed with intelligence. The enormous lizard's long body was wrapped around Juhrnus's waist, protected from the rain by his *ahalad-kaaslane*'s oiled cloak.

"Not what you're looking for, I'm afraid," he said. "Pots and pans, wire, a few swords and spears, nails, some brass. Not enough. I've scavenged all there is to be had for a hundred leagues around, and there was precious little left. If we want more, I'm going to have to go farther afield. Farther north up the Karnane, there might still be something that the royal troops haven't scavenged."

"No need," drawled Soka. "I'm going to get the metal."

Juhrnus gave him a sharp look. "Oh?"

"Lady willing," Metyein said. "Anything else? What about the plague? Koduteel? The Regent?"

Juhrnus scrubbed a hand over his face and glanced at the wagons behind, his expression forbidding. His voice dropped. "I'd rather wait. Is there word on Reisil?" His right eye twitched when the others shook their heads. "That's it, then." But he would say nothing more as they rode down to the stockades, the drizzle finally letting up, though the clouds hung low and menacing.

"You've made strides since I left," Juhrnus said, managing somehow to sprawl in a hard, straight-backed chair. Juhrnus sipped at his mug of mulled wine and sighed, patting his belly. "Best food I've eaten in more than a month." His face was thin and craggy beneath his beard, giving evidence to his short rations.

"It's filling, anyway," Metyein said, scraping his chair closer. "Looks like you could use another bowl." He shoved a plate of bread toward Juhrnus, who waved his hand.

"I'm tight as a tick. The new folks who came in with me will be grateful for a hot meal, I can tell you. I've kept the pace quick. It's getting dangerous out there." He flashed a grin. "Mind, they weren't sure about coming here. Surprised they stuck with me."

"You're *ahalad-kaaslane*," Kebonsat said. "That still means a little, outside of Koduteel. And it isn't as if they have anywhere else to go."

"True. The plague continues to spread, and the drought has made things worse. There are bandit gangs setting up trade wherever there's a bit of water and food. Families have been lucky to get out with their skins. And they're on their own. The local nobles are all still gated up inside Koduteel. There are no leaders and no soldiers to drive the scum out. It's ugly. When this is over, there's going to be a lot of work smoking the vermin out of their holes."

"If we survive, we'll put it at the top of our list," Soka drawled. "What's the word from Koduteel?"

"It still stands," Juhrnus said. "Plague fires still burn outside the city around the clock. Fishing boats go out every day. The men's families are held hostage against their return. Same with scavenge parties looking for grain, beans, vegetables—that sort of thing. Some of the bandit gangs in the Karnane are trading with them—whatever they can steal. The midden wagons are going out every day, but not much else besides. Aare's got soldiers riding with the drivers. Luckily Karina's got some of them in her pocket. She sent this." He pulled out of his tunic a roll of parchment wrapped in oilskin and bound around by leather strips. He handed it to Metyein, who slit the bindings with his dagger and unrolled the pages. After a few moments his face darkened. He looked at Juhrnus over the top of the documents.

"You read this?"

Juhrnus nodded. "Came back as soon as I did."

"What's it say?" Kebonsat asked.

Metyein sighed. "There's a description of the city. Marshal law seems to have curtailed the spread of the plague. There are food shortages. Water shortages. Most everything is going to mustering the army." He glanced at Kebonsat. "Karina says that Aare's staging in the foothills west of the city. He's been funneling

soldiers and supplies there. The Lord Marshal is overseeing the preparations. She figures they'll be coming
for us in the spring."

"What about the sorcerers?"

"Nothing good. Listen. Karina writes: 'After your
escape, the Regent tightened the noose. Wherever he
went, the Scallacians were at his side. They are using
their magic to aid the Regent's plans. The Regent's
hold on the city is absolute. His men follow him fanati-
cally. Even the nobles have stopped caviling. I can say
little of what the sorcerers are doing for him. Anyone
I set to watch them disappears within hours. There
are rumors of soldiers with the power of five men, of
arrows that do not miss their targets, of horses that
can travel for days without food or rest. But I fear
what they do now. They have withdrawn into the palace. We do not know why, but fear the worst. Be
warned. I hope your Reisiltark is very strong.' "

"Kedisan-Mutira. Her testing," Juhrnus said tonelessly.

Metyein paused. Kebonsat looked sympathetically
at Juhrnus, who was staring down at the scarred wood
of the tabletop, the muscles in his arms cording as he
clenched his fists. From the hearth, there was a moan-
ing chirp, and Esper lifted his head, his yellow eyes
shining with a hard light. After a moment, Metyein
continued reading.

" 'The sorcerers have made it nearly impossible to
buy loyalty from the guards. It is too dangerous now
to try to bring supplies into the city. Gather the folk
that you can and protect them. Protect Kodu Riik.
And pray to the Lady we survive the winter.' "

Metyein paused again, sucking in a long breath.
"Demonballs," he muttered, his lips pulling into a
snarl.

"What?" Kebonsat demanded.

"There's a postcript here. The writing is hasty and
smeared. 'I have news that the Regent is going to be
crowned Iisand at Nasadh.' "

"Chodha," Soka said into the turbid silence that followed. "How is that possible? As far as he knows, his father's still alive."

"We all knew he wouldn't wait. He's got the entire Arkeinik trapped in Koduteel. They'll agree to anything he wants if it means escape," Metyein said in a strangled voice. When Aare became Iisand, he'd have Lord Marshal Vare's complete support. And he'd have full command of Kodu Riik.

No one had anything more to say.

Metyein rolled up the parchment carefully, his fingers trembling. "Is there other news?"

Juhrnus rubbed his hand over his forehead. "Two things. I went to Gudsiil, before Koduteel." He nodded at Kebonsat.

Kebonsat held himself very still. "And?"

Juhrnus shook his head. "It's gone. Plague."

"Ceriba?"

Juhrnus shook his head, his expression tight. "They made pyres. I don't know how many bodies they managed to burn before it got out of hand. When I got there, the gates were open and the garrison had been deserted. Animals had been at the bodies that were left." He lifted red-rimmed eyes to meet Kebonsat's stricken gaze. "I looked for her. Went through the headquarters, barracks, and the dungeons. I saw no sign of her. It's possible they didn't capture her. Or she got away. Your man might have rescued her."

"I thank you for going inside. You should not have risked yourself." Kebonsat shoved to his feet and went to stare blindly out the window. His chest was tight. He felt as if he'd been holding his breath for months. Holding on to a fragile hope that now was slipping away like water into parched earth.

After Emelovi had revealed her brother's plans to kidnap Ceriba and hold her at Gudsiil, Kebonsat had dispatched Rocis to save her. Rocis was the best in the game. No one could sniff out information the way he could; few could match him with weapons. He was crafty and sly and didn't mind breaking rules. It *was* possible that Rocis had made it to Ceriba before the Regent's men. It was possible they were hiding, or making their way to safety somewhere.

Kebonsat bit his tongue. The memory of Ceriba's naked, battered body filled his mind. She'd been kidnapped on the eve of the treaty between Kodu Riik and Patverseme by a coterie of Patveresemese and Kodu Riikians determined to destroy any hope of peace. They'd raped and beaten her, planning to leave her on the palace steps, with a guilty Kodu Riikian confessing to the crime. In the face of such evil, they believed that the Karalis and Karaliene would withdraw from the peace talks. And they would have been right. The things they had done to Ceriba had been . . . unspeakable. Thank Ellini, thank the Lady, that Reisil had been there, had had the means to heal her.

A jagged sound tore past the constriction in Kebonsat's throat. He didn't know if he should hope his sister was dead, rather than suffering anything like that again. He started as Metyein squeezed his shoulder in sympathy.

"Would there were something we could do," he murmured.

Kebonsat swallowed. As sincere as Metyein's sympathy was, his friend was also recalling him to his duty. There was more at stake here than a single life. Than even a hundred or a thousand. He couldn't abandon Honor or Mysane Kosk. He gave a short nod, acknowledging Metyein's silent command, and turned back to the table, sending a silent prayer to Ellini and the Blessed Amiya that Ceriba was safe.

"I'll send word to Dannen Relvi. Soka, you'll leave at first light for Bro-heyek. Juhrnus, you make sure the new people are settled and then go see the *ahalad-kaaslane*. Kebonsat—" Meyein broke off, looking for words.

"I know. I'll see Emelovi."

"She has to know what's going on in Koduteel, if nothing else."

Kebonsat nodded. "I'll tell her."

Metyein waited a moment, as if expecting something more. Finally he lifted his shoulder in a shrug and turned to Soka.

"I'll give you an official message for your father."

Soka's teeth bared in a humorless smile. "Make it a sweet offering," he said sardonically. "He's a self-serving *ganyik,* and your blandishments had better outweigh any other temptations. He's not one for honor."

"I'll promise him Gulto and Scallas if he'll deliver us the metal we need."

"Better to promise him the throne."

Metyein looked at Kebonsat. "No, there's already another claimant," he said softly.

Kebonsat's stomach turned. Without a word he grabbed his cloak and strode out into the street. What was he going to say to Emelovi? *He's a self-serving* ganyik. . . . *He's not one for honor.* Soka might as well have been talking about Kebonsat.

He gritted his teeth and marched up the muddy street, gripping the hilt of his sword with iron fingers. He had time for weapons practice before joining Emelovi for dinner. They would be alone this night. Metyein would see to it. A romantic evening, and no one would interfere in his wooing. Or his confession. And after she knew the truth, they'd never have a meal together again. He doubted he'd even be allowed to empty her chamber pot.

It was no more than he deserved.

On the edge of the valley, Saljane perched high in a tall cedar tree, its bole larger than five men could encompass. Lower, an enormous branch splintering in his grip, perched Baku.

Saljane dropped down, touching her beak to his nose. This way, and only this way, could she hear him. The magic bubbling from Mysane Kosk and flowing through the valley below strangled his ability to speak mind-to-mind, except with Yohuac, his would-be *ahalad-kaaslane.*

~She told us to go talk to them.

~We cannot. We must wait, Baku said churlishly.

~She told us—

~She did not know, Baku interrupted. He shook his head as if pained in the ears, breaking contact with Saljane. He snapped at a nearby branch, shattering the wood in his jaws and spitting out the debris with a grunt. After a few moments, he extended his black-scaled head back to Saljane, the hide along his back and ribs twitching spasmodically.

~The magic here is . . . uncomfortable, he said. *The* nokulas *lie in wait. Reisil and Yohuac will need our help to break through. See?*

Saljane felt Baku's effort to draw her into his mind, to allow her to see, through his eyes. For a moment she saw whirling patterns of crystal light, sparkling brilliance, and translucent shadow. It reminded her of Reisil's spellsight. But there was a chaotic, unsettling feel to it.

After a moment she pulled away. She glared at Baku, considering. They had not bespoken their *ahalad-kaaslane* since Reisil's encounter with Sodur. That had been in the predawn hours. What progress the other two were making, they could not tell. Saljane was worried. But Reisil wanted their friends in the valley warned. . . .

~If we go down into the valley, down into the magic, we won't hear them if they call for help.

Saljane ruffled her feathers, preening an itchy spot on her chest. After a moment she straightened, opening her beak and hissing loud into the humid silence. She touched Baku's nose again.

~We will wait.

Baku turned his head to gaze down into the valley, the tip of his tail lashing back and forth.

~We will wait.

Chapter 5

There was a sound of agonized suffering, like a mountain lion trapped halfway beneath a mound of crushing rock, its back broken. The thin, high-pitched squeal went on and on. At first it was heartrending, then tedious in its unending agony. Hours passed before Kedisan-Mutira recognized that it was not some tormented animal causing the infuriating noise, but herself. And she was beyond the ability to stop. It was taking all the strength she had left not to die. She had passed the final trials of her *penakidah*. If she survived her victory, then she would at last be free.

Her body knew it felt pain. It had been stroked and massaged, then beaten and tortured. It had been pleasured past insensibility and then brutally raped. It had been fed deliciously and then starved. It had been given fine wines and then been given over to thirst. Now it craved water with an insanity of need. Bones were broken. Muscles and skin torn. Organs had shut down. She could not see through the swelling on her face, could not make words with the pulped flesh of her mouth, could not move her toes or fingers. But the agony was far distant, so great that her mind had fled from it. Her best, her only defense. The reason she yet lived. The reason she had not failed her testing.

"Should I fetch healing charms?"

"Let the *abi* take care of herself."

"She might well die, and we have declared her *pena-*

kidah. Are we not obligated? Will the Kilmet not find fault with us?"

"He will not. The moment she became *penakidah,* we relinquished all duty to her. She's on her own. Let her find her own way. Let her show us what she's made of."

"Haven't we seen? I've never tested anyone so rigorously. She ought to have died."

"Yes, she most definitely should have. But perhaps it is not too late. Let us go. We've left the Regent on his own long enough. Best go see what he's about."

The voices wandered away. Kedisan-Mutira was left with the echoes, stretching and distorting inside her skull. The first was Waiyhu-Waris. A toad. He'd taken the most lustful pleasure in her. The other was Menegal-Hakar. He was a man who liked to crush others under his heel, to gloat over them as they writhed and begged. The muscles around her mouth twitched as if to smile. She had not begged. She *would* heal. And then she'd teach them what fools they truly were.

Soon the charms she'd set into the bed frame and woven into the sheets would begin their work. All she had to do was not to die in the meantime. Her last coherent thought for some time to come was of a man with curling brown hair and a face she believed in with all her soul. She clung to his image like a tether in a storm, kept company by the unrelenting keening of her own agony.

Chapter 6

Reisil glanced back at Yohuac. His face was haggard beneath a layer of grime. He hunched in his saddle, one hand clenched around his pommel, the other knotted around his reins. He lurched from side to side with every jolting step. Reisil pulled up, easing back down to a walk as she turned Indigo up a steep path out of the defile.

The sun had sunk down behind the mountains, and fat drops of rain spattered her skin. Soon there would be a downpour, and the tiny creek running at the bottom of the narrow notch would turn into a raging torrent. Reisil shook her head, pulling her hood up. With any luck, it would catch their pursuers in its grasp and wash them down the mountain.

Her skin prickled, and she swiveled her head, smelling the clean tang of pine, cedar, and birch, and the rich scent of the damp loam. No sign of Tapit or his four companions. She'd glimpsed him just after dawn, following their trail down a ridge, only a league or two behind. She had increased their pace. But then the *nokulas* had interfered, scattering the wizards like dandelion fluff in the wind. Reisil could hardly regret their help, though the closer she and Yohuac came to Mysane Kosk, the more apprehensive she grew.

It turned out she could see the *nokulas* with her spellsight. She didn't know if that was a blessing or a curse. All through the day, she caught troubling glimpses of *nokulas* to the side and behind. Beams of moonlight wrapped around mosaics of colored glass. They were being herded.

Reisil shivered and stroked her hand down Indigo's neck, taking solace in his warmth. Sodur's warnings rang in her ears. She swallowed the dryness in her throat and pulled Indigo to a halt, waiting for Yohuac to catch up.

"Maybe we should split up," she said. "It might be they'll keep following me and you'll be able to get through to the others."

Yohuac's brows slashed downward, his jaw jutting. "I'll not leave you."

Reisil sighed. "One of us needs to get through—"

"*You* need to get through," Yohuac corrected. "I'm not leaving you to face them alone."

Reisil looked away, her eyes burning from lack of sleep. When the *nokulas* attacked, she didn't know if she would be able to protect him. And she wanted him safe. She thought of Sodur, of the metallic bite to his communications, of his alien difference. She couldn't let that happen to Yohuac. She didn't know if she could stop it.

"We'd better hurry. It can't be far now," she said brusquely.

She urged Indigo up the ridge into the thickening rain. Soon dusk gave way to night. Reisil pulled up and dismounted, wordlessly taking one of Yohuac's reins. Her wizard-sight allowed her to see in the inky blackness where neither the horses nor Yohuac could.

"I should walk," Yohuac said softly when the path narrowed and Reisil was forced to lead each horse separately through a maze of giant tree boles.

"So that you'll faint when it comes time to fight?" Yohuac did not answer, his silence hot and grim. Reisil pinched her lips together. That wasn't fair. His weakness wasn't his fault. If anyone's, it was hers. He'd never have been caught by the wizards if he hadn't come looking for her. He'd never have been tortured if she could have figured out a way to rescue him sooner.

"I won't slow you down," he said tonelessly.

Reisil stopped short. "What?"

"I will be able to look after myself. You need not worry about my weakness."

"I didn't say that!" she protested sharply.

"Didn't you?"

Reisil shook her head, saying nothing, starting to walk again. She knew how strong, how stubborn he was. But even at full strength, he could do little against *nokulas*. Unless he used his magic. And that was one thing he would not do.

On the other side of the trees, she unhooked Indigo's reins from a fallen log where she'd tied him and began up a steep, rocky deer track. There was a ledge just to the left. Trees thrust like hulking giants up from hundreds of feet below, their leaves pattering and rustling with the falling rain. Below, at the bottom of the steep drop, *nokulas* moved in a great horde. In Reisil's spellsight, they appeared like a river of moonlight and shattered glass. More trailed up the ridge on the right. And behind . . . Reisil swung around. Still more.

They were *converging*.

A shudder rippled down Reisil's spine, and fear porcupined in her chest. She handed Yohuac's reins back to him and mounted Indigo. "Gather your magic. I don't know how to fight the *nokulas,* but swords are going to do little damage against their numbers."

Reisil didn't wait for his reply. She trotted up the crest of the ridge. Indigo pranced and shook his head, sawing against the reins as he sensed her tension. Yohuac kept his gelding hard behind her. The rain hid the rustle and crack of their passage. Not that it mattered, Reisil thought. Neither Tapit nor the *nokulas* seemed to have any trouble tracking them.

Reisil pulled up inside the tree line at the top of the ridge. She stared.

The ground dropped away in a steep, rocky slope, gentling at the bottom and smoothing into a long, verdant valley. Six hulking stockades dotted the valley floor. A road ran east to west, curling amid the six stockades. On the east end of the valley, fields of grain and vegetables washed up against the road like a lush ocean. Juhrnus, Kebonsat, and Metyein had had a hand in this. How had they managed to do so much in so little time?

Reluctantly she looked past the stockades to the ruined city beyond. A mist hid the ruins themselves. Spreading out from it was a lattice of what looked like delicate blown-glass sculpture. The falling rain muted its crystal brilliance. Reisil wondered—

She blinked into spellsight.

The air went out of her in a whoosh and she jerked back. She pushed down her hood, feeling suddenly trapped inside its sodden folds.

The valley was on fire. Unformed magic eddied and whirled in jewel colors, pulsing and flashing as it undulated and bulged. It was not beautiful. It was bruised and bloated. It was angry and unbalanced. It was gravid with an evil that turned her stomach and made her skin feel as if it were crawling with maggots. Reisil recoiled, pressing her fist to her throat.

Slowly she became aware of the gathering *nokulas*. All around the valley like a living wall of menace. *Nokulas* piled together like a heaving, squirming tangle of rats. More poured down the hillside to the right and left, a steady stream of glowing bodies trickling down to swell the numbers below. As Reisil watched, the center softened and opened, giving away into a long gauntlet that led into the heart of Mysane Kosk. A dare? A taunt? Most definitely a trap.

"What do you see?" Yohuac asked.

"Trouble. This is going to be harder than I thought." Nearly impossible.

"We'll have to try to break through and get to one of the stockades," Yohuac said, when Reisil described the massed *nokulas* below.

She shook her head doubtfully. "There are so many of them. If we split up—"

"It won't help. The entire horde will just focus on

you. If I'm with you, at least I can distract a few of them. It could make the difference. *You* must get through. I don't matter."

"You matter to me," she muttered. He didn't hear. "What do you suggest?"

"We go down the slope slowly. No sense breaking our necks tumbling down the slope. If you can find one, angle toward a thin spot in their defenses. Try not to be obvious. When we're close enough, kick the horses into a gallop and try to break through to a stockade. I wish we had some sort of diversion."

Reisil dashed her fist at the rain runneling down her forehead and cheeks. It wasn't much of a plan. But she didn't have any better ideas. She drew her sword, watching the jumble of beasts below as they congealed together in hungry expectation. It was a fine line she walked. Though she wouldn't resort to tapping into the magic that gave them life, she didn't have any compunction about trying to kill them if necessary. She had a right to protect herself. She glanced at her sword. It wasn't much, especially with her feeble skills. Still, it felt good in her hand. Like she wasn't just a mouse surrounded by an ocean of cats.

She reached over to brush Yohuac's hand with her fingers, biting her cheek and tasting blood. He wouldn't be able to see the *nokulas* coming for him. *Please, Lady, watch over him.*

Reisil faced back down the hill, setting her chin. "All right. Let's go."

They picked their way down slowly, Yohuac allowing Reisil to guide their course. His gelding walked stiff-legged, its head high, its nostrils flared. Indigo twitched and snorted, but remained steadfast beneath Reisil's hand.

Every step twisted the wire through Reisil's entrails tighter. Suddenly the *nokulas* were mere yards away, divided from Reisil and Yohuac by a narrow creek at the bottom of a short, steep bank. Across it opened the mouth of the gauntlet.

"We'll have to jump," Reisil said huskily. "Ready?"

Yohuac nodded. Reisil gripped her sword more tightly, eyeing the distance over the creek with trepidation. Holding the reins and the sword, she was just as likely to lose her balance and fall off as not. Still, she was no cavalry rider who could make the horse obey by weight and leg alone. And she wasn't going to sheath her sword. She sighed. *Stop dithering and get on with it.* No sense keeping the *nokulas* waiting.

She glanced up into the night. She *would* see Saljane again.

Clutching the thought close, Reisil shortened her grip on the reins and clamped her legs tight around Indigo's barrel. Instantly he exploded. His hooves dug hard into the rocky soil. A spray of pebbles and mud spattered up behind. He bounded down the incline. At the top of the bank, he bunched himself into a tight spring and heaved himself aloft with a braying neigh.

They landed with a jolt. Reisil rocked forward onto the pommel and then back as Indigo launched into a desperate gallop. Beside her, Yohuac's bay gelding thudded to the ground and careened forward. Straight up the waiting gauntlet. Behind them, *nokulas* filled in the gap of their passing, closing the door on any escape.

All around her Reisil felt the pulsing magic of Mysane Kosk. They were down in it now. It pulled at her with a furious current, like storm-whipped ocean waves. The magic coiled and skurled, dragging against and swelling over her. Reisil cried out in primitive panic. It thrust into her mouth. She gagged and grappled at it with invisible fingers. It rose over her again, pushing into her ears and muting sound. She clung to Indigo, urging him faster.

They raced between the lines of invisible *nokulas.* Ahead loomed the crystal lattice and irridiscent mist surrounding Mysane Kosk. Reisil tore her gaze from its seductive beauty. Then she saw it. There, just ahead on the left. A thinning in the fence of beasts. She hunched over Indigo's withers, urging him faster. She pulled ahead of Yohuac. One breath. Two breaths. Three.

She yanked on the reins and Indigo swerved. He bowled into the thicket of *nokulas*. Reisil windmilled her sword, chopping a swath toward freedom. Her sword glanced off bony hide, sending needlelike tingles up her arm. She swung again. This time her blade cut into flesh and stuck fast. She shouted triumph. The sound turned to a scream as her arm was twisted behind and under as Indigo lurched sideways. Her arm wrenched and gave a stomach-churning *pop!* Pain erupted in her shoulder; tears blinded her. Indigo staggered, heaving himself around on his haunches. She heard thudding crunches as he struck out with his forelegs. All around them an unearthly, mind-curdling screech rose, hammering at her mental barriers. An instant later, warning bells clanged from the stockades.

Reisil scarcely heard it. Thirty *nokulas* crouched in a circle around her, with more closing in rapidly. Others surrounded Yohuac a dozen feet away. He slashed mightily with his sword. His muscles corded, and sweat and blood ran down his forehead and arms. Hardly aware of her own danger, Reisil shouted warning as a great *nokula* reared up, its mouth gaping, its claws cocked to shred Yohuac's exposed back.

She saw it in slow motion, as though the world were caught in syrup. Reisil forgot about her own danger. She snatched at her power. It rose in a volcanic flood. Without taking time to think, she released it, sending a bolt of burning magic into the *nokula* looming behind Yohuac.

The beast . . . shattered.

Reisil froze, stunned, as it simply exploded into shards of magic. Patterns appeared in the fragments, like phrases of *rinda,* the magical language of the wizards. Only mixed in with the *rinda* were characters and words she didn't recognize.

But there was no time to think. The *nokulas* around her paused a bare second. She could almost read the progression of thought in their blank expressions—if they couldn't have her for themselves, they'd not let her free to destroy them. In concert they turned on her, hunching against the ground, gathering themselves to sweep her off of Indigo. *A school of vicious fish,* Reisil thought wildly, recalling Sodur's description. *Rip. Tear. Kill.* It wasn't her imagination. She heard the words like a shout in the dark. Then she thought nothing at all, as the *nokulas* surged.

"We cannot send men in search of a fiction," Metyein said, pulling Kebonsat into a hollow between two buildings. "You have to tell Emelovi the truth."

"And what if she decides she wants to hightail it back to her *ganyik* brother?" Kebonsat demanded in a low voice. "You know he'll kill her."

"Are you suggesting we persist in the lie? To what end?"

Kebonsat blew out a harsh breath. "Of course not."

"Then what?"

Kebonsat looked away, unable to meet the condemnation in Metyein's gaze.

"Then tell her. And if she tries to go back to Aare, we'll stop her. But I doubt she will. Once she thinks it through, she'll realize she can't go back. She's a strong woman. She'll pull herself together and help us to rally the people here as no one else can."

Kebonsat rubbed his tongue across the inside of his lower lip, considering Metyein's inexorable expression. At last he nodded. "I'll do it."

"I'll be in my study if you want company after." Metyein gripped Kebonsat's shoulder sympathetically and then strode away.

Kebonsat had plenty of time to consider his words. An officious maid prevented anything but the most trivial conversation. The girl was the daughter of some minor Basham. She did not feel it proper that the Vertina should be left alone in the company of a man. Especially a Patversemese man. She tucked a blanket around Emelovi, brought a seemingly endless offering of food and drink, lit a fire, dusted a table in the corner, trimmed candlewicks . . . endless fidget work. All the while, Emelovi watched Kebonsat, her eyes dark and desperate. Much to Kebonsat's discomfort, she radiated an absolute faith that he would make everything all right. It made him want to slit his own throat.

It was too soon when Emelovi at last dismissed the maid. The girl left with a sniff and a swirl of skirts, promising to be "just a whisper away, Dazien." The look she turned on Kebonsat could have flayed the hide from a crocodile.

"Gelles thinks you will take advantage of me," Emelovi said, blushing.

Kebonsat smiled weakly. Something in his expression alarmed her.

"What is it? Is something wrong? My father?" Her voice rose breathlessly, her face turning gray.

Before Kebonsat could reply, an unworldly cry broke the calm night. Kebonsat leaped to his feet, the hair on his arms and legs standing on end. Before he could speak, bells began to clamor an alarm.

"What is happening?" Emelovi whispered, standing beside him and clutching his arm. "It's not . . . Aare?"

"No. Juhrnus said your brother is nowhere near Mysane Kosk."

"Then what?"

Kebonsat shook his head. "I must go. Stay here."

Emelovi nodded. Her voice trembled. "Of course."

There was no time to say anything else. The door burst open and the assiduous little lady's maid bustled in, her cheeks brilliant, her eyes snapping as if somehow Kebonsat were the cause of the danger.

She curtsied perfunctorily to Kebonsat, and then more deeply to Emelovi, wrapping the Vertina in a warm cloak and guiding her to a chair with determined hands.

"It will be all right, Dazien. You just rest and all will be well."

Kebonsat hesitated. He should tell her. He licked his lips. The bells clanged louder.

"I will send word as soon as I know something," Kebonsat said. Without another word, he snatched up his cloak and strode out the door. *You are a coward,* he told himself bitterly as he broke into a jog. *And you will surely pay the price for not telling her when you had the chance.*

Chapter 7

Yohuac whirled his sword. It felt as unwieldy as a stone club. His arm jarred and his teeth rattled with every thrust he made at the *nokulas* snapping and driving at him like rabid wolves. He fought hard against the drag of his wasted body. He moved sluggishly, two beats behind what his mind said to do. He couldn't find the rhythm that used to come so effortlessly. Instead he jerked himself from side to side, chopping and swinging with all the grace of a drunk donkey.

Fire cut across his thigh and raked down his calf. Yohuac hardly noticed. He was a warrior of the Cemanahuatl. He'd been inured to pain since boyhood. His horse shuddered, struck by a heavy blow. The gelding staggered and skidded, dropping to one knee. Yohuac's legs clamped down and he lunged backwards, driving his sword into the eye of a slavering *nokula*. His horse wrenched upright, rearing.

Then suddenly something exploded behind them with a rainbow light. The ground shook. A stinging wind rushed across the battlefield. As abruptly as it began, it dropped, heavy as lead. The air went still as death. Silence filled the valley from edge to edge.

It was shattered by a chorus of furious cries from the mass of *nokulas*. Their voices twined together, becoming a single sound that swelled and filled the night. It was unbearable, like teeth on metal. Every hair on Yohuac's body rose. Chills cascaded over his skin. It took several seconds to realize that he was no longer under attack, that the beasts' attention was fixed elsewhere.

He took hold of himself in the momentary lull. He twisted, seeking Reisil. He found her thirty paces away. The sound broke off abruptly. The *nokulas* surrounding Reisil heaved up. She lifted her sword. Magic blossomed around her hands. Too little, too late.

Yohuac didn't think. Instinct took hold of him. He dropped the dam on the magic that seemed always to fill him with torrential pressure. It rushed out with the force of an avalanche. He spun it in a whirlwind, shoving it outward with all his might. Magic-driven wind snatched *nokula* bodies up from the ground and flung them into the air. The funnel cloud expanded, eating greedily through their ranks.

The torrent roared through him, pulled up from the ground, from the air and the water. Yohuac flung his arms out, grinning madly at the destruction of his enemies.

A fist of pure power closed around him. It enveloped his funnel, crushing it in a grip that seemed careless in its extraordinary strength. It closed harder. Yohuac drove his magic furiously at the strangling hand. It ricocheted away and bounced back at him. Pain erupted inside him, fracturing through his flesh. He sobbed, faltering. The fist closed tighter. He felt his ribs crack. The whirlwind ceased. All around him pattered rocks and mud. *Nokula* bodies crashed down as if heaved from catapults. The pressure didn't relent. Yohuac gasped, his eyes bulging.

Suddenly he heard a shriek of elemental fury. It tore through across the blackness filling his mind.

~Baku?

The only answer was another shriek. And then the coal-drake was there. Baku tore at the invisible spell with talons and teeth, red fire crackling down his hide and flaming from his claws and maw.

The pressure released with a crack like thunder that shook the night. A flash of white light lit the valley for the blink of an eye. Yohuac slumped in his saddle, catching at the gelding's mane as he listed to the side. The gelding trembled and remained still, waiting for a command. Yohuac thanked *Ilhuicatl* and the Teotl that he rode a wizard's mount. None other would have stood so patiently as the world turned inside out.

Baku landed beside them, talons raking furrows into the dirt. His hide glittered as if he'd swallowed a sky full of stars. He lashed his head from side to side, snapped at the warily circling *nokulas*.

Yohuac mindsent inarticulate gratitude, feeling a hot rush of pleasure from Baku.

"Reisil!" Yohuac shouted suddenly, remembering the smothering attack of *nokulas*. He straightened, searching frantically in the darkness.

"Here!"

She hadn't moved, but between them now was the barest line of *nokulas*. Saljane perched on her shoulder. The goshawk hissed, gripping Reisil's shoulder tightly. The ivy on Reisil's face blazed gold, mirroring that on Saljane's beak. Both of their eyes had turned ruby red.

Reisil urged her horse toward Yohuac. The dun snorted and reared, and then canted forward in reluctant hops. As he did, long tendrils of magic flowed from Reisil's fingers. The sticky brown-colored strands coiled around the remaining beasts keeping her from Yohuac and Baku. She jerked her fingers, sweeping the *nokulas* aside into a piled jumble. Indigo leaped forward to the uncertain safety of the company of friends.

But even as she drew up next to Yohuac, the beasts sorted themselves out. They would attack again soon.

"Good to see you both," she said. "And thank you," she said with a weak smile.

Yohuac scanned her greedily from head to foot. There were scrapes on her face and hands, and her cloak had disappeared. A rent in her sleeve on her left forearm seeped blood, but she didn't seem to notice. Despite the unearthly red of her eyes and the brilliant stream of ivy on her face, she was herself, the woman he— He didn't even dare complete the thought. He was just glad, very glad, to see her alive.

"Lucky something stopped me before I killed you," he said.

"Lucky." She sounded more worried than pleased. "Can you do it again?"

She wasn't really asking if he could, but if he would. Yohuac nodded. "What do you have in mind?"

Rcisil flexed her fingers, wincing. "Hit them with everything we've got. And run like the demon hordes were after us."

"Aren't they?"

Reisil's mouth was tense. She looked at Baku. "Good to see you." She glanced up at Saljane, and Yohuac wondered what she said.

~I thought it wiser to wait and help, Baku said with a challenging snort.

Yohuac repeated the message.

"You just might be right," she said to the coal-drake.

"They're coming," Yohuac warned softly. During their exchange, the *nokulas* had regained their composure. Yohuac was appalled at how fast the beasts had reorganized. As far as he could see in the murky darkness, misty shapes flowed toward their position. Already the small bubble of open space around them was narrowing.

"We'd better not wait any longer." She turned her head to look at him. The ivy on her face burned bright enough to make his eyes hurt. Yohuac recoiled and barely kept himself from leaping to the ground in obeisance. "Don't worry about hurting me. Throw whatever you have at them." She paused. "And use Baku. That's what he's for."

Yohuac heard Baku's snarl in his mind and hesitated. For a second, when Baku had first touched his mind months ago, Yohuac had felt an exquisite connection, an endless wonder and delight in Baku that shook him to his core. And an instant later, he shattered the moment. He had a destiny and there was no room in it for Baku. Only he couldn't meet that destiny without the coal-drake's help. And so he'd let Baku guide him to Reisil. Even then, when he should have weaned himself from Baku's prickly companionship, he'd continued to lean on the coal-drake. Yohuac had been the reason Baku was trapped by the wizards.

It was time he drew a line. Time he stopped taking advantage. Time he stopped torturing this poor beast.

The pain that tore through his mind was a blade of pure rage. Yohuac's head snapped back and blood ran from his nose. Baku was nearly inarticulate in his fury.

~I am no poor beast. I am ahalad-kaaslane. *And my choice is not to be pitied. My choice is to stay with you, to defend Reisil, to save Kodu Riik.*

Baku didn't wait for a reply, but leaped after Reisil, who was pushing slowly into the ranks of the *nokulas,* her magic sweeping them aside. But she hardly went five steps before they pushed back, hardening themselves into an unmovable, unscaleable wall.

Reisil fell back a pace. The *nokulas* pushed forward. Another pace. They were being herded again.

Yohuac drew a deep breath. His power swirled inside like a raging nest of hornets. It was ever so. Releasing it . . . But the other choice was to fail, to allow the *nokulas* to drive them into the blighted city of Mysane Kosk. And then Kodu Riik and Cemanahuatl and all he held dear would be lost forever.

~Baku. Help me.

There was no hesitation. Baku was there, a bracing force, a half of himself Yohuac didn't know he was missing.

Yohuac released his power. Baku snatched at the torrent, spinning it into a fine ribbon, weaving it with his own elemental power. It was thread-fine, sparkling like diamonds and gold. And then he sent it snaking into Reisil's hand.

Reisil started as the thread wrapped her hand and spun up her arm. The ivy on her face burned incandescent, and Yohuac turned his head, tears running from his eyes. He clung to his horse, helpless as the power drained from him. He gasped, instinctively pulling more from the natural world around him. His hands and feet went numb, and he felt himself sliding from his saddle. He hardly felt himself hit the ground or Baku clutch him in his claws and drag him slowly forward.

Power buffeted them in sheets of fire. Yohuac screamed. He thought he screamed.

He couldn't see. He couldn't hear anything. His body felt wrapped in a shroud of moss and mud. He did not know if he had legs or arms or if his guts spilled out onto the ground. All he knew was the magic spiraling through him, grappling his soul and ripping it from his body. And he let it go. It was his sacrifice to Reisil.

Then he felt Baku's clutch on his mind loosen, as if the coal-drake mentally staggered. The tug on his soul lessened and icy screws began drilling through his insensate limbs. He heard explosions, though they seemed far away, and then a shock wave rolled through the air. The ground heaved and buckled, and the sinews between his joints stretched.

He thought he'd known pain. He was wrong.

He woke to jolting blackness. He was lying across Reisil's thighs as they trotted over muddy ground. He heard the rasping of Indigo's breathing, smelled the stench of horse sweat, blood, leather, and death.

"Come on, come on. Keep going. Not far now. Not far now." Reisil repeated the words in a broken chant.

Yohuac shifted, unable to get a breath with the pommel pressed against his cracked ribs and her knee digging into his stomach.

"Stop that," she said in a voice of marble and then went back to encouraging Indigo.

~Baku?

The coal-drake did not answer. Fear made Yohuac struggle against Reisil's hold. She slapped his head in the darkness.

"Do you want to fall off?"

"Baku . . ."

"Has got wings."

"What happened?"

"The wizards. They're busy arguing over us. Now
be quiet and stay still. We're far from free, yet."

The ride seemed endless. Yohuac coughed and
gasped, trying to be quiet. The rain that had stopped
sometime during the melee resumed. It trickled down
his neck and into his ears and nose. His dangling arms
burned and ached and his teeth clacked together. He
held his tongue to the roof of his mouth, trying not
to bite it in half. His knees banged into Indigo's side,
and one boot slid slowly from his foot.

The memory of pain haunted him, chewing and gnawing at the wounds the *nokulas* and wizards had made.
But it was vague. Troublesome in its endlessness, but
his mind had grown too fragmented to hold on to the
pain, to hold on to anything more than Reisil's voice,
repeating the endless chant of encouragement, as if
the sound alone carried all three of them to safety.

Reisil's voice cracked and her throat burned. Indigo's ears twitched in time to her constant flow of
words as he stumbled along under the burden of two
riders. He faltered only when she did. ". . . only a
little way . . . only a little way farther . . . keep it
up . . . keep going . . . steady now . . ."

Her hand was fisted in Yohuac's cloak, balancing
him across her lap. Her arm ached from the drag of
his weight. If it hadn't been for Baku's help, she never
would have grappled Yohuac up on Indigo. And thank
the Lady for the timely arrival of Tapit and his brethren. If Reisil had been capable of laughing, she would
have. As the wizards and the *nokulas* fought, their
prey was escaping. Reisil resisted the urge to look
back at the battle. Instead she focused on the narrowing distance to the nearest stockade. She clenched
at the stream of strength flowing from Saljane.

A nearby explosion made her body jerk, and Indigo
shimmied to the side, snorting. "Easy, boy, easy. Noth-

ing to worry about. Let's go . . ." She nudged him
with her heels.

Suddenly the temperature behind dropped, and a
rime of frost spread under Indigo and out to the stockades like wind over tall grass. In a moment the valley
turned white. A crust of ice crunched beneath Indigo's
hooves. His breath plumed in the air and steam rose
from his back. The rain turned to sleet, pattering Reisil's face with stinging blows. She hunched her shoulders, tucking her chin against her neck, her heart
pounding.

". . . easy now . . . steady . . . not far and then it
will be warm and you'll have a hot mash and hay and
a blanket . . ." The words were as much to settle her
own nerves as Indigo's.

A roar echoed through the valley. The ground shuddered. Reisil scrabbled for her magic, but she couldn't
hold it. The pain was too much. She moaned. Tears
streamed down her cheeks. Holding her breath, she
tried again. Her body convulsed and she listed to the
side. Yohuac started to slide off. She caught him with
a jerk, and heaved him back up. Her muscles screamed.
She swallowed the bile that rose bitter in the back of
her throat.

As they drew closer to the stockade, Reisil's strength
faded like a stone sinking in the ocean. She grappled
harder to Saljane, wordless in her need. Strength
flowed into her, and her stuttering voice firmed. "Just
a little farther . . . the gates . . . go to the gates . . ."

The walls of the stockades loomed high above them.
Reisil could hear voices calling to her, but couldn't
make out the words. Her head whirled and her hands
and legs began to tremble. She smelled sawdust,
woodsmoke, and manure. She blinked bleerily, but a
gauzy gray haze blurred her vision. She tried to shake
her head, but instead found herself sliding off Indigo.
She reached out to grab the saddle, but her arms
were leaden.

She thudded to the ground, Yohuac sprawling
across her. Her breath exploded in a rush. The frozen

mud was blessedly cold against her cheek and forehead. She sighed and told herself to get up. But her
body did not answer. Slowly night closed around her
senses, swallowing her in a soft embrace. Unable to
cobble up any strength to fight it, Reisil gave in, sinking into oblivion.

"Open the gates!" Juhrnus shouted as he leaped
down the ladder and flung himself toward the barred
gates. He slipped and skidded, sliding to his knees. He
swore, springing back up. The guards heaved aside the
two great beams. Juhrnus shoved between them and
out the narrow opening.

Reisil sprawled two dozen feet outside the gates,
Yohuac on top of her. Both were bruised and bleeding
and filthy. Saljane dropped out of the sky to perch on
Indigo's saddle, her piercing cry imperious.

Kek-kek-kek-kek!

Beneath the anxious bird, the gelding stood splay-
legged. His head dangled to the ground. His ribs bellowed with effort. Juhrnus dashed past the exhausted
animal and dropped to his knees. He checked Reisil.
Relief made his hands shake. She was still breathing.

Yohuac mumbled something unintelligible and grabbed
wildly at Juhrnus's cloak.

"It's all right now," Juhrnus said as other hands
grasped Yohuac. They lifted him, carrying him inside
Raven's walls. Juhrnus scooped up Reisil and followed, scowling at her slenderness and pallor.

Back in the walls, Nurema met him, her narrow,
dark face sharp with worry. "Take her t' your rooms
and put her in bed." She glanced at Yohuac, who was
being held up by two men. "Take 'em both. I'll send
a tark and some food."

Juhrnus strode away. He paused when shouting
erupted and wagon-sized black shape drifted down
into the commons area before the gates. Baku
snapped his wings shut, his wedge-shaped head darting
back and forth. He made a feint toward the men holding Yohuac, his teeth shining in the torchlight.

"Baku!" Juhrnus's voice cut through the babble, halting Baku in his tracks. Juhrnus said nothing more. He hitched Reisil closer and strode past, inside the main hall and up the narrow corridors to his room, the men carrying Yohuac following silently behind.

He laid Reisil on the bed, motioning the men to deposit Yohuac beside her.

"Fetch some water. And wood," Juhrnus ordered, flinging off his cloak and settling Esper onto the table. He paced back and forth, waiting for the tark.

~Saljane will tear out the entrails of those in the courtyard if you do not do something, Esper warned quietly.

Juhrnus suddenly became aware of high-pitched shrieking and shouts from outside.

"Demonballs! Watch them," he said to Esper, and then fled out of the room.

He came back into the muddy commons to find Saljane perched on top of Baku. Her wings were raised. As he watched, she leaped into the air, sweeping around the gathered watchers, screeching her fury and diving at the unwary.

"Saljane!" Juhrnus jumped between her and the man who narrowly avoided her talons by flinging himself to the ground. "Stop, Saljane! I'll take you to Reisil. Just come with me." He grabbed Yohuac's cloak and wrapped it around his arm, holding it out.

Saljane whipped up in the air, glaring at Juhrnus, and then she dove. She hit his arm as if grappling a rabbit. He staggered and stumbled beneath the blow. Saljane's talons clamped his arm in iron bands, the points biting through the protective cloak to draw blood. She snapped her beak in his face. The deadly curve scraped his eyelid. Juhrnus froze, and then eased around, holding his arm well wide of his body.

He entered the room on the heels of the tark. Saljane flung herself from his arm to the bed, nudging the unconscious Reisil with her beak and making low, distressed cries in her throat. Juhrnus pulled the cloak from his arm, wincing. He would have bruises later.

The tark was a tall, bony man, his knuckles red and knobby, his jowls drooping from a long jaw. He set his bag down on a chair and turned to scan Reisil and Yohuac, who remained unconscious. He wiped his nose with a wrinkled brown handkerchief and tucked it into the sleeve of his robe.

"Let's get them undressed," he said in a slow voice thick with a cold. At Juhrnus's hesitation, he flicked up a bushy gray eyebrow. "Are you squeamish? Shall I send for someone else?"

Juhrnus flushed and began wrestling off first Yohuac's boots, then Reisil's. The tark muttered under his breath as he stopped to examine bruises and cuts. He paused long moments over the welter of scarlet scars decorating Yohuac's body before moving on to the fresh wounds.

Juhrnus's own gorge rose at the sight of Yohuac's scars. He could imagine only one thing that could have made such wounds. "Wizards," he muttered, the word dripping with loathing.

The tark glanced at him. "Ah."

It took nearly two hours for Gamulstark to bathe and dress the wounds. Yohuac had revived and was sitting hunched in a chair dressed in Juhrnus's spare clothing, both hands wrapped around a cup of broth. He stared broodingly at Reisil's prone figure. Saljane nestled beside her in the bedclothes.

Juhrnus stoked the fire and paced furiously around the room, unable to elicit anything more than a one- or two-word response from Yohuac to his questions. Reisil's unrelenting stillness made him want to chew rocks. At last Gamulstark stepped in front of Juhrnus, his arms akimbo.

"I am sure your assistance would be appreciated on the walls," he said. His unrelenting expression allowed no room for protest.

Juhrnus looked again at Reisil. He wanted to be here when she woke up. Everything depended on her, and there was so much they needed to know. His hands flexed. He wanted to hit something.

"She will not wake up for some hours, I should think. She's depleted herself immensely," Gamulstark added, more kindly. "I will send for you when she wakes."

Juhrnus nodded. There wasn't anything else he could do.

"She's not going to . . . ?"

"Die? No. Not on my watch."

"Then I'll leave you."

~*Stay here. Call me if there's need*, Juhrnus said to Esper.

~*Be careful*, was Esper's response. Juhrnus turned and winked at his *ahalad-kaaslane*. With any luck, he'd finally get to hit something.

Chapter 8

Kebonsat fumed, pacing along the slick planking above the gates of Lion. A peculiar stillness hung thick and heavy over the valley. Not a breath of wind stirred, and Kebonsat's skin twitched at every stray sound. Now that the rain had let up, even the scuff of a boot or the jingle of a bridle sounded like a trumpet blast. Phantom shapes seemed to move beyond the torchlight, shadows slithering inside shadows. Kebonsat stared, his hands balling into fists, willing the darkness and mist to open up and reveal their secrets.

"What's going on?" Metyein came to stand beside him. Mud streaked his cloak and rimed his boots. He'd come through the tunnel from Eagle, where he'd been assessing Juhrnus's supplies and greeting the new arrivals.

"I wish I knew. We should be out there fighting. She could be hurt." Or worse.

The uncanny cry that had pulled Kebonsat away from Emelovi had ended with explosions of color that shook the ground and rattled the walls. These were followed by waves of heat and ice. Kebonsat knew Reisil was at the heart of it. What else could it be? And she faced an army of *nokulas*. They had streamed past the stockade walls not long after sundown, rank after silvery rank of them, none bothering to hide themselves. Their numbers had seemed endless. And not long after, the battle had begun. It had gone on for hours. Then, as suddenly as it began, silence fell.

"We don't know that Reisil needs help. You know better than anyone what she's capable of—what she did to the wizards in Patverseme." Metyein eyed the men gathered below. They stood stoic in drenched cloaks, their bedraggled horses saddled. Most had swords, but the pikes they carried were nothing more than sharpened spears. "We are ill-prepared to fight so many *nokulas*. We'll wait to see if there is need."

"What if she's trapped, waiting for us to help her?"

"What if she made it to one of the other stockades? Or she might have destroyed them all. We'll wait for word."

"You don't think she's really killed them?"

Metyein's lips twisted. "She's powerful. But it's more likely that Soka would become celibate."

"Send a scout to look for her."

Metyein pursed his lips and then shook his head. "I've considered it. But it's a waste of a man. Even if Reisiltark is waiting for rescue, a scout would likely be killed before he discovered that, much less reported back to us."

"So we wait."

"Until dawn and we can see what we're up against. Unless something changes."

Kebonsat swung around and peered again into the darkness. "And at dawn?"

"We'll go have a look. How is Emelovi?"

Kebonsat sucked his teeth. "I didn't tell her."

"Why not?"

"There wasn't enough time."

Metyein didn't reply. Kebonsat chafed at his friend's reproving silence.

"There was an officious lady's maid guarding her virtue. I couldn't drive the girl off long enough to say a dozen words." Kebonsat sounded more petulant than he would have liked.

"It cannot wait, Kebonsat. She must learn her new role. Our people need to know she is strong—that she is worth serving. That she will lead them in the battle against Aare."

Kebonsat looked over his shoulder. "And if she won't?"

"You have to let her choose her own path. She might surprise you," Metyein said. "Emelovi is loyal to Kodu Riik, and that means loyal to the Lady's law. Aare is breaking that law by trying to destroy the *ahalad-kaaslane*. He needs to be stopped, and once she finds out that her father cannot do it, she will find the courage to do it herself."

Metyein's argument made sense. But it made Kebonsat feel only marginally better. Because once he told her the truth, Emelovi would be lost to him.

He stiffened, disgusted with himself. *Coward! The way you are behaving, she would be well justified. You made a choice. You'd make it again. So stand up and accept the consequences.*

He nodded, jaw knotting.

"It must be soon. This news rots like dead flesh the longer it waits." Metyein drilled Kebonsat with his gaze. It was the look of a Lord Marshal to his subordinate.

"As soon as I see her."

"Good."

Metyein turned and descended the ladder. Kebonsat watched him go with a tight smile. Emelovi wasn't the only one donning a role she did not want. Like it or not, Metyein was the Lord Marshal of this rebellion. Of Kodu Riik, when they won.

Kebonsat turned back to the valley, straining at the darkness again. If they won. If their best chance hadn't died in this battle of magic. If Reisil wasn't even now spilling her heart's blood onto a muddy field.

He looked up in the sky. Dawn was hours away.

A guard on watch shouted, and Kebonsat jerked his head down and leaped to look over the wall. Filmy green light bloomed around Raven, the sixth stockade. It rose into the sky in a sheet of gossamer brilliance. He scrambled down the ladder, jumping the last six feet. Metyein was already calling out orders.

"Mount up. Four men deep, squads of twenty. Archers in front, cavalry next, footspears to the rear. On my mark, archers take down as many as you can. Release at will. When all arrows are depleted, cavalry moves up, with foot spears close behind. We'll drive the beasts into the wards and break them against the walls. You have fifteen minutes to make ready."

As Kebonsat approached, Metyein motioned three other men to join them. "Hopefully the other stockades are prepared. If not, rally them and send them after as soon as you can. We march in fifteen minutes. Kebonsat, take Wolf. Jiletes, take Fox. Yilek, you've got Hawk, and Nelus, you take Eagle. Go!"

Kebonsat took the horse a groom held ready. He was galloping before his right foot found the stirrup. The other two men were close behind. Outside the gates they split apart, each heading to rally his assigned stockade.

"They're coming, boy. Are ye ready?" Nurema's whisper was ominous. She pushed up her sleeves and flexed her fingers. "The wards may not hold. Wouldn't if them *nokulas* were coming full strength, but they've been worn down. Better hope them wizards tore their beasty hearts out."

"At least they can be killed." With four or five men on each creature, they could be taken down. But the cost in human lives would be very high. For every *nokula* killed, at least two men would die. And then, only if they could see them. When they went invisible . . . Juhrnus remembered seeing the remnants of a hunting party after a *nokula* attack only a week after they first arrived in the valley. How many beasts it had taken to tear the six men to stew meat, he didn't know. It could have been just one. After that, any team leaving the stockades had been made up of at least ten men.

Something shoved him. Juhrnus fell back a step, struggling forward against the steady gust. But the air was turbid and thick. It swelled and pressed against him. His ears felt full of water. He struggled to breathe, smelling the reek of heat and metal, like a

lightning strike. Nurema stood on the rail in the space
of a crenel, gripping the sharpened spikes on either
side, murmuring quick and low.

The force of the air eased and Juhrnus lunged for
the wall, yanking himself up to look over. Forty paces
from the wall, ghostly green lights flared and spread,
smearing and rippling and then fading slowly in streaking drips. Another buffeting gust of power pounded
against him. The palisade shuddered and creaked. He
lost his grip and fell to the plank rampart with a grunt.
He rolled to his feet, leaning into the pressure and
inching toward Nurema.

"Can you hold them?" he shouted. The sound came
out muted.

Nurema didn't reply. The muscles in her thin arms
corded, and her jaws clenched with the effort of rein-
forcing her wards.

Juhrnus hunched down and inched his way down
the wall toward the gate tower. The palisade's founda-
tions were made of log boxes that had been sunk into
ten-foot trenches and then filled with earth. Thirty-
foot-tall timbers were stripped of bark and then upended before them to create the palisade. More dirt
from the tunnels and the remaining dirt from the
trenches had been packed on top of the boxes and in
front of the walls for stability. Then the barracks and
living spaces had been built inside the walls on top of
the earth-filled foundation boxes. These took advantage of the palisade wall to save time and timbers
in constructing living spaces, and also reinforced the
palisade. Even with all that, the palisade continued to
shiver ominously.

Within the gate tower, the guards strained forward,
watching through the loops, bows ready.

"Where's the Captain of the Watch?" he yelled.

One of the guards pointed downward.

Juhrnus dropped down the narrow stairs. He
crossed the muddy commons to the barracks that lined
the back curve of the palisade. The captain stood next
to a sergeant who was loudly beating a length of wood

against the wall. The captain wore a leather helm, with strips of green and yellow banding his neckline, biceps, and the tops of his boots. The sergeant was marked by strips of green similarly placed, and a patch of yellow on either shoulder. The gaudy markings made him visible to his men in battle.

Soldiers poured out of the building past the two men, adjusting sword belts, pulling on coats and helms, and stringing bows. The only indication that they were soldiers were the helms and the strips of green sewn to their sleeves. Otherwise they looked like what they were—farmers, carters, miners, merchants, bakers . . . ordinary men. But their faces were full of determination and courage. Ordinary men they might be, but they were also the defenders of Kodu Riik, the defenders of Honor. Juhrnus nodded approval. He and Metyein and Kebonsat had chosen to call their settlement Honor to lend its new citizens pride and purpose. And it had.

The hodgepodge militia formed up in ragged lines. The captain turned and spoke to the sergeant, who gave up beating the alarm against the barracks and tossed down the length of wood. The two men marched down the lines, giving orders in each man's ear. The soldiers peeled away one after another, climbing onto the allure and taking defensive positions. They moved sluggishly, laboring against the waves of power that continued to leak through Nurema's wards.

And when the *nokulas* broke through? Bows and arrows and swords would be feeble defenses against magic. Juhrnus refused to consider it. One thing they had was plenty of arrows. The *nokulas* would pay a steep price before breaching the walls.

As the captain and his sergeant came to the end of the line, Juhrnus stepped in front of them. The burly captain jerked up from his conversation with his sergeant, his broad face annoyed. Seeing Juhrnus, he scowled. Juhrnus bent close.

"Wards aren't going to hold! Have to move the women and children to the tunnel!" he shouted.

"It's not finished! Nowhere to go!" was the captain's reply.

Juhrnus swore. Sending Reisil down into the tunnel would be nothing but a trap when the *nokulas* overran their defenses. The captain didn't wait, but strode off toward the walls.

~How is she?

~She sleeps still. She is restless, came Esper's troubled response. *The tark is worried. She is failing.*

Juhrnus didn't have to ask to know that Reisil was responding to the magical attack. It had to stop. But they needed help.

He turned, searching the compound. His eyes snagged on Baku. The coal-drake was pressed again the wall nearest to Juhrnus's quarters, his head nestled between his front feet. The tip of his tail thrashed back and forth, and his skin radiated a pearly light.

Juhrnus broke into a lurching jog, fighting the push of the heavy air. He squatted next to Baku, who lifted his head, his lips pulling back in a snarl. Juhrnus ignored the animal's threat, bending close.

"Can you fly? Can you bring the others?" he shouted.

Baku thrust his nose into Juhrnus's stomach. Juhrnus fell back at the blow, his breath exploding from his chest.

~Why? Baku's voice was a thin thread in his mind.

He coughed and sat up, holding a hand to his throbbing ribs.

~ Reisil can't take this much longer. I'm going to tell Nurema to drop the wards. When she does, we'll need help. The others won't know Reisil is here or that we don't have wards. They might wait until dawn to investigate. And dawn will be far too late.

Baku thrust his nose hard against Juhrnus again, blowing a hot, snorting breath.

~Why?

Juhrnus scowled, and then realization dawned. He set his hand on Baku's neck.

~Can you hear me?

~Yes. Why?

Juhrnus repeated his explanation.

~Can you fly?

Clearly Baku did not want to leave Yohuac.

~Yes, he said reluctantly.

~I'm going to have Nurema drop the wards. Go quickly.

Juhrnus scooted back as Baku launched himself up from the muddy ground and into the air in one elegant motion. The coal-drake vanished over the palisade.

"Hurry!" Juhrnus called after, though Baku could not hear him. He scanned the walls, looking for the captain. He glimpsed a flash of yellow near the gatehouse and plunged in that direction.

The waves of magic had grown denser and more turbulent. Once he was lifted off his feet, and the palisade groaned with the force of the blast. Juhrnus landed back on the ground, legs splayed wide. He gritted his teeth. Dropping the wards was a huge gamble. It wouldn't stop the *nokulas* from continuing their magical onslaught. But the beasts were well armed with teeth and claws and hides like armor. Tonight was the first time they'd resorted to magic. No one had even been sure the beasts could use it. So with any luck, they'd decide it was easier to use tooth and claw. It was Raven's best chance. Reisil's best chance.

Up on the battlements the captain was circling the allure. Juhrnus was panting and sweating by the time he overtook him.

"Captain!" he shouted, grabbing the other man's elbow. The captain spun.

"I don't have time for you!" he yelled, and turned away.

Juhrnus snarled and snatched the other man's arm again. The captain stiffened, staring down at Juhrnus's hand. His face mottled red as he swung back around. His lips pinched together. For the first time Juhrnus noticed the stitching of green ivy over the man's heart. The frayed threads indicated that it had been there for a while. Instantly Juhrnus understood. As far as the captain was concerned, Juhrnus was just another of those *ahalad-kaaslane* who'd turned against Reisil.

"We're going to drop the wards!" Juhrnus yelled against the other man's ear. Another blast of magic hit at that moment and he staggered, falling into the captain, who pushed him upright. The planks of the allure shifted and undulated as the walls shuddered. Now the captain grabbed Juhrnus's arm and yanked him close, his chest and chin thrust out. His fingers dug deeply into the tendons of Juhrnus's arm.

"You're going to what?" the captain bellowed.

"Drop the wards! This is killing Reisiltark!"

That took the captain aback. He waited for Juhrnus to continue.

"I sent Baku—the coal-drake—for help from the other stockades! Get your men ready!"

The captain thought a moment, and then nodded, dropping Juhrnus's arm.

"Tell the men!" He pointed back the way Juhrnus had come, and the *ahalad-kaaslane* nodded before retracing his steps, pausing to update each soldier. The captain moved off in the other direction.

At last Juhrnus returned to Nurema. He was out of breath. The air was thickening and becoming harder to breathe.

Nurema's face was pallid, even in the darkness, and her lip was bleeding where she'd bitten through it. She didn't falter in her unceasing chant, her mouth closing firmly around the words as she bit each off sharply.

Juhrnus approached her warily, settling one hand on her shoulder. Her body was rigid, and she flinched from his touch. He bent close. From her neckline, a tiny green snake rose up, its yellow eyes glittering as it opened its mouth to expose long needle teeth. Juhrnus drew back slightly. The *copicatl* was a pet of Yohuac's gods.

"Drop the wards, Nurema! Reisil's in trouble. We're ready!"

For a moment, he didn't think she'd heard him. She kept chanting, her gaze fixed on the colored dance of light beyond the palisade. Then suddenly . . . she stopped. Juhrnus caught her around the waist as she slumped. He held her firmly, chest tight as he watched the wardlights fail. *Lady, let this be the right choice.*

The flickering lights grew more feeble. They sputtered and faded. Suddenly, between one second and the next, Juhrnus could hear: the scuff of a boot, the heavy gasps rasping between Nurema's lips, the pounding of his own heart. The rest of the world was as quiet as an indrawn breath.

"Here they come!" someone shouted, and the twang of arrows filled the night.

Chapter 9

Kebonsat's horse skidded and slipped. The saddle canted steeply to one side as the animal's left hind leg sank deeply into the ground. There was an ominous *snap* and the mare shrieked. Kebonsat swore and jumped from the saddle, landing ankle-deep in soupy mud. The mare's left rear leg dangled, useless.

There was no time for mercy. He abandoned the animal. Wolf stood the farthest east of the completed stockades. By horseback, it was ten minutes from Lion. On foot, in this mire . . . Kebonsat refused to think about the distance. Instead he tucked his chin to his chest and focused on not falling.

Soon his lungs burned and his sodden cloak pulled heavily on his shoulders. He peeled it off and dropped it, tripping and catching himself with his right hand. He fumbled across the road, his boots making sucking sounds in the mud. He slogged across the field of barley, the young stalks swishing around his ankles. He had no sense of how much time had passed since he'd ridden out of Lion. He strained to hear the noise of horses on the march, of a battle begun. But his own harsh breathing drowned all other sounds. Faintly he thought he heard a roar like men shouting. But it could have easily been the sound of blood pounding in his head.

An animal sound ripped from his chest, and he forced his legs to churn faster.

When he came to the wall, his stomach heaved, and sweat made his clothing cling to his sides and back. He bent, bracing against the wall. His chest felt as if a pitchfork had been driven into it; his thighs were on fire. He dropped his head, sweat dripping down his nose, sucking in deep, sobbing breaths.

"Who's there, now?" came a deep voice from above. "I kin hear ye, so answer while I've a mind to listen!"

Kebonsat tried to answer, but was swept by a fit of coughing.

"No games now! Give yer name or I'll sieve your hide with arrows!"

Kebonsat dragged a breath into his lungs and then another. In a choked voice, he called, "To arms! Honor's Lord Marshal summons Wolf to arms!"

His rasped words were met with silence. Kebonsat banged his hand against the barked timber wall. "Do you hear? Raven is under attack! The Lord Marshal summons Wolf to arms!"

He heard shouting and the quick stamp of feet as soldiers collected above. Minutes ticked past. Kebonsat began wading around the wall toward the gatehouse. The rains had turned the newly built earthworks to bogs. He sank to his thighs and had to drag himself back up onto firmer ground. He'd hardly gone a few yards when an implacable voice called down from above.

"Name yourself, *ganyik*, or surely you'll not get much farther."

"Kebonsat cas Vadonis," he answered, holding on to his temper with both hands. "Raven is under attack by *nokulas*." He hesitated. Then, "Reisiltark has come."

There was a pause. "Why didn't the Lord Marshal send a rider?" The man's voice was filled with a wealth of suspicion. Kebonsat was Patversemese. That was reason enough to doubt him.

"He did. Horse busted a leg. Now, by the grace of

the Lady, get your lazy asses moving, or I swear by
the Demonlord's *ganyik* mother that I will carve your
heart out myself if Raven is taken!"

The man above did not answer, but suddenly Kebonsat heard boots pounding and more shouting. There
was the telltale booming thumps of the gate bars being
dropped and then the sounds of horses. Kebonsat
began struggling again through the mire, rounding the
curve of the wall to find himself face-to-face with a
young man, hardly more than a boy, leading a chestnut mare.

"Sir! Sergeant says you want a horse."

Kebonsat didn't bother trying to speak, conserving
his energy for the coming battle. He reached for the
reins, taking a moment to check the mare's cinch and
stirrups before dragging himself into the saddle. His
legs were trembling and so weighted with sticky mud
that he almost didn't make it. The boy grabbed his
doublet and yanked him up.

"Thanks," Kebonsat said gruffly as the mare
touched his boot with her nose and snorted dispar-
agingly.

"Sergeant says he wants you w' him." The boy's
voice cracked, and he made a gulping noise as he re-
joined the ranks of horsemen. They were fifty strong,
riding four by four, all carrying spears and bows. Kebonsat urged the mare into a trot, aiming for the head
of the column.

This sergeant was whipcord lean, with a seamed face
and close-trimmed yellow beard. He wore a leather
helm with green stripping and the sergeant's green
stripping and yellow spot on his shoulders. His expression was sour. When he saw Kebonsat, his face darkened and his lip curled. He spat.

"*Nokulas*, you say?" He sounded dubious. More
than that. He sounded insolent and hostile.

"That's right," Kebonsat said, gritting his teeth and
ignoring the insult. "Where's your captain?"

"Feeling poorly," was the curt reply. Something made

the hairs on Kebonsat's neck stand on end. Too poorly to fight?

"Oh? What's the matter with him?" he asked diffidently.

The sergeant spat again. "Be ye a tark too? Clever man, you are. 'Twill please the cap'n no end to have you at his bedside. Got himself a fever and some chills. Flux. Why don't ye go empty his slop bucket, then?"

Kebonsat hardly heard the last words shouted after him as he reined in the mare and spun her around. Fear made his mouth dry as he galloped past the ranks of soldiers. He urged his mount faster, unmindful of the treacherous footing. Mud splattered his face and chest as he swung the mare out around a clustered group of riders at the end of the column.

Then he was alone on the muddy road. They were swinging the gates closed, but he shoved inside.

"The captain! Where is he?"

"Barracks," said one guard, cowed by Kebonsat's imperious tone. "Over there." He pointed. "First door past the racks."

Kebonsat turned the mare and galloped the short space across the bailey. He swung down and pushed inside. He strode down the long common room, past the rows of bunked rope beds. At the opposite end was a set of doors leading to individual rooms and suites.

He found the captain's room just where the guard had indicated. He rapped on the planked door sharply, and then strode in without waiting for an answer.

The captain was sitting on the edge of his bed, drawing on his boots. He was pale and clammy, his hair damp with sweat. He wobbled from side to side as he eyed Kebonsat blearily.

"What do you want?"

Kebonsat hesitated. From the moment he heard the sergeant describe the symptoms, he knew—he *knew*—that this was Honor's first case of the plague. It was a miracle that it hadn't come sooner.

Kebonsat had nightmares about its arrival, of its devastation. Everywhere it had been, the plague had swept through like a harvesting scythe. No one who got it survived. And here, in Honor, in such close quarters—it would save Aare the bother of coming after them. He found himself scrutinizing every face, listening to every complaint of pain or fever, looking for symptoms. And now Honor's first plague victim was staring him in the face.

"Well? I don't have time for chatter, so state your piece or git out of the way." The captain rose, but his knees buckled and he fell heavily back to the bed, the air going out of him with an *oomph*. "Demonballs," he muttered, rolling back upright. "Weak as a kitten."

Kebonsat made no effort to step closer.

"You're weak because you've got plague," he said bluntly. "You've got to get into quarantine. Now."

The captain's eyes widened and then narrowed. He stared at Kebonsat, a red flush flagging his cheeks.

"What do you know, Pease scum?" he said, using the soldier-patois reference for Patverseme. "I got a touch of fever, is all. And a fight going on out there I'm late for. That's where I'm going. So git outta my way."

This time he kept his feet as he stood, but Kebonsat could see that he trembled and he gripped the bedpost for support. "*Chodha*," the captain murmured softly.

"It might not be the plague," Kebonsat conceded, sympathy softening his voice.

"And I might be a goat," the other man returned. He looked at Kebonsat, his weathered face pocked and scarred, his nose broad and unformed. His blue eyes were shrewd. "All right. Where are we going?"

"Fox."

The captain frowned in surprise. "Fox is quarantine? That's maggot-headed. There ought to be a place up in the mountains, away from healthy folks."

Kebonsat shrugged. "We can't protect any holdings outside the valley. And we'll not abandon our own."

The captain snorted. "Ain't yer own, is it?" He

shook his head. "That whelp of Lord Marshal Vare is a sharp one, but he's too soft. This is war. You ought to give me a blanket and some food and send me off to fend for myself. Nothing but trouble keeping the plague in Fox."

"I'll tell the Lord Marshal," Kebonsat said. "Now let's move."

He reached out a hand to steady the captain, who glared at the proferred aid.

"And if I touch you, you git sick too? I don't much like you, Pease, but I'm not gonna be the one who kills you. Lord Marshal says he needs you. So I'll manage on my own."

Slowly the captain gathered his bedroll and stuffed his pack with a few sparse belongings. Kebonsat waited for the other man to leave the room before marking the door with a charred stick from the fire. He drew a large black X. No one would mistake the message.

He followed after the captain as the man hobbled along, bracing himself against the walls and then the long row of bunks. By the time he reached the door, his face was slick with sweat and the skin of his head gleamed through his thining hair. He slumped onto a bottom bunk, his breath shallow and sharp.

"Better get a cart. Not goin' to make it much further on my own."

Without a word, Kebonsat went looking. He found a half dozen two-wheeled barrow carts upended against the horse barns. Their interiors were crusted with mud, straw, and manure. The barns were empty but for a swaybacked, spavined mule and six donkeys. Kebonsat manhandled one of the carts down on its tongue and hitched a brace of donkeys to it. He led them around to the barracks door, and the captain pulled himself inside. Kebonsat handed him a skin of water he'd taken from the stables. The captain took it with a grimace.

"Yer not so bad, for a Pease."

"And you're a pain in the ass," Kebonsat said, tying

his mare to the wagon and leading the donkeys to the gate. The guards opened the gates slowly, worry evident in their dour expressions.

"That's a fact, boy. What do you think is going on over there?" The captain jerked his chin toward Raven.

Kebonsat stared across the valley at the torch glow emanating from Raven. He could hear the sounds of clashing arms, shouting, horses neighing, and other, nonhuman, shrieks of fury and pain. He was needed there. He swallowed, pulling the donkeys along. If the captain really had the plague, then Kebonsat was needed here. One more sword at Raven wouldn't make much difference. But isolating the plague before it could take root—it could save every soul in Honor. He only hoped that Metyein could save Reisil.

Chapter 10

"Where is Wolf?" Metyein winced inwardly at the strain thinning his voice. He took a steadying breath, trying to slow his rushing heart.

The sergeant shook his head. "Dunno, sir." He was a seasoned soldier, one who'd abandoned Koduteel and the regular army when Aare began sweeping up the *ahalad-kaaslane*. Green stitching zigzagging along the collar of his vest testified to his loyalties. He stared expectantly at Metyein.

The young Lord Marshal of Honor scanned the columns of cavalry and foot soldiers. There were about three hundred men, with a hundred and twenty-five mounted. All seventy-five of the missing troops from Wolf were also mounted. They would be sorely missed. Men on horse were always better than foot soldiers, especially against opponents the likes of the *nokulas*. And the folk of Honor needed all the advantage they could get. But Raven could not wait.

"Let's move out," he ordered. The sergeant from Fox nodded and touched his fist to the red fox patch centered on a green triangle sewn over his heart. "Yessir." He jogged off at a sharp clip, relaying orders to the captains.

Metyein mounted his horse. He settled his buckler over his arm. Its leather surface was small protection against *nokula* claws, but it was better than nothing. His own helm was plain steel with a crossbar over the nose. He wore a mail shirt beneath his tunic, and steel greaves with steel-plated gauntlets. His plate armor had gone to the crucible for building the stockades.

He settled into his saddle and signaled for a roll call. When each company had sounded off, he waved his fist in a circle and clicked his mount forward. The stallion snorted and set off at a springy walk. Not prancing—that would be unmannerly and unrefined for a seasoned warhorse, one of a treasured handful in all of Honor. But the stallion's neck arched and his tail swished as he swaggered out, rattling his bit in his teeth.

Behind came the ranks of cavalry from Lion and Hawk followed by the regiments of foot soldiers from Fox and Eagle. Some of the men had fought in the Patverseme war. Many of those were missing bits of themselves, but could still wield a sword or a spear with skill. Not that most had swords. Already they felt the pinch of too little metal. He thought of Kebonsat. Where was he? Where was Wolf?

Raven was less than a quarter of a league from Lion. It would take a matter of two or three minutes for a man to gallop there on horseback, but the infantry and the mud slowed their pace considerably. They were little more than halfway when a runner came galloping from the rear.

The rider was a corporal. On his chest he wore a green triangle with the blue silhouette of a howling wolf. He was splattered with mud, his leather helm askew. He pulled up beside Metyein.

"Lord Marshal! Wolf's compliments, sir," he said breathlessly as he saluted.

"Well met at last, Corporal. What kept you?" Metyein glanced over his shoulder. "Where is Kaj Kebonsat?"

The corporal shook his head. "Sorry, sir. Kaj Kebonsat's horse busted a leg, so we was delayed getting your orders. As for Kaj Kebonsat, he left. Gone back to Wolf."

Metyein stared. "What in the three hells for?"

The corporal swallowed hard, his throat jerking. "Dunno, sir."

Foreboding prickled like icy pine needles across Metyein's skin. Something else was happening this night. Something important enough to pull Kebonsat from saving Reisiltark. "Dear Lady, help us," Metyein muttered.

"Sir?"

"Return to Wolf, Corporal. Tell your captain to split east at my command. Take twenty-five riders from Lion and half the complement of infantry. Distribute yourselves with archers in the fore, then cavalry, then footspears. We'll come round the northwest and close our noose. When the horn sounds, archers will let fly. After the arrows are depleted, cavalry begins its assault, with footspears supporting. Questions?"

The corporal shook his head. "No, sir. But the captain was feeling poorly. Sergeant Olivel commands."

"Then inform the sergeant. You are dismissed."

The corporal pounded his fist against his wolf patch and then peeled away, his horse kicking up a plume of mud.

Metyein urged his horse into a fast trot. There was one thing Kebonsat would abandon this fight for. *The captain was feeling poorly.* By the Lady, not the plague. Not yet.

Nighttime was a distinctly stupid time to wage a battle. Clouds covered the moon, and the ground was sloppy and uncertain. Raven itself gave off little light with its torches doused to keep the defenders from night blindness. The earthworks at the base of the walls was nothing more than a quagmire moat. The horses could not encroach too closely or they would certainly break their legs.

The *nokulas* did not seem bothered by the mess and the darkness and had no mind to wait until morning. The noise of their attack shredded the air. The beasts shrieked and growled as they scrabbled at the palisade walls. They clambered up the vertical timbers like cats, tumbling back to land on their companions when the defenders jabbed at them with fire-hardened spears and hails of arrows.

Mounds of silvery *nokula* bodies built up in discrete piles along the muddy earthworks. The beasts were attacking at three points that Metyein could see, and likely several more around the other side of palisade. In doing so, they divided the strength of the men on the walls. Soon arrows and spears wouldn't be enough to withstand the constant flow of *nokulas,* who clambered up the bodies of their fallen like stepping stools. Sooner or later, the beasts would be able to leap from the mounded bodies over the top of the palisades. If Raven didn't run out of weapons first. If the rest of Honor didn't come to the rescue.

Metyein's fingers flexed, unrolling and knotting around his reins. His eyes skimmed the ranks as the men jostled into place. The archers lined up in double rows, the first kneeling, the second standing. They busily adjusted strings and readied arrows. Twenty feet behind them, the cavalry massed, the horses snorting and pawing, eyes rolling white at the smell of blood. Their skins twitched and their ears flattened at the shrieking cries of the *nokulas.* Metyein hoped they'd hold together. Most of the horses had never seen a battle. Most were broken for the ordinary labors of travel, hauling wagons, or drawing plows. Behind the horses was a thin forest of footspears.

Metyein reined his horse to the side, cantering along the ring between the archers and the jittery cavalry. He was followed by his Guidon bearing the new colors for the Lord Marshal of Honor, and the Relay bearing a brass horn to signal Metyein's orders. Both wore yellow tunics with green stripes over armor made of boiled hide. They each had bucklers slung on their arms. Metyein pulled up opposite the gates at the intersection of his complement of men, and those who'd come around with Wolf.

"Sound the ready," he ordered.

The Relay blew a sharp blast that rose to the mountain peaks and tumbled back down, filling the valley with brassy command. The *nokulas* clawing at the walls took no notice.

Metyein's eyes narrowed. The lack of response meant that they had suddenly gone deaf, or they were too involved to notice their danger, or . . . He rubbed a hand across his mouth and drew a deep breath, his heart against his breastbone. Or they didn't care because they had little reason to fear the gathered men of Honor. Metyein spit, forcing himself to relax tense stomach muscles. Tonight they'd learn a little fear. "Sound the release."

The Relay blew two short blasts and one long one. Shouts rounded the ring of archers as captains ordered the archers to launch their volley. Strings snapped and arrows whistled. There was a sound like a hail of ripe plums, and then the *nokulas* screamed in fury and pain. The men on the walls gave a ragged cheer. Metyein smiled, his nostrils flaring. The *nokulas* were paying attention now.

Then *something* hit him in the head. *Inside his head.* He rocked back in his saddle, yanking hard on the reins as his eyes blurred and his ears thundered. His warhorse gave a startled snort and obediently backed several paces. Blood trickled from Metyein's nose. He struggled to draw air through his swollen throat, listing wide to the left as his right foot slipped loose. His stallion sidestepped beneath him, helping Metyein to regain his balance and pull himself back upright. Metyein stamped his foot back into the stirrup and shook his head to clear it, dashing at the blood running down over his lips with his fist.

"Sir! Are you all right?" It was his Guidon. The man was hardly more than a boy, with bird down for a beard and a soft curve to his jaw. He reached out his hand to steady Metyein. Metyein shrugged off the aid.

"I'm fine."

"What happened, sir?"

Metyein rubbed his forehead where it throbbed. His

eyes felt too big for his skull, and he heard the Guidon's words as if from far away. "*Nokulas,* I think." His voice came out raspy and reedy, his throat raw. What had they done to him? Struck him with some kind of magic bolt. They'd been paying more attention than he thought. They knew who was commanding the attack. He turned to the Relay, who waited on his left, horn half raised.

"Should I fall, immediately ride to Captain Lides. He'll take command."

He waited until the Relay nodded.

Bowstrings continued to twang and arrows struck again and again with a staccato pelting sound. The *nokulas* at the walls turned, finding themselves being chewed up in the cross fire. Even their armored hides and vast strength could not stand against the unceasing hail of arrows.

But the supply of arrows was not infinite. It dwindled far too quickly. The *nokulas* bunched against the walls and behind their dead to make more difficult targets of themselves. Now they stirred. It seemed to Metyein that they glowed as they crawled out of hiding, heads dropped in menacing fury.

"Call the archers to retreat," Metyein said.

The Relay blew two short blasts. The archers whipped their bows over their shoulders and scrambled back through the horses to the rear to act as the vanguard. They dropped their bows and snatched up spears from piles dumped by the supply wagons that had trundled around the perimeter. The exhausted men passed the wooden weapons from hand to hand in a bucket brigade and readied themselves for battle.

The *nokulas* bounded forward as the archers scurried away. The lines of riders broke into a ragged, milling mob. The men on the walls shouted, able to do nothing but watch, their arrow supply also depleted.

"Sound the charge!"

As the Relay blasted the notes, Metyein clapped his heels to the warhorse's flanks. The horse erupted, thrusting ahead of the loose line of cavalry. It was stupid. He was the Lord Marshal. He should stay behind and give the orders. He was too valuable to risk. He knew it. But there were too few men to fight and too many *nokulas*. Trained swords were especially needed. Metyein drew his sword and dropped the reins, guiding the animal with his knees and weight.

The first and last coherent thought he had for a while was that the *nokulas* leaped absurdly high, higher than the head of his horse. They slashed and bit as they flew overhead. Their eyes glowed jewel-bright—ruby, emerald, sapphire, tourmaline, jasper. Four converged on Metyein. He swung his sword, slicing through the paw of the first. The warhorse deliberately collided with another. A blade of fire ran across Metyein's left shoulder. He grunted, gritting his teeth against the sudden pain, and whipped his sword up and down, chopping at the next beast. His sword barely bit into the tough armored plates on the *nokula*'s back. The impact jolted up his arm and through his chest. Then he was through, on the other side of the line of *nokulas*.

The warhorse wheeled. Metyein found himself face-to-face with his Guidon and Relay. Both wore scrapes and deeper lacerations, blood dampening their tunics. The Relay had blood running down his scalp and over his right ear. He clutched his horn close to his chest, fear turning him pale as a *rashani*. Metyein swore.

"What in the blighted demon-pits are you doing here?" Then he shook his head. "Never mind. Stay behind me here. Sound the ready."

The relay hesitated for a bare second; then he raised his horn with shaking hands and blew the call.

The officers were shouting orders and the riders were already reestablishing lines as the *nokulas* flung headlong into the footspears. Metyein bared his teeth.

"Sound the charge. Crush the *skraa*-eating bastards."

The horn blared out and the charge began. This time Metyein remained behind as the riders plowed into the *nokulas*. His horse snorted and lifted his feet, but remained in place.

The cavalry pushed the *nokulas* back through the footspears to where the archers waited with their spears. Metyein held his breath. The cavalry pushed them through and beyond, leaving behind hundreds of silver carcasses and far too many fallen men. In the darkness came a ragged cheer, and those on the walls responded in kind as the *nokulas* retreated back toward Mysane Kosk.

"That's it then. They've routed. Sound recall."

The relay blew the blasts. The cavalry riders came cantering back in no order, and with them came the footspears and archers jogging and limping, grins on their faces.

"Send for tarks. Check the *nokulas* and kill any still alive. Captain Lides!"

The captain galloped across the muddy field, pulling up with a sharp salute. "Lord Marshal, sir!"

"Set up a perimeter and get the wounded inside Raven."

"Not Fox, sir?"

"No. Not until we can be sure the *nokulas* won't be back tonight."

The captain accepted the explanation, touching his fist to the orange hawk on his green chest patch, and cantered away. Pretty soon men from Raven appeared carrying hide slings. Spears were slid into the sleeved edges to create stretchers.

Metyein toured the battleground, followed by the Relay and the Guidon. Honor had lost forty-eight men, with another ten severely wounded. Many bore lighter wounds, but a merriment permeated the troops. It was relief and joy that they'd won, and they knew Reisiltark had come at last.

"Sir!"

The sergeant from Hawk squelched through the mud as Metyein approached. "What do you want done with the dead *nokulas*, sir?"

Metyein's head felt muzzy; his arms and legs felt sodden. His vision went blurry and he swayed in the saddle. When he spoke, his voice sounded hollow and far away. "Burn them, I suppose."

The sergeant nodded and stepped away. Metyein clutched at his pommel as a sudden wave of vertigo struck him. He blinked, clenching his hands tight, but his muscles didn't want to obey. He tried to draw a deep breath to steady himself, but could only gasp shallowly, like a fish flopping on the shore of a lake.

"Ho, Metyein! Well played, and just in time. Nurema sent me to tell you— *Chodha!* Grab him!"

Metyein felt himself falling. His face felt hot and his chest was cold. Hands caught him and lowered him to the ground. Numbness spread through him, and he began to shiver.

"What's this? Lady's eyes! He's been wounded. You! Bring a stretcher! Now! Hurry it up!"

Metyein felt himself turned onto his stomach and lifted on a stretcher. Wounded? Ah, he remembered. The fire down his shoulder.

"Blighted fool. Get him to a tark as fast as you can. Hurry!"

Then Metyein felt the ground roll. He jolted, and now a fire burned in the numbness. He convulsed and vomited weakly. Then he slid into a stupor. Voices sounded, and a whirl of sounds and smells he couldn't identify.

"I don't care what your orders are. If the Lord Marshal wasn't busy bleeding to death—" Juhrnus glared accusingly at the bristling sergeant from Hawk. The man was smeared with mud and blood, and his clothing had been torn in the fighting. The sergeant glowered back, his jaw jutting as he squared his shoulders and pushed his chest out menacingly.

"He didn't say nothing about bein' wounded—"

"Maybe if you opened your blighted eyes, you could have seen it for yourself. Did you think he'd complain and take himself from the field? It's *our* job to make sure he takes care of himself. If he dies, where will

we be then? Who'll lead Honor against his highness
the Regent?"

The sergeant sucked his teeth and spit, just barely
avoiding Juhrnus's foot.

"Well," Juhrnus said softly. "So long as you have
someone in mind, that's all well and good. It's always
good to see such loyalty."

The sergeant's nostrils flared and he sneered. "Ain't
you one to talk. After chasing off Reisiltark? And she
the only *ahalad-kaaslane* what cares about us."

Juhrnus's hand shot out and he snatched the sergeant's collar at the neck. He yanked the other man
close, his fist twisting as he lifted the beefy man up
on tiptoe. Juhrnus's lips brushed the other man's bristled cheek.

"Reisil. Is. My. Friend. And so is Metyein. I would
die for them, for you, for Kodu Riik. I am *ahalad-
kaaslane.* And I'll thank you not to forget it."

He shoved the sergeant away, fury churning in his
stomach. It wasn't directed at the other man, but at
Sodur and Upsakes. If it hadn't been for their lies and
machinations . . . Now the people hated the *ahalad-
kaaslane.* Didn't trust them even to drive a midden
wagon. Only Reisil.

The sergeant was watching him warily. Juhrnus grimaced inwardly. One day the *ahalad-kaaslane* would
win back the trust of Kodu Riik. He'd make sure of
it. But not today. He swallowed his fury and spoke
slowly, without inflection.

"The *nokula* bodies cannot be burned. They have
to be returned to Mysane Kosk."

As soon as he began, the sergeant began shaking his
head stubbornly. "My orders is from the Lord Marshal
himself. He said to burn 'em."

"And I say take them back to Mysane Kosk." Juhrnus's eyes narrowed. "I am the Lady's hands and eyes
in Kodu Riik. Do you refuse my authority?"

The sergeant hesitated. The men piling the *nokulas*
in the back of the wagon had come to range themselves behind him. They eyed Juhrnus with no little

malice. Juhrnus ignored them, his gaze drilling into the sergeant.

Finally the other man nodded. "As ye wish."

He stalked away without another word. Juhrnus let out a sigh.

"Your balls must be half-shriveled from the heat," came Soka's sardonic voice from behind.

Juhrnus spun around. Soka stood twenty paces away. He was on foot, leading his mount. The horse held its right foreleg in the air.

"You'd know, if you had a pair," Juhrnus returned. "I see you survived. I'd have thought you'd be with Metyein."

Soka shrugged, his long hair loose around his shoulders. "When the call came, I was . . . busy. Had to argue over a horse and arrived late for the festivities."

"He's wounded."

Soka stiffened. "What? How bad?"

"Lost blood. Can't be too bad. Went touring around after it was over, not telling anyone he'd been hurt. Fell off his horse. I sent him to the tarks."

"How did he get hurt?"

"Decided to join the attack, the blighted fool."

"Did his brain dribble out his ears?" Soka asked incredulously. "Why didn't Kebonsat stop him? He, at least, should've known better."

Soka had begun striding toward the gates, where the wounded were being carried on stretchers or staggering along under their own wind. His horse hobbled behind, making pathetic whistling noises. Juhrnus kept pace beside him.

"Kebonsat wasn't there. I was watching from the walls. I never saw him."

Soka slowed. "I don't like the sound of that. Where is he?"

"Lady knows."

"This could be bad. On a night like tonight, it would be all too easy to slit his throat and drop him into a ravine without anyone noticing. There's been a lot of talk about him being too close to Metyein and Emelovi. He's a Pease *ganyik,* is how most have it. I wouldn't put it past someone to stick a dagger in his back if they got a chance. And Aare has to have spies here. One of them could have done something to him."

"So I thought too. But where to begin looking? And who do we trust to send?"

"We'll ask Metyein. If I don't kill him first."

Soka's lips tightened in what might have been a smile. Juhrnus heard the click of the poison bead against the other's man's teeth. A shudder rippled down his back. If it had broken, if Soka had accidently bitten through it in the battle—there would be another dead man on the field.

"And if he doesn't know? Or is unconscious?"

"Then I'll go to Emelovi. She's the only other possible reason Kebonsat would desert Metyein in a fight. And if she doesn't know, then I'll scour the valley until I find him."

Metyein had been carried into the Raven captain's quarters. Juhrnus and Soka passed down through the outer rack-room where the other injured were being laid on the rope bunks. The wounded men moaned and cried out pitiably. Other soldiers pressed make-shift bandages to their wounds and comforted them in low, urgent voices.

"Anybody sent to Fox for the tarks?" Juhrnus asked.

Soka pushed back his hair with an annoyed hand. "I would say our Lord Marshal had done so, but apparently he has gone witless." He glanced around, scowling when he didn't find what he was looking for. "There should be one stationed in Raven. Where is she?"

"He," Juhrnus corrected. "Gamulstark. He was with Reisil and Yohuac."

Soka nodded. "So they did make it. I thought as much. Are they . . . well?"

Juhrnus shrugged, shaking his head. "They barely made the gates. Dragged 'em in unconcious."

~*How are they now?* he scnt to Esper.

~*Restless. Especially her. But they sleep.*

Juhrnus hesitated, torn. Metyein needed care, and if there was nothing more to be done for Reisil and Yohuac . . .

~*The tark is needed for the wounded,* he told Esper at last.

Long moments ticked past with no reply.

~*Esper?*

~*Saljane will not permit him to leave. She guards the door.*

Juhrnus stopped walking, closing his eyes and rubbing his hand over his face. "Damn."

~*All right. I'm coming.*

"*Chodha,*" he muttered, and met Soka's impatient gaze. "Saljane's trapped the tark. Go on without me. I'll be back soon as I can. Make sure someone's sent to Fox."

Soka nodded, and Juhrnus hurried back up the corridor and across the muddy compound He jogged down the packed-dirt corridors, pausing outside the door of his room. He could hear the Gamulstark's frantic and furious tones, then the sounds of flapping wings and Saljane's high-pitched shriek. Gamulstark hollered inarticulately, the sound like a bull caught in the mud.

Juhrnus shoved inside. The tark was crouched in a corner, his hands raised to ward off Saljane, who was circling around to perch opposite the terrificd tark on the footboard of Juhrnus's bed.

Seeing Juhrnus, Gamulstark pushed himself upright against the wall, his long, droopy cheeks blotched red. "Thank the Lady!" He made to step from the corner to join Juhrnus, but Saljane leaped at him again with a shriek, beating at his head with her wings.

Gamulstark cowered back down, clutching his arms over his head and spreading his hands in front of his

face. He swore a string of oaths to make even Soka
blush. If Soka had been there. Juhrnus wished heartily
that he were.

"What are you standing there for?" demanded Gamulstark as Saljane flapped back to her perch to eye
him balefully. She snapped her beak and pecked at the
footboard with sharp rapping sounds. "Do something!
That, that . . . bird . . . will not let me leave," Gamulstark sputtered.

Juhrnus drew a breath, glancing at Reisil and Yohuac. They remained unconscious, appearing much the
same as when he'd left. One of Reisil's arms was flung
out to the side, her hand curled in a fist. Her lips
were clamped tightly so that there was a ring of white
around them.

He understood Saljane's concern. He looked at
Esper, stretched lengthwise along Reisil's side, and felt
again the endless emptiness when he'd nearly lost the
sisalik. In the same position, he'd shackle Gamulstark
to the bed.

Juhrnus let out his breath in a gust and stepped
between Saljane and the tark, motioning the man to
stay still. Saljane mantled. Juhrnus eyed her razor talons. Licking his lips, he bent so that he was eye-to-
eye with the distraught bird.

"Saljane," he said softly. "Hear me. Metyein is
wounded, as are many others. Gamulstark is needed.
Reisil would not want anyone to die because of her."

Saljane's only answer was to snap her beak at him.
Behind him Gamulstark made a strangled sound and
shifted his weight.

Kek-kek-kek-kek!

Saljane's body flexed, her wings extending. The
tark froze.

"Saljane." Juhrnus bent closer, mouth drying as the
curve of her beak swung within inches of his eye. He
blinked, holding his ground. Suddenly he became
aware of the stench of sweat and blood mixed with
the scents of the cooling kohv, bread, and stew that
sat on the table waiting for Reisil and Yohuac to

wake. His stomach lurched and he swallowed hard. "Saljane. This is necessary. Reisil will be well. I will stay with Gamulstark. If he is needed, Esper will tell me and I will send him. The battle is over. The *nokulas* have gone for now. All will be well. I promise."

He waited. Saljane opened her beak and hissed. *Damn.* What was he going to do now? He'd told Soka that Metyein's wounds weren't too serious, but in truth they could be mortal, for all he knew. Even now Honor's Lord Marshal might be bleeding to death. How was he going to make Saljane listen to reason?

But before he could think of anything else to say or do, Saljane relented. She ducked her head and glanced at Reisil and Yohuac, and then made a show of shaking out her feathers. She turned her back on Juhrnus, studiously ignoring him as she began to preen herself.

Juhrnus didn't wait, grabbing Gamulstark under the arm and hauling him into the corridor.

~If either of them so much as twitches, I want to know, he sent to Esper.

~I will watch.

Gamulstark sagged against the wall, bracing his hands on his knees and drawing deep, hollow breaths. Juhrnus watched him with a frown. Was the man going to piss his pants? Metyein needed help now. Not to mention all the other wounded men leaking buckets of blood. Every moment counted, and this fool was wasting people's lives. He caught himself. It was more than a little unnerving to be held prisoner by an angry goshawk. Saljane could have killed him if she wanted. The tark had a right to a few moments to pull himself together.

"Are you well? Can I help?" Juhrnus asked curtly.

Gamulstark waved a hand in the air. "A moment is all I need." He took several more breaths while Juhrnus fidgeted, shifting his weight back and forth and tapping his fingers against his thighs.

At last the lanky tark straightened, offering a wan smile. "I have always hated ducks and geese. Vicious beasts, they are. Peck you to death for crossing their path." He shuddered delicately, glancing back at the door hiding Saljane. "But that . . ." His voice faded.

Juhrnus grinned. Suddenly he liked Gamulstark a whole lot better. "Felt a little dribble down my leg, myself," he said confessionally.

Gamulstark stared for a long moment and then chuckled. He stood, rubbing his hands together. "Let's get to business, shall we? The Lord Marshal is hurt, you say? How did it happen?"

"He decided to join the battle," Juhrnus said as they paced briskly up the corridor. "The wards fell and it was looking pretty ugly; then Himself turned out with the rest of Honor to save us. Blighted fool decided he ought to jump in and do some fighting instead of telling everyone else what to do. Didn't know he was even hurt until he fell off his horse after the battle was over."

"Anyone send to Fox?"

Juhrnus nodded.

"Good. They'll bring supplies. In the meantime, I'll need more than I have here." He patted the satchel hanging from his shoulders. "Can you get the rest of my things . . . ?" He trailed off as Juhrnus shook his head emphatically.

"We'll send someone. I'll not have Saljane stripping the hide off my back for breaking my word."

"Indeed. Well, if you have a weak stomach you'd better get yourself a basin, because if you're going to be underfoot, I am going to make use of you."

"As you like. But be warned, if Esper calls, I don't care what you're in the middle of, you're going back to them"—he jerked his chin in the direction of his quarters—"if I have to drag you by your hair. Or let Saljane fetch you herself."

Gamulstark glanced at him as if expecting a joke, but Juhrnus's expression remained sober. The other man nodded slowly. "Agreed."

Chapter 11

By the time Kebonsat had led the donkey cart to the gates of Fox, the Wolf captain had fallen into a heavy slumber. Kebonsat tied the donkeys to a log pile outside the palisade and went to talk to the guards on the gate. Across the valley he could hear the sounds of battle. Horses screamed and *nokulas* wailed. The eerie harmony was punctuated by odd silences lasting only a matter of moments. Kebonsat ignored the battle. There wasn't anything he could do that Metyein wasn't already doing. He pulled his dagger from his belt and pounded on the gates with the hilt.

"Open up!"

"Who's asking? Name yerself!"

Kebonsat stepped back and looked up. He could see the rounded shape of a helm between the crenellations.

"Kebonsat cas Vadonis. Open the gates. I have need of a tark."

Silence answered. Kebonsat sheathed his dagger and waited, forcing himself not to pace and fidget. He heard the sound of boots on the allure and another voice called down, in the same rough tones as the first. Kebonsat rolled his eyes at the darkness. It never ended. He was Pease scum as far as the Kodu Riikians were concerned; he was as much the enemy as the *nokulas*—if not more.

"What's yer business?"

"I need a tark. Open the gates."

"Be ye hurt?" This came from the first guard.

Kebonsat gritted his teeth at the unmasked hopefulness in the tone. "No. I have brought someone who is ill."

"Wounded? From the battle? How fares Raven?" demanded the second guard.

"Not wounded. He is ill. Get a tark. Now." His voice was as unrelenting as glacier ice.

"Hold yer water, then," he heard, and then shouts. The gate swung open.

"Whatcha dawdling out here for? Ye coming in or not? Don't want to leave the gates hanging open for any beast to just trot in."

The guard stepped into the gateway, one hand wrapped around his hilt. He was older, probably in his fifth decade, with stringy gray hair topped by a battered leather helm. His clothing was worn and patched, with green laces closing the neck of his tunic. His paunch bulked over his waistband. He glared at Kebonsat, his jaw moving as he chewed something— probably tobacco or willow bark, Kebonsat guessed.

"Send a tark out here," he said evenly.

"Out here? What for?" The grizzled guard glanced from side to side, not seeing the donkey cart parked out of sight. His gaze returned to Kebonsat and he took an uneasy step back as he pulled his sword half out of its sheath. "What's the game, Pease?"

Kebonsat blew out an annoyed breath. "Do it."

The guard twitched and hesitated, clearly torn by the command in Kebonsat's voice and the strangeness of his arrival.

"Now. There's no time to waste," Kebonsat said, weariness and tension sharpening his voice.

The guard retreated, returning several minutes later with a short man, his blond head coming barely up to the top of Kebonsat's ribs. He had broad shoulders and was nearly as wide as he was tall. He bore a bulging pack over his right shoulder and carried an oil lamp in his other. He marched out to stand in front of Kebonsat, his boots squelching in the mud.

"Well, then? Where's the patient—and it had better not be you, because you're still standing and I don't have time for hangnails and jokes." It all came out in one breath, and before Kebonsat could answer, he began again. "They're going to be sending us injured and we've got to be ready for them and to go take care of those that can't be moved and this had blighted-well better be as urgent as you seem to think."

"It is." Kebonsat motioned the other man to follow and led him around to where he'd tied the donkey cart. The captain had not woken or even moved. The tark reached for the blanket covering the unconscious man, and Kebonsat stopped him.

"The Lord Marshal sent word today—we're going to house plague victims in Fox."

"Yes, I heard," the tark said, shaking off Kebonsat's hand. "We're going to start moving over to Hawk tomorrow—or we were, until this battle. We'll have to wait now, but it won't matter much until we get our first . . ." He trailed off, realization striking him. He rested his hands on the side of the cart. "How bad?"

Kebonsat shook his head. "I don't even know for sure that it is the plague. But he's got signs. Fever. He's weak. Could hardly walk to the cart."

The tark looked at him, his gaze shrewd. "You don't think it's just an ordinary illness?" Despite the terseness of his question, miracle of miracles, there was not the slightest hint of ridicule in his tone. Instead he leaned above the captain, holding the oil lamp over him as he tugged the blanket back.

"Could be the first stage. Not much sets it apart from other sicknesses until the second stage." He glanced at Kebonsat. "I hope you're wrong, but better safe. We'll have to clear out Fox before we can bring him in. We'll set a guard on him in case he wakes or in case the donkeys take a notion to go wandering. You didn't touch him?"

Kebonsat shook his head no.

"Where'd you find him?"

"Wolf. I didn't see the tark."

"Biidestark is assigned to Wolf. Probably rode with the troops to Raven. I would have. They'll be needing him. Well, nothing to do for him right now, and dawdling won't get the people of Fox moved, and it won't be long before the Lord Marshal sends someone to fetch us—"

"If they drive the *nokulas* off." Kebonsat's words didn't faze the tark in the least.

"No sense borrowing trouble when it's always so eager to climb into your lap like a puppy born of demons—" He broke off suddenly, turning to thrust a broad hand out at Kebonsat.

Kebonsat grasped the proferred arm, bemused by the tark's unflagging patter.

"Name is Remuntark. Been put in charge of the passel of tarks, and it's no great privilege I can assure you, with all that gabbling and bumping heads and snits over this or that, but of course it must be done or we'll all fall to pieces, and Honor is going to need its tarks." He barely paused for a breath and then began again, resuming his course to the gate. Kebonsat walked beside, trying to sort meaning from the piled words.

"It isn't just luck that there are so many tarks in Honor, because of course the Regent's only been thinking about containing the plague even if it means killing whole families or towns, which means he hasn't needed tarks." Remuntark frowned. "We got in his way. Like maggots spoiling his meat. He didn't like that." He paused as if remembering something unsavory. Then he shook himself, reminding Kebonsat of a wet dog.

They returned to the gate, and again Kebonsat rapped on the wood with the hilt of his dagger. Remuntark continued, "In the end we felt it best to come to Honor and see what we could do to help. That *ahalad-kaaslane* Juhrnus said we would be needed, and really it isn't safe to go down into the Karnane with all the bandits and suspicion, and we couldn't refuse the Lady's call either, and he said Reisiltark would come."

The gate swung open and the two men slid inside. Fox had been stripped of men, all but a few guards, grandfathers, and gangling boys answering the Lord Marshal's call to arms. Still it was neither empty or quiet. The commons bustled with activity. They were loading medical supplies into wagons and preparing the hospital barracks for wounded.

"We'll have to move everyone out into Hawk tonight," Kebonsat said, surveying the commotion.

"That will take more than the night," Remuntark said.

"No. We'll stockpile all our supplies and necessary goods outside the gates. You have enough people here to do that much. It can be moved later after the battle is over." *If it ends. If the* nokulas *are driven off.* He didn't say it. "The real problem is keeping everyone from panicking."

"I'll tell my folks first. They'll manage things. This won't be the first time they've had to soothe fears—in these times it seems that's what we do most. Won't be that much of a surprise. Most folks have been looking over their shoulders, waiting for it to jump out at them. Speaking for myself, I'm glad you're keeping the hospital in Honor. People will too. They'll want to know that if they get it, they won't be swept into a corner to die."

"I'm surprised. I would have bet you'd want to keep the quarantine outside the valley."

He shrugged. "Not much point to it, really. We don't know how the plague spreads. And we don't know how much time passes between exposure and the onset of symptoms. It could have been in the valley from the moment we first arrived. Or more likely, we brought it in with us. Only the Lady knows. But even if we didn't, we couldn't very well build all this"— he waved his hand at the surrounding palisade— "without all available bodies."

Remuntark held his hands before him palm-up, and then weighed them up and down like a moneylender's scale. "No way to win." He lifted his right hand higher. "This way you bring the plague in with you but build shelter and defenses for everyone." He lowered the right hand and raised the left. "This way you make sure—as best you can—that the plague stays out, but everyone starves or freezes in the winter or is eaten by *nokulas* or murdered when the Regent's army comes." He shrugged again. "Not a ship I'd like to steer, myself, but if you're asking me, then you made the correct choice."

"I hope you're right."

"Of course I am. And now I will get this lot moving. I'll also set someone to watch the captain in case he wakes. You might see about the Vertina. The news will be better coming from you, I think."

Kebonsat nodded, his chest filling with sand, remembering his promise to Metyein. *As soon as I see her . . .*

He left Remuntark calling out orders and wandered through the flurry of preparations with leaden steps.

Emelovi marched jerkily back and forth between her door and her bed. Her arms were crossed hard over her breasts, her fingers gouging into the flesh of her biceps. She hardly felt the bite. The door was firmly closed and latched. Every two or three minutes, with teeth-grinding promptness, the officious little brat of a ladies' maid knocked and queried whether Emelovi needed anything—a posset, hot kohv, her hair combed, help to change into her nightclothes, a warm brick for her bed. . . .

If she could have strangled the girl, Emelovi would have. But instead she smiled and politely said no, she merely wanted some time alone. After the ninth or thirteenth query, Emelovi had resorted to locking the door and refusing to answer the benevolent badgering. Which merely served as a challenge to the girl's tenacity and eagerness.

The knock came again.

"Dazien Emelovi, are you well? May I get you something? Surely you would like me to stir the fire?"

Emelovi didn't answer, and after a few moments she heard the rustle of Gelles's skirts and the set of her foot on the plank floor—not quite stomping, but clearly annoyed nonetheless. Emelovi smiled, her teeth gritting together so that her jaws ached.

The minutes ticked by with maddening slowness, bringing no word. Emelovi strode back to the bed, to the door, clutching her arms tighter and biting her lower lip. She didn't want to think about the battle. But the harder she pushed away the errant thoughts, the stronger they rebounded, pecking at her like angry crows.

What if something happened to Metyein? Or Kebonsat? She gasped, a low moan escaping from her lips. Tears prickled hot in her eyes as she shook her head fiercely. No. They would be fine. They had to be. If they weren't . . . She choked back a sob and sank down on the edge of the bed, bending forward over her knees, her stomach roiling. By the Lady, what would she do without them?

The question filled her mind, pushing out everything else. Sweat sprang up over her body, followed by a wave of gooseflesh. She stared at the floor, unseeing. She had no idea what she was supposed to be doing. Find her father. That was what she'd come for. That was why she'd left Aare. Guilt gnawed at her. She pressed her palms hard against her temples. She'd done nothing, less than nothing, to find him. But what could she do? She couldn't go looking herself. Nor could she ask to take men from the all-important task of establishing Honor so that the people, *her people*, would survive the winter and be safe from *nokula* attacks. That was what her father would want. To save Kodu Riik from Aare's selfish arrogance. But how in the Blessed Lady's name was she going to do that if she didn't start looking for her father?

She sat up, dragging her fingers through her hair,

pulling the pins loose with feral intensity. Her mouth twisted as she fought the blistering emotions that clawed up her throat, demanding a voice.

Emelovi lunged to her feet, striding across the floor again, beating her thighs with her hands. What *could* she do?

"What can I do?" she wailed at the room's white-washed walls.

She opened her hands, staring at the alabaster skin and manicured nails. A pink pearl set in an etched gold band circled the middle finger on her right hand, and another band of sapphire circled the index finger on her left. They were the hands of indolence and idleness. She dropped her hands, hiding them in her skirts.

A knock on the door made her start and jerk around with a gasp. There was an exchange of voices: Gelles's and a deeper, masculine voice. The knock came again.

"Emelovi? Are you there?"

Hearing Kebonsat's voice, Emelovi leaped for the door, scrabbling at the latch and yanking it wide. Her mouth opened, but nothing came out. Her arms twitched to reach out and snatch him in an embrace, but she held herself rigid. Gelles stood just behind him, peering over his shoulder, a frown furrowing her brow.

"You're here," Emelovi said in a thick voice. Then, "Come in. Please. What news?"

Kebonsat strode past Emelovi, catching himself up short as he encountered her bed. Emelovi shut the door firmly on Gelles, who followed a half-step behind. She leaned back against the door, examining Kebonsat for wounds. He was filthy, caked in dried mud that flaked off as he walked, despite the fact that he'd clearly sought to brush himself clean outside. His hair was matted and his face smudged. Tension pulled his mouth down. His eyes were bloodshot. He smelled strongly of sweat. But he was not wounded. Relief made her almost giddy.

Silence pooled thickly between them as Emelovi

tried to think of something to say. Kebonsat stared at her, saying nothing.

"Would you sit?" Emelovi asked at last, unnerved by the intensity of his expression. He shook his head, glancing down at his muddy clothing.

"Is there news?" she asked breathlessly when he continued in ominous silence.

"Of the battle? No. It goes on, I think. I can't really say."

Emelovi's brows furrowed. "You can't say?" she repeated uncertainly.

Kebonsat chewed his lower lip. Something seemed to click in him and he straightened, speaking briskly. "You know we wanted to move you to Hawk? Make Fox the quarantine?"

"Yes," Emelovi replied with an uncertain frown. What did that have to do with the battle?

"I'm afraid we'll have to move you now. Have your girl pack what she can, but you'll have to be ready as soon as you can."

Emelovi pressed her hand over her mouth so that he wouldn't see her chin tremble. "The plague." It wasn't—quite—a question.

He didn't try to soften it. Emelovi was bolstered by the confidence he showed in her strength to handle the news.

"Probably. It's early to tell. But we're moving everyone out tonight."

"Fine." A hard lump rose in Emelovi's throat. "Is there anything . . ." Her voice faded as he gave her that spellbinding look, the one that made her body flush with unfamiliar heat. He looked at her as if she were the only woman in the world. As if he couldn't live without her. Her heart thumped. If he'd reached for her, if he even stretched out his hands . . . she would wrap herself in his warmth forever. She licked her lips, not even blinking as she searched for some sign. But he did not move. "Is there anything I can do to help?" she asked at last, forcing her voice to be calmly firm.

But he began shaking his head even before she finished speaking. "Nothing. Just be ready to move. The rest is carrying and fetching."

"I could do that," Emelovi offered quickly. Her cheeks heated when Kebonsat smiled.

"It's not the work of a Vertina," he said.

"Then what is?" she asked sharply, the words spilling out before she could stop them. "I came to here to find my father, and all these months I've done nothing. He's the answer, the only way to stop Aare. I know we can't afford to take men from Honor, but we can't afford not to, especially now that the plague is here. Promise me that as soon as this battle is over, you'll send out searchers."

He stiffened, his face paling. His expression rippled with discomfort and something else she couldn't read.

"I—" He looked away, wiping his hand over his mouth. "We'd better get going."

Emelovi stared, waiting for more. He only crossed to the door and grasped the handle firmly. Just like that he was going to leave? He paused. He began to turn to face her, and Emelovi's chest tightened in hope. But then he yanked open the door and strode out.

Immediately Gelles filled the empty doorway, her long, narrow face a study of annoyance, worry, and solicitousness. "Dazien Emelovi, are you all right?" The girl grasped Emelovi's suddenly limp arm and settled her into the chair. "Would you like some wine? Mint tea, perhaps—kohv would be too heavy, I think. My mother always said so. Are you cold?"

Before Emelovi could begin to answer the patter of questions, the girl had snatched up a throw from the foot of the bed and swaddled Emelovi within it; then she began digging furiously at the fire with a poker. Ash puffed up and clouded the room.

Emelovi rubbed her eyes, pressing her fingers hard against her eyelids. She took a deep breath. It wasn't Gelles's fault, she told herself. The girl wanted to serve well; she just had no idea how. But she was

about to have a lesson. Emelovi dropped her hands
to her lap and sat straight.

"Gelles, please pack my things. We will be moving
to Hawk as soon as possible."

At the sharp authority in Emelovi's voice, the maid
jerked up as if stung. When she would have expostu-
lated about the lateness of the hour and the Dazien's
health, Emelovi narrowed her eyes, chin jutting.

"Begin now, if you will. I shall wait in the other
room."

With that Emelovi returned to the sitting room. She
went to stand at the window. It was barely a foot tall
and only half again as wide. It was set high in the
wall; her chin barely reached to the bottom of the sill.
To keep invaders out. If she hadn't been who she was,
they would not have allowed it at all. She shuddered.
Without windows she may as well have been in a
prison.

She pushed open the shutters and peered out. There
was a startled grunt below, the soft squelch of boots in
mud, and the rustle of clothing. She frowned. At a time
like this, the guard remained outside her window?

She abruptly pulled the shutters closed and latched
them, tearing a fingernail as she did. Blood oozed
from the torn skin. She stuck the offending finger in
her mouth and wandered across the room and back,
hearing Gelles packing in the other room. Sudden purpose prodded her. She snatched up her cloak, tying it
about her throat. She *would* fetch and carry. It might
not be the work of a Vertina, but at least it was something she could do to help. And her guards too.

She nodded to herself and went to the door, ignoring the nauseating worry swirling in the pit of her
stomach.

Chapter 12

"No. It cannot be. I *will* not and you cannot."

Reisil sat huddled in a chair. She was shivering, despite the two heavy quilts tucked about her and the roaring fire on the hearth. Saljane nested in her lap. Juhrnus stood in shirtsleeves near the door, as far from the fire as possible. Sweat glistened on his forehead. His *ahalad-kaaslane*, Esper, lay blissfully on the hearth, his tongue working slowly in and out of his jaws as he tasted the air.

Gamulstark fussed at Metyein, who had arrived leaning on Soka, his face gray. Soka was propped in the corner, arms crossed. A scratch down his left cheek made him look all the more rakish in combination with his customary crimson eye patch stitched garishly in gold. Yohuac slumped against the headboard, mottled with bruises and bandages. He too was layered in quilts and shivered like a frightened kitten. He held a hunk of bread in one hand, hardly able to get it into his mouth.

But he was alive, thank the Lady. Reisil closed her eyes, stunned by the feelings that spiraled through her. When had he come to mean so much? She reached wordlessly for Saljane, steadying herself in the goshawk's fierce strength.

~*What about Baku?*

As if in answer, a wailing howl surged through the walls, vibrating in the bones of Reisil's skull and making her teeth ache. It went on and on until she thought she'd throw up. At last it ended, but only long enough for Baku to draw a breath. Then it rose up again.

"Get him in here." Reisil gasped, dropping her cup of broth with a clatter. "He needs to see Yohuac himself, else he'll never stop."

Juhrnus left without a word.

Nurema closed on Reisil from where she had been standing near the fire. Her face was set in rigid determination beneath the bristled, steel-colored hair. She'd lost too much weight since Reisil had last seen her. And she'd aged—like a pumpkin left outside through the winter. Still, she had the presence of a battle-scarred sword. For all her age, she was still tough and dangerous, with an awful bite.

Reisil dragged at herself, trying to collect the whirling fragments of her mind. Suddenly Baku's ferocious wail cut off. Reisil rocked back in her chair as if a hand pulling on her had let her go.

"It must be done. You haven't any choice. They'll be coming again and again until you're dead or worse."

Reisil shook her head vehemently, and then stopped as pain drove screws through her head. "No. We'll be as bad as the wizards. . . ." She trailed off, looking at Yohuac.

At that moment the door thudded open as Baku thrust his head against it. He was too big for the opening, and it shouldn't have been possible, but his body *shifted* and changed. For a moment it seemed as if he were made of shadow and oil. And then he was through. He humped up onto the bed, his hindquarters trailing onto the floor, his tail snaking to curl around the footboard. He pushed his muzzle beneath Yohuac's elbow, careful to keep his weight off the injured man's body.

Reisil smiled at the momentary sheer happiness that suffused Yohuac's hawklike features. But as quickly as it came it faded. A knot rose in Reisil's throat. She looked away, stroking Saljane. The goshawk rubbed her beak against Reisil's arm.

"You'd best stop now with all that piddle," Nurema said sharply.

Reisil's gaze snapped back to the other woman.

"You have to be healed to fix Mysane Kosk. Everybody's makin' sacrifices. They have to, too." She scowled as Reisil shook her head.

"They've *been* sacrificing. The wizards have been stealing their power. It *kills* them."

Nurema shrugged, unimpressed. "Doesn't change what has to be done. You still got to be healed if yer going to save Kodu Riik and the beasties too. I ain't got enough magic. They do. All's you gotta do is let me borrow it."

"There has to be another way."

"Mebbe there is. But we ain't got time. We was lucky this time—them wizards helped you weaken the *nokulas*. That was the only way we could drive 'em back. But they'll be tryin' agin. And when they do, my bitty wards won't hold 'em. And yer not going to be able to stop them, weak as ye are. They'll raze Honor. And it'll be that"—she snapped her fingers—"for Kodu Riik. Is that what you want?"

"Of course not. But I'm supposed to protect all of Kodu Riik, including the *nokulas*," Reisil said, unconvinced.

"Some have to sacrifice so the rest can live," Juhrnus said slowly, grimacing as Reisil's head jerked around to look at him. His brown eyes were both unrelenting and sympathetic. "I don't like it." He shook his head. "That's not true. I'd raise a glass if the Demonlord saw fit to sweep the *nokulas* into his third pit and we never heard from them again. But if we *are* to protect them, then they'll have to pay part of that price, whether they want it or not. Just like the rest of Kodu Riik. No one has asked for it, but it's what we have to do. Call it duty, call it pride in your country, call it bad luck.

"And we all know that you dying means we won't have a snowflake's chance in summer to save Mysane Kosk or Kodu Riik, and then what's the point? If they could be reasoned with, the *nokulas* would agree. But they can't. So. Get yourself healed, get out of that chair, and get on with it. 'Cause sure as anything, the Regent and his army will be coming before long, and then we'll really be in a mess.''

Reisil continued to stare at him, unable to break the lock of his gaze. At last she closed her eyes, head drooping back against her chair. For a miracle, Nurema held her tongue.

~I don't know what to do. How can I use them that way? I know they've tried to kill us and we've killed them, but that was battle. This . . . this feels so wrong. Like Kvepi Uldegas and Kvepi Debess. What they did to Yohuac and Baku . . . what I helped them do!

She squinched her eyes tighter, chills radiating harder as she pulled herself inward, struggling with the morality of the decision.

Saljanc didn't respond to her right away. Reisil felt her *ahalad-kaaslane* thinking and didn't intrude, but waited, hoping her friend and heart-companion would know the path through this bramble-patch. But when Saljanc replied, she did not offer the solution that Reisil wanted to hear.

~The path of the ahalad-kaaslane *is never easy, never safe, never straight. Upsakes made wrong choices. This may be also. But I can see no other. You must allow it.*

Reisil stilled, feeling as if a wagon of sand had been dumped on top of her. Her heart sounded loud in her ears, and her lungs refused to draw breath. Heat filled her throat with an unending ache. Upsakes had thought he was saving Kodu Riik, even as he betrayed his country and the Lady. Was this the same?

She sighed, opening her eyes and looking at Nurema. She nodded slightly.

"Good," the old woman said. She held out a cup for Reisil. "Drink it. It's laudanum. It'll go better if yer unconscious, what with yer power. I don't want to have to fight it."

Reisil hesitated, her gorge rising. The sickly-sweet smell of the drug reminded her again of Upsakes.

He'd become addicted to the stuff. Had it been that that turned him traitor? Convinced him that what he was doing was right? Her stomach twisted, but she grasped the cup firmly. It had been mixed in a cup of cool water and flavored with mint leaves. She held her breath and swallowed.

Before long, her eyes grew heavy and the room turned misty. As she began to fade entirely, a thought struck her like a bolt.

"Nurema," she graveled, trying to lift her heavy arm.

~Saljane . . .

Kek-kek-kek-kek.

The piercing cry shredded the murmuring silence inside the room.

"Nurema . . ."

"What's it now?" Nurema bent close, a smudge of darkness against the gauzy brilliance of the fire.

"Yohuac . . . drug him too."

Silence met Reisil's words and she struggled to open her leaden eyes. "Nurema?"

"Yes, girl. I understand."

And the obsidian sharpness in the other woman's tone indicated that she really did understand. Well, and she was one of the nahuallis who'd bred Yohuac to be what he was. Could she really be angry that they'd succeeded? And then she thought nothing at all as consciousness slipped away like oil from wet skin.

Reisil swam out of the murk slowly, drifting toward consciousness. She felt a sensation of warmth and . . . no pain. The searing, aching rawness that had bound her like chains was gone. Since the night she'd freed Yohuac and Baku and the plague-healers— Dear Lady! The plague-healers! She flailed against the darkness of her mind. She had to tell them!

She kicked upward toward the surface of consciousness. It was . . . there . . . just beyond her fingertips. . . . She stretched—and recoiled. Tapit's face swelled in front of her, looking bloated and swollen. He smiled, his lips widening past the point of reality, cutting his head in half. Blood cascaded down his forehead and dripped into his eyes, staining them crimson. But nothing disguised the brutal cold there, the unending animosity.

But Reisil wasn't running any longer. She wasn't playing desperate rabbit to his fox. She bared her teeth and thrust herself at him, through him. And he was gone, dissolved into nothingness. She woke smiling.

She pushed away the pile of quilts and swung her legs over the edge of the bed. Yohuac grumbled sleepily. She yawned and stretched, reveling in the feeling of strength and health. Her stomach growled loudly. She licked her lips, making a face at the sticky sweetness lingering from the laudanum.

Baku whuffled, and she turned to find him lying at the foot of the bed like an enormous hound. He peered at her with brilliant yellow eyes. The bloodred striping across the center reminded her of her dream. She closed her eyes. Then she opened them, firmly setting aside her fears. Wherever Tapit was, she'd deal with him when the time came. But for now . . .

A hand curled around her wrist. Yohuac yawned at her. His jaws cracked. He sat up, the covers falling from his chest. He slid his hand up her arm to curl around her neck. Pulling her close, he kissed her. Reisil tasted the laudanum and something uniquely him.

The kiss intensified as he held her tighter, sliding his hands over her back. Reisil sank against him, tangling her fingers in his hair—

"Your hair?" she said, pushing him away.

It fell in a thick black wave to his shoulders. Reisil threaded its coarse length through her fingers. He lifted his own hands to follow hers, his eyes widening.

"How?"

"Nurema. She healed me. You too. Apparently she didn't like the shorn look."

Something hollowed out in his eyes, turning them inward and dark. Baku lifted himself from the floor, making a gravelly noise in his throat.

"What is it?" Reisil asked, stroking Yohuac's cheek with her fingers, smoothing the graven lines that pulled his mouth tight.

Yohuac pulled away, climbing out of bed and reaching for the stack of clean clothing that had been left in readiness.

"Yohuac?"

He said nothing, continuing to dress silently. She touched her lips regretfully and then got out of bed, eyeing her new clothing with a raised brow. It was not meant for fighting, but for comfort and ease. She hadn't worn such things since . . . since before becoming *ahalad-kaaslane*. The Reisil from back then would have been delighted with the pretty garments.

This Reisil wrinkled her nose at the soft sage-colored cambric, fingering the green ivy embroidery around the cuffs of the tunic and the hem of the skirt. The fine threads snagged on the rough skin of her fingers. She pulled them back with a grimace. It was delicate work, made for a noble lady. Hardly the kind of garb in which to go fighting *nokulas* and wizards.

She chuckled at the image, then gave a little shrug. Someone had gone to a lot of effort and trouble to present her with something special. It would be unforgivably crass and rude to complain.

She picked up the tunic, and then noticed the grime on her hands and arms. Her hair was stiff and gritty with dried sweat and mud, and she didn't doubt that she smelled like she'd been wallowing in a pigsty.

"It would be a crime if I wore this before taking a bath—with a wire scrub brush," she announced, then looked over her shoulder at Yohuac, who was turning his slippers over in his hands, a look of unertain incredulity on his face. Like his clothing, the slippers were midnight-blue watered silk with orange and yellow embroidery. Reisil laughed out loud at his bemusement.

Yohuac's brows angled down in a frown, and then he smiled slowly, the tension draining visibly from him.

"Dirty or not, there's nothing too fine to touch your skin," he said. His eyes snared her in a net of fire and Reisil shivered, her mouth going dry. The more time they spent together . . . The feelings she had had for Kaval and Kebonsat were nothing like the storm of emotions that Yohuac sparked inside her.

And equally futile, she reminded herself, shifting her gaze away. He was going to return home to be the champion he was bred to be. And that was that.

She drew a steadying breath, pushing away the loss tightening around her throat. He wasn't gone yet. They still had time. And if there was one thing she'd learned since becoming *ahalad-kaaslane*, it was that you didn't waste time mourning for the future. You just got on with the present, taking gladly what the Lady offered while it lasted.

She met Saljane's ember gaze, the goshawk perched on the headboard of the bed, feeling the bird's silent amusement.

~So, I've learned my lesson. Don't be smug.

~The fledgling matures.

Reisil stuck out her tongue at Saljane, who bent to preen her feathers.

"Reisil?" Yohuac had come to stand behind her, ignorant of the exchange. He caught her hand in his and pressed his lips against her knuckles. "Do not be angry. I—" He broke off, searching for words.

Reisil's fingers tightened on his. "I'm not angry. And you don't have to explain."

"I want to." He pulled her after him as he picked up his pack from where it had been deposited in a corner. He settled onto the bed with her, levering Baku's head to the side. The coal-drake whoofed but allowed himself to be pushed a few inches. Yohuac dug in the pack, pulling out a makeshift pouch that Reisil had constructed from the corner of a blanket and strips of rawhide. He untied it and emptied the contents into a pile on the bed.

There were two heavy beaten-gold earrings shaped in hoops. There was a geometric pattern etched in them. There were three gold bands—two for his wrists, one for his bicep. The fourth was a melted blob. Reisil had used it to store magic when destroying the cages holding the plague-healers and then Baku. Then there was a series of beads made of wood and metal. These were intricately carved. Some were enameled and painted, while others were plain. All in all, there were probably thirty of them.

Yohuac swept the beads up into his fist, staring down at them. "There are elders in the tribes who wear hundreds of these," he said, emotion making his voice thick. He pinched his lips together and then let the beads fall between his fingers. "The first bead is tied into a boy's hair as soon as it is long enough to braid. This is his name, his family." He touched two beads. "Then more are added as he grows—they mark his prowess and his deeds."

Yohuac's face contorted and he pushed the beads into the pouch. Reisil said nothing. It wasn't as easy as braiding them back into his hair. She could see that. He'd lost something. The wizards had stolen it. And growing back his hair did not solve it.

Yohuac drew a heavy breath. "A man marks his life by his beads. A man who loses them is *chiltoc*. He is . . ." Yohuac frowned, searching for words. "He is suspended—between. He loses his name, his family, his tribe, all his belongings. He has no status at all. He must now prove his worthiness. If he does, his tribe may invite his return, give him a new name, and he may begin anew. If not, he must leave. He may try to prove himself to another tribe. It is rare that any other will take someone who has been so careless, however."

"That's stupid," Reisil said hotly. "Careless? You were taken prisoner by the wizards when you were trying to rescue me! I'd call that heroic."

He fingered the armbands and earrings. "These were gifts." He pushed them back inside the pouch, tying the rawhide and tucking it in his pack. His fingers lingered on the flap. "It does not matter. I must still do what I was born to do—win the *pahtia* and become *Ilhuicatl's* son in the flesh. Anyone can compete, even a *chiltoc*. I have no need of a name or tribe."

Reisil took his hand between hers. She didn't know what to say. Words seemed inadequate. Finally she said, "If it counts for anything, your name is written on my heart. I don't think you can change that." She smiled impishly, trying to break the heavy mood. "Not even if you cut your hair again. Or take a bath. So if you were worried about that . . . don't."

He grinned. "Do you say I smell?" He picked a chunk of dried mud from her hair. "The tiger laughs at the skunk's stripes."

"At least I didn't already get my clothes dirty," Reisil said, sniffing and pinching her nose. Then scrambled away with a giggle when Yohuac tried to tickle her.

"How about I tell them we're awake and see if they'll take pity on us?"

"More likely they'll not let us out until we do bathe," Yohuac pointed out. "But perhaps we can hurry them up. And food. Don't forget to ask for food."

Reisil went to the door. A girl sat against the opposite wall, embroidering. Seeing Reisil, she scrambled to her feet.

"Oh, I'm sorry. I didn't realize . . ." She caught herself and stopped, then began again with a speech she'd clearly practiced. "I have been assigned to help you with anything you need. As soon as you are feeling ready, I am to notify the Lord Marshal and—"

"The Lord Marshal?" Reisil interrupted.

"Yes, ma'am, Reisiltark, I mean," the girl answered, paling and clutching her embroidery ring to her chest.

"I don't understand—the Lord Marshal Vare? Here?"

"Yes, ma'am. I mean, no. He's our Lord Marshal, not that other one." She sounded both proud and more than a little in love.

Reisil nodded thoughtfully. "I would be grateful for a bath and some food. Could you arrange that?"

The girl nodded eagerly. "Be just a few minutes," she said, and then trotted off, her skirts swirling around her ankles.

In twenty minutes, a wooden tub had been set in front of the hearth and filled with steaming water. The fire had been stirred so that the flames danced in furious abandon. Yohuac insisted that Reisil bathe first.

"Mmmm," she said, as he ladled water over her, rinsing away the soap. "I have missed baths."

Much as she wanted to soak, Reisil traded with Yohuac as soon as she was clean. She hoped the promised food would be arriving soon. She dressed quickly, helping to rinse Yohuac, then tackled her hair. She picked up the comb that had been left beside the clothing. There was also a silver hair clip.

She yanked at the snarls, muttering annoyance. It seemed that she'd torn out as much hair as not. "I think I'd like to shave *my* head," she announced, throwing the comb at the wall.

Yohuac bent and picked it up. "You must have more patience," he said, combing gently through her hair.

Reisil closed her eyes. "It is much better," she agreed. If she could have purred, she would have.

She didn't know how much later it was when there came a sharp rap on the door. She woke from her doze with a start. "Is it the food?" She yawned as her stomach rumbled.

Soka and Juhrnus entered, bearing two heavy platters loaded with steaming dishes. They were followed by Nurema, who carried a brace of fat rabbits, gutted and skinned for Saljane. Behind her came Metyein, walking stiffly upright. Kebonsat and the Vertina Emelovi brought up the rear.

Reisil responded to their various greetings with an absent wave, her attention narrowing on the succulent smells emanating from the food platters. She snatched the one from Soka, taking it to the table and tucking into the food ravenously. She burned her tongue on the stew, and gulped milk to cool her mouth before plowing ahead. Yohuac settled across from her.

"They certainly look better," Juhrnus commented dryly, "though their manners could use a little work."

"Just so. And they do smell better," Soka replied with equal gravity. "Though to be sure, it is difficult to keep clean in such barbaric accomodations." He flicked imaginary dust from his sleeve, which was made of utilitarian broadcloth died green and covered by a leather jerkin.

Reisil couldn't help but laugh at his mincing aristocratic tone, spraying crumbs back onto the table.

Soka sniffed and looked down his nose. "Barbarians," he repeated.

Reisil giggled again, but didn't answer, too hungry to join the banter. All the same, she felt good. She felt like she was *home*. Her mind flashed back to her time with the wizards, and she went still at the memory. For a while, she had been . . . comfortable. At home. The wizards had respected her, welcomed and encouraged her.

It wasn't that they hid their true natures. She could have seen, if she wanted to. What else should she have thought when Kvepi Kaisivas blithely dismissed Reisil's killing of a hundred wizards in Patverseme?

She should have known. It had been everywhere to read. But she hadn't wanted to. She wanted the peace that had seemed to pervade the stronghold. She wanted the warmth of friendship without demand.

She wanted to be a coward.

She closed her eyes, hating the memory of herself. Of the way she had sought to earn their praise even as she pretended to despise it.

Yohuac's foot bumped hers beneath the table as he shifted himself in his seat, recalling her to the present. Reisil began to chew again, no longer tasting the food, eating by rote, her hand tightening on her fork until the wood began to bow with the press of her thumb. She forced her fingers to relax, one by one.

Resolutely she brushed aside the recriminating whispers that buzzed insistently inside her skull. She'd not behaved well. She admitted it. But in the end, whatever her feelings, she could have done nothing different. To have any hope of saving Kodu Riik, she had *had* to learn how to use her magic, and how to read the *rinda*. She had had to make the wizards trust her, make them believe in her.

She swallowed and took a bite of buttered bread, savoring the yeasty flavor. She'd done what was needed, and Yohuac had forgiven her. Even Baku understood the necessity, whether he was ready to forgive or not.

"Let them eat," Metyein said in a thin voice that cut the threads of Reisil's meditations. He sat on the bed, leaning gingerly against the headboard. His face was pinched and his eyes were sunken and heavy, as if he'd not slept. "We'll tell them all our adventures and by then they'll be ready to tell us theirs. There's no time to waste." He looked at Kebonsat. "And we'd better start with the plague."

Morning dawned a brilliant, warm blue. A mist rose from the muddy fields. The valley bustled with activity, from women and children tending the fields and trying to mend the damage of battle, to men hauling bodies away. It was a most disorganized and chaotic scene. Perfect for Tapit's purposes.

He picked his way toward one of the stockades. The image of a pair of talons clutching a spear had been carved into the green beams above the gate, then painted brown. The gates themselves were open. A wagon was cocked sideways just in front, one wheel sunk to its hub in mud. The guards argued with the driver, even as people swarmed in and out around them. Tapit's lip curled involuntarily at the disorder, even as he took advantage of the guards' distraction to slip through the gates.

Once inside, he walked briskly across the commons to a long building that was clearly a barracks or dormitory. He entered purposefully, as if he belonged. Inside his eyes swept the racks of bunks, all deserted. He paced down the aisle until he found an empty one on the top. From beneath his cloak he pulled his roll of bedding and spread it out, setting his bundle of clothing at one end to act as a pillow.

He then drew his dagger and pricked the side of one finger with expert deftness. Blood welled in the wound. He smudged it on his chest, over his heart, and then along his neckline. He murmured words and the blood flared and suddenly on his chest he wore a green triangle emblem with hawk's talons clutching a spear in brown. The blood on his collar had transformed into a crude stitching of green ivy.

Tapit examined his handiwork, nodding satisfaction. He then made his way back to the entry. Before he opened the door, he closed his eyes, sensing the *rinda* painted on his face with his own heart's blood mixed with pine sap—they wouldn't easily wash away.

His lips tightened in something like a smile. They remained strong. With the thick flows of magic swirling through the valley, no one would notice them. At least not from farther than three or four paces. Not even Reisil, powerful as she was. She wouldn't know he was there until he was ready.

Tapit allowed himself a long, slow smile and then opened the door.

Chapter 13

Emelovi sat on a stool in the corner, trying very hard to be inconspicuous. She pleated her skirt between her fingers, burningly conscious of how oddly she fit into this company.

Her eyes skipped to each of the occupants of the room. Metyein, his face drawn and gray. Soka, with his rakish eye patch and cutting tongue. Juhrnus, returning Soka's feints with sardonic ease. Nurema, her eyes stormy, impatience written in every line of her body. Kebonsat standing near, silently reassuring. Yohuac, powerful and raw and forbidding, even as he ate like a starved dog.

Emelovi's gaze settled last on Reisiltark. She appeared much the same as she had in Koduteel. Ebony hair, pale skin, moss-colored eyes. She was beautiful, in a masculine sort of way. There was no fat on her, no soft curve to her chin or jaw or hip. This she had been in Koduteel. But she *was* different.

Emelovi's brow furrowed as she sought the alteration. In Koduteel, Reisiltark had been determined and fierce, but at the same time she'd been uncertain and diffident. Then Emelovi had felt a certain affinity with the other woman, as if they shared similar fears and frustrations. Like Emelovi, Reisiltark had held herself tightly in hand, flinching at noises and strangers. But all that was gone, burned away perhaps, in fires that Emelovi couldn't imagine.

Now Reisiltark crackled with energy. She seemed assured and in control of herself. Emelovi envied her the change. Envied the way the others leaned toward her, like sunflowers chasing the day. Even Kebonsat.

Emelovi bit the inside of her cheek. And why shouldn't he? Reisiltark was a match for his strength and swift mind. *She* was no wilting flower who needed care and support to survive from day to day. *She* didn't need protecting. If Reisiltark's father were missing, she would be out hunting him herself.

Emelovi slumped, staring down at her hands. The pale skin covering them was scratched and blistered on the palms. She'd made them let her help load the wagons and empty the Fox stockade of its contents. She hadn't done much. She'd tired quickly and had to rest often. The muscles in her legs and arms ached from the unfamiliar labor. And she was glad of it. The pain was proof of her contribution, minor as it might have been.

It had given her a taste to do more. To do something more than sit in a corner while the others made plans and fought battles.

The noise in the room dropped suddenly. Emelovi raised her head, stiffening.

"The plague?" Reisiltark asked sharply, setting her fork down, riveted on Kebonsat.

"We aren't sure," Kebonsat replied.

Reisiltark quirked her brows, her silence commanding. Emelovi sighed unconsciously. To have such presence—to be able to speak so, as an equal, amongst such men!

"The captain from Wolf has a fever, weakness, headache. We've put him in Fox under quarantine."

At Reisiltark's look of confusion, Juhrnus handed her a rolled map of the valley. She opened it, holding it above her food as she examined it.

"I see." She scanned the others above the edge of the map. "You decided to put the plague right in the valley?"

"We won't abandon our own," Metyein said simply.

Unseen, Emelovi nodded warm approval of his answer. Why couldn't Aare be more like Metyein? Care more for Kodu Riik and his people?

Reisiltark went back to examining the map. But she didn't seem to disapprove of the decision. She lowered the map, rolling it up and handing it back.

"When I was able to free Yohuac and Baku, I also freed some other people," she said, with an odd inflection in her voice when she said *people*. Utter silence gripped the room as Reisiltark recounted her adventures, from breaking free of Koduteel to Saljane's kidnapping, and the wizards' unexpected welcome. Emelovi strained forward, enthralled.

"I thought I had destroyed their stronghold and killed many of them. I had hoped it would give us some breathing room to stop what's happening here. Because they aren't going to give up Mysane Kosk easily. Whatever spells they did might have gone terribly wrong, but they've reaped the benefits anyway. They capture the *nokulas* and steal their magic to fuel their spells.

"But that isn't the worst of it." Reisiltark paused, her expression smoky. Her lip curled. "I don't know exactly what they are or if what they say is true, but the other . . . beings . . . I rescued from the wizards, they called themselves plague-healers."

For a moment there was silence. Emelovi stared, repeating the words in her mind, trying to make them make sense. The others seemed equally taken aback.

"Plague-healers?" Kebonsat repeated.

"That's what one of them said." Reisiltark shook her head perplexedly. "She said . . . the plague has no harmony. They sing it back to joy."

"What in the Hag's name does that mean?" Soka demanded.

"Lady knows. There was no time for questions. All I could do was send them out of the stronghold, hoping they'd get away. Have you seen them? They look almost human but with a *nokula's* silver eyes. Their cheekbones are ridged and their brows wide. All four of them were pale as grass that's never seen the light of day."

Everyone shook their heads. Everyone but Juhrnus. He began to swear.

"You've seen them then?" Kebonsat asked eagerly.

"Maybe. I don't know. There's been sightings. *Nokulas* are what we thought they were. They had the eyes, you know. And strange faces. People thought— I thought—they were in the middle of the change to *nokula*."

"What did you do to them?"

Juhrnus shook his head. "Killed a few. Others we chased." He looked around the assembled group, his face dark and hard. "We didn't know what they were."

"Well, we do now, and we'd better find them," Reisiltark declared. "If the plague has really arrived, we need them."

"Do you think . . . Do you think they can reverse the effects of Mysane Kosk?" Kebonsat asked, a peculiar intensity burrowing through his voice.

Unexpectedly, everyone looked at Emelovi. She flushed, averting her eyes. Their combined regard lay over her like a heavy net. She squirmed, and then blessedly their attention returned to Reisiltark. Emelovi gathered her scattered composure, her heart fluttering, ice hardening in her lungs. What had caused that *look* . . . ?

"I . . . doubt it," Reisiltark said, answering Kebonsat's question. "I think the plague and these . . . alterations . . . are two different things. The plaguehealers and the *nokulas* aren't decaying; they are simply different from what they were. They can still think and talk.

"And that brings me to the last thing. A couple of days ago, Sodur found us. He said he'd been waiting." She paused. "He's *changed*, and so has Lume. They've both become *nokulas*, just like the Iisand."

She said more, but Emelovi could no longer hear the words. Her chest hurt and she felt cold, so cold.

Her head reeled. She felt herself sway, and hands gripped her shoulders. She looked up into Kebonsat's face. His mouth was drawn down and his skin had gone gray. But it was his eyes that caught her attention. There was knowledge there, and guilt.

Emelovi's tongue clung to the roof of her mouth as if mortared there. Her jaws felt like stone. She could not speak. Not that she knew what to say. Fragments of thought spun in her head, wanting to make a pattern, wanting to settle into an awful picture. She couldn't let them. She didn't want to know.

The palms of her hands were pressed against her cheeks, and her fingers dug hard into her scalp. But she could not push out what she'd heard. She could not stop the puzzle pieces from falling together as understanding slowly emerged from the maelstrom in her head.

Her father was . . . a *nokula*.

She lowered her hands. Once again they were all looking at her. And suddenly she realized that they knew. They *all* knew.

"Why?" she croaked. But she knew the answer. She would not have come. She would not have deserted Aare—*he was the rightful ruler of Kodu Riik now*. Fear spawned in her blood. But it could not win against the tide of bitterness sweeping through her. They'd lied. Kebonsat had lied. Something inside her screamed in agony and snapped in two. It was all a political game. She was just a pawn on the board—spoils in the war against her brother. But at least Aare was honest about it.

Her stomach bucked and heaved. Her body twisted, and Kebonsat caught her as she spasmed forward, retching onto the floor. The noxious flavor burned in her throat and nose. Kebonsat rubbed her back, murmuring soft words.

Something exploded behind Emelovi's eyes at the caress.

She wrenched away, falling off her chair. She shoved Kebonsat's helping hands away and lurched to her feet, staggering drunkenly. Kebonsat made to reach for her again and her hands cracked loudly against his. She glared at him, panting, unable to get enough air into her constricted chest.

"Do. Not. Touch. Me. Never again." Her voice came from deep in the earth and her eyes burned with tears she *would not* let fall.

Reisiltark was standing, pity and something akin to impatience coloring her expression. "Why don't you all give us some privacy," she said briskly. "The Vertina and I need to talk."

The others rose and left in embarrassed silence. Emelovi didn't look at them. When at last the door shut and she was alone with Reisiltark, her legs sagged and she melted to the floor, sobs jumbling in her chest and tearing free of her throat. Reisiltark knelt beside her, pulling her close and stroking her hair.

Emelovi didn't know how long they remained thus, with Reisiltark murmuring softly, unintelligibly. Slowly the torrent of her emotions lessened and Emelovi sat up. Her nose was stuffed and her eyes felt swollen and gritty. Her head throbbed. She took the handkerchief Reisiltark offered, blowing her nose and rubbing away the tears. Reisiltark helped her to the chair that Yohuac had occupied and sat down opposite, picking again at her food, saying nothing.

At last Emelovi could stand the silence no longer. "You said you wanted to talk?" Her voice was raspy and thick.

Reisiltark sat back, wiping her hands on her napkin and crossing her arms over her chest. She scanned Emelovi up and down, as if examining a crystal vase for cracks. Emelovi flushed and stared at her hands knotted together in her lap.

"I don't know why they didn't tell you the truth. They should have," Reisiltark said.

Emelovi jerked up, eyes widening. She didn't know what she'd expected. Recrimination, maybe, something about decorum or behaving herself.

"They should have, but they didn't, and you've a

right to your anger, but you'd better get over it, or at least put it aside until there's time to indulge it. Your father isn't coming back. Kodu Riik is in danger. Your brother is going to get the throne, and when he does he's going to bring an army and the Scallacian sorcerers down on us. You can help, if you want."

"I wouldn't have come if I'd known!" Emelovi cried. She wanted to defend herself. She should have stayed with Aare. She *couldn't* be a traitor!

Reisiltark stared and then shook her head, the pity returning. "I'm sorry for that. Sorry for you. But you're here now. You can't go back. He'll kill you. Or worse."

She held Emelovi's gaze, demanding truth. At last Emelovi gave in. "He wouldn't kill me. It would not be enough, and it would be wasteful. My brother never wastes what he thinks will profit him." She hesitated. "You told me Kebonsat was honorable. You said he was dependable and loyal and that you would trust him with your life."

Reisiltark sat back, her head tilting up as she remembered. The day the Scallacian sorcerers had arrived in Koduteel, the day Reisiltark and Emelovi had first spoken.

"I still trust him. With my life. And yours. But the rest—that you will have to take up with him. His honor is his to defend."

"I cannot—" Emelovi broke off. She could not, she would not speak to Kebonsat. She felt . . . like she did when Aare had ordered her to lie with the Scallacian sorcerer. Trapped and naked and helpless. Kebonsat had done this. He'd taken something precious from her. *Choice.* He'd . . . he'd raped her. She recoiled from the idea. A small voice inside ridiculed the notion. *No, he hadn't. He'd saved her from Aare, from having to bed the sorcerer, from losing her pride and becoming a whore. He'd given her exactly what she wanted—a way out.*

Her fingers curled, her nails chewing into her palms. But he'd lied to do it. Lied about her father. Lied about caring for her. Or maybe that part was genuine. But that only made it worse. He'd treated her like a bitch to be taught to fetch and heel.

A hot blush suffused her body as she realized the depth of her gullibilty and stupidity. Her stomach twisted again, and she clenched her teeth against the tide of bile that rose up on her tongue. She *would not* make a spectacle of herself again.

She lifted her chin, her lips clamped tight. She met Reisiltark's pitying gaze with a hard glare.

"I am no child. Is there more I should know?"

Reisiltark smiled, and the pity transformed into respect. She leaned forward over the table, her voice solemn. "You came here to find your father. But he's gone. I don't think there's any way to change him back, and that isn't what I'm trying to do. My goal is to stabilize the spell the wizards cast and keep Kodu Riik from being destroyed. To keep the entire world and Yohuac's world from being destroyed, if Nurema is right. You know what's happening?"

Emelovi nodded. Since leaving Koduteel, she'd been privy to most everything Metyein, Kebonsat, Juhrnus, Soka, and Nurema had discussed, from the planning of Honor to the dangers of Mysane Kosk. Though she had had nothing to say to add to it, she'd listened avidly.

"Good. You say you wouldn't have come if you'd known the truth. That's water down to the ocean. You can't go back. So it's time to think about what you're going to do here."

Emelovi frowned. "What I'm to do? What do you mean?"

Reisiltark pushed away the stray hairs tickling her face. "They brought you here to save you. I doubt they even thought about what it would mean. Not that they would have done differently." She smiled bitterly. "People will do awful things to one another in the name of friendship. But you have choices here."

She sat back, examining Emelovi closely. Emelovi struggled to keep from fidgeting. Finally Reisiltark spoke. "You still have choices. You can lock yourself in your room and feed your anger. No one will bother you. Or you can start doing what's in your blood. You can lead your people."

Emelovi stared. "Rule?" she repeated.

"Why not? You're of royal blood. You legitimize this rebellion. The *ahalad-kaaslane* will support you. People will rally to your banner if you call them. No doubt your brother thinks that's why you're here. No one else can do it. The only question is, will you? Will you do what your father can't and protect Kodu Riik from your brother and the Scallacians?"

"Yes."

The word escaped before Emelovi could catch it. She covered her mouth with her hands, stunned at her audacity. But an eagerness burned inside her, steadying her pounding heart. Slowly she lowered her hands. "Yes. Yes, I will. Can I really?"

"I think you have to. If you love Kodu Riik and want to serve your people. It's going to be very ugly. There's going to be a lot of fear, pain, and suffering. They'll look to you for leadership. But it means leaning on Metyein and Kebonsat. They know about ruling and war. They'll have to teach you. You'll have to let them."

Reisiltark leaned forward and caught Emelovi's hands between hers. Her skin was warm and calloused. "They can teach you a lot. Juhrnus can advise you too. He's smarter than he knows. But trust yourself. Trust your instincts. Listen to their wisdom, but do what you know is right."

Emelovi's ears rang, She studied their hands clasped together. Was she really going to do this? Was she really going to declare herself a challenger against Aare?

Fear spiked through her, and for a moment she was paralyzed. But she forced herself to breathe, to grapple with her fear, and pushed it down inside. Reisiltark was right. For her father, for Kodu Riik, for herself: She had to face Aare. And defeat him.

Chapter 14

"My wards aren't gonna hold against the *nokulas*.
That's a fact. And if the wizards come at us too . . .
we have no choice."

"You keep saying that," Reisil replied. The lack of
inflection in her voice gave nothing away. She smiled.
She was learning. And not just about politics and in-
trigue and leadership, but also about necessity.

She thought of the Vertina. She knew exactly how
the girl felt. Reisil had felt the same way when she'd
learned of Sodur's lies. Of Kaval's betrayal. All for
her own good, for the good of Kodu Riik.

She remembered that sickening feeling in her stomach that wouldn't go away. The burning humiliation
of having been so completely fooled. Of having been
manipulated so easily. And by someone you loved.
And Emelovi did love Kebonsat. Or had. Reisil didn't
know if her feelings had turned to hate, the way Reisil
had come to hate Kaval.

She thought of Sodur. The bitterness was still there,
but she didn't hate him. She didn't know how she felt
about him. He was suffering his own horrors now.
That was retribution enough, if she wanted it.

"You smile. Does that mean you agree?" Nurema's
voice cut through Reisil's musings.

She turned her head to look at the other woman. It
was hard to imagine that Nurema was one of Yohuac's
nahuallis. That she could work magic. Reisil remembered her as a contentious, sharp-tongued woman who

didn't suffer fools at all, and who told the painful, unvarnished truth. She was staring, her mouth pinched in a line, her forehead wrinkling as she lifted her brows.

"Well?"

"I smile because I am pleased to see you again. You have not changed."

Nurema barked out a laugh. "Sure, I have. My magic's come back to me."

"So you're a witch. Most people in Kallas thought that after about two minutes with you."

Nurema laughed again and slapped her thigh. "Ye always were sharper than most gave you credit for. And not so green as ye were, either. Y' know enough to listen. Yer friends, too."

"Even Juhrnus."

"Even that one. Found his feet, didn't he, and grew up. Not the bully he started out to be. Found out having balls didn't have to make his head soft. His grandmother'd be proud. Shocked dead, mind, but proud."

Reisil chuckled and glanced behind. Juhrnus and Yohuac were just coming through the trees and up the steep ridge. Metyein was in no shape to ride, though his injury was not so great that it required magical healing. Not that Soka would have permitted it.

"He'd blighted well better learn his lesson and remember it! I'm not going to be around to watch over him, and if he goes waddling out into the fray like the gibbering idiot he's acting like and gets himself killed, Honor's going to suffer for it. So let him suffer now!" Soka's belligerence didn't mask the concern he felt for his friend.

"He does it again, I'll curse him," Nurema had said, crossing her arms and leveling that deadly gaze of hers at the injured man. "Shrivel up the bits of himself he likes best."

Metyein had acquiesced with his ears burning, offering chastened apologies. None of which pacified Soka, who remained at his bedside as Reisil's little group wended their way to a rocky knob overlooking Mysane Kosk. Reisil wanted to see it for herself; she wanted to see it with spellsight.

Reisil stretched. The sun was bright and the breeze hardly enough to rustle the leaves. The battle had been only two nights ago. It felt like a lifetime. She had few memories of that night. A blur of light, unending terror and pain. She hadn't tried to summon any magic since Nurema's healing. Nor had she tried her spellsight. It felt too good to be whole and safe with friends. But there was no time for a lengthy respite.

"They'll be comin' agin. Soon. We need to anchor the wards to Mysane Kosk. To the power in the valley. Then the wards will match 'em, every step. Keep the wizards out, too. It's the only way t' keep Honor safe. No choice."

Reisil might have screamed at that. She was tired of not having choices. Not that she really disagreed. The wards could only hurt the *nokulas* if they attacked, which, as far as she was concerned, would be no more than they deserved. All the same, she wished she could explain it to them. That it was necessary to buy time until she could figure out how to stop the spell without killing everyone. Not that they would listen. Sodur had seemed sure of that.

She wondered if they'd caught him yet. If the *nokulas* had overrun his mind. And if they had? She shuddered with a sudden chill. Should she have killed him, as he wanted?

Reisil had no ready answer. But if the *nokulas* had taken him, had learned all he knew, then on top of all the other knowledge they stripped from him, they would also have learned what she intended to do. She rolled her eyes. That is, her plans as far as she knew them. Which wasn't much. But at least the *nokulas* knew of the promise she'd made.

Reisil shoved those thoughts away. There wasn't anything to be done about Sodur or what the *nokulas* might learn from him. Or what they might do with that information. Her concern now was Mysane Kosk.

She glanced ahead through the trees. At the top of the slope was an overlook that would allow her to see the entire city and valley. Or as much as could be seen through the occlusive mist. They pulled up, tying their horses to some gooseberry bushes. Reisil plucked a few of the green berries. They were tart, not quite ripe, but tasted good all the same.

Reisil scratched the forehead of the copper-colored gelding she'd been given to ride as she untied her water bag. Indigo was in desperate need of rest and feed. When she and Yohuac and Soka departed from Honor in the morning, she wouldn't be riding him. She patted her new mount regretfully. It couldn't be helped. Even if she used her magic to heal Indigo, it wouldn't be enough. She couldn't do for him what food and rest could.

She took a long drink and slung her water bag back on her saddle. Then she joined the others to climb the last fifty paces to the top of the overlook. The ground was gravelly and loose, and by the time she reached the top, Reisil was damp with sweat and breathing quick and heavy. Nurema, Juhrnus, and Yohuac scrabbled up behind.

Baku waited, his bony skull nestled between his forelegs like a dog's. His sides bulged with the two deer he'd slain and eaten that morning. His eyes drifted open halfway. He shifted his wings and settled them. Saljane perched on his back. She leaped into the air, and Reisil caught her on her fist, raising her to the padded perch on her shoulder. The artfully designed gauntlet that protected her hand, arm, and shoulder from Saljane's powerful talons had been a gift from Sodur. Reisil stroked Saljane's chest, remembering the pleasure she'd taken in his thoughtfulness.

He'd been infected then. Reisil sighed and followed the others to the edge of overlook. Every memory she had of Sodur was tainted. Had he ever really been a friend? Or had it all been the urgings of the growing *nokula* influence on his mind?

~He was Sodur. He was our friend, Saljane said, dipping her head and nipping Reisil's fingers in her beak.

Was.

~It would be nice to think so.

And then she forgot about Sodur.

She gazed down at Mysane Kosk, peering between Juhrnus and Soka. "By the Lady," she whispered. "It's beautiful."

"Pretty as an ice storm," Nurema said, leaning on her walking stick. " 'Cept more deadly. And hungry. It's going to swallow up the valley before long."

The diamond mist drifted on unseen currents, like a deep-bedded river. It was constantly in motion, lifting and falling. Not like a river, Reisil thought, unease gripping her. The motion was more like breathing, as if the mist below were merely the skin of a living thing—a dreadful beast lying in wait.

The sun glittered on the crystalline shapes that surrounded the mist in a sparkling bezel. The leading edge of a storm. Those twisted, sculpted, tortured figures hinted at what had become of Mysane Kosk, gulped down by that slothful beast.

"I didn't realize how big it was," Reisil murmured, her hands clammy. She knelt, trying to see more clearly.

"It's been growing. When I was first here, it hadn't reached but halfway to that stand of trees, and look now; it's almost swallowed them entirely."

Reisil followed Juhrnus's pointing finger to a stand of aspen along the far edge of the valley.

"How long before . . . ?" She waved at the stockades.

"At the rate the mist is growing now?" Juhrnus shrugged. "Metyein figures we have a year at most before we lose Fox. But it's been expanding faster than it was. I figure it's only going to go faster, so late

spring is more likely. Right around the same time we
expect the Regent. It'll be a grand party. We'll have
cake and ale.''

Reisil's lips quivered with the beginnings of a smile
at Juhrnus's gallows humor. She swiped her hand over
her mouth, pinching her lips in a hard grip. By spring
the world would end or she'd save it. And she still
didn't have the slightest idea how.

Maybe doing what she'd come up here to do would
help. She sat, resting her elbows on her knees. Taking
a breath, she blinked into spellsight.

She flinched and gasped.

"What is it? What do you see?" The others bent
over her, searching.

"Magic."

Solid waves piled up in rainbow colors. They
mounded up as if held by a dam. Then the layers
slowly dissolved, melting like wax into pools, swirling
and running through the realm of Mysane Kosk in
slow, spreading rivers. The colors themselves never
mixed, but pooled inside one another and then
stretched in skeins, twisting and curling, knotting and
stitching together, creating intricate patterns of lace
and filigree.

Within this tapestry of raw magic, sparks flashed.
They grouped, moving in unison, separating and re-
forming in elaborate patterns. They reminded Reisil
of flocks of starlings . . . or schools of fish.

In the middle of it all, directly over where the city
had stood, swirled a sluggish hurricane. Here the colors smudged into a muddy red. It turned, turbid and
slow, like an enormous screw. Even from the overlook, Reisil could feel its power. Its pull. Its wrongness.

She concentrated, narrowing her gaze. Shock turned
the marrow of her bones to ice. She bent closer, hardly
believing. But yes . . .

The rocks beneath her shifted and she wrenched
forward into thin air. Saljane screeched and leaped
into the air even as hands caught Reisil by the shoul-

ders, dragging her back to safety. Reisil clutched her stomach, breathing hard, ignoring the questions that peppered her. She looked at Baku, who watched her with his half-lidded, knowing eyes.

"You see them too? The *rinda*?"

He whuffed and she felt a tickle in her mind that might have been his attempt at a reply. She swore and scrabbled over to him, setting a hand against his hide.

~Well?

~The spell words? Of course.

Reisil gritted her teeth. Baku had a right to his antagonism, she reminded herself. No matter how infuriating his bare-bones, and uncooperative answers were.

~All of them. Can you see all of them? Even . . . the wrong ones?

~Wrong ones?

~Yes!

Baku lifted himself up, his eyes wide-open now. Reisil followed him as he paced to the edge of the cliff.

~I see chains of letters and words. They are like . . . bricks and water. He sounded baffled. *What should they be that they aren't?*

Reisil settled next to him so that her thigh touched his extended foreleg. Saljane flapped down from the tree branch where she'd perched when Reisil had nearly fallen over the cliff. The heavy weight and firm grip on Reisil's shoulder were welcome.

Reisil opened her mind to Baku, picturing the *rinda* from the book she'd borrowed from Kvepi Debess. Then she pictured the various spells she'd encountered in her sojourn in the wizards' stronghold.

~Do you see? The letters, the words? See how they are so rounded and fluid, like fancy script? Now look down there at Mysane Kosk. See how some of the rinda *are different?*

They seemed sharp-edged and oddly shaped. They had abrupt lines, rather than the scrolling fluidity she was used to. Some were so small that they seemed no bigger than rosemary seeds. Others were larger, nearly readable. She could see what Baku meant in calling them bricks and water. Every shape below was formed from *rinda*. The spell-chains were both skeleton and flesh to even the *nokulas*.

Without warning, Baku swept inside Reisil's mind and dragged her into his. Reisil clutched at him for balance, her stomach twisting at the sudden disorientation. She tasted acid and gooseberries on the back of her tongue and swallowed hard. She felt him pause, as if waiting for her remonstrance. Not far under the surface seethed a boiling pool of resentment and rage. The slightest challenge from Reisil would trigger a volcano. Instead she waited patiently for Baku to show her what he wanted her to see. At last he gave her a gentle mental *push*. Suddenly she was looking out at Mysane Kosk from his eyes. She gasped and strained forward.

Baku's eyesight was much sharper than her own, and he had natural spellsight. It was almost as if she hung a few feet above the crystal-floss landscape of Mysane Kosk. She could see the *nokulas*, could see the *rinda* that shaped their flesh and bone, that shaped everything inside this magically constructed land. Inside that ugly, slow-turning hurricane, she could see the spell-chains twisting and breaking. They whirled and floated and fit together in random patterns. Here and there, a knotted tangle fell out of the twisting, sucking mass, as if too heavy to remain inside any longer.

"Blessed Lady," Reisil breathed, feeling a thrill of excitement. She was beginning to understand at last. . . .

"What? What is it?" Nurema demanded, grasping her wrist in a wiry hold.

Reisil closed her eyes, slowly withdrawing from Baku's mind.

~*Thank you.*

~*You're welcome.*

His tone was testy and accompanied by a shove that sent her precipitously into her own head. Reisil smiled, patting his neck.

~You have helped me a great deal. I may have learned the key to figuring out what to do.

Baku snorted and turned his head. But he did not draw away.

"Well? You gonna moon all day or tell us what's going on?"

Reisil opened her eyes and picked up a twig. She brushed a flat, clear space on the damp ground with her hand and carefully scratched a figure in the dirt. It was angular and with sharp points and protruding stubs. It looked nothing like any of the *rinda* she'd learned from the wizards. But it was *rinda*; Reisil was sure of it. And she had a feeling Nurema would recognize it.

"Do you know what this is? Have you seen it before?"

The poleaxed expression on Nurema's face was worth gold.

"It is the ancient language of nahuallis," Nurema said slowly. "It is one of their most closely guarded secrets."

"Do you know what it means?"

Nurema shook her head. "Only those who had passed the highest trials were taught the language. I had not yet progressed so far. How can you know this?"

Reisil jerked her chin at the edge of the cliff. "They're called *rinda*. The language of spells. Only this"—she pointed to the design in the dirt—"this is different from the *rinda* that I learned from the wizards. Everything in Mysane Kosk is constructed from a combination of the two *rindas*. Somehow spells from Cemanahuatl have fused with the spell the wizards cast here.

"Which means," she said slowly, "that trying to get to Cemanahuatl is the right step to make after all."

"Didn't I say so? Well, then, you've seen all there is to see. Let's go fix them wards," Nurema said.

Reisil rolled her eyes as the other woman marched off, stabbing the ground with her walking stick.

"I didn't say *that* was a good idea," she muttered, clambering to her feet and dusting herself off.

Nurema halted, swinging around, her smile stinging. "My gift is t' see the future. Course yer goin' to Cemanahuatl. And ye'll fix the wards. Should've saved yer arguments and just listened." She turned and started down the path. Juhrnus grinned at Reisil and followed after.

Reisil resisted the urge to stick her tongue out. She sighed, leaning into Yohuac, who slid an arm around her waist.

"If she can see the future, why doesn't she just tell me how to fix this mess?"

Yohuac tightened his arm and smiled at Saljane, who chirped at him. "She's nahualli. But she wishes the safety of Kodu Riik and Cemanahuatl. She is doing all she can to help. She would not withold information that would help you."

"I'd like to believe that," Reisil said darkly. "But she could have told me a lot more, and sooner." Sodur had kept secrets and manipulated her "for her own good." For the sake of Kodu Riik. He'd caused more harm than not. Nurema might very well be doing the same.

"Perhaps."

"But she's right. I guess we go to Cemanahuatl. I hope the rest of the nahuallis are more eager to talk to me."

Yohuac smiled grimly. "Don't wager on it."

Chapter 15

Evening had fallen on Honor after a busy, but blessedly uneventful day. Reisil and Nurema had reestablished the wards around each stockade, anchoring them to swollen flows of magic from Mysane Kosk. The people of Honor had worked hard to move the hospital to Hawk, build funeral pyres for the dead, clear the fields of arrows and debris, and make repairs to Raven. And then they went about the regular business of preparing for war.

Much against protest, Reisil had visited the Wolf captain.

"If I see him, I can confirm he's got the plague," she declared.

"We'll know soon enough. You get too close, you might end up with it," Kebonsat argued flatly. "We can't afford to lose you." He looked gray and sort of deflated, as if something had gone out of him. His eyes were sunken and smudged, and a hard, glittery desperation swam in the dark depths.

Reisil disliked seeing him in pain, but couldn't scrape up much sympathy for his predicament. Much as she agreed that Emelovi's life in Koduteel under her brother's thumb would probably have been hideous, Reisil couldn't help feeling disgusted with Kebonsat. Emelovi was no child. She knew what staying in Koduteel would mean, what it would cost her. Stupid, maybe. But her choice to make. Except Kebonsat had decided she was wrong—wrong enough that he felt compelled to trick her. And now he was learning the cost of his duplicity. It was steeper than he imagined.

Why was it that perfectly honorable men chose lies when they couldn't have their own way? First Sodur, and now Kebonsat. But not this time. Not today. This was a choice Reisil had made and was determined to accomplish.

"Are you going to get out of my way?" she asked, hands on her hips, her brows lifted.

For a moment she thought that Juhrnus, Kebonsat, and Soka, who formed a gate across the doorway, were going to wrestle her into submission. But then Juhrnus stepped aside, his expression stoic. Soka followed suit.

"As we are to take a journey together, I'd rather you didn't catch the plague," he said sardonically.

Reisil grinned. "I will do my best to oblige."

"Hmph," was Soka's only reply.

She cocked her head at Kebonsat, who remained boulderlike in the doorway. At last he moved aside, his teeth gritting audibly.

"This is stupid. There's no point to it," he said.

"The point is that we will be certain."

"What difference will it make if we know now or in a week? We've quarantined him. Knowing for sure won't change anything."

"If he's got it, then I will check everyone I can before I leave tomorrow. We may be able to cut off the head of the snake and control the outbreak before it's too far out of hand."

"It's a waste of your strength," Kebonsat argued. "You need to save all you've got for this journey. If you fail, we'll all die anyway."

Reisil bit her tongue. She drew a breath and let it out slowly, counting to ten. "Thank you, but I believe that I can manage well enough," she said in a carefully bland tone. But Kebonsat felt the point nonetheless. He flushed. He stepped aside jerkily.

"As you see fit."

"Exactly so," Reisil said tartly as she walked out

the door. He was right. But so was she, and as an
ahalad-kaaslane, she couldn't walk away from Honor
without trying to do something about the plague. If it
was here.

The captain from Wolf *was* infected. He was still in
the innocuous first stage, with a low fever, dysintery,
body pain, and nausea. It would not be long before
his fever increased to blistering and any light would
cause him extraordinary pain. He would be too dizzy
to stand. Within a few days after that, the horrors
would begin. First the rash and jaundice, then bleeding
from every orifice, including his gums and fingernails.
After that . . . his fingers and toes would begin to rot
from the inside out. It would travel up the arms and
legs, killing him inch by inch as his blood pathways
deteriorated.

"So I'm a goner, am I?" the captain asked when
Reisil sat back, pulling her hands from his chest.

She nodded her head wearily.

"Demon-blighted Pease was right. That's the real
bite of it."

Reisil smiled with effort. He had his pride and
didn't want her to see his struggle with the bleak fear
sweeping him. Not of death. He was a soldier, and
Reisil had enough experience with such men to know
that death was not the horror to them that it was to
most people. But *such* a death. That was the dragon
he was fighting.

She spread her hands and turned them over. She
tried to imagine them swollen and black, blistered with
yellow, seeping pustules— Reisil shuddered, crossing
her arms and tucking her hands beneath them. Her
eyes burned with tears of anger and frustration. She
refused to let them fall.

"I've heard some have survived," the captain said,
his thick fingers tightening around his cup of kohv.

Reisil looked at him squarely, not wanting to offer
him false hope. "There have been a few, here and
there. A very few. The plague made them blind. That
happens in the second stage, when light becomes so

very painful. But when it goes past that into the third stage . . . you will certainly die."

"That be a blessing, to my thinkin'," he said.

"I believe you are right."

With nothing else to do and no comfort to offer, Reisil left him. A tark was looking after him as well as or better than she could have.

She brought the news back to the others as they settled in to eat supper. It was a sober group, with Emelovi seething quietly at one end of the table, and Kebonsat as far away as possible at the other end. Between sat Metyein and Soka, with Reisil perched opposite of Emelovi, Nurema and Juhrnus flanking her.

Silence drowned the room. All that could be heard was the scrape of knives, the clunk of mugs returning to the table, and the merry crackle of the fire. At last Metyein pushed back his trencher.

"All right. I still don't like it. Reisiltark just arrives, and in the nick of time, I might add, and already she's leaving. We have two unfinished stockades, a fifth of the crops were destroyed in the battle, and we will be once again without means to fend off the *nokulas* when they attack."

"The *nokulas* wouldn't have attacked at all if it hadn't been for me," Reisil pointed out for the twentieth time. "And I doubt you'll have trouble from the wizards. The *nokulas* aren't going to let them come stealing power from Mysane Kosk. Sodur was in my mind. He's seen what the wizards do to the *nokulas*. They're not going to stand more of that."

Truth be told, the night before, when Nurema had first declared that Reisil would have to leave Honor immediately and return with Yohuac to Cemanahuatl, Reisil had been astounded.

"Go to Cemanahuatl? Why? How? Now?" The words burst from her lips in stuttering staccato.

"You've got no choice. I've *seen* it."

There was no arguing with a foretelling. Nurema had proven herself and her abilities, and she'd never

been one to lie or muddle the truth for her own ends.
Reisil believed her. And after seeing the mix of nahualli *rinda* in the spells today, she was more than
convinced.

The others had been harder to win over, but at last
they'd agreed, grudgingly. Not that they had any
choice. No more than Reisil.

At that thought, Reisil found herself studying Emelovi across the table. The other woman was eating,
her movements jerky and graceless. She clearly was
having to force the food down, keeping herself from
throwing it back up again by will alone.

It said a great deal for her that she wasn't hiding
in her room with her head under a pillow. And though
she kept her gaze fixed relentlessly on her trencher,
her attention was riveted on the rest of the conversation. Reisil smiled, reaching for a crock of sweet butter. Metyein's voice interrupted her musings, and she
turned her attention back to him.

"Since we won't have Reisiltark with us, obtaining
metal for weapons becomes even more critical. One
important item we have neglected to discuss is what
gift we might send to Thevul Bro-heyek. Whatever it
is should show that we are a force to be reckoned
with, and not merely rabble with nothing to our
names. It should also be of great enough value that it
is not perceived as an insult."

"A gift?" demanded Soka. He set his knife on the
table, his hands flattening on the rough planks. His
lips were white, his voice high and tight. He reached
up and touched his fingertips to his eye patch. "The
goat-loving *ganyik* already has my eye. What more
does he have a right to ask? He *owes* me. Far more
than a few paltry wagonloads of iron and steel."

Metyein sucked in an audible breath, casting a sideways glance at Emelovi, who'd paled at Soka's coarse
outburst. He twisted his head, his nostrils flaring as he
faced Soka. His voice was relentless and cutting. "Yes,
your father does owe *you*. But he does not owe *us*—
he does not owe Honor. And despite his attacks against

his neighbors, as far as we know, he is loyal to the crown. We are traitors. After all, we're the ones building an army to drive Aare off the throne.

"We have to convince your father to support us. He will expect us to follow political protocols. If we don't, he'll lose any respect he might have had for us. We'll be cut off at the knees before we get started. *Think*, Soka. We're asking him to commit treason. We'd better demonstrate our worth."

"I'd sooner castrate him," Soka said, picking up his knife to dig deep gouges in the table.

"You said you could do this," Metyein reminded him, his temper fraying.

"I said I would go ask for the metal. I did not say I would fawn at his feet. I'm not going to bend over and stick my ass in the air. I'm no molly."

"I'm not asking you to do anything of the sort. I *am* asking you to act as befits your rank and your mission. We can't afford for you to fail." Metyein's voice had turned cold and implacable. "Say so, and I'll send someone else."

Soka's teeth bit white dents into his lower lip. He pushed up, swinging his leg over the bench. His sword got caught and he jerked it free, going to stand at the end of the table by Kebonsat. He stood there, arms straight at his sides, his feet braced wide. He stared at Metyein, his eyes stark with fury and hurt.

Reisil gave a silent sigh. Did the betrayal never end? And yet Metyein was not wrong, any more than Soka was wrong. It was the situation. And at least there was truth between them.

"He will go. And he will do as he must to secure the metal for weapons." Reisil had not seen Emelovi stand. Her body was rigid, her face pale. She stood straight, imperious even, and resolute. No one spoke; everyone stared.

"It must be done. And there is no one else to do it. You will take a gift. You will do what is necessary. You will return with the metals we need to build weapons. Is that clear?"

Soka hesitated a long moment, the tendons in his neck tenting. Then he gave a short, jerky nod. "As you command."

There was a long moment of tense silence when no one moved. Then Emelovi sank back down to the bench, folding her shaking hands in her lap.

The silence continued. Emelovi remained as she was, head bowed down. Soka retreated to a place near the fire, where he leaned with pretended casualness. At last Metyein spoke, his voice raspy.

"That still leaves the matter of a gift. Does anyone have suggestions?"

"We can't afford anything that a man the likes of Bro-heyek would value. Horses, livestock, weapons— we need everything we have," Kebonsat said.

"Agreed," Metyein said. "What *do* we have?"

No one answered. Finally Nurema spoke.

"Best be something as can be carried easy. Speed is going to matter."

"I have jewels," Emelovi said abruptly.

"I don't think jewels will interest the Thevul much," Metyein said. "But thank you."

Emelovi gave a slight nod.

"A bargain, then," Kebonsat said. "Against the future. Against us winning and . . . the Dazien . . . taking the throne."

Metyein nodded, considering. "A charter of land? Trade rights?" He rubbed his upper lip thoughtfully. "He's hungry for land and power. There's no doubt that if Aare wins, sooner or later he'll march up north and put Bro-heyek in its place. The Thevul has a lot more to gain from supporting us than not."

"Offer him the position of the North Warder," Emelovi said softly.

"North Warder? Is there any such thing?"

"There will be, if he says yes. It will entitle him to rule his neighbors in the name of the crown. He will be entitled to a portion of all taxes collected north of the Sawtooth Range. If he is as hungry as you say, he will not refuse."

"I will craft a letter, Dazien," Metyein said respectfully.

Emelovi smiled slightly. "Very good, Lord Marshal."

Vertina to subject, Reisil thought. Emelovi had been raised to rule. Or at least to be the wife of someone in power, whether a Kijal or a prince from another land. Perhaps she could learn to rule in her own right. At least she'd decided to put aside her hurt and anger to try. It was a good choice.

Chapter 16

They departed before dawn the next morning. A steady rain had begun in the early morning, and Reisil's boots caught in the mud, pulling free with sticky squelches as she and Yohuac crossed the central compound to the stables. She carried a mug of kohv in her hand. A bedraggled Saljane perched miserably on her shoulder, making unhappy grunting sounds. Yohuac walked beside her, his expression somber. He'd braided his new locks of hair, but the beads were nowhere in evidence. Reisil wondered how he felt to be going home.

She gave a small sigh. She was going to have more time with him. She was going to be able to consult with his nahuallis. For the first time, she had reason to hope she might solve the problem of Mysane Kosk. Still her throat ached with the lump that she could not swallow. He wouldn't be coming back.

~I don't remember losing Kaval or Kebonsat hurting this much, she complained to Saljane.

~You were not heartbound, then.

Reisil gave a silent nod. No, though she'd cared deeply for them, she'd never felt for Kaval or Kebonsat what she now felt for Yohuac. She didn't know why he claimed her heart so completely. Except that in the short time they'd spent together, he seemed to understand and accept her in ways that the other two never had. Just like she accepted him. Accepted that he was going to return to Cemanahuatl. She'd gained a short reprieve with Nurema's insistence that she go too, but when she learned what she needed from the nahuallis, that would be the end. She'd return to Kodu Riik and he'd become *Ilhuicatl*'s son-in-the-flesh, or die trying.

~Baku will be devastated.

~He already knows.

Reisil glanced up, startled.

~He does? And then— *Of course he does. It's just that he's always been so determined that he could change Yohuac's mind.*

~He no longer hopes for such. Baku will accompany Yohuac as far as possible, and then . . .

And then? Would he even survive the parting? She thought of how the wizards had torn Saljane from her. The sudden, endless emptiness. A silence so profound that she couldn't hear her own heartbeat. Reisil had been driven past reason with the pain of it. And yet later, once Saljane was restored to her, the pair had calmly decided that should either die, the other must continue on, must protect Kodu Riik. An easy decision to make with your heart's ease sitting on your shoulder. Whereas Baku faced exactly that hopeless choice and carried on. Reisil's chest hurt. Never again would she chastise Baku for his ill humor.

She lifted her hand to stroke Saljane's wet feathers, searching for Baku in the wet darkness. There— He crouched by the gate. She doubted anyone else saw him. To anyone else without spellsight, he would be invisible.

~He will not grieve alone, Reisil said.

Soka was checking his saddle and packs when Reisil and Yohuac arrived outside the stables. His face was set. He jerked on the cinch to check it, then picked his horse's hooves. What would it be like, Reisil wondered, to come face-to-face with a father who'd made him a hostage to the court, who'd been responsible for Soka losing his eye? What would it be like to swallow his pride and ask for help from that man?

Beyond Soka, the four soldiers who would be escorting him to Bro-heyek were also readying their mounts. Juhrnus and Kebonsat waited alongside. They would accompany the travelers to the edge of the valley. They were already mounted, their hoods pulled low against the pattering rain.

Reisil shook off her melancholy with an effort. She yawned, her jaw cracking. She turned. "Where's Nurema?"

"You two're the late ones, not me," Nurema said. She stood out of the rain in the wide doorway of the stable. "I'll not hold you up longer than needs be. Come on, then."

She led the way inside to an empty stall, a lantern dangling from a hook on the wall. She rolled up her sleeve, exposing her tanned arm. Reisil watched, repulsed, as a lump formed just beneath Nurema's skin above her wrist. It bulged sharply, and then the skin split bloodlessly. What emerged was a tiny snake, perhaps four inches long. Its skin was a brilliant green, the color of new grass on the first day of summer. Its belly was bloodred, its eyes topaz yellow. It was a *copicatl*, a messenger of *Ilhuicatl*, the father-god of Cemanahuatl. It wriggled down to coil in Nurema's palm, its yellow tongue flickering.

She held out her hand toward Reisil. "The *copicatl* will open the gate between Kodu Riik and Cemanahuatl. The same location where he and I came through," she said with a nod to Yohuac.

Reisil hesitated. The idea of the reptile burrowing into her flesh was repellent to the point of turning her stomach. But she need carry the snake for only a little while. Just until they traveled across the Karnane Valley to the point where first Nurema, and later Yohuac, had entered Kodu Riik. There was no time for squeamishness. Every passing moment brought Kodu Riik—brought the entire world—closer to destruction.

Taking a breath, Reisil slowly exhaled, extending her left hand palm up.

Before Nurema could move, Saljane shrieked and

lunged off Reisil's shoulder. She knocked heavily against Nurema, dumping the *copicatl* to the ground and leaving a long gash in the older woman's forearm. Then the goshawk landed and snapped viciously at the hissing emerald snake as it dodged back and forth.

Nurema stumbled backwards, swearing like a river rat. She bent to snatch up the *copicatl*, narrowly avoiding losing a finger. Saljane leaped back up to Reisil's shoulder, shrieking loudly, the ivy pattern on her beak flashing gold in the lantern light.

Reisil tried to soothe Saljane, but the bird was inarticulate in her fury. That worm had no right to invade her *ahalad-kaaslane*'s body. She would shred it with her talons, crush it in her beak.

Rage. Resentment. Possession.

"She won't allow it," Reisil said, spreading her hands helplessly, inexpressively relieved. "I can't carry it."

Exasperated, Nurema turned to Yohuac, but found herself facing Baku. The coal-drake's head wove back and forth, his tail lashing from side to side. The message was clear: Neither Reisil nor Yohuac would be allowed to carry the *copicatl*.

"What are we going to do?" Reisil asked.

"Get yer animals under control," Nurema said.

"They are *ahalad-kaaslane*," Reisil corrected sharply. "They act as they see fit. Neither of us can carry the snake." Despite her relief at not having to let the snake burrow inside her, she wished she understood Saljane's response. It isn't as if the goshawk hadn't known the plan.

Saljane startled her, breaking free of her wordless fury.

~*I thought you would carry it in a sack, or a box.*

Reisil suggested this to Nurema, who nodded. "I s'pose we could do it that way."

Saljane mantled, tension radiating from her stiff body.

~*I do not trust it. It wants inside you. I will kill it first.*

Reisil shook her head. "Saljane seems to think it's gone past that point. She doesn't trust it."

"Baku says he will carry it," Yohuac volunteered, sounding surprised. "He says it cannot inhabit him." At the questioning looks cast by the two women, he shrugged. "I do not know. But Baku is certain."

"Fine," Nurema said. Before the coal-drake could change his mind, she raised her hand. Baku bent forward. The snake lifted up tall on its tail on Nurema's palm. It stretched up straight as an arrow, touching its nose to Baku's. The coal-drake's nostrils fluttered gently.

They remained thus for a moment, and then the *copicatl* slid up the bridge of Baku's snout. It wriggled up between Baku's eye ridges and over the bony knob at the top of his skull. It nestled down in the hollow behind, coiling into a knot the size of an apricot.

"Done," Nurema said briskly, dusting her hands together. "Best get off then. Time's wastin'."

"Take care of them," Reisil said, grasping the other woman's hand. Nurema's grip was strong and firm. "Keep them safe until I get back."

"Do as I can. But I left Cemanahuatl 'fore I had much training."

"Just hold. That's all I ask."

"Don't take overlong," Nurema said, her fingers tightening on Reisil's. "The wards'll hold awhile, but if the Regent comes callin' with his pet sorcerers, I can't speak for what'll happen. Can be sure them wizards won't sit silent for the Scallacians to steal their prize. *Nokulas* will have their say too."

What would happen in that tug-of-war, Reisil didn't want to imagine. But it would be bloody. And Honor would be the battleground. She shivered. She *had* to find an answer and get back before the Regent arrived. Before spring opened the passes.

"I'll be back in plenty of time," Reisil promised. She hoped it was true.

"Be sure to put up wards when ye camp. Just like I showed ye. Don't get lazy. Don't forget."

"I won't. Lady's luck to you."

With that, Reisil pulled her hand away to follow Yohuac.

"One more thing," Nurema said abruptly, sounding angry.

Reisil stopped and turned, warily. What now?

"Bein' as how we might not see each other agin, I figure I ought to speak of this. I told ye how I came to Kodu Riik, followin' after Kinatl. She was young and I goaded her into somethin' stupid. Which is how she ended up here, and I ended up chasin' her. Never did find her. Stopped lookin' after I met the Lady.

"Anyhow, she met a man. An *ahalad-kaaslane* who'd lost his animal. One of those *magilanes*. He was sore hurtin' and not far from dyin' hisself. But Kinatl was desperate, like a trapped animal. She was about starvin' and had no clothes and her magic had stopped workin'. He took pity on her and helped her. And she helped him right back. Made him want to live. Fell in love, they did. Bound together closer than soul to body. They stayed up high in the mountains until she got herself pregnant. That's when they decided to come down an' find a tark. Feared somethin' goin' wrong and losin' the baby.

"Like I said, I didn't find her. She found me. In Kallas. Course I knew she'd be comin'. Had a vision. She was glad to see a face from home. Until I told her she'd have to leave her baby. And the necklace her man had given her." Nurema's eyes flicked to where Reisil's tunic hid the Lady's talisman—the same one Nurema had given her before leaving Kallas.

Reisil's mouth dropped open. She couldn't speak. She couldn't breathe. Nurema had gone pale, but she continued on doggedly.

"They didn't want to leave the little thing. Broke their hearts. But Kinatl knew I *see* true. Celidan had been *ahalad-kaaslane*. With the mark of the Lady on my hand, he couldn't refuse either. They gave it a name and went away." Nurema looked down at her palm, rubbing a finger across the gold gryphon seal inscribed there. Then she looked back up at Reisil.

"What—?" Reisil could hardly push the word out. Her knees were shaking. She stiffened, trying to keep the fractured pieces of herself from flying apart. "What happened to them? My parents?"

Nurema shook her head. "Don't know. They never came back. The visions never spoke of 'em again."

Bleak silence fell between them. Reisil had more questions than she could begin to ask. And she had a journey to make. She glared at Nurema for a long moment, then spun around and strode out into the rain.

The coppery chestnut was drenched. But he remained steady and unflustered. Reisil patted his neck, hardly aware of what she was doing. She checked her cinch and packs with rote method, then swung up into the saddle.

"You all right?" Juhrnus asked cautiously. His eyes were fixed on the golden ivy unfurling on her cheek.

"Let's go," Reisil said harshly. She chirruped to her gelding and trotted out to the gate.

Nurema still stood in the doorway of the stables. Reisil did not look at her.

There was no conversation as the little group made its way to the edge of the valley. Reisil paused to say good-bye to Kebonsat and Juhrnus as the rest of their expedition began winding up the path into the mountains. As Reisil watched, Baku crawled up the path after Yohuac to disappear behind a tor, his legs and belly clotted with thick, red mud. Reisil wondered absently why he did not fly. She shrugged. She turned to her two companions.

"Are you all right?" Juhrnus asked again. "Has something happened?"

Reisil wiped the rain from her eyes with icy fingers. Her mother's name was Kinatl. Her father was an *ahalad-kaaslane*. A *magilane*. He too had been paired with a predator bird. She swallowed jerkily, feeling a maelstrom of emotions pulling at her. She couldn't deal with this now. There were more important things to do. She pushed the revelation about her parents far down in her mind. She'd think about it later.

"Nothing that matters," she answered at last. "At least not to anyone but me. Just more secrets." She felt Kebonsat flinch at the bitterness in her voice, as if she'd pointed a finger at him.

"You should have stayed in bed," she said to Juhrnus, trying to lighten the mood.

He shook his head. "I'm on my way, too. Down to the Straits of Pleanar to meet Dannen Relvi, and then back to Koduteel."

"I thought Karina said she wouldn't be able to send out any more information."

"I can still spy on the Regent's preparations. He's got to have a staging area for his army. And I might discover something about the Scallacians." He gave a lopsided smile that lacked humor. "Don't want 'em sneaking up on us unawares."

"Have you heard from her?" Reisil asked with a pang of guilt. She'd forgotten about the sorceress—or rather, about how important Kedisan-Mutira had become to Juhrnus. She was different, he claimed. Exactly how different, Reisil didn't know. Nor did Juhrnus. He didn't believe that she was going to turn against her fellow sorcerers or the Regent Aare. He seemed sure of that—sure that he could not trust her. But still he hoped. So did Reisil, for his sake and Honor's.

She nudged her horse close to his and pulled him into a hug.

"Don't be stupid," she said softly.

"Look who's talking," he jeered. "Come home soon."

"Soon as I can," she promised.

"Try not to die first."

"Yohuac says the nahuallis have spirit-catchers. I'll come back one way or another," Reisil promised, pulling away.

She turned to Kebonsat. His face was white and sunken beneath his hood. His skin wrapped his skull tightly. He looked eerie and hopeless, like a *rashani*— one of the soul-destroyed, condemned to roam the land long after their bodies rotted away and their sins had no meaning. Reisil suddenly regretted the jibe she'd made. She reached out and grasped his hand. He wore gloves, but he seemed to radiate cold. The same cold that clutched her, only far more bleak. Hopeless. Her grip tightened.

"You cannot let go," she said. "You cannot abandon Metyein and Emelovi. They need your experience and wisdom."

He looked at Reisil, his eyes fathomless. "I am forbidden to see or speak with her. She does not trust my word." He paused. "I have no place here. I have no place anywhere. I have no family and no country." He cocked his head in an oddly unemotional way, as if considering the price of dishware or candles. "I have no claim any longer to my name. Do you know the suffix *sat* refers to the titular heir? I have been disowned. I am nothing more than Kebon, a blank shield."

Reisil wanted to grab him and shake him out of his apathy. No, that wasn't it. It wasn't that he didn't care. It was more that everything that anchored him to this world had been torn away: his name, his family, his country, his purpose. She knew how that felt. She had felt the same way when her magic had failed, and the *ahalad-kaaslane* and nobility had shunned her. She'd never felt so alone, so useless. More than useless; she'd felt as if she were causing harm to those she was supposed to be protecting.

She pulled him close, so that her nose nearly brushed against his. "You are Kebonsat cas Vadonis. You are *my friend*. I trust you. I need you to look after them. I need you to keep Emelovi safe, and to help Metyein fight the Regent and his father. Do you understand? There's no one else who can do it. Can I rely on you?"

Reisil released him.

He was still, everything but his cheek. It twitched just below his right eye. Reisil held him snared, refusing to let him look away, refusing to let him withdraw any farther.

"I—" He closed his mouth, clamping it shut. A full minute passed. The horses shifted uneasily. Reisil's copper gelding pawed the ground, shoving his nose out against the reins.

"I . . . yes. You can." The words were low and tight, barely audible.

It was enough.

"Bright journey, then," Juhrnus said, extending his arm.

Reisil grasped it firmly, and then Kebonsat's. "Lady hold you in Her hands while I'm gone," she said. And then she wheeled and urged her chestnut up the hill. Kebonsat would not fail her. He'd broken his word once. He would never do it again.

Tapit learned of Reisil's departure two days later. He was trundling a barrow of dirt from one of the tunnels to fortify the earthworks of Raven when he overheard the worried conversation of two guards.

"Them's sayin' she's gone off agin, Reisiltark. Since two days."

"Gone? Where? What fer? What we gonna do without 'er?"

"Ain't no tellin' where. And now, when the plague's got us by the balls. I tell you square, not much sense stayin' here now. Ought to be gettin' goin'. Git away from this cursed place and take . . ."

The rest of the conversation was lost to Tapit.

He upended the barrow, seething. Gone? Where? And why? He lowered the barrow, swinging it around to push it back toward the mounds beside the tunnel opening. He strained against the mud, his face slick with sweat, his undertunic damp and clammy.

She'd come to the wizards' stronghold to learn what had been done to Mysane Kosk, and to ask how to reverse the spell. Her shock had been laughable when she learned that no living Kvepi knew what had happened. And neither did they mean to undo the spell. Though it hadn't happened in the expected way, the original goal had been accomplished: the creation of a vast source of power. And it had also unlocked the door to using magic inside Kodu Riik. What had happened at Mysane Kosk had turned out better than they hoped.

Tapit reined in his thoughts, scowling. She still meant to reverse the spell. Where else could she go for help? He thought hard, but his mind remained empty. A niggling thought. Unless . . . the Whieche? He almost laughed aloud.

That gaggle of weak-stomached cods wouldn't know *rinda* from a chamber pot. They called themselves wizards, but had never wanted to make the necessary sacrifices to learn their craft. What puling few there were left after the Nethieche had purged them. No, the Whieche wouldn't be able to help her. But crossing into Patverscme to find them meant she'd be in Tapit's homeland. He chortled. It would be almost too easy to get ahead of her and set a trap.

The lean wizard parked the barrow, making a show of grasping his gut and pretending the need to void himself. The other men hardly paid attention to him as he wandered toward the trees for a moment of privacy. His mind raced. He'd circle the valley for her trail. He could track her. A two-day trail was not so difficult, even with the smothering magic of the place, even with the rain. A fierce smile spread across his face. She could not hide her path so well that he could not find it. It was his gift. And capturing her would be all the sweeter for a good chase.

Chapter 17

The grueling journey east and north across the Karnane Valley to the Melyhir Mountains took six weeks.
At every stop, Reisil checked the horses, healing
bruised hooves, pulled muscles and tendons, scrapes,
torn frogs, and twice sprained fetlocks. It was easy
enough to do, and tired her no more than hauling
wood for the fire or cooking, both of which the others
delegated entirely to themselves. Harder was setting
the wards in the evenings, though practice made it
easier. They each still took watch, to call a challenge
and recognize a friend, but more than once the wards
proved their worth by killing marauders that meant
them harm.

"Handy, that," Soka said the first time they were
attacked. He knelt, turning over the body of a ragged
man who sprawled lifeless, a battered sword clutched
in his hand, his body emaciated beneath his filthy
clothing. "Be nice if the buggers worked when we
were moving."

"Nurema said it was impossible."

"Why?"

"It's the spell. Wards guard places. You have to lay
them out in a pattern so they connect to create a kind
of fence, with everything inside protected. But it won't
work on water, horses, or even a man walking. You
walk right out of the spells. I don't know why you
can't make them more portable."

But the question niggled at her. It occupied her so

that she didn't have to think about her parents, to wonder if they still lived. In the evenings while the food cooked, Soka, Yohuac, and the four soldiers sparred and wrestled with one another. As much as Reisil could use the practice, she ignored them in favor of studying the ward spells. She tried modifying them, but it was no use. She hadn't any idea how to read the nahualli *rinda*, much less use them. They could be letters, words, or entire sentences. Or numbers. Equations. The possibilities seemed endless and hopeless. And she hadn't learned enough of the wizard *rinda* to create much of anything.

"I should have taken that blighted book," she said in disgust, throwing the rock upon which she'd been trying to set the changed ward spell.

"You were otherwise engaged," Yohuac said, panting as he settled behind her on the ground, his hair damp with sweat. He rubbed gently at her shoulders. "Saving me and Baku. Not to mention the plague-healers."

"I'm not sure I didn't dream them," Reisil said, leaning back against his chest, breathing in his scent. She wasn't in the least embarrassed at their intimacy, though Soka wasn't above the occasional teasing jibe.

"You did not. Baku and I remember them."

"You weren't entirely in your right mind."

~I was. I remember.

Reisil smiled. "Saljane says she remembers too."

"Remembers what?" Soka sprawled flat on the ground, groaning. "I wouldn't refuse a shoulder rub of my own, preferably from the lady." He waggled his brows at Reisil.

Yohuac shoved his foot against Soka's thigh and the other man rolled onto his side, affecting an expression of pitiful desolation.

"What I wouldn't do for a hot bath. All those years in Koduteel, envying those who had the freedom to ride for days and weeks, anywhere they wanted to go—sheer madness. I didn't know what I had. Feather beds, rich, remarkable delicacies, the best liquors, and the women . . ." He flopped onto his back, his arms outstretched above his head. "I was a colossal fool."

"Was?" Reisil said. And then before he could retort, she went on. "I said I wasn't sure the plague-healers were really real. But Yohuac, Baku, and Saljane insist they remember them as well."

"So then, your mind is not going soft. That must be a comfort."

"I'm not so sure about that. I can't figure out how to make these ward spells work on the move. If only I hadn't left that book—I just don't know enough *rinda*! And without knowing more, I'm stuck."

"You can't do magic without these *rinda*? But of course you can. You've been keeping the horses sound." Soka hitched himself back up on his side, leaning his head on his hand. "So what's the problem?"

Reisil sat up, drawing with a finger in the dirt. "Well, with *rinda*, you can set spells to trigger without you there. You can set them to use stored magic. It keeps you from exhausting yourself every time you want to do something. And you can create more powerful and complex spells by laddering the *rinda* on top of each other and interweaving them. The wards do that. But they want to guard a space, not a thing. So it isn't that the wards are protecting us, so much as they are protecting the ground we stand on. And I don't know how to change it. At least, not with the *rinda* I know, and I left the book I was using to learn them in the wizards' stronghold."

For a moment she remembered Tapit's derisive words—*the stronghold still stands and only a handful of us lost*. Was the book lying where she'd left it? On her bed? In the workroom? She couldn't remember. Much as she wanted the stronghold to have been destroyed, obliterated by fire and the falling mountains, she hoped the book had survived.

"What's so special about these *rinda*?" Soka asked, breaking into her thoughts. "If they're just words, why not just use ordinary ones?"

Reisil opened her mouth, but couldn't think of an answer. Why not?

"The *rinda* are the sacred language of the gods," Yohuac said, pulling Reisil back against his chest and encircling her warmly in his arms. "Other words are just . . . words."

It was a reasonable answer. Still, Reisil wondered. . . .

"Ah," Soka said mockingly. "Just like the language of love. The right ones unlock the bed and drawers of the most coy lover."

They continued east until they came to the Elii River, which meandered through the Karnane Valley and ended in the salt marshes in southeast Kodu Riik. As they descended out of the Suune Vaale Mountains and into the southern part of the valley, the rainstorms ceased and the ground turned hard and dry. Dust puffed with every step, clogging their noses, mouths, and eyes. The air was still, the sun unrelenting. Saljane and Baku scavenged constantly for food, bringing back snakes, scrawny rabbits, and occasional squirrels.

Most of the villages they passed were either deserted or burned to cinders. The blackened husks of the latter served as grave markers for the victims of the plague, for the victims of the drought, for dead hopes and stillborn dreams.

The repeated devastation robbed Reisil of any appetite. How many had died in the flames, burned by their friends and families? Or had entire villages been annihilated by neighboring towns in fear of the plague?

As the days passed, she found herself growing silent and somber, her stomach churning with bile. Her resolve hardened. She had to—no, she was *going* to—find the answer to saving Mysane Kosk. She ate because she would not permit herself to become sick or weak. She slept for the same reason, ruthlessly repressing her dreams and nightmares. Her land and people were dying. Time was running out.

They forded the sluggish Elii River, its flow turbid and less than half of what it should be. Because of this, they crossed easily and started north. On flat land and close to water, they could make much better time. Game was more plentiful as well. But this path also brought them dangerously close to those towns and villages yet inhabited. These were forbidding, hostile places, and attempts at approach resulted in hails of arrows and shouted warnings. No one new was allowed. *Take the plague back where you came from. Come near and die.*

But far more perilous were the raiders. They gathered in voracious packs, hunting travelers and those who strayed too far from the walled towns. Their fear of the plague could not withstand their greed for horses, for weapons, wealth, and women. They reveled in the lawlessness that came with the plague. They could rape, pillage, murder, and steal, and no one would stop them.

Except Reisil.

The first bodies they found were of a family. The father's throat had been slit, his eyes gouged out, his intestines spilled out on the ground. The mother and five children had been raped. The youngest was a boy, could hardly have been more than three. Reisil could hardly look at his battered body. His teeth were knocked out, his arms twisted at unnatural angles. His pale skin was washed crimson in his own blood.

Reisil retched when she turned and found the rest of the family, her stomach convulsing. She grasped the Lady's talisman at her neck, its hard edges cutting into her hand, recalling her to herself.

The other children were stair-stepped up in age to about ten. Like the youngest, like their mother, they were blond with brown eyes. And they'd also been brutally raped. The mother had clearly died trying to fight the men off her children. Her jaw had been knocked askew, her breasts nearly carved off her chest. Animals had been at the bodies, birds and wild dogs. The stench of decay was thick in the air, like putrid syrup, mixed in with a sharp smell, and Reisil realized with horror that the men had urinated on the bodies.

She started violently when from the trees, magpies, jays, and crows screeched furiously. Above, the vultures that had drawn their small party circled lazily.

Yohuac gripped Reisil's shoulders, pulling her away.

"There's so much blood," she said, her sobs knotting in her chest, tears streaking her face. Again her stomach twisted and she retched, her ribs convulsing in short, chopping heaves. "Who—what—could do such a thing?" she gasped.

"Juhrnus spoke of raiders," Yohuac said, his voice like molten steel.

~*Unnatural, evil men*, Saljane added darkly. She gave her piercing cry, chasing the scavenger birds from the trees. Baku roared and joined her.

They built a pyre. Reisil blasted it. The destruction did little for her fury and frustration. The tinder-dry wood exploded in flames, the bodies burning quickly in the inferno. The smell of cooking, crisping flesh turned Reisil's stomach. She staggered away up a knoll, to sit with her arms wrapped around her knees. She lifted her head to let the breeze stroke her face, cooling the heat of her tears.

It was to be only the first of many atrocities they encountered, each as brutal and sickeningly gruesome as the first. And when they found themselves becoming the hunted, Reisil hungered for retribution.

The wards worked only when their group stopped and Reisil established the magical boundary. When they rode, they were protected only by their own strength of arms, and Reisil's magic. Yohuac was too unskilled to direct his with any purpose, and he remained unwilling to learn. And Baku . . . He had done no magic since he'd saved Yohuac from the *nokulas*. Reisil still did not know what Baku could do. Or what he would do. Nor did she ask. If he wanted her to know, he would tell her. He could, and did, fight with his teeth and talons, but never did he mount any other defense.

Reisil didn't care if he did. She wasn't going to let her companions risk their lives against the butchers who'd begun to hunt them. She smiled in ruthless anticipation. None of the cowardly *ganyiks* would get close enough to send an arrow, much less torture and maim. As far as she was concerned, anyone who'd do what they did, deserved to die. Painfully.

The idea should have appalled her, but it didn't.

She'd been trained as a tark, taught to heal and to preserve life. As such, she found death a bitter thing, an enemy to be fought against, tooth and nail. But on her journey from tark to *ahalad-kaaslane*, she'd learned sometimes death was to be welcomed. Sometimes killing was necessary. Sometimes killing a person meant saving others. Some people needed extermination.

She touched the Lady's talisman at her neck. These men were rabid. They reveled in torture. They were depraved, vicious monsters, and they couldn't be allowed to continue on.

Saljane warned her of the ambush. The riders from Honor were riding along the thinly wooded river bottom. To the east, the hills rose in long, easy swells. To the west, the river glinted. The ground was dry and the grasses were brown. A stiff breeze blew from behind them, blowing up clouds of choking dust.

~They wait.

Reisil slid into Saljane's mind, seeing what the goshawk saw. There was a small army of them. They had taken position where the river made a sharp turning to the east, its banks becoming steep and narrow as the ground beside it rose in several thickly forested hummocks. It was a good trap. The river was impossible to cross there, and its crook provided two sides of the box. The trees gave cover ahead and to the east. The travelers would cross a large meadow in between as they approached the timberline, and the ambushers would erupt from hiding and seal the box.

"They are ready for us," Reisil said, describing the

trap for their companions, who pulled up in dismay. "There must be a hundred of them."

Soka swore, and Clano, one of the soldiers assigned to escort Soka home, signaled the two men riding point to return.

"Our only chance is to go up into the hills and try to outrun them," said Temles, another of Soka's escort. He did not sound hopeful.

The others nodded agreement, already turning their horses.

"No," said Reisil. "They must be dealt with. They cannot be permitted to continue terrorizing the valley."

"But we can't—" Soka broke off as understanding glinted in his eye. "Of course. *We* can't. You can."

Reisil nodded, her face feeling like it had been chiseled from obsidian.

"Wouldn't hurt my feelings any to see them get paid for what they've done," Soka said with a sharp grin.

"Me either," Temles said feelingly, then blushed when Reisil looked at him. He was young, not yet twenty, with a boy's slenderness and grace. Nevertheless, he was deadly with a bow and quick with his blade.

Yohuac said nothing. Reisil searched his face. He answered her unspoken question by touching his fingers to his heart, and then dropped his hand to his sword.

"What do you need?" he asked.

Reisil let out the breath she hadn't known she was holding. He thought of her as a kind of nahualli—but he feared the nahuallis as much as he respected them. Reisil most definitely did not want him afraid of her. Not the way so many had feared her after she killed the wizards at Vorshtar. Their fear had quickly turned to hate. But then, Sodur had had a hand in stirring that frenzy up, she reminded herself. But it didn't really matter. There wasn't any time to worry about Yohuac's reaction. She'd know soon enough.

She nudged her horse into a walk, taking the lead. The horses' hooves made a loud clopping sound on the parched dirt. "It's just over that hill," she said, pointing. "They'll let us get into the flats and close off the escape before we're supposed to know they're there."

At the top of the hill, just below the crown, she dismounted. She told the others to do the same, handing her reins to Yohuac. "With what I'm going to do, the horses might bolt. Don't go far from me. It won't be safe."

She caught each man's eye, and one by one they nodded. Clano's throat jerked as he swallowed, his eyes fixed on her cheek. Reisil lifted her fingers to touch the glowing ivy pattern there and smiled. It was a cold, menacing smile.

They walked down the slope toward the meadow. Reisil was aware of the hundreds of eyes watching them. She could smell their sweat, feel their lust. For blood, for gold, for flesh. Her fingers curled into her palms. For a moment, her footsteps faltered. Then she shook herself. This was necessary. She remembered the Lady's words that fateful day when Reisil had healed Ceriba. *You have shown yourself to have judgment, to be capable of making the right choices for Kodu Riik and all her people.* She thought of all the dead, tortured bodies littering their journey. This was the right choice.

Almost leisurely she reached for her magic. It came to her in a long, whirling trail of sparks and fire. It thrust upward, hot and prickly and hard. Suddenly she felt six inches taller. Her bones felt anchored in the soil, deep, down to the fiery core of all life.

She turned her head, scanning the landscape to the sides. Through the trees and rocks and dirt, Reisil could sense each soul's flame. *Wind*, she thought. *Wind to blow them all out.* Or fire. She remembered. She could *be* lightning. She could strike them all to a cinder. *Yes*.

She turned her head up, searching the sky. She caught sight of a black speck circling above.

~Come to me, my Saljane!

And then her *ahalad-kaaslane* was plummeting out of the sky. Ten feet above Reisil's head, Saljane's slate wings popped wide, sending a puff of hot air across Reisil's cheeks. Her talons clamped around Reisil's upraised fist. The goshawk's eyes glowed garnet, the ivy pattern on her beak shining like the first sliver of sun at dawn.

~Are you ready?
Kek-kek-kek-kek!
~Then let us weed our garden.

The words were lava in her mind. She smiled. *Weeds, yes. Just so.*

Reisil lifted Saljane to her shoulder, their minds locked together. The power continued to flow up through Reisil, but seemed tame beneath their shared strength. Reisil shoved deeper into the flow of magic, and deeper still. She began walking again, down to the level ground of the meadow.

A hand caught her arm. She turned ponderously. It was . . . Soka. He yanked his hand back, a look of uncertainty and fear rippling across his face. He hunched his shoulders resolutely forward, firming his jaw.

"We will want their weapons," he said.

She nodded and smiled. He blanched, faltering. Reisil swung back around.

Wind, then.

The attackers waited until their prey crossed through the center of the meadow. Then they swarmed out of hiding. Most were mounted. They all wore a garish hodgepodge of clothing and jewelry—all clearly stolen. They wore helms and armor, and each carried a sword.

Yohuac, Soka, and his four escorts drew their weapons, turning nervously in a circle.

The attackers halted as their commander raised his sword high over his head. Theatrics, Reisil realized. To create panic. So that their victims might know how well and truly trapped they were, and how hopeless their plight. But not today.

"Ye are trespassing on our lands! Put down yer swords and leggo yer horses, and ye may plead yer case to the Master of the Rum Bluffers," shouted a stout fellow who rode a squat, mutton-withered palomino to the left of the commander. There was a swell of cackling laughter from the raider ranks. "If'n he decides ye have crossed us innocent-like, ye will be free to leave, tendering only a small token for our trouble."

Reisil snorted.

"There is no innocence here," she whispered so that only Saljane could hear, her fingers knotting around the talisman at her neck. "Hold tight to the horses," she said more loudly over her shoulder. "If they bolt, let them go. It won't be safe."

A ragged cry went up from the besieging riders as the men standing behind Reisil swiftly sheathed their swords and took a tight hold of their mounts.

Reisil did not bother talking, either to ask questions or accuse. She'd already passed judgment. Nothing they could say could change her mind. There was only carrying out the execution.

The force of magic within her had built to such a peak that it felt as if her skin would split. Abruptly she grappled with it, pushing it down, under the ground, and sending it streaking away in a half-wagon-wheel pattern. The lines of power burrowed outward with breathtaking speed, tunneling beneath the enemy ambushers and beyond. With a mental jerk, she halted it, bending the spokes upward into the air. They were the color of water, the color of sky. No one noticed them. She pushed against them, flattening them. Columns became walls and the walls connected seamlessly. Nobody was escaping today.

"Did ye not hear? Be ye deaf? If'n ye don't do as yer told, ye'll be jiggered!" Another cackle of laughter spread its way around the line of ambushers.

"I'd like to jigger a few of them," Clano muttered.

The power flowed up and out of Reisil in a thick

current. It wasn't enough. Not for what she wanted. She reached for more. It rose up faster, stronger.

"Hold tight," Reisil warned.

The ambushers had lost patience and began to advance. Their ragged lines pushed inward, slowly at first. Then faster.

Reisil slipped again into spellsight. Every body had a hint of magic inside, the magic of a beating heart. The flame of the soul. All around her, Reisil could see the flames burning. The beauty of it was enough to make her throat ache. But not enough to stop what she was about to do.

Rashanis. The soul-shattered. Spirits trapped between death and life, without physical form, without hope. Most were tortured by a need for vengeance. They rode the winds and haunted the dark nights, shrieking their fury, their hunger for retribution against those who'd harmed them so dreadfully that their souls had shattered. Reisil wondered how many *rashanis* these Rum Bluffers had created.

However many, they were about to get their justice, their freedom.

"Hold tight," she repeated, her voice sounding hollow and distant. "Don't move."

Around her companions, she built another wall of magic, thin as glass, reaching up into the cerulean-blue sky. The horses snorted, pulling and rearing. They felt the crack and bite of the invisible walls. Reisil's own hair rose in response to the crackling energy swirling in the walls. The men hung onto the animals, speaking softly, urgently.

The Rum Bluffers had crossed half of the parched meadow. They were shouting, the sounds muted. Reisil waited for them to come closer. She had to see their faces. Her fingers clenched, sweat dampening her brow and trickling beneath her breasts. The magic sang through her, swelling, demanding. She held it in check. Not . . . quite . . . yet.

The faces began to resolve. A redhead with freckles

and a wide, mobile mouth. He was perhaps seventeen. A grizzled grandfather, missing his arm below the elbow, his green eyes squinting against the brilliant sun. Their leader, a well-built man, tall, with white scars hashing his face in a chicken-scratch pattern, and teeth that were snaggled and gray inside wet, smiling lips.

Reisil shifted away from him and scanned the enemy line up and down, looking at each man, remembering each face. She was about to do something truly awful. She would not do it carelessly, from a distance. She would see the results of her handiwork. Otherwise she would be no better than they.

Wind.

She reached out spectral hands, grasping the air and tugging on it. It came easily. She stirred it faster. Outside the core wall, dust rose. The sharpening breeze caught clothing and hair. Faster. The line of attackers fumbled to a confused halt, the riders looking at one another in surprise.

Reisil shoved hard, and the gust blew several men to the ground. Horses coughed and fought their riders, pawing and rearing, sawing their heads up and down. Reisil shoved again, and once more. Each gust sent more men sprawling on the ground. One mare panicked and began to buck. Suddenly she bolted, dragging her rider after her, the man's foot caught in the stirrup. The flame inside him vanished as his skull bounced over a rock. *Lucky.*

The wind swelled until the dirt stung and the men were forced to hide their faces in the crook of an elbow. It was a steady blow, relentlessly pushing. Reisil lowered her head, concentrating. The wind divided into strands. They wriggled, becoming long, probing fingers.

Wind!

Each lash of Reisil's wind-whip struck. In through a mouth, an ear, a nostril, an eye. They squirmed inside, invisible, weightless. Each length of air spread, filling every hollow space, spinning in a tiny cyclone, down and down, tighter and tighter.

One by one the flames inside each man flickered. But Reisil wasn't content simply to snuff them out. There was no justice in that. All around she could feel a new pressure building, a gathering of hunger, rage, pain and fear. And hate. The sounds of the whirling wind had disappeared, replaced by the banshee calls of congregating *rashanis*.

"Soft, now," she whispered. "You will have peace soon."

Then she reached out and *shoved*.

The cyclones burst outward.

Flesh shredded. Bones splintered. Blood sprayed.

Reisil tightened her grip on the flow of magic and hauled back on it.

Between one breath and the next, the winds halted. Fleshy detritus pelted down in sodden thumps. Reisil ignored it. The men's bodies were gone, but their souls yet remained intact. She held them in her net of magic. She began to twist the net like a wet dish towel. The soul-flames inside exploded in little pops, like harvest-corn over a winter fire. The fragments of flame did not snuff out, but drifted like dried petals on a sullen breeze. Slowly they collected into discreet clusters. And then . . . faded.

Gone but not gone. Soul-shattered. *Rashanis*.

They would slowly gather the remnants of themselves and begin haunting the land. They were helpless and harmless. In time, as their fury or pain diminished, the lucky would dwindle until their voices could no longer be heard. Some would scream forever.

Reisil lowered her magic walls. Equally slowly, she retracted the long lines of energy, pulling them back inside her interior reservoir, and then letting it drain back down into the current of the earth. The roiling magic resisted, spurting back up. Reisil snatched at it and shoved it down.

The warm breeze twirled the dirt. Gobbets of blood,

flesh, bone, and brains littered the field. It was a gruesome sight. Already the smell was thick with decay. Magpies and crows hopped across the ground, screeching and squabbling over the banquet. The horses snorted and leaped to the ends of their reins, crow-hopping.

Reisil closed her eyes. There was a drift of current, more than air, not quite magic. Like phantom fingers.

A thank-you. A farewell. A benediction.

Reisil drew a breath. Justice served. She knew that, even if her stomach didn't.

She opened her eyes, turning to her companions, keeping her voice steady. "It's messy, but gather the weapons and arms. Make a pile. I'll ward them for when you return. No one will find them. Be quick. I doubt any of us want to sleep here."

They nodded, saying nothing. Reisil avoided their eyes, not wanting to see what might be there. She left them to their grisly business, wandering down toward the river. She stood above it, the bank dropping away in a sheer drop. She knuckled her eyes, pressing her forehead to Saljane, feeling sick.

~What have I done?

~Balance. It is right.

~How come it feels so . . . horrible?

~It should not be easy to kill, even those who deserve it. It should always be a struggle.

Reisil nodded. She would never want it to be easy. She would never want to enjoy it. She would never want to feel nothing after. What she regretted was having to do it at all.

~Maybe I won't have to do it again.

But, somehow, she knew she would.

Chapter 18

"This is for you," Reisil said, handing a Lady's-head coin to Soka. Its silver surface was scuffed and dented. There was a hole in the middle with a leather string knotted through it. She lifted it over his head so that it rested against his chest.

Soka lifted it, turning it around, and then quirked his brow at Reisil.

"Jewelry for me? I'm flattered, though I should have thought you'd be more discreet." He leered and glanced meaningfully at Yohuac, who only shook his head and made a show of ignoring the other man.

"It's a ward," said Reisil. She grimaced. "Maybe. I mixed *rinda* and ordinary words, as you suggested. Hopefully whoever wears it will be protected, even as they move. But it might not work. And if it does, it may be good for only one attack. It could also explode in flames and boil your brain in your skull."

Soka twirled the coin on its cord and then wrapped his hand around it and tucked it inside his tunic. He grinned. "I'll be sure to stand close to my father then." He opened his arms. "If I may thank you and wish you luck?"

"I'm sure your father will wonder at your show of affection," Reisil said sardonically as she stepped into his embrace. Yohuac made a growling noise in his throat. Soka laughed, his chest rumbling against Reisil's cheek as he tightened his arms.

"Don't raise a breeze, now. You will have her to

yourself for weeks. But be warned, I will be waiting to assert my claim, and then, my friend, you will have a hard battle on your hands. I *am* known for my way with the ladies, don't you know." He chuckled at Yohuac, who did not answer.

A knot rose hard in Reisil's throat as she pulled away. Yohuac was going to stay in Cemanahuatl. He was never coming back. Now was all the time they had. All they were ever going to have. But Soka didn't know that.

She schooled her expression, painting on a mask of cheerfulness and wagging her finger at him like a child.

"Keep your pants tied up tight in Bro-heyek. You don't want to be gutted by some cuckolded husband before you get the metal for Honor," she said. "And do *try* not to chomp too hard on that." She tapped the bulge in his lip where he held the poison bead ready against need. "The ward won't work against stupidities you commit against yourself, and I won't be around to heal you."

"The ward may boil my brain in my skull—did you not say so?"

"And it may not," Reisil returned, wondering if she should have given it to him. He was right. It was more dangerous than not. But Soka was grinning rakishly, the gold threads of his eye patch gleaming against the crimson silk.

"Not to worry. The Blessed Lady will not let me die such a dull death as this would cause," he said, clicking the bead against his teeth.

Reisil smothered her grimace at the sound. "Then I'll see you in Honor. Soon I hope."

The last was said with frowning worry. Less because of Soka, and more because of the journey to and from Cemanahuatl. Though the nahuallis would certainly help her all they could, who knew how long it would take to learn what she needed to know? If she would find the answer at all?

And then the long journey back . . . She could return too late to save her friends and Kodu Riik. The thought burned in her stomach.

"I'll not spend any more time in Bro-heyek than absolutely necessary," Soka declared, trying to reassure her, reading her expression as concern for his reliability. "Preferably not longer than a single hour," he added darkly, his blue-topaz eye turning hard.

"So long as you get what you came for," Reisil said. "Honor needs it."

"What they need," he countered, swinging up onto his horse, "is a miracle. I'll leave that part to you."

Reisil said nothing as he and his four companions rode away north toward Bro-heyek. None of them turned to look back. She bit her lip, hearing Soka's last words echo in her mind.

"Best not tarry," Yohuac said in his low voice. "Our journey will not be a swift one."

The western slopes of the Melyhir Mountains were covered with sparse grasses, prickly pear, and sage. A few juniper and spruce trees were huddled in creases and in the lee sides of hulking boulders. As Yohuac and Reisil climbed higher, the air grew thin and dry. It was hard to breathe. At last they passed through a notch between two great, snow-covered peaks, and plunged down the eastern slopes into a wide, flat valley with winding streams and red-stemmed willow thickets. Wapiti and smaller, fleet-footed white-tailed deer grazed along the valley bottom, flicking their ears at the biting flies and gazing in mild surprise at the two intruders.

Baku pounced out of the air and crushed one of the big wapiti to the ground, tearing the flesh from the animal with powerful jerks of his head. Saljane sailed down to join his feast. Reisil was surprised. Since she'd rescued him from the wizards, Baku's mind had been spiny against her own, and he rarely offered more than terse responses to her overtures. But he seemed to have developed a fast friendship with Saljane.

She glanced at Yohuac, who was watching the two feeding on the wapiti. His face was troubled. He never spoke of Baku. The conversation between them was always silent. Sometimes Reisil wondered if they spoke at all. She couldn't remember the last time she had seen the telltale, faintly cross-eyed look on his face that usually accompanied such communication.

"How far, do you think?" she asked, breaking his reverie.

Yohuac started. "Not more than three or four days. We must cross into the next mountain range." He pointed to the blue-misted mountains rising in fading blue layers from the opposite side of the valley floor. "I'll know better once we find the trail. Baku . . ." He trailed off, turning his head away. Then, with obvious effort, he turned back to her. "Baku will remember better than I do, I am certain."

They said nothing further as they picked their way between the willows, across the weave of streams, to make camp at the base of the mountains. They went about the business of setting up camp without speaking more than a bare handful of words.

For Reisil, silence was a balm. Throughout the long journey from Honor, she'd never let her mind rest. She'd practiced the wards. She'd pestered Yohuac for information about Cemanahuatl and the nahuallis, and spent hours contemplating the problem of Mysane Kosk. When that grew stale, she returned to tinkering with the wards. The task had kept her mind busy, too busy to think about what was to come. It kept her from feeling the bite of her greatest fear—what if she couldn't find a solution? What if she failed?

She glanced down at her hands as they turned a duck on the spit. They were calloused, tanned, and scarred. She'd always thought of them as healing hands. She remembered Kvepi Debess's pronouncement in the wizards' stronghold—how long ago? Only weeks? It seemed like lifetimes. He'd said she wasn't really a healer. Her skill, her calling, her gift, was to destroy. Reisil sighed. He was right. She couldn't heal the plague, but she could grind a hundred men to sausage with hardly an effort. It was . . . monstrous.

A sickening feeling made her stomach lurch and spread wintry fingers to encircle her heart. She closed her eyes. It might be so. But there was no time now for guilt. When Kodu Riik was safe . . . there would be time later to cry over the thing she'd become.

But now the uncertain future loomed large, casting her in its bleak shadow. She could no longer distract herself from what was to come. Apprehension made her so nauseous that she had to force herself to swallow every bite she took. When she was done, the duck sat in her stomach like carrion. She sipped her mint tea, taking slow, steady breaths, her stomach bucking. Through their mental bond, Reisil could tell that Saljane was equally unsettled. They did not speak. It had all been said.

Later, as she curled up against Yohuac, her head nestled in the crook of his arm, she watched Saljane settle on Baku's back. The yellow eyes of the *copicatl* glimmered like stars against the coal-drake's black hide, inches from Saljane's talons. So it had been since their journey began. Saljane and Baku guarding the magical snake. Neither trusted it.

Reisil tugged her cloak up under her chin, squirming close against Yohuac's warm strength. He tightened his arm around her, his legs twining with hers. She smiled, a tight, thin curve that withered as soon as it bloomed. She closed her eyes, feeling anew the dull saw of uncertainty and fear. Deliberately she turned her mind to something else. Instantly she snagged on the other question that had been chafing at her: Where was Tapit?

Reisil squirmed, reaching under her to push aside the rock digging into her shoulder. Did the wizard still live? Or was he stalking them even now? Reisil's skin tingled and her exhaustion dropped away as her muscles clenched. She held herself stiff and still, her gaze sweeping the valley.

Her wizard-sight revealed the landscape as if lit by

a noontime sun. She saw nothing out of the ordinary. But then, Tapit was an exceptional hunter. A chill rippled through her and she pushed out of Yohuac's embrace.

"What is it?" he asked, sitting up with her.

"Probably nothing," she said, stirring the fire and sitting with her back to it and facing the valley. "Sleep. I'll keep watch." With the wards, they hadn't set a watch since separating from Soka and the others. *Stupid*. But if Tapit *was* out there, he'd missed his chance to take them unawares.

Yohuac hesitated a long moment, and then pulled his cloak about him and settled back down on the ground. "Wake me when it's my turn."

His breathing steadied into a slow, steady cadence. Baku chuffed and let out a deep sigh, stretching out on the ground. Saljane mantled and settled down to sleep.

Reisil blinked into spellsight. Baku sparkled with silver motes, as if he were made of night and stars. Saljane gleamed a soft, burnished gold. The *copicatl* was like an orange flame. Reisil glanced upward toward the sky, half expecting to see an *ilgas* floating down to trap them in its magic-deadening folds. But the sky was clear, except for a few curling wisps of silvered cloud.

She turned to survey the valley. The *nokulas* did not seem to have followed her either. That bothered her almost as much Tapit. Why not? Because they knew she'd return? Were they even now preparing an ambush?

She set her teeth, pulling her cloak tight and hunching against the cold. A memory seeped up from the darkness in her mind: Sodur's warning. Of course they were. And if she thought getting to Honor had been hard the first time, it was going to be a whole lot worse the second.

It took Tapit more than two days to pick up Reisil's trail—going east, not west into Patverseme. He was perplexed. Where could she be going? He followed

her east, down into the Karnane Valley. It was an
easy enough trail, marked by the vestiges of the work-
ings of large magics. Not spells, he thought, his lip
curling slightly. Witless smashing and bashing—all the
finesse of using a club to catch a fish. But, he admitted,
surveying the stinking carrion covering a wide battlefield, effective. At least against helpless worms such
as these men had been.

He yawned, glancing up at the sky turning sapphire
with the lowering sun. He was only a day or so behind
his prey. They'd turned north. It made no sense.
Where were they going? And why?

The subtle tingle of a warding distracted him from
his musings. He pulled up his horse, tilting his head
and blinking into spellsight. He had a special talent
for finding magic, for feeling it on his skin like a lover's touch. Better. Intimate in ways that no lover could
match. He gave an involutary sigh and forced himself
to concentrate. Ah. There.

He found the wards protecting a copse on the top
of a low hillock. He nudged his way inside the thicket
of trees and leafy underbrush. The wards covered a
small grassy patch between a triangle of silver-skinned
birch trees. The shielding rippled with iridescent light.
It was a strong warding. He reached out his hand,
feeling the crackle of its energy. He nodded with pro-
fessional approval; then he bent, squinting. What
was this?

The spells contained *rinda* he'd never seen before.
Jagged-edged and complex. A jigsaw puzzle of convo-
luted shapes, all hard lines and sharp points, patterned
in geometric snowflakes. Elegant in simplicity and
more than effective.

Tapit stood, considering. He could break the wards.
He was certain of it. But he couldn't reconstruct them.
Reisil would know someone—a wizard—had been
here. It would not be difficult to guess it was him.
Tapit turned and retreated. The wards guarded something she wanted to keep safe until she returned, that
was clear enough. Whatever it was would wait.

He caught sight of Reisil and her companions just after noon the following day. He still could not fathom their destination. Their hurried pace was curious, and Tapit was inclined to bide his time, see what they were up to. Five days later, Reisil, her lover, and the coaldrake split off from the other four, heading east. Hungry anticipation flamed inside Tapit. He reached down to pat the saddlebag containing the three *ilgas* he'd prepared. Then he frowned, tapping his fingers against his thigh. He could capture them easily enough. He didn't doubt it. He had trapped more difficult prey. But his curiosity continued to prod him. What were they up to?

The mystery made him still his hand, though his prey grew lax with their watch. Tapit maintained a wide distance as he followed them high into the Melyhir Mountains. He constantly sniffed the air, searching for traces of magic, of something that would lure Reisil here. And the higher they climbed, the farther east they went, the more Tapit wondered how he would return them home when he captured them.

He winced, his teeth clicking together. Home. His lips pulled back in a bitter, exultant smile. Reisil had done her damage, but many of his brethren had escaped her attack. And they were waiting eagerly for him to return with her. She would help them repair and rebuild. She would be made to serve until she learned her place. As for her companions— Tapit's nostrils flared. They had value too. And no one escaped from him. These would not be the first.

He scratched his bristled jaw, not having taken time to shave in more than a week. Still, there was a problem of getting her back. Or was there? Certainly she was looking for something that would help save or destroy Mysane Kosk and defeat her myriad enemies. Surely she must be searching for a magical answer, for nothing else could help. Eagerness quickened Tapit's heart. What could it be? He wanted it. He had to have it.

Tapit smiled. Let her do the work. Let her think she was safe beyond his reach. She could retrieve her weapon and return to Mysanc Kosk. When she did, he would spring his trap. He would have her, her lover, the coal-drake, and the weapon she was looking for. The hand resting on his thigh closed in a fist.

Bro-heyek was situated on a squarish bulb of land north of the Karnane Valley. It was divided from the the rest of Kodu Riik by a low, dull-edged parade of mountains at the northwestern end of the Melyhir Mountains, called the Sawtooth Range. These merged into another, more aggressive march of mountains known as the Tornaat Mountains. These peaks thrust up higher than any other in Kodu Riik. Their heights were never free of snow, and there were no roads through them. The steep, rocky slopes were daunting even to mountain goats.

The towering Tornaats ran north between Guelt and Kodu Riik, dividing the two countries and providing the western boundary of the Bro-heyek lands. North of Bro-heyek unfurled rolling farmlands that ended abruptly in high, sheer bluffs overlooking the cold waters of the Jartain Ocean. These same waters curled south, filling the harbor at Koduteel and flooding the fens and salt swamps east of the Karnane Valley.

Soka tasted the salt of the ocean in the back of his throat as he rode through a pass and began his descent out of the Sawtooths. The sunny slopes were heavily forested with redwoods whose boles were as wide as two horses nose-to-tail. The ground beneath was a dense mat of rust-colored needles, brightened here and there by leggy bushes sporting dark, wide leaves and brilliantly colored flowers. Soldier-jays squawked furiously at the five intruders.

Clano and Temles flanked Soka, watching the trees warily. Ahead, Ferro and Slatts rode point. It had been four days since leaving Reisil and Yohuac. Soka's stomach tightened. Fewer than that to reach Bro-heyek. He blinked, his single eye feeling suddenly gritty.

The closer they came to his childhood home, the more Soka found himself sinking inescapably into the memory of the last time he'd seen his father. The day he'd been taken as a hostage to the court.

He'd been standing on the deck of a royal ship surrounded by men wearing the night-blue and gold of the royal house of Varakamber. He'd been a month shy of eight years old. He remembered searching for his father in the crowd along the dock, waiting for him to come, to rescue him.

Soka swallowed, tightening his lips against the tremble in his chin, despising himself for his weakness.

At last his father had come. He'd swaggered up the gangplank, uncowed by the Iisand's soldiers. He'd come wearing his sword and dagger and his mail coat. He was sandy-haired and slender, the bones of his face rather fine. But his slightness was deceptive. He was made of iron and diamonds. His eyes were the same piercing blue as Soka's, with a commanding, unrelenting quality that made men quail before him. The guards holding Soka were no exception. They ducked their heads deferentially and stepped back, leaving Soka to stare worshipfully up at his father.

Thevul Bro-heyek stood, legs spread wide, square chin jutting, one calloused, long-fingered hand resting on the pommel of his sword. His beard was neatly trimmed, his earth-brown clothing plain and dusty from the day's work.

Soka remembered swelling with pride for him. Thevul Bro-heyek was rare amongst the nobility, getting his hands dirty with his men, spending his sweat and blood on the land. This was the sort of man Soka wanted to be.

Had wanted to be.

His father had stooped. Soka had tilted his head back as far as it would go, blinking in the brilliant sunlight. His father squeezed Soka's shoulder in a bony pincer-grip.

"Be brave, as I know you are. I will see you soon as may be."

The words had jolted through Soka like blows, and his body jerked with the impact. His father was *supposed* to save him. Supposed to take him by force if necessary. Tears had blurred his vision and he'd savagely knuckled them away. His throat tightened and strangled his voice. But if he could have spoken, he didn't know what to say. He wanted to beg, to cling to his father's legs and go home.

But as quickly as he'd come, his father straightened and strode away to the gangplank, turning and lifting his hand in farewell.

"Don't let them cow you, boy. Have a mind for the blood that runs in your veins and make me proud. You'll hear from me soon."

And Soka had. When it came, the message had been all too clear. Was Thevul Bro-heyek proud now?

Soka reached up and touched his eye patch. What had become of his eye? He couldn't imagine his father's reaction upon receiving it. He doubted it had been a cause for mourning. Or that it had been the reason for Bro-heyek's succumbing to the Iisand. It was more likely that the war had caused his father to behave himself. Soka was lucky not to be missing a hand. He thought of Aare. His cheek twitched and the muscles in his thighs contracted. Or his balls.

He flicked the poison bead from his cheek and caught it in his teeth.

Twelve years since he'd lost his eye, and he was coming back at last. Thanks to Metyein, he was a man—the kind of man his father couldn't ignore. Soka touched the hilt of his sword. He would show his father exactly what kind of blood ran in his veins.

He called a halt in the early afternoon, setting up camp on the edge of the Old Forest. It filled the horizon between the mountains like a shadowy wall.

"We gotta go through there?" Temles asked, gaze fixed on the thick undergrowth and foreboding shadows beneath the contorted trunks of the ancient trees.

"Yes." He drew out a map from inside a round, oiled-leather case and carefully rolled it out. "There's a good road through the forest that will take us clear to Bro-heyek. Part of its borders are inside the Old Forest. We can be there in two days." Not home. Bro-heyek hadn't been home since the day Aare had stolen his eye. As far as Soka was concerned, he'd been orphaned that day.

"But—" Temles swallowed and then went back to work, furiously chopping the stray limbs from a log for the fire.

"But?" Soka pushed, knowing full well what was bothering Temles.

"It's just . . . I've heard stories."

"Have you? Do tell."

"The Old Forest—they say . . ." Temles's voice dropped, and he glanced over his shoulder. "Things live there. They'll tear your heart out while you sleep. Rip your spine out and steal your soul!" His eyes had widened and he stared, face pale.

Soka smiled lazily, rolling up the map and standing. "Half of Bro-heyek lies inside the Old Forest," he said. "And it's true. There are things—beasts and sprites and likely hordes of demons inside that you don't want to encounter. But the terrible truth is, the monster you ought to fear the most is the one we've come to see. So I wouldn't worry so much about the ring of eyes in the night; I would worry about the dagger in your back at Bro-heyek."

Chapter 19

Metyein sat alone at the long plank table. Yellow candles made of tallow burned smokily in wood sconces along the walls. He twirled the stem of a crystal wineglass between his fingers, watching the ruby liquid swirl. He had taken such things for granted before coming to Honor. But now . . . wine and glasses were a luxury. Most everything else hauled to Honor was necessary and useful. And the myriad of things they didn't have would fill a book.

He sighed and set the glass back on the table and rubbed his face with his hands. By the Lady, he was tired. The plague was spreading slowly. In the six weeks since Reisil had left, there were seven more cases. There was no pattern to them. They'd come from a variety of stockades, work assignments, dining halls, social groups, families, and arrival dates. There were three men, two women, and two children. Only the two women yet survived. For now. But they were in the early stages yet.

The good news was that since Reisil's departure, there had been no incursions by either the *nokulas* or the wizards. Metyein brushed a loose strand of hair out of his face. With any luck, the *nokulas* had killed the wizards. He yawned and rubbed the knotted muscles at the base of his neck. Not likely. But for the moment, he didn't care why they were holding off from attacking. All that counted was that they were.

Metyein drained his glass and refilled it before

reaching for the sheaf of papers in front of him. Tonight was his meeting with Kebonsat and Emelovi.
They met every three days to review the happenings
in the settlement and make decisions. He didn't look
forward to it. Emelovi didn't bother to hide her frigid
hostility for Kebonsat, refusing even to address him
except through Metyein. Meanwhile, Kebonsat boiled,
a slow, black simmering of guilt and resentment.

It was, Metyein thought mordantly, almost enough
to make him want to go back to Koduteel and beg
his father's forbearance and forgiveness.

The door slid open and shut again with a thump.
Metyein turned with a careful smile. "You're early
tonight—"

But to his astonishment, instead of Kebonsat or Emelovi, a thin, gray Juhrnus slouched inside. His beard
was ragged, his hair matted. Esper rode across his
shoulders, his fleshy, black tongue slowly tasting the
air. The sisalik's skin was dry and sunken over his
ribs, and his eyes were dulled. Juhrnus's foot caught
on the rough floorboards and he staggered. Metyein
leaped to steady him.

"Bright heavens! You look like you've been dragged
the last twenty leagues behind your horse." Metyein
hooked a chair with his foot. Juhrnus dropped into it
with a thready sigh. Esper crawled down to the floor
and parked himself between Juhrnus's cracked and
dusty boots. Metyein thrust his wine into the other
man's hand before perching against the edge of the
table.

"I left word at the gate to fetch me when you
arrived."

Juhrnus gave a limp wave of his hand as he swallowed the wine in a gulp and handed the glass to
Metyein, wiping his mouth with the back of his hand.
It shook. "Faster to come myself. Sent the guard for
food." He scrubbed his hand over his face. "Been a
couple of days."

"That bad?"

"News isn't good," Juhrnus said. "Came fast as I

could. Ran into trouble with raiders outside Koduteel and again in the foothills."

He patted his ribs, and Metyein realized that there was a makeshift bandage tied awkwardly around Juhrnus's chest. A bright crimson blotch spread inside the brick-red blossom of old blood.

"*Skraa!* How bad is it? I'll call a tark," he said, not waiting for an answer.

Juhrnus didn't protest as Metyein yanked open the door and disappeared. He returned a few minutes later, followed by a panting guard carrying a platter covered with a square of burlap. The man deposited his burden on the table.

"Fetch some more," Metyein ordered. "And plenty of ale and water. We'll need fresh, raw venison too."

The guard departed with a doff of his forelock. Metyein knelt beside Juhrnus, whose eyes had closed. Metyein frowned, seeing bruises beneath the dirt on his face and hands. Juhrnus blinked and raised his head.

"I'm awake."

"There's food. A tark will be here soon. The Dazien and Kebonsat as well."

Juhrnus let Meytein help him to stand. He lifted Esper up on the table and pushed aside the burlap covering the tray. There was a loaf of brown bread flavored with garlic and rosemary, a heaping trencher of stew, a crock of butter, and a bowl of huckleberries and rhubarb sweetened with honey.

"There'll be fresh meat in a few minutes," Metyein said as Esper eyed the offerings with obvious disdain.

"Wait if you want," Juhrnus told the sisalik around a mouthful of bread. "But I'm eating while I can. Lesson well learned."

Esper tilted his head as if thinking, and then bent and nibbled at a chunk of meat.

Metyein paced as Juhrnus ate, taking a hard rein on his impatience. What had forced Juhrnus to take such a grueling pace to get back, and with such a wound? What *was* the news?

He fairly snatched open the door when the tark arrived. It was Gamulstark. He carried his healing satchel on his back, along with a brazier, a bucket of water, and a sack of coal. He offered no greeting as he dropped his burdens on the end of the long table, lighting a fire in the brazier and filling a pot of water to boil.

"Well, now. Let's have a look," he said when he was ready. Juhrnus grimaced, but sat back to let the tark cut away the bandages. Juhrnus had tied them over his clothing, and his tunic clung to the seeping scabs. Gamulstark *tsk*ed and began snipping away at them with a pair of scissors.

"You're filthy," Gamulstark said accusingly. "You'll be lucky if the wound hasn't turned septic."

"Wounds, actually. Three, and if I'm going to die soon, you may leave me in peace. The Lord Marshal is waiting."

"The Lord Marshal can wait, if it will keep you alive," Metyein commented sardonically.

"The tark says I am filthy and septic," Juhrnus said.

"The tark says you are filthy. Whether you are septic remains to be seen," Gamulstark corrected.

He helped Juhrnus peel off his tunic, bending down to examine the seeping gashes. "Ugly. The edges are torn and ragged. What caused them?"

Juhrnus caught his breath as Gamulstark probed with his fingers. "A makeshift blade. Like a saw, but with a handle."

"There is some infection. I need to clean them to know more."

Juhrnus continued to eat, despite the obvious pain of Gamulstark's ministrations. Metyein watched with narrowed eyes as the wounds were exposed. Two of them were about seven inches wide and sickle-shaped. They chased each other along the left side of Juhrnus's rib cage with red fury. The other was smaller, but deeper. It dug deeply into the flesh of his shoulder just under his collarbone and seeped blood and pus.

"Want some more wine?" Metyein offered as Juhr-

nus shoved aside his trencher, turning white as ice.
Metyein sloshed a healthy measure into the glass.
Juhrnus slugged it down in a long gulp and dropped
the glass back onto the table, his face twisting with
pain.

At last Gamulstark stood back, wiping his hands on
a towel. "The two on your ribs aren't too bad. In-
flamed with some infection. This other on your
shoulder—we'll have to cut into it and clean it out.
You're lucky you weren't hit lower or you'd have died
about a minute later." He stood and busied himself
over the boiling water. As he mixed his potions, Juhrnus guzzled two more glasses of wine and began on a
third. Metyein continued pouring without comment.

Juhrnus flicked a fuzzy glance at Gamulstark, who'd
unrolled the pocketed cloth that held his surgical
knives and begun laying them out on the table. Esper
made a forlorn noise in the back of his throat and
clambered up Juhrnus's arm to curl around his neck,
his nose tucked under his *ahalad-kaaslane*'s bearded
jaw.

"I'd best tell you what I know before I keel over,"
Juhrnus said, his voice slightly slurred and focused, as
if he were concentrating on pronunciation. He
squinted, his eyes bloodshot. "It's nothing good."

Metyein's chest tightened and he sat down, his face
stiff with anticipation.

"The Regent's started staging his army in the foot
hills west of Koduteel," Juhrnus began carefully.

Metyein nodded. "We knew that."

"Here's what you don't know. He's been con-
scripting. If you can carry a sword and walk and you
don't have the plague, you're in. He's got more than
a thousand men already. He's got plenty of gold to
pay, and it means decent meals. There's not a lot of
complaint about his methods, so far."

Metyein leaned back in his chair, his hand slowly
curling into a fist, shock curdling his stomach. Honor
could muster near five hundred. "A thousand? What's
he doing for supplies?"

"Taking them from us, for one. He's found out about Dannen Relvi's supply dumps and he's raiding our pack trains and caches."

"Demonballs," Metyein muttered, his mind whirling. "That means . . ."

"Gonna have to change locations, find safer harbors, start shifting schedules. Need to be more unpredictable. I sent word to Dannen Relvi. Don't know when it'll catch up with him. Sent word to the camps, too. Folks will start taking precautions, but we're gonna have a hard winter. Regent's not gonna give up. He needs the supplies bad as we do."

"How much have we lost?"

"Least two shiploads, maybe three. Haven't heard from the one coming up from Nardal."

Metyein tapped his fingers, thinking. This was bad. It could hardly be worse. He thought of his father and Aare. It could. He looked at Juhrnus.

"What else?"

Juhrnus cast a suspicious glance at Gamulstark, who was threading a needle. The tark looked up from his work and rolled his eyes.

"I could leave, I suppose, but then you could die," he said. "Which would you prefer?"

"Do it," Metyein said to Gamulstark, and Juhrnus snorted. "Tell me now, before you pass out, what else?"

"Two things. First"—Juhrnus held up a finger—"can't find the Dazien's family. Not where they're supposed to be. Her brother stashed them somewhere else. Or . . ." He looked away for a moment, unwilling to finish the thought. "Anyhow, the *ahalad-kaaslane* are still on the trail. If anyone can find them, they can."

Metyein stood, pacing back and forth and dragging his hand through his hair. "*Skraa*. Emelovi—the Dazien—doesn't need to hear that. She's hardly begun settling into the notion of standing up to her brother. The idea terrifies her."

"What about Kebonsat? Can't he settle her down?"

Metyein shook his head. "She won't say a word to him. The whole thing is wearing thin, I can tell you. I need both of them. Honor needs both of them. But she won't so much as look at him, and he's so tarred-and-feathered in guilt that he won't fight back. This news will only make things worse."

There came a knock on the door and a serving man arrived with meat for Esper. Metyein waved for him to set it on the end of the table. Esper scrambled to it and began bolting the food. Juhrnus waited to continue his report until the man departed.

"Want the rest of it?" He leaned back gingerly.

"Quickly," Metyein said, flicking a glance at Gamulstark, who came to stand impatiently over Juhrnus.

"And then you can climb up on the table," Gamulstark added with a sharp smile.

Juhrnus glowered at the tark before returning to his report.

"Ceriba."

"You found her?"

"Whispers say he's got her. I don't know where. But she seems to be alive. That's the only good news."

Metyein swallowed. Dear Lady. She'd be better off dead. He thought of the poison bead Soka carried tucked in his mouth, on top of the dozen other poisons secreted on his body. Soka clung to the edge of death, never wanting to stray too far from its safety that he couldn't jump over at a moment's notice. When it came to getting caught in Aare's clutches, death was the only sanctuary. Metyein brushed the thought away and focused back on Juhrnus, whose face looked old and lined. He knew it too.

"On the table now. No more time to waste," Gamulstark said firmly, helping Juhrnus to his feet. He handed him a small wooden cup to drink from and then settled the injured man on the table. Soon the drug he'd swallowed put Juhrnus into a deep slumber.

The tark had finished stitching the ugly wounds and was binding them up when Kebonsat and Emelovi arrived a half hour later. She came in first, stiff-backed, her face pinched tight. Kebonsat trailcd after, keeping his distance, his expression set and haunted.

Seeing Juhrnus lying on the table, both tensed and drew closer.

"What's happened?" Emelovi asked in a weedy voice.

Metyein winced at her fear. He'd worked hard the last six weeks to shore up her confidence, but while she'd grown more assertive and self-assured in his company, it was little more than a veneer. One that disappeared as soon as she was challenged with something new.

"Juhrnus was attacked by raiders on his journey here."

"Is he—? Will he—?" Emelovi pressed her hands over her mouth.

"He'll be fine, providing he sleeps and eats and takes the medicines I give him," Gamulstark declared. "He won't wake for at least a day. He needs to be put to bed. I'll call for help."

A few minutes later, the unconscious Juhrnus had been carried off on a stretcher, accompanied by Gamulstark. Metyein summoned servants to scrub off the table. At their departure, he invited his remaining companions to sit. Emelovi sat at one end of the table, with Kebonsat at the other. Metyein sat between, cushioning the tension. He gave a low sigh, eyeing the bloodstain on the table that the servants had been unable to remove. A narrowed glance at his companions revealed they'd noticed it as well. Emelovi was the color of milk, wringing her hands together in her lap.

What followed was the most unpleasant task Metyein had faced since donning the mantle of Lord Marshal to Honor. He would have cheered at the flame that flared in Kebonsat at the news of Ceriba, but he had to stamp it out.

"You can't go after her," Meytein declared sternly, making it an order. Before Kebonsat could argue, he lifted his hand, looking pointedly at Emelovi as he spoke.

"I sympathize with your fears for your sister," he said, never taking his gaze from Emelovi. He couldn't order *her*. But it was time she got over her resentment and thought about what her tantrum meant to Honor. They couldn't afford it. "I sympathize, but you are needed here. I need your expertise to help prepare the valley for war. I have never been in a battle. I've read books and treatises and I've been taught by the best. It will not be enough. Not against my father and the might Aare has already amassed. You cannot go. Do you understand?"

Patches of color had risen in Emelovi's cheeks and she averted her eyes, giving a faint nod. Meytein's head swiveled and he snared Kebonsat in the same hard, demanding gaze.

For long moments he didn't answer. The vein at his temple stood out prominently, and he nearly trembled with the effort of restraining his emotions. He looked as if he were dangling over the edge of a cliff, hanging on by his nails. Metyein bit the tip of his tongue. What if he let go?

But Kebonsat's lifetime of training and ingrained sense of duty overrode his roiling emotions, and he answered with a clipped "yes."

Metyein closed his eyes, relief flooding through him. "Good. Then we'll review our inventories and draft a plan for the winter. With any luck, Soka and Reisil will return long before Aare comes knocking on the door."

Chapter 20

Reisil sniffed thickly, huddling in her cloak. She'd caught a cold. The mustard smear on her chest had done little to alleviate her symptoms. Neither had the licorice, featherfoil, and slippery elm lozenges she'd been eating since the previous morning. She sneezed, the explosive sound making the chestnut gelding's ears twitch. He turned his head to eye her curiously.

Reisil resisted the urge to stick out her tongue at the animal and instead reached for her water bag. She'd filled it with a honey-sweetened horehound-and-catmint tea that morning. Though it was tepid, it soothed her sore throat. She took a long draft and then broke into a hacking cough. Yohuac reined in and patted her on the back, concern darkening his features. Reisil waved away his solicitations.

"I'll be fine," she said, her head throbbing, as she tucked another lozenge in her cheek.

Yohuac said nothing more, but his forehead remained creased with worry as he again took the lead.

They'd been another two days in the mountains since camping in the great valley. Six days since splitting from Soka. And they were very close to their destination. Reisil could feel it. There was a subtle vibration, one that she felt in that nebulous place between flesh and magic. It was unsettling. She found herself grinding her teeth and clenching her body tight. But the closer they drew to their destination, the more intolerable it became.

Two hours later, the sun had begun its slow descent. Yohuac pulled up and waited for Reisil to ride up alongside.

"Another hour or two. Perhaps we should stop and let you rest. Start fresh in the morning."

Reisil shook her head, grimacing at the flare of pain spidering beneath her brow and the bridge of her nose. "No. We need to get through now."

"You're ill. A few hours will make little difference," Yohuac argued.

Didn't he feel it? Reisil swallowed, feeling phlegm thick in her throat. She opened her mouth to speak, but found herself coughing instead. Finally she collected herself, breathing slowly through her mouth.

"That's not it. It's . . . uncomfortable." Pitiful word for the thing she was feeling.

Yohuac considered her for a moment, his face expressionless. Finally he nodded. "All right."

"Let's hurry," Reisil added, wiping her raw nose with a handkerchief and starting to cough again.

They rode up the rocky trail, the trees closing in hard around them. The gray and black walls of the mountain rose up steeply on either side, blocking out the pink-and-orange sunset, the beauty of which Reisil was in no mood to enjoy, anyway.

They climbed through a narrow passage in the rock. It led up and up. Saljane flew ahead in small hops while Baku coasted on the winds above. They crested a ridge where the mountain walls opened for a space before narrowing again. The space was grassy, a creek tinkling merrily down the center through a tapered fissure in the rock. Yohuac reined in and dismounted.

"This is where we leave the horses. We'll have to walk the rest of the way."

He stripped the saddle and packs from his horse and removed the mare's bridle. Reisil slid to the ground with a groan, sniffling and wiping at her running nose. She sneezed. The sound echoed. She fumbled at the cinch straps and finally Yohuac came to help her. She settled on a rock and watched as he

quickly denuded her mount of its burdens and tack.
The horses gazed at their riders in mild surprise and
then went to cropping the sweet meadow grass, swishing their tails at the biting flies.

"Better eat," Yohuac said, digging in a pack. He
brought out some cold meat and a doughy hunk of
flatbread they'd cooked a couple of days before. Reisil
chewed mechanically, tasting nothing. Her head felt
swollen, and her forehead and cheeks ached. A feeling
like biting ants crawling along her bones made her
twitch.

When Reisil had managed to choke down the last
of it, Yohuac stacked their saddles beneath a rocky
overhang. They set off again. Instead of proceeding
up the trail, as Reisil expected, Yohuac led them into
the tapered fissure from whence the stream issued.
They splashed through the frigid water, struggling over
the moss-slicked stones and clambering over boulders.
It was slow going. Reisil quickly lost her breath and
had to stop every twenty feet or so to calm her pounding heart and heaving lungs. Coughing fits overtook
her so that she was forced to bend and brace against
her knees.

Yohuac was patient, carrying both his own and her
packs, and lending her a strong brown hand over the
most difficult terrain.

Reisil lost track of time as the sunlight turned pearly
and then gray. She concentrated on her feet, settling
each step on firm ground before risking the next.

Up they went, steeper and steeper, like climbing a
ladder. Reisil's lungs hurt and her throat was raw. Her
head was one big ache, with bars of steel thrusting
beneath her browbone. Her eyes watered and her nose
was stuffed full of cotton. She stopped to rest, leaning
against the bare-rock wall that ran alongside their
path. She was standing in the stream, the floor of the
crevice so narrow that the streambed offered the only
path. Her feet were numb. She sniffed, a wet, con-
gested sound. Her breathing sounded loud and ragged.
The vibration she'd been feeling had increased, mak-

ing the marrow of her bones ache. It was that alone
that kept her moving. Otherwise she would have
gladly collapsed in a heap and slept for days. Reisil
sighed and closed her eyes, wishing for a hot bath, a
soft bed, and a pile of blankets.

"Are you all right?"

Reisil opened her eyes and nodded at Yohuac.

"Uh huh. Come on; I'll help you. It isn't far."

In fact it was only another fifty feet or so. But it
was a hard scramble up a nearly verticle slope. Yohuac
stayed next to her, steadying her and pulling her up
when her strength failed. At last she crawled over the
top and sprawled on flat ground, her ribs heaving. She
rolled onto her side as a coughing fit overtook her.
Yohuac sat her up and pulled her against his chest,
holding her until it subsided.

"What now?" she croaked, shivering as the vibrations sent splinters of sharp-edged ice up her nerves.

"I don't know." Yohuac sounded tense. His arms
were tight around her.

Reisil caught hold of herself and sat up, biting back
the moan as agony spasmed through her muscles. If
they didn't get through to the other side soon, she'd
end up with Yohuac slinging her over his shoulder
like a sack of barley.

"Help me up."

He did as she asked, keeping an arm around her
waist to steady her as she wavered.

"This is it?" she asked in a voice deepened by her
cold. She stared around blearily, wiping her nose absently with her sleeve.

They stood on a shelf on the side of the mountain
peak. Green grass carpeted the ground, and sheer rock
walls rose high overhead on three sides. The stream
they'd been following bisected the grassy space and
ended in a waterfall that plunged from high above.
The fourth side was the precipice overlooking their
trail. Looking out, Reisil could see for miles. The sun
had fallen below the horizon and the sky gleamed brilliant gold against the twilight sky.

"This is it," Yohuac confirmed, rubbing her upper arms restlessly. "Nurema said the *copicatl* would open the door between our worlds."

"Call Baku then."

~Come to me, Saljane. It's time.

The goshawk coasted down from her perch on a tree that had rooted itself in the rock wall some twenty feet above. Baku circled once and landed, his wings nearly soundless. He settled and shook himself, opening his mouth in a wide, toothy yawn. The *copicatl* wriggled up over his head to drop down on the ground. It coiled into a ball no bigger than a walnut, its triangular head extended above, its red belly like a streak of blood in the dusky light.

Its pinpoint topaz eyes gleamed as it looked at the four companions—Saljane on Reisil's shoulder, Yohuac beside her, and Baku, just out of reach of the man who would never be his *ahalad-kaaslane*. Reisil twitched, a sudden shaft of pain driving up through her heels as the *copicatl* opened its mouth wide, its yellow, forked tongue flicking.

Then suddenly all sound ceased. Reisil couldn't hear the birds or the sough of the wind. She could not hear her own stertorous breathing. Her ears rang with the emptiness. Before panic could set in, the *copicatl* flared with emerald light, so bright Reisil had to close her eyes. Then, equally suddenly, the ground dropped away. Reisil felt herself scream, the sound tearing silently at her tented throat.

And then the *copicatl* vanished. The world went black and she was falling.

~Saljane!

~I am here.

Reisil felt Saljane's talons clench tighter. Her wings buffetted Reisil's ear and cheek. Fearing that they might be separated, Reisil reached up and grasped hold of Saljane's legs. Wind rushed past. Her stomach lurched sickeningly. Reisil braced herself, expecting to slam against the ground at any second. But the fall didn't end. Down they plunged. On and on.

She did not know how much time passed. After a while, Reisil began to get used to the feeling of falling. She remained tense, but her mind began to work.

~*Are you all right?*

~*What is happening? When will it stop?*

Saljane sounded panicked, her mindvoice shrill.

~*I don't know.*

Reisil stroked Saljane's chest with her free hand, unwilling to chance letting go of the bird's legs. Saljane's feathers were stiff and puffed up, as if they were standing on end. She trembled with every sweep of Reisil's fingers.

Reisil began a soothing chant, exactly the sort of thing she might have used to calm a frightened child.

~*It's all right . . . nothing to fear . . . we'll be all right . . . it'll end soon and we'll be just fine . . .*

The blackness was oppressive. Yet Reisil couldn't force herself to keep her eyes closed and just pretend. Gradually she became aware of light—a pink-and-silver glow. It was the size of the Lady's-head coin she'd given Soka and hung in the blackness just beyond her face. Or so it seemed. Slowly it grew larger, and Reisil realized it was much farther away than she imagined, and it was coming toward her. What was it?

She reached for her magic, half believing it would fail her in this emptiness between worlds. But it came to her in a golden rush, filling her with a rhapsody of joy and vigor. She extended it around Saljane, and felt the goshawk shudder and hunch down to snuggle close against Reisil's neck. Reisil twisted a ribbon of magic around Saljane's legs and released her handhold.

The pearly-pink glow continued to grow, a glistening jewel in the eternal night. As it drew closer, Reisil began to make out its shape. By the Lady! It was Baku!

Shock made Reisil go rigid. Magic flowed around her, crackling hotly over her skin and billowing in the darkness. She clamped down on it, reeling it back under her control, staring openmouthed at Baku's approach.

He was . . . beautiful. Exquisite. Dazzling. The words couldn't begin to describe his aching beauty. He was a collection of stars inside a veil of shimmering rainbow droplets. He was fluid and graceful, winding through the void like a dolphin through the waves, his outstretched wings gauzy silver, his tail a streamer of diamonds behind him.

The coal-drake held Yohuac clutched tight against his chest. Yohuac's face was pale and rigid, the muscles of his arms bulging as he gripped Baku's claws for dear life. His feet kicked helplessly in the emptiness.

Yohuac's mouth moved, his eyes riveted on her. She shook her head, pointing to her ears.

Baku swam closer, his eyes the same yellow and red as always. He opened his mouth in something like a grin and rolled himself over and around. As he did, a shocking realization struck Reisil, and her mouth fell open.

~*He looks like a* nokula. *Sort of. But more . . . right. Like he was meant to be.*

~*He looks happy*, Saljane said, a note of peevishness in her voice. Her grip on Reisil had not relaxed, but her heartbeat had slowed and she was not so stiff.

~*Doesn't he? Like he belongs here. Like he's . . . home?* Reisil's voice turned up at the end. Could it be? Was this void the place Baku called home?

~*It matches his under-memories.*

~*Under-memories*? Reisil had never heard such a term.

~*Under his thoughts where he has no words.*

Ah. That made it all clear as murky, stagnant water.

Suddenly the rushing wind grew hot, bearing a rich, wet, green smell. It was overlaid with a complex web of other, unfamiliar smells. At the same time, a green tinge slowly suffused the velvet darkness. Baku's rich paleness turned the color of new wheat. Reisil's stomach clenched. She held tight to her magic, pulling it into a shield.

It was several moments before she realized they were slowing. They drifted gently like autumn leaves.

Reisil twisted and struggled to turn herself over, to see what was below. But she labored in vain. Something held her fast.

Abruptly they landed.

Reisil grunted. The air burst from her lungs. Her magical shield collapsed as she struggled for breath. Saljane squawked and rolled completely over. She scrabbled to her feet with a screech, her wings raised, the ivy on her beak burning brightly. Baku alighted gracefully, one moment a being of crystalline brilliance, the next his sinuous self. He let go of Yohuac, who dropped to his knees on the sandy ground. Instantly he lunged to his feet, crouching, his sword in his hand.

Their packs plopped to the sand as Reisil sat up. She ducked and twisted, narrowly avoiding being hit in the head. Saljane lunged into the air, wings flapping as she squawked furiously.

Reisil's attention snagged on the emerald radiance lighting the small chamber. She turned, watching the *copicatl*. The glow diminished, seeping back into its tiny body. Its mouth closed and it slowly uncoiled. It looked at Reisil for one burning instant, and then plunged its head into the sand. It wriggled, burrowing down to disappear altogether. Reisil fisted her hands on the sand, abruptly becoming aware that it was warm, as if the sun had shone on it all day.

After a long moment, Yohuac slid his sword back into its scabbard and extended a hand to Reisil. "Welcome to Cemanahuatl."

She let him help her up, dusting herself off before examining their surroundings. They were inside a small rock bowl shaped like an oval. If she stretched, she would just be able to reach the lip with her fingertips. There were no doors or stairs, and the gray stone was smooth. Clouds hid the stars above. As Reisil tipped her head up, fat drops of rain splattered on her forehead and chin. Seconds later it turned into a downpour.

"Come on! We've got to get out of here before the place fills up."

With Baku's help, they struggled out, climbing onto the coal-drake's back and levering themselves up. The rain pelted them unmercifully. It drove straight down, the drops full and hard, like ripe grapes. Reisil covered Saljane in her cloak and tucked the goshawk against her stomach. Yohuac tossed the packs over Baku's shoulders and motioned for the others to follow.

He set off across the enormous plateau, shoulders hunched, steadying himself against Baku. Reisil followed. She watched the ground carefully, so as not to misstep. Slowly she became aware that the entire plateau was carved with intricate pictures and words made of the strange, angular *rinda* she'd first noticed at Mysane Kosk. She paused, blinking into spellsight.

Reisil gaped. The entire mountaintop was a mass of intricate spellwork in a multitude of jewel-tone colors. They pulsed and flared and shimmered as if alive. Reisil glanced down at her feet, at the tendrils of magic swirling and coiling around her legs like seaweed on the tide.

"What's wrong?" Yohuac shouted beside her. He and Baku had returned to her once they'd realized she was no longer following.

"What is this place?" she shouted back.

"The Monequi. Home of the Teotl—the fifty-two gods! Are you able? We should not tarry here! It's a long way to shelter and it's not safe!"

As he spoke, a jagged streak of lightning seared across the clouds, followed nearly instantly by a crack of thunder that throbbed through the stone beneath their feet. Reisil jumped, her stomach clenching as goose bumps prickled across her skin. She nodded vigorously at Yohuac and waved for him to proceed.

She followed closely, glad of her wizard-sight that allowed her to see in the dark, though the rain was nearly blinding.

They hobbled along slowly. Saljane wriggled in her sodden cocoon and made high-pitched whistling noises.

~Easy, sweetheart. It will be better soon.

Wet. Aggravation. Hunger.

Reisil smiled at the blend of peevishness Saljane sent back at her and concentrated on walking through the pounding storm.

She didn't know how long they walked. Her arms were aching with the weight of Saljane and her sodden cloak. Her teeth were chattering and she was so hungry that she was dizzy. The only thing she had to be happy about was that she could breathe and her throat no longer ached. Her cold had vanished entirely when she'd used her magic in the long fall.

Her magic. For one yearning moment, Reisil considered creating a magical umbrella above them, but then dismissed the thought reluctantly. It was too dangerous. Anyone could be watching. And she'd rather have the benefit of surprise when she met Yohuac's nahuallis. Though they'd sent Yohuac to find her, Reisil remembered all too well her reception in Koduteel after she'd destroyed the wizard circle and stopped the war. Everyone had questioned her loyalties and her motives, frightened of her magic. It would not do to repeat the same mistakes with the nahuallis. She'd wait until they knew her, until they trusted her, to reveal her abilities.

Reisil stumbled and staggered into Baku.

~He says it is not far to the path down.

Baku's gravelly voice startled Reisil.

~It can't be too soon, she replied feelingly, infusing her mindvoice with her pleasure for his consideration. She had a sense of a mental blush from him that made her smile with hope. Maybe he was coming around.

Indeed they came to the path at last. But it was not what Reisil was expecting. It was a narrow stairway that plunged down the side of the mountain. Rainwater drained from the plateau in a tumbling cataract. Reisil couldn't even see the stairs beneath the flood.

"Be careful! It will be slippery! I'll go and then Baku and then you! Watch out for snakes!" Yohuac waited for her nod before stepping onto the stair.

It was the longest journey of Reisil's life, and the most difficult. Harder even than escaping the wizards' stronghold. The water rushed around her calves, pushing her off balance. The steps were a scant six inches wide. She turned and edged down sideways, clutching Saljane tight against her stomach, feeling the bird quaking.

~It will be all right. I won't let you fall. Reisil wasn't sure Saljane believed her. She wasn't sure she believed herself.

Step by slow step, she descended. Her legs began to shake, and her neck and back ached. Her head was thick and heavy with exhaustion. At last she had to sit, bracing her elbows against her knees to keep Saljane out of the water.

~He wants to know if you are all right. Baku's voice cautiously insinuated itself in her mind.

~Tired, was the only answer Reisil could muster. She hung her head.

~You must keep going. It is dangerous to remain here.

It was the worry in Baku's mindvoice that made Reisil push to her feet and begin again. The cascading water pushed at her. She slipped, crashing to her knees and onto her side, the steps biting hard into her ribs. She slid down half a dozen stairs and slammed against Baku's hindquarters, scraping her elbows, shoulder, and hips. Baku whipped about agilely, catching her with his claws and tail.

~Saljane!

The goshawk was flailing inside the cloak, shredding it with her talons as she fought for freedom.

~Saljane! It's all right! We are safe! We are safe . . . all is well . . . all is well.

Saljane slowly subsided under Reisil's mental and verbal reassurance, her body racked with shudders. Reisil held her, stroking Saljane's wet feathers while the rain battered them. Reisil's body throbbed painfully, floodwater sluicing over her shoulders and thighs. Tears overflowed and were washed away.

Suddenly Yohuac was beside her, having clambered

over Baku to get to her. He took Saljane, cradling the bird against his chest. Saljane didn't even protest, her crimson eye whirling with distress. Yohuac helped Reisil to stand, holding her steady against the flood.

"We must continue!" he shouted urgently above the hammering of the rain. Reisil nodded weakly. They had to get down. If they didn't walk, they'd be washed away by the torrent. This time Baku led the way with Yohuac in front of her. She steadied herself with a hand on his shoulder, concentrating on keeping her feet.

Down and down they went. A hundred steps. Two hundred. Reisil counted to help keep her mind focused. But soon she found herself eagerly anticipating reaching the bottom, reaching a place to rest. But they didn't. On and on they went, always down. She gave up counting, holding back sobs of frustration and fear.

She almost couldn't believe it when the stairs gave out. They stepped joltingly out onto a path, perhaps five feet wide, and flat. It ran away in either direction, girdling the mountain. Reisil stared back and forth, her mind sluggish. The push of the water from above eased here, swirling gently around her ankles. But the rain continued to pummel them mercilessly. She turned to Yohuac, her silent question written on her face: Where now?

He jerked his head for her to follow and set off on the left-hand path. Baku came alongside her, guarding her from the precipice. They stumbled on until they came to a small basin carved in the rock and hanging out over the vast emptiness below. It was filled with water. Opposite it, on the mountain's wall, was a small shrine. It was little more than an arched hollow carved in the rock, with bands of the jagged-shaped *rinda* carved in intricate lacings and bands around the entrance and in the interior. It was empty.

Yohuac stopped, pulling at the ties on his pack with one hand, hampered by his grip on Saljane.

"Have to make an offering!" he yelled when Reisil touched his arm.

An offering? What kind of offering? Reisil watched him struggle a moment, a thought trying to coalesce in her muddled mind. It came to her at last, and she reached out and grasped Yohuac's hands. His dark gaze was heavy on her, his own movements becoming ponderous with exhaustion.

Reisil dug in the side of her pack and pulled out her rosemary candle. She rarely burned it anymore. Only when she stayed anywhere long enough. The last time she'd lit it was . . . She couldn't remember. She banished the pang of sorrow that thrust through her. She'd made her choice to be *ahalad-kaaslane* long ago.

She turned the candle in her fingers, smelling the sharp, woody scent of rosemary. Lit by a tark, it would burn endlessly. At least in Kodu Riik. Here, she didn't know. But it didn't matter. It would send a message to the gods of Cemanahuatl, to the Teotl: She had come to help heal their land.

She set the candle on the flat, carved bottom of the shrine's niche. Taking a deep breath, she steeled herself, tensing every muscle. Then she drew on her magic, touching her finger to the candle's wick. It flared to light, filling the hollow of the shrine with a rich yellow glow. Reisil let go of her magic and a wave of fatigue swamped her. She swayed and her knees buckled. Yohuac caught her around the waist before she fell.

A glance at the tight concern in his face told her that they still had a long way to go. She fought against her sudden urge to slump to the ground and give up. Instead she straightened, holding herself erect by will alone.

She nodded to Yohuac and then turned to the shrine and gave it a slight bow.

"We have come. We will not give up. So long as we breathe and blood flows in our veins, we will not give up."

The words were as much to convince herself as a promise to the gods who'd sent Yohuac to find her. Suddenly the flame of the candle flared. The *rinda* around the shrine flickered with green light. Reisil stepped back, bumping against Baku.

"What's happening?" she shouted at Yohuac.

"I don't know!"

The hollow opening of the shrine distorted. It stretched and grew. Taller and wider it expanded, the interior become a shallow cave, the bottom lined with golden sand. Reisil's rosemary candle suddenly burned at the center of a crackling fire, the wax unmelting despite the heat.

Yohuac's lips curved in a shaky smile as the green light flickered and dimmed and then vanished altogether. He went inside and she followed, Baku bringing up the rear. Instantly the sound of the rain quieted.

"Quite a welcome," Reisil murmured. She looked around, becoming aware of the warmth emanating up through her sodden boots. "Thank you," she said to the air, to whoever had created their shelter. "Thank you."

The flame of her candle shot up high into the air like a streamer of sunshine, and then subsided.

"You are welcome here," Yohuac said, his weary voice full of wonder. "The Teotl welcomes you to Cemanahuatl."

Chapter 21

Soka touched the ward Reisil had given him where it lumped beneath his shirt. Would he need it? Would it work if he did? He drew a long, unobtrusive breath and let it out soundlessly, flicking the poison bead in his mouth against his teeth with a click. He scowled. Didn't matter. He had his own solution.

With an effort, he schooled his features into an expression of boredom and glanced at his four companions. Clano and Temles both looked nervous, twitching back and forth at every sound or flit of a bird. Ferro and Slatts were alert, but relaxed, uncowed by the shadowy Old Forest, or by its rumored strangeness.

A streak of inky shadow caught Soka's attention. He looked at it from the corner of his eye. Yes, there it was. A crumpled shape, like a discarded rag, gathered in a heap in the crook of a great elm tree. It suddenly gathered itself, thrusting stiffly out over the road like a diseased limb. Its attention was fixed on the balding Slatts about to ride below. The soldier had removed his leather helm, and his long gray hair dangled down his shoulders in a thin tail. Soka turned, staring hard at the tattered shadow. Instantly the thing shifted, rippling as if caught by a breeze. Soka knew better. It was *seeking*. It froze, awareness of Soka's attention making it fade to a sickly gray. Suddenly it leaped away into the shadows.

Soka raked the trees, searching for more *kivis*. One of the many creatures that inhabited the Old Forest, they were mostly harmless, though a nuisance. They would fling themselves over the head of an unsuspecting man or woman, casting illusions over all their senses. Once attached, they became invisible. *Kivis* feasted on emotions, and their illusions drove their victims to the extremes of those emotions until they passed out or they dropped off on their own, sated.

Mostly they hunted alone, dropping out of trees onto their unsuspecting prey, as this one had been about to do to Slatts. They were easy enough to drive off, if you noticed them. Another story entirely from the ravenous *delgeskes* that had swarmed their camp the night before. The crab-like creatures had overrun them in a slow-moving mass. With Clano's warning, there had been ample time to collect their gear and escape. *Delgeskes* were dangerous only to the unwary and slow. However, neither Clano nor Temles had yet recovered from seeing the chittering family horde rolling and tumbling into the camp like an errant tumbleweed.

Soka's lips quirked. The *delgeskes* made an appropriate appetizer for the bitter meal of Bro-heyek.

They'd kept riding through the night, the men too unnerved to camp. Now it was approaching noon and they had just crossed into the boundaries of Bro-heyek, marked by a stone lintel supported by two rough-carved plinths. The lintel was square-shaped. In the center was carved a set of twisting antlers tipped with wicked points, and woven together by a winding of bull-thistle.

Soka didn't pause as he rode beneath it. But immediately he felt a chill roll down his back, followed by a spurt of hot anger in his belly. He straightened, his thin lips pinching together as he wrestled with his fury. Honor couldn't afford for him to lose control. Metyein was counting on him.

They'd not gone more than half a league when he

became aware that they were being watched. The birds and insects went silent, and his skin prickled warning. Slatts and Ferro noticed at the same time.

"Got company," Slatts said softly out the side of his mouth, reaching up in a nonchalant stretch.

Ferro nodded and laughed as if Slatts had said something funny and looked over his shoulder at Soka.

"Friends or foes?" he said, just as quietly as Slatts, his gaze sweeping the great boles of the gray-skinned trees promenading beside the road.

Soka smoothed a hand over his jaws and mouth. Either. Neither. Both. "Let's find out," he murmured. Then in a loud voice, "Ho, there! In the trees! If you be friends, let's see you."

Behind him he could hear Temles and Clano shifting in their saddles. Temles lifted his bow from his lap, the arrow already nocked. Clano swung his over his shoulder and followed suit.

The five travelers stood thus for several moments. They were perfect targets, if those watching had a mind to shoot at them. Soka suddenly rushed back to the winter afternoon in the Jarrah Gardens and the arrows that had pounded into him from unseen hands. His shoulder and ribs ached with the memory of the wounds. Sweat trickled down his back and over his belly. He gathered his reins tighter, preparing to bolt to safety.

A crackle of underbrush to the right and a jingle of a bridle to the left warned them that they were surrounded. Slowly a necklace of twelve men emerged from the forest, their faces hard and suspicious. Each carried a longbow, arrows pointed squarely at the five intruders.

"Quite a welcome," Soka said sardonically, fear draining away in a surge of emotion he couldn't quite identify. He rolled the poison bead on his tongue.

"Name yourself and your purpose," came a gruff voice from behind Soka.

He turned. The speaker was a hale man, twice as

wide as Soka in the shoulders and boasting a robust paunch. He was near to forty summers, dressed in the grays and greens of the forest, the antlered Bro-heyek coat of arms stitched over his heart. His black beard bristled from a thick jaw, and his eyes were flat and hard. His nose had been broken at least once, and a pink scar slashed his face from his left temple to the corner of his lip, lending him the false appearance of good humor.

Soka stared at the man, sorting through his memories. His face was not familiar.

"Bright day to you," he said, his nostrils flaring as he reeled in hard on the recklessness pushing at him. "We are on our way to Bro-heyek."

"And who be you?" the bearded giant demanded, raking them with a suspicious gaze. "What be you wanting in Bro-heyek?"

They'd been riding hard for weeks. The five of them didn't look like much. Shaggy and ragged, dirty and rough. More like highwaymen than not. Soka smiled inwardly. If his father expected his eldest and heir to have turned out a court fop—or worse, a weakling with no skills—then Thevul Bro heyek was in for a rude surprise. Thanks to Metyein. And if his father thought Soka would have forgotten who was responsible for the loss of his eye . . .

The fingers of Soka's right hand curled into a hard ball. He cocked his head. He'd been told he looked like his father. They had the same blue eyes. Or rather, his father had one extra. He touched his crimson eye patch, one eyebrow flicking up. "I am Soka cas Raakin. I've come to see my father."

The other man remained still for a long moment, studying Soka from head to foot, his face expressionless. Then he nodded.

"I'll escort you then."

"As you wish. Though I know the way." His fingers brushed his eye patch again, touching the gold threads that picked out a map of Bro-heyek. It matched the network of scars on his eyelid. Aare's handiwork.

The other man stared at the eye patch. Soka saw him swallow hard.

"Name's Prefiil," the other man said. "Huntmaster. Any of you be sick?" The question was asked matter-of-factly, but there was a biting chill to his tone.

Soka looked over his shoulder at his men. "Feeling all right?"

They nodded. Temles and Clano continued to aim their arrows at their besieging challengers.

Soka turned back to Prefiil. "Nothing a bath and a woman wouldn't cure."

The Huntmaster's lips turned slightly, but his expression remained dour.

"Is my father in residence?" Soka asked, suddenly remembering his father's habit of roaming. It might be they had to hunt farther than Bro-heyek to find him.

"Certes he is. Celebration begins tomorrow. Nelle is going to be married."

Nelle? Soka felt the muscle in his cheek spasm. His sister. Younger by two years. They had not been close. It was the habit of the household to keep the girls separate from the boys except at meals and family gatherings. And even then they rarely spoke. But he remembered she had auburn hair with pale green eyes and freckles. She looked like the portrait of their mother that hung in the morning salon. Mellisaan cas Bro-heyek had died while giving birth to Anliv, who had been four when Soka was taken to Koduteel. He had almost forgotten he had a sister and a brother. He wondered if they had forgotten him.

While Soka digested the news, Prefiil called out orders to his men, sending four back into the forest, no doubt to collect the bounty of their interrupted hunt. The rest fell in behind Soka's party—at a distance—with the burly giant riding beside Soka.

They were a silent group as they rode through the dappled afternoon. The trees rustled and soughed in the breeze, a mixture of black spruce, sugar maple, aspen, elm, and white cedar. The undergrowth was dense, lending the road a tunnel-like quality. The sense of being underground was oppressive, further darkening Soka's bleak mood.

The sun was drifting down to rest when they arrived at the gates of Bro-heyek. The massive portals were made of fire-hardened oak and banded with iron hung between two flanking towers. An enormous coat of arms wrought in copper was riveted to the outside of the great slabs. It flamed forebodingly in the lowering sun.

The walls were of kelamite stone from the Tornaat Mountains. The cream-colored stone was streaked with pink and red minerals and glimmered here and there with metal ores. The walls were fifteen feet thick and twenty-five feet high, with a cleared field of fire fifty yards around—an island in the trees. Square bartizans were spaced every thirty feet along the wall, with machicoulis in between and arrow loops interspersed along the top third. A dry moat filled with brambles, stinging nettles, and sharpened stakes was sunk deep around its base. Thevul Bro-heyek always expected an attack.

The riders stopped before the bridge on the other side of the moat, and Prefil called a greeting to the guards on the walls.

"We got guests."

There was a pause.

"They clean?"

"Appear so."

There was silence. Soka eyed the walls with receding patience. Every hall, every town—it was necessary to be sure of visitors, to be careful of plague. But it gritted anyhow. To return at last, and to be left waiting outside like a beggar.

There was a sudden bustle of activity on the walls and the gates were swung open, the great coat of arms dividing down the middle. The inner portculis was raised with the measured creaking of a capstan. Prefil led the way inside.

As the Huntmaster and his men dismounted, Soka examined the castle. The place was the same. Smaller

than he remembered. Not as grand. But then, he'd
lived the last twelve years in the palace of Koduteel.
There he'd witnessed a kind of luxury and decadence
that Bro-heyek had never seen. Had never wanted to
see. His father had always eschewed such things as
vanity and foppishness.

The castle was laid out in a square, with tall towers
anchoring the corners. The bailey was an open, grassy
square, with room enough for the entire garrison to
assemble. Near the gates were the barracks, kennels,
and stables. Beside it on the eastern wall were the
servants' quarters. Next to it were the kitchens and
granary, and on the north wall were the hall and family living quarters. On the western wall were the visitor
quarters, steward and household offices, blacksmith,
and saddlery. Cellars beneath the hall stored provis-
ions. Cisterns were located along the interior of the
buildings to supplement the well. In the center of the
bailey was a firepit and a small stone altar to the Lady.
A flame burned low on the top.

Had that been there before? Soka's brow furrowed
as he searched his memories. He didn't remember his
father being devout. But yes, the altar *had* been there.

Stable hands came to claim the horses. Soka stepped
slowly down out of his saddle. He was stiff and covered with grime. Guardsmen in brown livery and polished mail watched the visitors with hard suspicion.

"I'll take you in. Bexten'll see to your men," the
Huntmaster said, nodding toward a grizzled man, a
head shorter than Soka and four times as wide, the
buttons on his shirt straining.

Soka motioned for his companions to follow Bexten,
and then accompanied Prefiil across the grassy bailey.
The smells of roasting meats drifted on the air, and
his stomach clutched painfully. They arrived at the
wide steps leading up to the entry of the Great Hall.
It was imposing and martial, designed for defense and
intimidation. The only ornament was the coat of arms
carved in relief above the doorway. Soka passed be-

neath, feeling his bladder tighten, and he was disgusted at the nervousness that quaked his muscles.

An iron chandelier filled with smoky candles cast a dull shine on the brilliant streaks in the kelamite stone. The walls were hung with tapestries depicting battles and hunts and interspersed with a variety of weaponry. From inside the Great Hall, Soka heard merry music, laughter, and a jumble of voices. Prefiil paused outside the heavy doors to speak to the two guards outside. Soka faltered a moment before forcing himself to follow.

He remembered this place as if it were a potent dream. He remembered chasing through the hallways while the scullery maids scrubbed the floors. He'd slipped and slid and shouted with laughter, accompanied by a pack of boys he'd befriended. He remembered romping with his father's hunting dogs, learning to shoot his child-sized bow, swimming in the river and ocean, galloping swiftly on his pony. . . .

He caught himself short, his expression flattening into a death mask. Once, everything about Bro-heyek had been limned with a halo of gold. It had been a perfect place—an idyll for the child he had been. And then his father had let him be taken hostage. Now the memories were steeped in the bitter juices of betrayal, loneliness, and hatred. Returning here at last, where once he'd imagined himself happy beyond words, was a grinding ache. A pain too deep and vast to speak.

Still, he had promised Metyein, and if there was a soul in this world Soka did not want to disappoint, it was Metyein.

He set his teeth as the guards swung the doors open.

Animal heads lined the walls. A half dozen iron chandeliers reigned over four rows of trestle tables and a dais at the end where people of importance sat. Two enormous hearths on either side contained roaring fires. Fresh rushes covered the floor in a thick carpet, and dogs yipped and chased between the benches.

Though the tables were full and the ale flowed freely, the dinner had not yet begun. The company paid little attention to Prefiil and Soka as they walked toward the dais.

Thevul Bro-heyek sat in the center. He'd aged well. His sandy hair was threaded with gray, his face more lined. But he remained lean and powerful, radiating an air of energy and power. Soka could feel it halfway across the room. He still commanded the worshipful respect of his liegemen and retainers.

Despite himself, Soka had hoped to find his father mad or decrepit—some weakness to explain why he'd abandoned his son and heir. The fury Soka had kept tamped down since he was nine rose scaldingly. All this time and his father had never come. Never tried to free him. Suddenly his empty eye itched like it was being gnawed by ants.

He walked stiff-legged to the front of the dais, his gaze locked tight to his father. The sounds of the room faded. All he heard was the thunder of his heart. His father turned sideways to talk to the woman next to him. He laughed, his teeth white against his sun-bronzed skin. He lifted his cup to his lips and drank.

Prefiil and Soka halted at the foot of the dais. Thevul Bro-heyek turned curiously, raising his brows at his Huntmaster. And then his gaze flicked curiously past to Soka.

There was a moment when nothing seemed to move, when sound ceased and the air corroded inside Soka's lungs. For the space of a breath, his father's expression melted into dumbfounded shock. Then he caught himself and straightened, his face solidifying into basalt.

"Soka. I did not expect you."

"Didn't you?" Soka said, his voice taut. "I thought maybe you would. I came to get my eye back."

Chapter 22

At Soka's announcement, his father stiffened. His cheeks blotched red as his jaws knotted. He stood, pushing back his chair with a loud scrape.

"Let us take this to my office." He spun about and strode to a nook behind the dais, where he pushed open a door hidden by the drapery.

Soka was conscious of a sudden hush and the ripple of muttering voices spreading across the hall, and the might of more than a hundred eyes screwing into his back. He ignored them, following his father out through a passage ending in a long stair. At the top was a set of carved doors that entered into an expansive office suite. The walls of the outer office were covered with weaponry and hunting trophies and shelves of bound records. Four tables littered with papers, maps, nibs of pens, and charcoal pencils crowded the floor.

Thevul Bro-heyek led the way to an interior office. It was furnished with heavy walnut chairs upholstered in red leather and brass. The floor was covered in a thick green carpet patterned with artful images of trees and vines picked out in yellow. The walls were bare of ornament, except for the Bro-heyek coat of arms inlaid above the fireplace in copper, silver, and gold. Behind his desk a bank of mullioned windows overlooked the bailey.

Soka's father closed the door and went to stand behind his desk, pouring a glass of black Gueltan whiskey and drinking it in a gulp. He poured himself another, then looked up at his son, examining him from head to foot, his gaze lingering on the eye patch. Soka resisted the urge to squirm, resenting that he cared about his father's opinion of him.

"I hadn't thought Geran would let you leave the court," his father said, sipping from his whiskey. "Given the reports, I figured you would be more useful there."

Soka went rigid. *Useful?* For years he'd imagined what his father might say when at last they came face-to-face. Nothing he dreamed up ever seemed adequate. But this . . . His father didn't even bother to try.

Something ugly clawed to life in Soka's gut.

"I thought you ought to have the chance to admire your handiwork," Soka said, touching his eye patch.

His father flicked an eyebrow up, reminding Soka of himself. "Gaudy, isn't it?"

"True. But I wouldn't want anyone to think I'd forgotten, would I?" Soka reached up and hooked the eye patch with his fingers and tossed it on the desk. "Of course, it was a fairly memorable occasion. I doubt *I'll* forget."

His father swigged the rest of the whiskey, setting the glass on his desk with a hard click. He picked up the eye patch, turning it over.

"Bro-heyek is grateful for your sacrifice," his father said at last, dropping it back on his desk. He sat down and leaned back, his gaze sharp.

"So you didn't get permission to come to the wedding. Should I expect Geran's troops on my doorstep, ready to drag you back?"

Soka frowned. That was the second time his father had mentioned the Iisand. Didn't he know? How could that be possible?

His father continued on, his fingers tapping on his desk. "He could very well call it treason, leaving without permission. He already took one eye—do you want to lose another?"

A slow, disbelieving smile spread across Soka's lips, bitter as arsenic. "If I am caught, Father, it will not

be running away that wins me a romance with the
torturer. It is the least of the things I've done."

His father snapped straight. "And you scuttled to
Bro-heyek for safety? Explain yourself," he demanded harshly.

The ugly thing inside Soka thrashed. He reached
for the whiskey and a glass. "Do you mind?" he
asked, not bothering to wait for an answer. He poured
himself a drink and dropped heavily into a chair,
slouching down and crossing his ankles. He took a pull
of the fiery liquid, savoring its smoky, woody flavor.

"Why, by the Demonlord's warty horn, would you
think I'd come *here* for safety?" he asked derisively.

If Soka expected his father to flinch from the none-
too-subtle accusation, he was disappointed. Thevul
Bro-heyek merely scowled impatiently.

"Are you saying the Iisand has sent troops after
you? What have you done?"

Soka set down his half-finished whiskey, staring.
"You really don't know."

"What? What don't I know?"

"The Iisand—he's . . . gone. Aare was made Regent
more than four months ago."

"Gone? What do you mean?" His father sat forward. There was an implacable, relentless quality to
him. This was the man who'd let his son be tortured.
This was a man who'd invaded his neighbors. A
conquerer.

Soka licked his lips, once again feeling the urge to
squirm. His thoughts scattered and he grabbed at
them, forcing himself to think. Few knew the truth
about the Iisand. If Aare should learn his father had
become a *nokula*, he would be free to take the crown.
When he did, any resistance that Metyein's father
made to Aare's dictums would cease. Worse, Lord
Marshal Vare would be forced to carry out Aare's
commands. Something Honor could ill afford. The
longer they could delay that inevitability, the better.

Soka looked at the crumpled eye patch on the desk.
Trusting his father was out of the question. Soka could

no more trust him than he could Aare. They were cut of the same cloth.

"He's gone missing. About four months ago. The *ahalad-kaaslane* named Sodur disappeared at the same time. Some say they went together, others that he was kidnapped." Soka spoke matter-of-factly, enjoying the shock and consternation pinching his father's expression. "When it was discovered, Verit Aare had himself declared Regent, and then sealed the gates of Koduteel— to help get hold of the plague. Shortly after, he began hunting down the *ahalad-kaaslane* and locking them up. He's also allied himself with three Scallacian sorcerers."

He paused, taking a slow sip of his whiskey, well aware of his father's glowering impatience.

"Is there more?"

Soka shrugged. "Well, some of the *ahalad-kaaslane* escaped with the Vertina Emelovi and gathered what loyal people they could. They established a rebel camp outside of Mysane Kosk."

"Rebel camp? At Mysane Kosk?" His father shook his head. "Why there?"

Soka rubbed his hand over his face, feeling the dry roughness of his skin beneath the stubble of his beard. There was so much to explain, and he had to, if he hoped to get the metal Honor needed. But he couldn't give too much away. He had to be careful, *careful.* . . .

"You know the wizards attacked there during the war?"

His father nodded, eyes narrowing.

"Have you heard of Reisiltark?"

"She's *ahalad-kaaslane*, isn't she? With wizard powers." His father's lip curled in repugnance. "She refuses to use her magic to heal the plague. Some say she caused it."

He knew that and not the rest? Soka bared his teeth without humor. If he were his father, he'd relegate his spies to the fields. They were worthless.

"That's what Aare would have you believe, anyway," he said mockingly. "It's true she cannot heal the plague. But she's looking for the cure. The wizards caused it with whatever they did at Mysane Kosk. They caused the plague and the *nokulas*—you *have* heard of them?"

His father nodded, sitting back again in his chair, his fingers tapping slowly. He radiated fury at Soka's insolence. Soka smiled again, touching the poison bead with his tongue. But he must not antagonize his father too much. He sobered, sitting forward earnestly, his elbows on his knees.

"According to Reisiltark, Mysane Kosk must be protected. If it falls into the wrong hands, if it is destroyed, the consequences for Kodu Riik will be dire."

"You believe her?"

If he answered yes, his father would call him a fool. Soka could read it in the disparaging lift of his eyebrows, the way he relaxed into his chair, as if his concern had been for nothing.

"Yes."

"What's your proof?"

"She's *ahalad-kaaslane*; do I need more?"

"If you've got any sense."

Soka *tsk*ed. "I hope the Lady doesn't overhear."

"The Lady can—" His father broke off, swallowing. "The Blessed Amiya does not reward stupidity and blind obedience to folly."

"Your estimation of my intelligence is flattering."

"Once again, what's your proof?"

A snake, a witch, a gold hand tattoo, and a *nokula* that used to be the Iisand. Not to mention a coaldrake and a man from another world. Even if his father would believe it, Soka wasn't willing to tell him. Still, he needed to say *something*. Metyein was counting on him.

He sat back, considering.

"Tell me you have some proof for this . . . tale," his father said contemptuously.

"I do."

"Well?"

Still Soka hesitated. Then, just as his father opened

his mouth again, Soka spoke. "I have seen evidence that the *nokulas* and the plague come from Mysane Kosk. I have seen other proofs to convince me of the rest."

"Tell me," he ordered, as if to one of his retainers. The thing inside Soka howled and writhed.

Soka gritted his teeth together. Cool, unfamiliar air rubbed at the exposed eyelid of his stolen eye. It itched. He reached up and rubbed at it, feeling the fine lines of the scars.

His father's gaze followed the movement. "If you were one of my men," he said, "I'd turn you out. Your insolence is reprehensible."

"If I were one of your men, I'd still have my eye," Soka retorted, jerking to his feet. "And if I told you what you want to know, I'd be ensuring Honor's destruction. You're about as trustworthy as a whore with the pox."

His father's face purpled and he leaped to his feet, bracing his hands on his desk as he thrust forward, his voice lethal. "Honor? You ride in here with your tail between your legs, looking to hide from the Regent's wrath, and you speak of honor? You disgrace your name."

Soka leaned over so that his nose was only inches from his father's. His voice shook with rage. "I am not here to hide, Father. I am here on business. And since I am well aware that your integrity is malleable, I know I can count on your greed and ambition to silence any qualms you might have in dealing with me."

He straightened, reaching into the interior pocket of his vest, and removed the letter from Emelovi. It was wrapped in an oilcloth pouch. He slapped it down on the desk.

"Read that. It will tell you all you need to know. If you want more, get better spies. You'll have nothing from me."

His father's nostrils flared, his lips turning white.

"Don't be so cocky, boy. If I truly want the answers, I *can* get them."

Soka smiled venemously. "Torture? Try it."

The absolute surety of his words took his father aback. His gaze narrowed, and he pinched his lip consideringly, but he made no reply. Instead, he picked up the letter and opened it, perusing it in silence.

Soka reached for the decanter and poured himself another whiskey. Fury stitched through his flesh with threads of fire, tightening until he felt like he was about to choke. He grimaced at the tremble in his fingers as he set the glass back down.

His father finished reading and folded the parchment back up.

"Geran thought keeping you at court would put polish on you, while affirming your loyalty to the crown. He was very angry to have to take your eye."

"He overestimated your interest in my welfare," Soka said, crossing his arms over his chest. All of a sudden he felt like the boy he'd been when he'd left—young, gawky, gullible.

"And yet you come here, looking for help from me," his father said scornfully. "Though you think I'm the worst kind of scoundrel, still you come begging."

"Oh, no, Father. You are mistaken. I have not come begging. I know exactly what you are. That letter offers you a chance at power and prestige in the new government. It's a bargain you will be loath to pass up. You let the Iisand cut my eye out for your ambition. You have little to lose. If we win, you will profit. And if we lose, then it won't matter. We'll all be dead. We may all die anyhow, if Reisiltark doesn't succeed."

"So you say. But if you fail, then Geran will be severe with me."

A long moment passed and then Soka spoke, choosing his words carefully. "It is not believed that the Iisand will ever return."

This time his father did not ask for proof. He rubbed his chin, lost in thought. He did not appear particularly disturbed by any sentiment he might harbor for the Iisand. But then, Soka knew better than anyone that his father didn't make a general habit of letting his attachments interfere with doing business. His father sat slowly back in his chair. Soka followed suit, feeling the tension of the moment lessening.

"Are you going to win?"

The question startled Soka so much his mouth dropped open.

"What did you say?"

"Are you going to win?"

"Getting the metal will help."

"That doesn't answer the question. Are you going to win?"

Soka thought of the *nokula* attack, of the wizards and the Scallacians. He felt for the ward tucked under his shirt, and thought of Reisil's annhilation of the raiders.

"Pray we do. Because there's nowhere to hide from what's coming if we lose."

His father was toying with his dagger, turning it in his hands. The hilt was made of elkhorn inlaid with the Bro-heyek crest. It gleamed and flashed in the light.

"Yours is the first information I've had in some time. There's a pack of raiders south of here—an army really. Of late, every man I've sent down that way has vanished. The same with those shipping down the coast or those traveling the mountains. Everywhere there used to be peaceful villages, there are now nests of raiders. They are like anthills. It speaks well of you that you made it through."

"You don't need to concern yourself about the rabble near Millcote anymore. They're gone."

"Gone?"

"They raped and tortured children. Reisiltark put an end to it."

His father's expression darkened. Soka knew the cause: fear of her power and the urge to stamp it out, twined with an opposing craving to own her leash.

"How?"

Soka leaned forward. "She shredded them like meat in a grinder and spattered their guts for leagues. I've never seen such slaughter. Enough to make you soil your pants.

"But here's the thing, Father, and it's the only thing that matters in the end. Kodu Riik is going to be destroyed. The only way to save ourselves is to protect Mysane Kosk until Reisiltark can stop the storm of magic the wizards unleashed with their spells. To buy her the time she needs, we have to arm ourselves with better than rocks and sticks. So we need you to give us the metal we require. It's up to you. Reisiltark isn't going to come here and twist your arm for it And I don't have the time or army it would take to murder you in your sleep, inherit, and take care of it myself.

"There's not a lot for you to lose. I know you don't care about being called a traitor. If you did, I certainly would still have my eye. But you *are* hungry for land and power. You can have both, if Honor wins. You'll even be called a hero." Soka sat back, tossing out his hand. "It's a gamble. You may not want to risk it.

"But there's one more fact you should know. This map"—he touched his vacant eyelid—"this is Aare's work. A message for you, just from him. Now I don't expect you to take revenge for my sake. I plan to get Aare myself, one day. But you should know that when he becomes Iisand, he isn't going to look kindly on you. He'll very likely strip you of your title and lands. And that would be the least of it."

His father stared up at the vaulted ceiling, his hands steepling together. At last he stood. "I must return to the Hall. You are invited to join us. I will have someone show you to a place where you can clean up. I'll think on this other and give you my decision later." He came around the desk, pausing to examine Soka, who had risen to his feet as well.

"Geran was sure that living at court would turn you into the right sort of man. It may be he was right, though I'm not certain he would agree."

With that he left, calling for a servant. Soka followed slowly, feeling at once wrung like a rag and exhilarated. A thrill of pride rippled through him for what had seemed like praise, followed almost instantly by a flood of self-disgust. What did it matter what his father thought of him? Thevul Bro-heyek was nothing better than gutter trash. And once Soka walked away with the metal Honor needed, he never intended to return to Bro-heyek or see his father again.

Chapter 23

Just two weeks since his return to Honor, and Juhrnus was itching to leave. His wounds had healed well enough. They ached sometimes, keeping him awake, and there was an uncomfortable tug to his flesh when he twisted or raised his arms above his head. He wasn't back to normal, but he was good enough to get going.

Juhrnus pulled on his shirt and laced his jerkin over it, then stamped his feet into his boots. He fastened his hair into a tail at the nape of his neck, and buckled on his sword. Esper was splayed in the middle of the bed. The tip of his tail twitched as he watched his *ahalad-kaaslane* with somnolent interest. Juhrnus stroked a hand down his back, feeling Esper's contented croon vibrate down his spine.

~Don't be getting too used to all this pampering. Is there anyone who hasn't been coddling you?

~I must keep up my strength, Esper returned loftily, shifting onto his back so Juhrnus could reach his belly. It was rounded and tight.

~I hope you built it up well, because we're leaving.

~Where are we going?

~Did you sleep through the entire meeting last night? Lazybones. We're going back to keep an eye on the Regent. And none too soon. I think I'd rather have the plague than try to keep the peace between Kebonsat and Emelovi. I don't know how Metyein can stand it.

Juhrnus had found himself suffering through hours

of icy tension between the two, his injuries making it impossible to escape. Though according to Metyein, this was an improvement. Now at least she spoke to Kebonsat, albeit grudgingly, and more important, she listened. But everything about her, from the tightness around her eyes to the way she held her head stiffly to the side and refused to look at him directly, showed her intense repugnance.

On the other hand, Kebonsat was morose and spoke in short, jerky sentences—to the point and nothing more. He habitually prowled the room like a trapped wolf, keeping as far away from Emelovi as space allowed. As soon as permitted, he escaped, spending the rest of his time schooling the troops in weapons and battle tactics.

~*They are hurting.*

~*They need each other and they are being stupid about it,* Juhrnus retorted.

~*She feels betrayed.*

Juhrnus scratched his head, relenting slightly. She *was* entitled. And still . . . He couldn't blame Kebonsat. At least Emelovi was safe from her brother. For now.

He thought of the sorceress, Kedisan-Mutira. An ache pulsed through his chest. She was far better prepared to defend herself from the likes of Aare than Emelovi was, he reminded himself. But the Regent wasn't the reason he worried for her. It was her companions—the two Scallacian sorcerers. They were her mentors, her teachers, her torturers.

Since her coming to Kodu Riik, he'd felt a connection to her, stronger than friendship, stronger even than love, though he thought he might love her. It was kinship. A soul-deep understanding of each other—it came with a primal urge to protect and defend her. He thought she might feel the same about him. He didn't know. They were, after all, enemies. The Scallacians were no friends of Kodu Riik. They had come to harvest power, to get ahead in the violent political game back home. And in that political game, Kedisan-

Mutira had plans of her own. Plans that made Juhrnus afraid for her. He couldn't wait to get back to Koduteel and learn how she was.

A knock on his door made him start. Metyein entered, his expression grim.

"You're ready then? Good. I've assembled your gear and had your horse brought around. But there's a change of plans. You're not going back to Koduteel. You're going to Patverseme."

For a moment Juhrnus could not speak. Kedisan-Mutira's face rose up against his mind's eye. The last time he'd spoken to her had been just before escaping Koduteel. Aare had been hunting the *ahalad-kaaslane*, but Juhrnus had gone to the palace anyway. He couldn't leave without seeing her. She'd been cold and distant. She'd been wearing almost nothing, her skin smudged with bruises—evidence of what her companions did to her, were doing to her still. Her pale hair had been mussed, her dark eyes troubled. She had been worried for him.

"Why?" he croaked out at last, turning to put on Esper's carry-sling.

"We're going to ask your friend Edelsat for help. And we're going to send word to the Karalis and to the Wizard Guild."

Juhrnus turned back slowly. "You think they'll help?"

Metyein shrugged. "Can't hurt. They certainly won't support Aare."

"Why now?"

"It'll take time for them to get here, if they're going to come."

Juhrnus's jaw jutted and he shook his head. "That's the story you're telling everybody else. But there's more. Why now?"

Metyein's lips pulled into a grimace and he pulled a parchment from a pocket sewn inside his vest. "I found this on my bedstead this morning when I woke up. It's my father's seal. There's no doubt it's authentic."

Juhrnus took the parchment in his fingertips as if it

would burn him. He studied Metyein's face a moment, seeing his pallor, the tightness of his skin and the fear and sorrow lurking deep in his eyes.

"What's it say?"

"Read it."

Juhrnus opened it up gingerly. It didn't say much. Three nonsensical sentences. He read aloud.

" 'The sun rises. Foxes eat the hens when the lace-flies hatch. What duty and honor require.' "

There was no signature, but for the Vare family seal. Not the seal of the Lord Marshal. Juhrnus looked at Metyein.

"What does it mean?"

The other man moistened his lips. "It's a warning. One that he won't repeat. Aare's taking the crown—that's what 'the sun rises' means. It also means my father will swear fealty to him. He'll be leading the army when it comes. And they'll be coming for us when the lace-flies hatch. They'll get here in late March, I'd guess."

"That's what that fox business is?"

Metyein shook his head, an air of hard-suppressed emotion about him. His cheeks were flushed and his fingers shook as he took back the parchment and tucked it back into his vest. When he spoke, he sounded faintly out of breath.

"I don't think so. He has to be talking about the Scallacians. They've committed to Aare. Before we left Koduteel they hadn't shown their magic, except for that first night of their arrival when Reisiltark took them down a peg. But if I'm reading this right, then he's got them. That's why he's warning us. He distrusted Reisiltark because of her magic, but at least she was *ahalad-kaaslane*. The Scallacians are greedy *ganyiks* and he knows it. Being in bed with them is like being in bed with a pox-ridden whore. Sooner or later she'll give you the pox or stick you in the stomach and spill your guts on the floor, then step over you to steal your money."

"You get all that from those few lines? How can you be sure?"

Metyein's face went even grayer. He swallowed hard. But when he spoke, his voice was crisp and businesslike. "The last line. 'What honor and duty require.' It's the message I wrote to him when I left. It has to do with a conversation we had about Aare's rule. I as much as told my father that if Aare came to power, I was going to fight him. It is what honor and duty require." He tapped his fingers against the parchment in his vest. "My father's loyalties are dreadfully torn, especially with Emelovi here. He loved Iisand Samir like a brother. And he loves Kodu Riik. He knows Aare is going to make a pestilent Iisand. He'll destroy Kodu Riik for his own avarice and glory. Inviting the Scallacians here is proof enough of that. But my father is the Lord Marshal, and he's sworn to fulfill that office. Breaking his oath would kill him. And that means serving the rightful Iisand. Who will very shortly be Aare.

"But he has a little time before Aare takes the crown. And so he's sending us this warning. Because duty and honor require it, whether to me as his son or for Emelovi or for Kodu Riik, I don't know. It doesn't matter."

Juhrnus gripped Metyein's shoulder. The other man's muscles were hard as stone. Metyein gave him a little nod of gratitude and stepped away. Juhrnus understood. Metyein and his father had never been close. This note was a declaration of affection. By bending his infamously inflexible honor, the Lord Marshal Vare had told Metyein how much he loved him. But it didn't change the fact that father and son were about to go head-to-head in war.

"So I go to Patverseme," Juhrnus said.

"I'm sorry. I know you wanted to return to Koduteel and find out about your sorceress, but—"

Juhrnus held up a silencing hand. "This is more important. There's nothing I can do for her. Anyhow, she's in Aare's pocket. I should be hoping something happens to her, not trying to stop it."

It was Metyein's turn to sympathize. "Doesn't work that way. You're besotted, and the heart will choose what it wants, regardless of politics. But she's strong. And Lady willing, she'll turn against her fellows. She *did* hint at it."

Juhrnus gave a thin smile. "She's got to have something to take back to her Kilmet that is better than Aare and better than Mysane Kosk. Something to give her the political edge. Such as we are now, it isn't us."

"Have faith in Reisiltark. She'll return and she'll have the answers. That should be enough for the sorceress. She wants to help you. If she can, I think she will."

With nothing left to say, Juhrnus loaded Esper into the sling and followed Metyein outside.

"What's this?" he said, seeing Reisil's dun gelding waiting for him.

"He's a good mountain horse. Take this." Metyein handed him a courier's pouch wrapped in oilskin. "You've got food enough. You remember how to get there?"

"Who could forget?" Juhrnus said dryly. It was on the way to Mekelsek Keep that Upsakes had tried to kill him, Esper, and Reisil. He'd not forget a step of that trail for as long as he lived. Juhrnus checked the cinch and then swung into the saddle. He reached out a hand to Metyein and grasped his arm.

"Best speed," Metyein said. "Bright journey."

"I'll be back before the snow flies."

"See that you are. And if you happen to find any of those plague-healers wandering about, bring them back too."

The corner of Juhrnus's mouth lifted in a half-smile. They'd been scouring every corner of Kodu Riik looking for plague-healers, but so far, no one had found any. If he didn't trust Reisil, he'd have doubted they existed. Bringing one back would make this trip worthwhile, even if no other help came of it.

Juhrnus wheeled Indigo and trotted him toward the

gates. He'd gone no more than halfway when shouts sounded from the walls and a rider stumbled in, his horse sobbing with great, gasping rasps. The animal wove a drunken path, and then stopped short. It swayed, then dropped ponderously to the ground. Its rider pushed off, staggering. Men grabbed him to hold him up as his legs buckled. Metyein ran past Juhrnus, who'd pulled up.

"A message! News from Koduteel!" came a bellowing voice.

"Let me in," ordered Metyein. His commanding voice cut through the tumult, and a corridor opened. He strode forward. The rider was scraped and torn and clearly half-starved. Exhaustion made his hands shake as he proferred the courier's pouch with trembling hands. Metyein took it, putting a gentle hand on the man's shoulder. "Good work. Honor recognizes your bravery and is proud," he said as he took the pouch. He turned to the men supporting the exhausted messenger. "Take him inside and get him some food. Send for a tark."

With that he retreated. Juhrnus dismounted and followed after. The messenger was helped away, but the rest of the gathered men did not disperse, waiting in an uneasy knot. Metyein glanced at them. Then he blew out a breath and opened the pouch. The message was lengthy. He read it, his face turning bleak.

"*Chodha*," he muttered.

"What is it?"

"It's from Karina. I was right. Aare's got the Scallacians. They've begun helping him. Karina says they've wiped out the Fringes—scorched it to the dirt. And they've begun helping him find and question our people. As if he needed it." He looked away for a moment, his teeth biting white dents into his lower lip. "And they are putting charms on his army's weaponry and armor. They're going to be invincible against ordinary swords. Even if Soka brings us the metal to forge our own, it may not help. Who knows how long the wards will hold against their attack."

Juhrnus nodded and leaped back up onto Indigo. "I'd best get going then," he said tersely.

"Don't get caught. And hurry."

Juhrnus hesitated a moment. "Reisil will be back in time. She won't fail us."

With that he galloped away out the gates, west toward Patverseme.

Chapter 24

Yohuac caught Reisil's arm, pulling her away from the long, dangling frond of an enormous tree.

He pointed to the handful of large black ants crawling along the underside of the leaves. "Volcano ants. You do *not* want to get bitten by even one."

Reisil nodded, giving the ants a wide berth and continuing on. Her legs ached and she was drenched to the skin. Her boots seemed full of lead and they were beginning to fall apart from the constant wet. Yohuac had sloughed his sometime that first dreadful night and went barefoot. She thought of the volcano ants and all the other spiders and bugs they'd encountered in their trek through the tangled jungle and shivered. She was keeping her boots until there was nothing left.

Yohuac had pulled a leech off the back of her neck, and she doubted it was the only one she'd find. Her stomach quaked and she firmed it by willpower alone. Reisil glanced upward, trying not to think of a horde of the creatures getting fat on her blood. The light was gray, but at least the rain had stopped. For now. The water dripping from the trees and the dense moisture in the air didn't allow for their clothes to dry. She would almost welcome another storm to get rid of the itchy, sticky heat that prickled her skin and made *everything* chafe.

Misery. Frustration. Agitation.

Saljane hunched low on Reisil's shoulder. Periodically she mantled and shook herself, flicking droplets of water across Reisil's face. It did little good. She was soaked through. A ribbon of fear twisted around her unhappiness. She could not fly. If she could not fly, she could not hunt or help. She was useless.

Reisil stroked Saljane's chest, smelling the animal mustiness of wet feathers.

~It will be well.

But it wouldn't if things kept going this way. Every night, when the rain stopped, Reisil broke her own self-imposed rules on using magic. She set the wards and dried Saljane's sodden feathers. She worried that if she remained wet, mold or mildew would grow, or that the goshawk would catch a fever. But it wasn't enough, and her aid was causing other problems. Saljane's skin was getting scaly, and cracked from the frequent dousings and dryings. It had been eight days since they'd arrived in Cemanahuatl. It would be another eight until they reached Yohuac's village. And then who knew how long after to learn what they need to know and get back. Saljane couldn't keep going this way. Reisil had to fix it.

That night they camped next to the bole of one of the great trees. *Brischil*, Yohuac called it. It was a tall tree, spreading its leaves far above the rest of the canopy. Its roots gripped the ground with knotty fingers. The jungle floor beneath it was mostly clear of undergrowth, but for the stranglevines twining up the ancient column. It was on slightly higher ground, and so they were out of the puddles and rills interlacing the rest of the jungle floor. Silvery-green rodents the size of Reisil's head came to watch them build their fire. Their blunt noses twitched eagerly until they caught sight of Baku. They scurried away, chittering loudly.

Baku gave a loud *hmph*! as he curled up on the ground. Reisil chuckled. Yohuac built a fire while Reisil dried Saljane. Then she began her quest for leeches, removing them with a zap of magic from her finger, pressing herbs against the triangle-shaped bites to stop the bleeding. She found three: one on her ankle, one on her lower back, and one just beneath the collar of her tunic. She examined Yohuac, disgusted when there were none on him.

"How can you keep them off? Does your blood taste bad? Look at all the yummy flesh you've got exposed and still they jump on me and not you."

Yohuac shrugged. He'd returned to wearing his native clothing: a short, sleeveless tunic that barely covered his stomach and short, tight trousers. They were a kind of greenish gray. They were made of the skins of one of the great predator eels that hunted the great river, and they shed the rain like duck feathers. He wore a loincloth over his trousers embroidered in brilliant colors with symbols of animals and plants. He carried a blowpipe on a baldric. With it, he could blow tiny poisoned darts farther than fifty yards.

But even though he wore the same clothes, he didn't look like he had when he'd come to Kodu Riik. The beads were missing from his hair, kept now in the pouch at his side. His hair, like hers, was twined into a single braid down his back. Neither did he wear his gold armbands, two for his biceps, two at his wrists. One of the first, Reisil had destroyed when combating the wizards during their escape from the stronghold. But the others were with the beads in his waist pouch.

"How do you keep them off?" Reisil demanded, crossing her arms and tapping her foot.

He looked shamefaced and glanced away.

"What?"

"It is . . . my magic."

Reisil stared with narrowed eyes. His magic? He'd not done anything with it since they'd left Honor. He'd refused even to talk about the battle against the *nokulas.*

"I make them think I'm a tree," he added with a little shrug.

"A tree."

"I think— I think I've done it all my life. I didn't know I was doing it. But since . . ." He trailed off.

Reisil didn't push him. It was a hard confession. "You do it with the mosquitoes too?"

He nodded.

"And everything else . . . you just send out a magic message that says, 'I'm not tasty, I'm a tree.' What happens when termites get the message? Or a wood-pecker?"

He smiled stiffly. "Then I become earth or water."

Reisil stuck her tongue out at him and his smile widened.

"Can't you tell them I'm a tree too? Or show me how." she demanded, scratching a welt that looked like it had been left by a mosquito the size of a horse. It was a mistake.

"No!" he said sharply, and then marched away into the trees.

Stupid, Reisil chastised herself. And pointless. He was never going to need magic. Not really. He wasn't going to fight the Scallacians or the wizards. He wasn't going to fix Mysane Kosk. She had no reason to push him.

"I guess the leeches and mosquitoes are entitled to their dinner," she said sourly, and added some wood to the sputtering fire.

The rain began just as Yohuac returned. He carried one of the tree beasts that chattered and hectored them from the canopy. Its fur was black with crimson and white patches around its eyes and it had a long, ringed tail. Reisil tried not to see any more as he set about gutting it. The little animals had a human qual-ity that made the eating of them uncomfortable. Still, her stomach growled and gnawed at her backbone, convincing her that no matter what they looked like, the beasts were tasty.

Yohuac put the meat on to roast with some pinkish tubers he'd dug up. Reisil, in the meantime, set the wards and began working on something to keep Sal-jane dry. If she could make a ward for Soka, then surely she could make something to keep the rain off Saljane. She used a wood button, no bigger than the

nail on her little finger. As with Soka's ward, she set
the spell with her words. She thought about borrowing
from the *rinda* she'd learned from the wizards and the
few she'd learned from Nurema, but decided against
it. At least she knew exactly what these words were;
she knew exactly what the spell was supposed to do.

With a yawn and a groan, she struggled to her feet,
going to where Saljane perched on Baku's back. From
her pack she had taken a thick thread. She strung the
button on it and tied it to Saljane's leg.

~*It's not too tight?*

~*No. It will keep the rain away?*

~*I hope so.*

In fact, much to Reisil's surprise and pleasure, not
to mention Saljane's, the ward did work. The rain
sheathed off a finger's breath from the goshawk's
body. She was able to fly and hunt, though she could
do little of either in the middle of a pounding rain.
Pleased with her success, the next night Reisil made
one for herself. She added a bit to keep the leeches
off. Yohuac refused her offer to make him one.

"The *pahtia* begins soon," he said. "I must prepare
my body for it."

There was more to it than that. Reisil could see it.
He'd not pulled away from her, but there was
something. . . . She couldn't put her finger on it. But
there was a subtle shift, as if part of his mind were
somewhere else, somewhere dark. She didn't press
him to talk about it. She had her own secret fears.
Not the least of them was meeting the nahuallis and
getting the answers she needed.

On the sixteenth day in Cemanahuatl, the travelers
came to Yohuac's home. Oceotl, Yohuac's tribe and
village, was situated in a lush pocket-valley at the base
of a thundering waterfall. The sides of the valley were
terraced, the floor an undulating field of yellowing kalmut grain growing to Reisil's waist. The village sat at
the far end of the valley on a rocky hummock surrounded by young *Brischil* trees. Dome-shaped houses
covered the hummock like bees on a hive. At least

two hunded of them. They were made of stranglevines
planted in circles and trained up a central post. These
were interwoven with other vines and strips of bark,
and roofed over with palm fronds. Small holes in the
fronts provided doorways. There were no windows in
any of them.

The houses surrounded a flat, cleared space on the
top of the hill that had been paved with red glazed
tiles. The borders held a pattern of a black jungle cat
running and leaping. There was a great red-clay bowl
in the center, fully eight feet across, where a fire could
be built. Next to it was a large building, capacious
enough to hold several hundred people. Two large
Brischil trees anchored its ends.

The fields and terraces were bustling with people,
the first they'd seen in Cemanahuatl. It had surprised
Reisil until Yohuac drew a map of the terrain. There
was a sacred circle surrounding the Monequi, the
mountain of the fifty-two gods. No one was permitted
to live inside this circle. The Oceotl's tribal territories
were the closest going eastward.

The noon sun shone bright and hot, giving relief
from the constant rains of the past two weeks. Steam
rose up in misty tendrils from the ground and forest,
and rainbow light sparkled in the air. Reisil could hear
the sounds of singing and babies crying and dogs barking. Birds chirped and warbled; insects whirred and
chittered. She could hear the creak and rustle of the
trees, and the crash of arboreal animals bounding
across a trail only they could see. There was a smell
of heady richness to the air, of fertile growth and ex-
otic flowers.

Twining with the natural fragrances were the delec-
table odors of roasting meat and baking bread. Reisil's
stomach growled loudly. She made a face at Yohuac,
who handed her a smooth-skinned red fruit from those
he carried in his pack. Its flesh was yellow and sweet.
Reisil took it gratefully, eating it quickly and wiping
her hands on her pants.

"Ready?" His face was remote and expressionless.

She nodded, her stomach tensing. She resisted the urge to snatch Yohuac's hand, as if she could keep him by her side that way. He'd played his part to bring her here. Now he would go his own way, competing in the *pahtia* so that he could breed magic back into Cemanahuatl, while she learned what she needed to save both their worlds and return home to Kodu Riik. But the sorrow of that loss was eclipsed by the fear that surged suddenly through. The fear she'd managed to ignore until now.

~Do not underestimate what you can do.

~And what if I can't figure it out? Reisil asked, putting words to the dread that threatened to smother her with its impossible weight.

Saljane was silent for so long that Reisil thought she wasn't going to respond.

~If you cannot mend the spell, then everyone will die and no one will be left to care, came Saljane's unhelpful response at last.

~That's encouraging.

Saljane nipped Reisil's ear sharply, making Reisil yelp.

~It is what is. You did not cause this.

As if that were any reason to feel better. Reisil rubbed her ear.

~If I don't find an answer here, I don't know where else to look. And she wasn't all that certain there was an answer to find anywhere, but she didn't say it.

~We won't give up.

~We won't give up, Baku repeated, startling Reisil. She turned to look at him as he crawled down the path behind. His black hide was daubed with mud and dusted with yellow pollen. But his presence was solid and sure, and Reisil took comfort in it. She nodded to him.

~We won't give up. She squared her shoulders and thrust out her chin. There. That was one thing she could be sure of.

They proceeded a few hundred feet along the path. It zigzagged in a long switchback, through trees and

open ground. They came to a wide spot where a
carved post had been set upright on the valley's verge.
The wood was satiny and dark, almost black, and
carved like the face of one of the tree beasts. It was
snarling and its teeth were long and sharp. Yohuac
halted beside it, making a hooting-whistling sound
through his fingers and then resting his palm on the
top of the animal's wooden head.

Reisil felt a tingle of magic sweep her skin and eyed
the post suspiciously. She blinked into spellsight, and
saw that the post was a ward. It was inscribed with
four of the nahuallis' unfamiliar *rinda*. They were
overlaid on one another in an intricate puzzle-shape.

"We must wait here until they come for us," Yohuac said, not removing his hand from the post. Reisil
wondered what would happen if he did.

The minutes ticked past slowly, and Reisil found
herself drawn to the edge of the clearing. The brush
and trees had been cleared from all around their van-
tage point, allowing them a good view down into the
kalmut fields. The village was hidden by the mountain's stone shoulder, and as she watched the play of
the cataract frothing into the pool below, Reisil realized that they made prime targets, exposed as they
were on the hillside. Which was, no doubt, the point.

~They are here.

Saljane mantled, straining herself upward, her head
twisting from side to side. Baku gave a low, warning
snort and went very still, only the tip of his tail flicking
back and forth. He'd clearly sent a warning to Yohuac,
who stood rigidly, as if expecting a blow.

A host of warriors came out of the grasses on either
side of the trail. They had Yohuac's dark coloring,
his black hair, blunt, prominent features, and strong,
graceful limbs. They wore their hair braided with
beads, and each wore a treasure's worth of gold. They
were quiet and predatory. They carried bows, spears,
short swords, and blowguns, and several had other
weapons Reisil couldn't identify.

No one spoke. The warriors ghosted out of the grass

and stood waiting with weapons aimed, eyes inscrutable and hard. Reisil flicked a sharp glance at Yohuac, but he continued to wait, hand resting on the post.

Reisil didn't know how much time had passed. Sweat trickled down her back, and the bottom of her right foot itched horribly. And she had a strong urge to urinate. Still, the ring of men surrounding them didn't look particularly sympathetic to her need. She shifted her weight and the nocked arrows before her lifted a hairsbreadth. Reisil froze.

At last the nahuallis came. She knew they were coming long before they emerged from the trees and rocks obscuring the trail below. They radiated power and a kind of *presence* that hinted at the beating heart of the world. For a moment, before they came into sight, Reisil thought they must certainly be superhuman, like the Lady with her crystal talons and unworldly eyes. But they were just women.

There were seventeen of them. They walked up the trail in two parallel lines, with one in the lead. They were dressed simply, with short tunics, trousers, and belt pouches. They wore their hair loose and long with none of the braiding the men favored. They wore an Iisand's ransom in gold and stones: earrings and necklaces, wrist and armbands, rings and headbands. Everything about them was graceful, seductive, and primal. None carried anything more threatening than a knife, but Reisil could feel their menace. She swallowed, her throat dry. No wonder Yohuac wanted to throw himself on the ground when he was around them.

The nahuallis reached the outer edge of the surrounding warriors and broke apart, threading through until they'd grouped around the travelers. None spoke, but paced in a circle, scrutinizing each intruder from head to toe. Now that Reisil could see them up close, she realized the women represented a range of ages, from a girl just stepping into womanhood, to a middle-aged mother whose hair was liberally streaked with gray. They were each strong, supple, and fit.

Finally they came to a halt as if by command. Reisil wondered if they had some sort of silent speech, the way the *ahalad-kaaslane* did. A younger woman, perhaps a few years older than Reisil, approached. Her nose was crooked and her eyes were a pale honey-brown. Her teeth were bright white and her lips were sensuous and full. She stopped, her legs spread, her gaze fixed on the golden ivy trailing down Reisil's jaw and neck. She lifted her hand as if to touch it, but Saljane snapped her beak and the woman pulled her fingers back, rubbing them together thoughtfully.

She opened her mouth and spoke, rattling off in a language Reisil didn't understand. Reisil frowned, shaking her head. By the Lady, she'd gotten so used to the fact that Yohuac spoke the Kodu Riikian language that it hadn't occurred to her that she would need to learn his!

~I can give it to you as I gave him yours, Baku said.

~Too late now. They know I can't. It'll be strange if suddenly I can. And I'm not sure they should know about you and Saljane being able to speak, or do magic.

~They will know my nature, if they care to look.

~I know, but they might think you're some kind of pet. Let's leave it that way for now, all right? Until we know more about what we're getting into.

Reisil couldn't say what drove her caution. But the wizards had seemed friendly and welcoming before she realized what they were—when she already knew what they were. The nahuallis might be no better. Reisil wasn't going to take the chance.

~Tell Yohuac. Don't let on about you and Saljane.

Baku agreed. The nahualli turned away from Reisil and went to Yohuac. There proceeded a lengthy conversation with her asking short, clipped questions and him making long, humble explanations. His hand never left the post. Could he even lift it? Reisil blinked into spellsight, trying to decipher the ward. It was interwoven so tightly, she couldn't tell what it did. But as she looked closer, she could see that his hand was held in a pair of what looked like spectral jaws with cruel, hooked teeth.

Anger made Reisil act without thinking. She reached for her power. It whipped out, catching the jaws of the ward and snapping it in two. There was a loud *crack!* like summer thunder. It echoed from the valley walls and scorched through the air as the ward shattered and the post burst into flame. Yohuac jerked his hand free just in time.

There was a moment of frozen stillness. Suddenly the nahuallis whirled on Reisil. There was a rush of friction in the air as magic collected in a vortex. Their impassive masks dropped and their faces came alive with emotion. Yohuac began yelling. Reisil drew on her own power, feeling it erupt into flames around her hands. Saljane shrieked, her wings snapping wide, buffeting Reisil's cheek.

Yohuac leaped forward, standing with his back to Reisil and facing the nahuallis, ratcheting out words in a sharp staccato. He dipped his head so that he was staring at the ground, his hands lifted in suppliance.

Seeing his attitude, shock struck Reisil like a physical blow and she realized her mistake. Bright Lady! What was she doing? But her anger flared again when Yohuac dropped to his stomach. Reisil could barely hold herself in. She lifted her gaze to stare at the nahualli witch who'd first questioned her. Their eyes locked and held. Reisil's vision began to swirl with a red haze, and she knew her eyes were turning red and the ivy on her face was flaring gold. She smirked when the nahualli's arrogance faded for a moment and uncertainty made her frown.

And then the uncertainty was gone. She stiffened, staring arrogantly at Reisil. She reached out deliberately with her foot and set it on Yohuac's head. His voice cut off. There was a growl in Reisil's head from Baku. The coal-drake's talons cut deep gouges into the dirt.

The nahualli's smug expression dared Reisil to do something. Reisil's fingers curled, and sparks of magic danced hot and sharp across her skin. But she held back. This was not what she'd come to do. Nor would Yohuac forgive her for rescuing him. It wasn't her place.

For long moments she waited, neither bowing nor battling. They had sent for her to help. She would not come as a servant or a beggar. The moments stretched and finally the nahualli stepped back and said something to Yohuac. He rose fluidly to his feet. The nahualli examined him, reaching out to touch his hair. He flushed, staring at the ground, answering her questions in short, dull phrases. She stood back, her expression dark with emotion Reisil couldn't read. She spoke again and now Yohuac turned to Reisil.

"I've told her who you are. She asks if you will come to the village."

Reisil's brows flicked up. "Asks, does she? I bet. Well, tell her I'll come." *And tell her she might learn some manners.* But Reisil didn't say it. Antagonizing them wouldn't help. She let her magic seep away, the red haze clearing from her vision. A sign of good faith.

Yohuac relayed her message and swiftly the group began down the path. The nahuallis arrayed themselves around Reisil and Baku, with Yohuac squeezed out to trail behind. The warriors followed, their weapons still held at the ready.

~*Quite a welcome*, Reisil said waspishly to Saljane.

~*Be careful with them*, Saljane replied, her steel mind sharp with suspicion.

~*They are hungry*, came Baku's gravelly voice, tight with anger. *They covet you.*

Covet? The word sent a chill through Reisil's blood. She thought of the wizards and the *nokulas*. She was beginning to feel like a juicy bone amongst starving wolves.

She lifted her chin. Let them do their worst. They'd find she was harder to swallow than they thought.

Chapter 25

It grated on the nahuallis that they could not communicate with Reisil without Yohuac's help. Reisil couldn't help but enjoy their consternation. Their haughtiness reminded her of the arrogant Scallacians, and she did not like the scornful way they treated Yohuac. She thought of Juhrnus and his doomed feelings for Kedisan-Mutira. Trust them both to choose such impossible, hopeless loves.

As they descended down the trail into the village, people crowded around in watching silence. There was a wariness to them, a tautness that came from living with constant danger. She didn't see any children.

~*They have hidden them*, Baku inserted suddenly.

Reisil started, wondering if Baku was going to continue to pass her information. It would be a whole lot easier if he could just tell her what the nahuallis were thinking. She sighed quietly. Or maybe not. She already didn't like them much. And if she actually knew what they were thinking, she had a feeling she'd like them less. And her stealing their secrets wouldn't make them interested in helping her. They'd probably do the opposite. Better to just negotiate her way normally and hope Baku would warn her if they were plotting something truly dire.

The nahuallis took them to a small, round building on the river side of the village. Unlike the rest of the houses, it was made of clay brick. They stopped, the lead nahualli turning to Yohuac and spitting out a long speech. He bowed deferentially and turned to Reisil, still looking down at the ground.

"You must go inside and bathe. They will bring you clothing. When you are done, they will come for you."

"What about you?"

"I must be cleansed as well." There was a peculiar twist to his tone that Reisil didn't understand. "Baku will stay with you. They should think he belongs to you."

With that he bowed again and backed away. He was then escorted away by a half dozen warriors.

There was a short walkway up to the bathhouse, its entry bracketed by two carved doorposts, much like the wardpost along the trail. These were covered with strange, violent-looking creatures and painted in vivid yellows, oranges, and reds. The lead nahualli motioned Reisil to pass between and inside. Reisil blinked into spellsight. Spells glowed softly in the posts, matched by those set into the walls of the building itself.

She took a breath and crossed between, feeling a *zing* across her skin like a corpse's cold touch. She started and eyed the nahualli askance. The witch only looked down her nose with that superior, arrogant look and gestured impatiently. Reisil swallowed her suspicion and went inside, leaving Baku to wait for her.

The walls were covered in a mosaic of precious stones set in gold and silver. The pictures were bold and stark and more than a little grotesque. They were of animals and the jungle, and everything seemed out of proportion. As she scanned the walls, Reisil gave a little shudder at the violence and lewd sexuality of the images. Her gaze snagged one image. Fully half the curved wall was devoted to a single god. *Ilhuicatl*, Reisil guessed, remembering what Yohuac had said about the nahuallis being favored by the greatest of all the fifty-two gods.

This image was as garish and repulsive as the others, more so because it pushed out of the wall as if the god were coming alive. His legs were outstretched, his feet like the roots of the great *Brischil* trees. His penis thrust out between his legs. Made of blue-green stone, it was broad and hollow. It formed a great spigot that reached out more than six feet and sprayed steaming water into the large pool that curved in front. His arms were twisted around by serpents, and in the palms of his hands were eyes. Each of his fingers was tipped with red mouths from which protruded long, supple tongues. He wore a feather headdress of rainbow hues, and from his ears dangled bloody heads like earrings. His nipples were each the sun and moon, and above them, his expression was seductive, lustful, his tongue curling hungrily from his mouth. His eyes were faceted obsidian.

The central steaming pool into which *Ilhuicatl* poured himself was large enough for a dozen people. It was surrounded by smaller pools containing water of varying degrees. Along the walls were woven mats and baskets of brushes, combs, soaps, and towels. The nahualli led Reisil to a corner and, by pointing, ordered her to strip. When Reisil hesitated, the witch drew herself up and stared, her pale eyes like shards of glass.

Reisil drew a breath and blew it out.

~I guess I wouldn't mind a hot bath, she said to Saljane.

And as she thought about sinking into the hot water, she had a sudden sense of the grime on her skin, the itchy greasiness of her hair, and the general bad odor emanating from her. She wrinkled her nose.

"If I were you, I'd want me to have a good scrub too," she said to the nahualli, who only frowned, not understanding.

Reisil lifted Saljane down to perch on a stool, and then removed her clothes. The nahualli watched, pointing to a basket where Reisil could deposit her dirty things, and another for her gauntlet and weapons. As Reisil finished disrobing, the nahualli stared askance at the gold leaf pattern chasing down Reisil's cheek and neck and across her ribs. Quickly she caught herself and pointed peremptorily to the main pool.

Reisil hesitated, flushing, suddenly recalling with force how full her bladder was. She pointed to her stomach and looked around meaningfully. The nahualli led Reisil to a small alcove where tall clay pots were set in a line on the floor. They had wide rims for sitting, and lids. Beside them were baskets of fresh, fuzzy green leaves. The witch waited outside while Reisil relieved herself.

After, she followed docilely to the large pool. The water was far hotter than comfortable, and Reisil yelped when she dove in, swallowing some water and coming up choking. When her coughs subsided, she turned to look for the nahualli and blushed fiercely when she realized the woman was right behind her in the water, also naked. She was toting another basket and from it pulled a scrub brush and a handful of what looked like sticky sand.

The witch pushed Reisil to the shallow end of the pool, until she was standing only ankle-deep. Much to Reisil's mortification, the nahualli began to wash her, starting at her feet. The brush had stiff bristles and scraped painfully against her skin. But the other woman's hands were like iron shackles around Reisil's leg, uncaring of any pain she might be inflicting.

~*Or she's enjoying it*, Reisil said, gritting her teeth and forcing herself to stand still. She couldn't help but flinch when the nahualli's ministrations went higher. The other woman prodded Reisil's legs wide as she scrubbed into Reisil's intimate places and higher. When she was through, the nahualli dropped the brush back into the basket and set to work on Reisil's hair. She unraveled the braid and pushed Reisil back into the deeper waters. Reisil's skin stung painfully as the hot water closed around her.

The nahualli was no less vigorous with Reisil's hair, scrubbing her scalp with fingers Reisil could have sworn were tipped in stone. Then she combed out the tangles with equally little heed for any discomfort she

might be causing. When she was through, Reisil was
clean and sore and bright red. She touched her head
gingerly, feeling as if she'd been scalped.

The nahualli nodded satisfaction and motioned for
Reisil to go to the pool farthest from the entry door.
Reisil swam over and lifted herself over into the indicated pool, letting out a startled squeal. It was as cold
as icemelt. The nahualli laughed and jumped in beside
her. They shivered there for fully a minute before the
nahualli indicated they could step out.

The basket of Reisil's filthy clothes had disappeared.
In its place were tribal garments. The nahualli helped
Reisil to dry herself and then dress. Last she combed
Reisil's hair out, waving her finger disapprovingly
when Reisil would have braided it up again.

"All right," Reisil said, lifting her hands up. "You
win."

Reisil caught Saljane's amusement at Reisil's tone
of defeat. The nahualli waited impatiently as Reisil
strapped on her weapons and donned her gauntlet,
lifting Saljane back on her shoulder.

~You are supposed to be on my side, she told the
goshawk.

~I am always on your side.

~Well, try not to find it so funny, then.

There were no shoes. Her tattered boots were gone,
and when she asked, pointing to her feet, the nahualli
shook her head, lifting her own bare feet. They were
hard with calluses. The other woman smiled, more
than a little maliciously, and then led Reisil out of the
bathhouse. As she caught her reflection in one of the
pools, Reisil realized that, dressed as she was, she
looked a lot like her guide. The realization made her
stomach tighten. Bile flooded the back of her tongue.

For a while, at the wizards' stronghold, she'd worn
their robes and let them call her Kvepi. They thought
she was one of them; they'd wanted her to be one of
them. For a while, she'd almost lost herself there,
wanting so much to belong that she forgot what the
wizards were. She'd not repeat her mistake here, she

told herself somberly. She knew who she was. No matter who or what her mother had been, she was not nahualli. She was *ahalad-kaaslane*.

Baku was nowhere in sight when they emerged from the bathhouse. Reisil craned her neck about, but he was gone. Maybe to find Yohuac, or possibly to investigate the village. She gave a little shrug. There were dozens of things he could be doing. He was well equipped to take care of himself, and he'd return in his own time. He certainly wouldn't be grateful if she made a fuss over him not staying put.

The witch led her through the village. The ground was muddy and full of sharp pebbles. Reisil hadn't gone without shoes for more than a year, and not regularly before that, and her feet were tender. She stumbled and limped along, her teeth set. She was sure that the nahualli was taking pleasure in her discomfort, and she wasn't about to give her the satisfaction of complaining.

They arrived at the red-tile circle on the top of the hill. A fire had been built in the great bowl, waiting to be lit. There was an eerie silence. Though the jungle sounds continued, the sounds of the people were gone.

The nahualli pointed to a place on the tile, gesturing for Reisil to remain standing. Her back was to the valley and she faced the large building on the opposite side of the circle, its ends fixed in place by two of the great *Brischil* trees. The nahualli turned and disappeared among the buildings, leaving Reisil alone. She stood awkwardly, feeling eyes on her. She shifted in place, feeling exposed.

~*What happens next?*

~*We will see*, came Saljane's unhelpful answer.

~*Some hospitality*, Reisil said, beginning to feel peevish. Her skin still felt shredded by her bath, and she was hungry. *If this is the way they welcome friends, how do they welcome enemies?*

Reisil continued to wait, gritting her teeth against the sudden itch that attacked the instep of her left foot. Suddenly, a deep, throbbing gong sounded. It echoed from the valley walls and faded into silence. When the last reverberation had died, it sounded again. And then once more. With each booming throb, Reisil twitched, feeling a vibration in the tiles beneath her feet. Then silence descended again. This time it was complete. No animals, no jungle sounds, nothing.

At last there came a slow, steady cadence of several drums being beaten together. Then out of the large building came two lines of women carrying copper drums shaped like hourglasses and etched with geometric patterns. The women were young. They wore their hair long, with silver bands around their upper arms, wrists, and ankles. Each wore a silver circlet around her neck etched with *rinda* and set with a red ruby the size of a walnut.

They were dressed as Reisil was, but their clothing was decorated with the mysterious *rinda* symbols in a wide spectrum of vivid colors. And there were a lot of different symbols. Reisil lost count as the women entered the tile circle, splitting apart and going around until they met in a ring. As one, they turned inward to face the fire and Reisil. All told, there were twenty-eight of them.

Their measured drumming sped faster, developing a complex pattern. The women stared at the unlit fire, their hands slapping and pounding, their muscles bulging with effort.

Suddenly they stopped.

The silence was profound. Reisil felt herself slumping, as if she'd been holding herself against a great wind that ceased without warning.

Across from her, four women stepped back, opening the circle. Now the senior nahuallis emerged from the great building. Their jewelry was predominantly gold, set with a black-veined blue stone Reisil had never seen before. Their hair was also long, but it had been dyed a deep purple, the color of a humid summer sky before a terrible storm. Instead of drums, they carried small copper bowls of various-colored paints.

These women bore with them a tide of inexorable power. It was so thick it made it difficult to breathe. They filed inside the outer ring, surrounding Reisil in a second circle. The outer ring closed. Reisil flinched when the drummers struck a thunderous clap. At the same moment, the interior witches dropped to their knees. The drums began a low, rumbling beat, like rapid heartbeats. The kneeling nahuallis crawled forward to the great stone fire bowl. Then they began a slow, deliberate inscription of *rinda* on the exterior of the bowl. Each would dip her finger into her copper pigment bowl and inscribe a series of figures. Then she'd move left and paint some more.

Slowly a vibrant, intricate pattern emerged as the symbols overlapped. When the fire bowl was completely covered, they spiraled outward on the paving tiles. Reisil watched avidly, trying to understand the arrangement and the purpose. To no avail. There were too many *rinda,* and the layering was too intricate.

When they came to the tile Reisil stood on, they made a single inscription between her feet in midnight blue. They finished at the feet of the drummers. When the painters stood, they too were outside the design.

~I don't like this, Reisil said with foreboding.

~We must be patient, Saljane said, but she ruffled her feathers uneasily, twisting her head and sweeping the gathered nahuallis with a crimson glare.

They *had* sent for her, Reisil told herself firmly, eyeing the spell apprehensively.

Now the elder nahuallis began inscribing symbols on the faces of the young drummers, turning once again from left to right. Soon their faces were covered entirely.

As if on cue, the cadence of the drums changed suddenly, becoming short and slow. Reisil felt her heart slow with it. She breathed deeply, forcing her tense muscles to relax.

The senior nahuallis stepped outward between the drummers, who stepped inward at the same time and fell to their knees, nestling their drums between their thighs.

The drums stopped. The silence was turgid. Reisil's stomach clenched in anticipation.

Then, without warning, one of the elder nahuallis extended her arms upward, tilting her head back. She began chanting a series of three words. The sounds were guttural and hard. One by one, each woman in the outer circle added her voice to the thickening rope of words. Their voices wove together, building louder. Softly the drums joined in, a rumble beneath the thunder.

At first Reisil thought it coincidence when the wind picked up. But quickly it gusted harder and clouds scudded across the sky from nowhere, piling overhead in blue-black billows. Beneath her feet, the ground began to quiver. Reisil started and braced her legs as the vibrations tickled over her skin.

Lightning flashed, spreading across the northern horizon like the roots of a great tree before closing in a net around the valley. Thunder cracked, shaking the air. The hairs on Reisil's arms prickled. Saljane shrieked, clamping her talons tightly, but Reisil could hardly hear her.

Closer and closer came the storm, spiraling tighter, pulling downward like water down a drain. Reisil felt the pressure of the air against her chest. Her wildly beating heart ached inside her ribs. She felt her hair lifting, floating on the invisible currents in the air. Around her the nahuallis' hair did the same. Their eyes gleamed in the bruised darkness, making them look almost demonic. Reisil's stomach jerked and bucked. She wanted to reach for her power, but held herself firmly in check. Who knew what adding a bit of magic to this maelstrom would do?

Suddenly the elder nahuallis spun to face inward. They grasped one another's hands and pointed toward the fire bowl. Their faces twisted and their necks tented with the effort of their shouted chant.

Sound stopped. Fear bulled through Reisil. The junior nahuallis continued to shout and pound with furious energy, but Reisil could no longer hear anything, not even the beat of her heart.

~What is happening? Saljane's mindvoice was taut with fear, but Reisil grasped at it like a lifeline.

~I don't know. But look!

The painted spell on the tiles, fire bowl, and faces had begun to glow with a harsh light. A tightening in the air caught her attention. It was as if someone were winding the threads of the world around a spindle, pulling them tight. Reisil looked up and gasped, her stomach flip-flopping.

The clouds and lightning had pulled together in a massive finger cloud. They spun together tightly, elongating, dropping lower and lower. The revolving tip gleamed with pure, silver energy, as if all the lightning had been sucked inside and concentrated into a single point of ferocious intensity.

Lower and lower it danced in a bumbling path, winding back and forth. The closer it came, the brighter the painted *rinda* grew. Reisil held her breath. The funnel swung wide, and trees on the eastern lip burst into flame. The nahuallis strained, their faces screwing up with effort. Still silence smothered sound. Even the wind had ceased.

Lower still it came. Reisil could feel the heat of the contained energy as the tip of the funnel swung close and then far. She smelled the odor of burnt hair and metal. The point of the cone slowed, becoming steady. It dropped purposefully, speeding toward the spell circle and the gathered women. Reisil turned her head away from the white heat.

The tip of captured lightning touched the wood in the fire bowl. The ground heaved. Reisil swayed, flinging out her arms to steady herself. Instinct told her that moving from her place would be deadly. She caught herself, flexing her knees and tightening her muscles.

White, blue, and orange flames shot from the fire bowl, stretching hundreds of feet high inside the fun-

nel. Reisil could now feel the pull of the compressed
wind, deflected by the painted *rinda*. Then suddenly
the nahuallis in the outer circle stepped forward, onto
the border of the spell.

Time slowed. Reisil watched in disbelief as the flames
shot higher, attentuating, and then sucking back down
with a shriek that shattered the veil of silence and set
her teeth on edge. They plunged down to the fire bowl
and erupted outward. The painted *rinda* flared incandescent. Reisil closed her eyes, but continued to see
phantom flashes across her eyelids. Heat rippled over
her in waves, each one more searing than the last. She
held her breath, feeling as if the insides of her nose,
mouth, and throat were on fire. Raw power flowed
around her, thick and fast as molten lava.

But it did not burn. It caressed.

Reisil opened her eyes, blinking into spellsight.

Her jaw dropped. The funnel and clouds were gone.
Inside the circle was a column of power, quiescent and
biddable. Each of the nahuallis, including herself, was
anchored into it, like the pegs on a loom, sharing the
weaving between. The power inside was not merely
raw energy, but it had been channeled into a pattern
that could exist beyond the nahuallis. Like the recep-
tacles that the wizards used to hold magic until they
wanted it later.

But as she looked, realization hit her. A worm of
ice burrowed into her stomach. All the nahuallis were
on the exterior edge of the tapestry. Only she was
within. She blinked out of spellsight. The nahuallis had
broken off their chants and their drumming. They
were looking expectantly at her.

Reisil caught her lip in her teeth, looking down at
her feet. The test was clear. She was caught in the
spell. To live, to be free, she had to get to the edge.
And she had to be careful. Any wrong move would
kill her. She could read it in the impassive challenge
in the eyes of the watching women. If she was the one
they'd sent Yohuac to find, she would be able to get
out. If she wasn't, then she didn't deserve to.

Chapter 26

Reisil swore under her breath.

~And I just let them stand here and paint us into this mess. Maybe the test isn't whether I can get out, but whether I'm stupid enough to walk into a trap in the first place.

~We are here now. What can be done?

Which meant stop whining and get on with it. Reisil drew in a quiet breath and blew it out. The nahuallis were watching her. All right. They wanted to see what she could do; she'd show them.

She flexed her fingers, surveying the spell with a quick glance. She had no doubt she was meant to leave it intact. All that work wasn't meant to be wasted. It was a good test. Shattering the spell would be easy enough. And bloody. But not disturbing it while she withdrew—that was finesse. She looked at the figure they'd traced between her feet. It was painted in midnight blue. An uneven triangle contained several symbols within. The first was shaped like a three lying on its back. Above it were three horizontal dots, and above them a jagged line with four points, reminding Reisil of mountains. The ends of the line were hooked inward, and the left side was taller than the right. She frowned. What did it mean?

Reisil blinked into spellsight, and the symbol changed colors, turning white. The rest of the *rinda* were shaded in rich rainbow hues. Hers was the only white one in the bunch. Which likely meant it really wasn't part of the larger spell. So moving wouldn't likely destabilize the tapestry. Did that mean she could just walk out?

She gave a slight shake of her head. No. What kind of test would that be? She rubbed her mouth, considering.

When she'd freed the plague-healers and Baku, she'd unraveled the wizards' spells, pulling much of the power through herself. Could she do the same here? She eyed the spell doubtfully. She wouldn't know where the weakness was—where the *rinda* weren't drawn quite right, or where they were spaced too far apart. And even if she did know, she didn't think she could draw that much energy into her. Rupturing this spell would kill her, and maybe all the nahuallis too. There had to be another way.

Reisil racked her brain. She dared not call on her own power, and tapping into the tapestry might unravel it, unleashing the tremendous power it contained in an uncontrolled *snap!*

Which left her with walking out.

It was too easy. It was suicidal.

It's our only choice. They'll not wait forever.

~*Then let us be quick.* Saljane sounded more irritable than frightened, and Reisil smiled.

~*Yes, let us be quick. But first*—

She held up her fist and Saljane hopped onto it, lifting her wings for balance. Then Reisil bowed to the fire bowl. She had no doubt it represented *Ilhuicatl*, the father of the gods. She then turned in a circle, bowing her head to the nahuallis, careful to remain on her tile. Then she bent and smudged her finger through the midnight paint, obliterating the symbol. She hesitated. It *was* too simple.

But hard on the heels of that thought came an idea. She smiled. Would it work? It was worth a try. She dipped her finger into the paint and began writing. She didn't use the wizard *rinda*. Her own words had worked well enough on the wards for Saljane and herself. And they felt right. Two words, twined together, repeating in an endless chain around the edge of the tile.

Silence.

Stillness.

When she was satisfied, Reisil stood. The nahuallis watched impassively. Reisil traced the words on the back of each hand. That should do it. She hoped.

~Ready?

~As ever.

~Let's give it a try.

Reisil reached for her magic. It roared up furiously, like a pack of rabid dogs. She was ready for it. She caught it tightly and fed it into her *rinda*. Power ran around the letters. Her hands felt like they were being gnawed. For a moment the pain was everything. Then it faded. And so did the *rinda*. First they turned gray and then vanished altogether. Reisil stared down at her hands. The paint was gone. But when she blinked into spellsight, the *rinda* were still there, glowing a pale white. *Yes!*

Reisil turned and faced the edge of the circle closest to her. The watching nahuallis were glancing askance at each other. Reisil smiled. One moment the strange nahualli from another world was trapped in the middle of their spell; the next she'd vanished.

Without hesitation, Reisil stepped out onto the spell. Nothing happened. Her jaw tightened in triumph. The power of the nahualli spell swirled around her. It felt almost alive. She took another step. Another. Slowly she walked the ten steps to the edge, passing between the kneeling nahuallis and out.

She staggered, feeling suddenly light, as if a tremendous weight had been lifted away. She panted, her lungs filling with warm, moist jungle air, fragrant with flowers and greenery. The nahuallis neither moved nor spoke, but they were clearly unsettled by her disappearance. Deliberately Reisil rubbed the backs of her hands against her legs. The painted *rinda* smeared, and there was a small jerk as her spell snapped. Inside the tile circle, the giant column of power flinched and quivered in response.

"All right then," she said out loud, knowing they couldn't understand her. "When's dinner?"

Her words acted like a goad on the nahuallis. They began chanting again. They rose to their feet, the outer circle walking a path around, stitching in and out of the drummers. The paint on the faces of the inner circle of younger nahuallis slid away, down to the ground.

Slowly they pushed farther inside, spiraling back to the smoldering fire bowl. Reisil watched, using her spellsight. With every step, the senior nahuallis pushed at the tapestry of power they'd created, shrinking it. As they did, the column at the center compressed and shrank.

When they reached the fire bowl, they stopped. The power had condensed into a thick, glowing mat. Reisil marveled at its complexity and the immensity of the magic it contained. What would they do with it now?

Even as she watched, she was answered. A young nahualli witch who had not participated in the ceremony now approached. She was perhaps thirteen summers old. She was naked except for the jeweled copper bands around her arms and ankles, and the yellow *rinda* blanketing her skin. Her head was shaved. In her outstretched hands, she carried an obsidian box the size of Reisil's fist.

The girl ducked between two nahuallis and climbed into the fire bowl, unmindful of smoldering coals. She crossed to the center, beneath the spell tapestry. She lifted the lid of the box. Inside was a large blue stone heavily veined with black, like the one in the jewelry worn by the elder nahuallis. It was oval-shaped. Reisil winced as the girl knelt in the coals and ash, her knees splayed wide, lifting the box up level with her forehead. Her face remained expressionless. Reisil hoped the *rinda* painted on her body protected her from the heat.

The nineteen elder nahuallis now began to lower their arms, keeping them extended as they switched into a new chant. The drummers joined in, closing ranks behind them. As Reisil watched, the weaving of power grew smaller. Slowly it shrank, brightening into a point of shimmering silver light. The nahuallis eased their hands down, guiding it onto the black-veined rock inside the box. The girl shuddered as the compressed weaving settled onto the stone. Her arms shook as if suddenly loaded with an extraordinary weight. Then with a sudden flourish of drums, the nahuallis fell silent.

One reached down and set the lid on the box and took it. The girl rose awkwardly. Her skin was reddened, but otherwise unblemished.

The nahualli with the box now turned to Reisil, motioning her to follow them into the large building. Reisil did as directed.

She passed inside the door of what could only be the village meeting house. The walls were lined with a smooth, green wood polished to a high sheen. The east and west ends were the knotted trunks of the ancient *Brischil* trees. The floor was a mosaic of blue tiles of every hue, none larger than Reisil's thumb. It slanted downward to the center, where there was another firebowl made of red clay, this one much smaller than the one outside. Overhead, a chimney hole had been cut in the roof. One of the younger nahuallis rushed forward to light it, while others lit the candle bowls scattered on shelves around the walls and in shallow inlets in the floor.

Cushions were piled against the walls in a tumbling array of brilliant color and pattern. The junior nahuallis dragged these forward, setting them in concentric circles around the fire.

One of the elder nahuallis gestured for Reisil to sit in the innermost circle. She acquiesced, more than pleased at the chance to rest. She sat cross-legged. Saljane settled in her lap.

The elder nahuallis filled out the rest of the interior circle. The younger ones rushed in and out, bringing platters of food and drinks. Reisil ate hungrily. She wouldn't have cared if it were carrion. But in fact, the food was delicious. The meat was cut in strips and marinated in hot spices and fruit juices. The effect was a sweet heat that exploded on her tongue. The vegetables were crunchy, with an intense citrus flavor. The bread was spongy and hot and flat. The drink she was given was a fruit juice that was cold and refreshing. Saljane was content to watch Reisil gorge herself, having hunted that morning.

At last the dishes were gathered and bowls of hot water passed around for washing. Reisil dried herself on a proferred towel. The food and the heavy fragrance of the candles made her sleepy, and she struggled to remain awake.

She started when a gong sounded, echoing brassily through the chamber. Her blood surged and the sleepiness vanished. The door opened and Yohuac was escorted inside, two nahuallis bracketing him.

Like Reisil, he'd been scrubbed and dressed in fresh clothing. He wore the gold jewelry he'd worn before, including a new armband to replace the one Reisil had destroyed. His hair had been braided, though without any decorative beads or ornaments. What was appallingly altered were his expression and carriage. He bore himself humbly, even ashamedly. His kept his head bowed, staring at the floor. Anger flared in Reisil, and she bit the inside of her cheek. This was Yohuac's choice, she reminded herself.

They led him to an open place, his escorts stepping back a pace. Yohuac remained standing, the firelight gleaming on his skin. A staccato question was launched at him. He answered quickly and obediently. Another question, this time a longer answer.

The questions lasted for more than four hours. The nahuallis interrupted often, arguing amongst themselves, then prodding at him for more information.

They directed nothing at Reisil, and she understood nothing they said. Baku did not respond to her questions. She was forced to wait with gritted teeth.

The nahuallis' voices rose. Yohuac blanched, looking sickly. He argued weakly. They rebuked him. Even Reisil could understand that. She bit her tongue, her lip curling when he dropped down to the floor, wiggling forward on his belly. The witches observed Yohuac with a mixture of aloof disdain and complacent privilege. They let him lie there until Reisil thought she'd scream. Her fingernails cut dents in her palms.

~If they wanted to make a good impression, they failed, she snarled to Saljane.

~This is for you. They want you to know their power. Saljane sounded equally angry.

Reisil thought about that column of tremendous magic. Reisil eyed the many black-veined blue stones that studded the nahuallis' jewelry. Each was a twin to the stone from the ceremony. Reisil blinked into spellsight. A chill like ice slid down her throat into her stomach. The room glistened like a pouchful of tiny suns. The collected power was immense. She shivered. They could swat her like a mosquito if they wanted. What did they need her for?

~Some doors cannot be opened but with a key. Might is not all.

It wasn't nothing either.

Reisil stroked stiff fingers down Saljane's back, forcing herself to remain impassive as Yohuac continued to abase himself. She scanned the austere, proud faces of the assembled women. There was a tightness to their expressions, a hard-held fury. Reisil licked her dry lips. They needed her, and they hated that they did. They wanted her to know how puny her power was compared to theirs. She was supposed to feel small and helpless, obligated and grateful. She was supposed to feel flattered just to be able to serve them.

~I don't think so, she said caustically to Saljane. But brave words aside, Reisil knew she had to be careful.

And very fast. The nahuallis were caught between the mortar of their need and the pestle of their pride. It was an intolerable situation. If their patience failed before Reisil succeeded, they'd turn on her. It was as certain as the sun.

At last Yohuac was given permission to rise. He did so, his head hanging low. Reisil sensed his anger, leashed tightly. One of the nahuallis addressed him again, her words unrelenting. Then to Reisil's surprise, he turned, his gaze fixed on the ground before her.

"I am to tell you that you are welcome as a magician. You could not have survived their test otherwise. But while it is accepted that you have power, you must prove your worth to the Teotl. You must make a journey to Atli Cihua, the sacred ground where *Ilhuicatl* first breathed life into the nahuallis. You will be given no food, water, weapons, or clothing. It is a far journey, one that will take an entire turning of the moon. It will be fraught with many dangers. When you arrive there—" Yohuac broke off, his muscles knotting with the effort of controlling his emotions. When he spoke again, his voice was frayed. "When you arrive, you will be judged by the Teotl. If they find you worthy, you will be permitted to speak and be heard."

Reisil stared in disbelief. Their world was being torn apart and they wanted to waste an entire month testing her? She shook her head, scowling. It was ludicrous!

~He says you must not refuse. There is no other way. Baku inserted in her mind abruptly.

~And what will happen to him?

~He will prepare for the pahtia. *It begins very soon. They do not believe he can win.* The last was said resentfully.

~They underestimate him, Reisil said, sensing Baku's stout agreement.

"I will do as required," Reisil said aloud, aware that the nahuallis were waiting for her response.

"Then I wish you speed. If we do not see each other

again, know that you are cherished. I will not forget
you, in this life or the next." He spoke in a monotone,
as if discussing what to eat for breakfast. He turned
back to address the gathered women, relaying Reisil's response.

Meanwhile, Reisil sat stricken, realization slowly
seeping through her. This was it. Good-bye. This was
where her path and Yohuac's forked. Chances were,
after today, they would not see each other again.

She bit her tongue hard, swallowing back the hot
grief that burgeoned up inside her. Already they were
leading him away. Reisil watched him go, her chest
burning as if she'd been skewered by a hot poker. It
seemed unreal that he could leave her life so suddenly
and absolutely. And not even a chance to say good-
bye.

~Tell him— She started to Baku, and then stopped.
What could she say? Nothing seemed adequate. *Tell
him to be careful. Tell him . . . there will never be
another man for me.*

And it was true. There had been Kaval and Kebonsat, and losing them had hurt. But this was different.
Reisil was rooted in Yohuac in a way that seemed
impossible in so short a time. But it was what it was.
Whether she saw him again or not, they were bonded
as tightly as she and Saljane.

Reisil sucked in a quiet sob, her hands beginning to
shake. Saljane lifted her head and rubbed her beak
against Reisil's cheek, wrapping her in wordless
sympathy.

~He wishes me to stay with you. Baku sounded hurt
and forlorn and more than a little desperate. *He
wishes me to help you. He says that the* pahtia *is not
my concern. You are, and helping to save Kodu Riik.*

Reisil licked her lips. Baku would be helpful. Not
only to make this journey to the sacred place, but also
to help when she returned home. Logic told her to
ignore his pain and endorse Yohuac's direction. But
she couldn't. Part of it was Baku's pain. He *needed* to
be with Yohuac. But more than that, instinct told Rei-

sil there was something more for Baku and Yohuac
to do. Something besides just delivering her into the
hands of the nahuallis.

~Go. I'll be well enough.

She felt Baku's thrill of hope, followed by uncertainty and hesitation.

~If I need you, I will call. If he didn't go so far she
couldn't hear. If the wild magic of the land didn't
interfere, the way it did at Mysane Kosk. It didn't
matter. He needed to be with Yohuac, and she needed
to pass this next test on her own. *Go.*

Yohuac disappeared out of the meeting house, and
the nahuallis wasted no time with Reisil. They stood
her up and indicated that she should remove her clothing. Reisil hesitated a bare moment and then complied
with a shrug. When she was done, her exposed skin
gleamed white in the firelight, the gold leaf pattern
like burnished flame. She flushed at their stares but
did not look away.

She had not removed her gauntlet or the talisman
she wore around her neck. The nahuallis pointed to
both insistently. Reluctantly Reisil pulled off the
gauntlet, but shook her head adamantly when they
continued to gesture at the talisman. One of them
reached for it, but Reisil pincered the woman's hand
in an iron grip.

Tapping it with her fingertip, she said, "*Ilhuicatl.
Teotl.*" It was a gift from the Blessed Lady. She wasn't
going to give it up.

The nahuallis frowned and muttered amongst themselves. At last they seemed to accept Reisil's refusal.
Now two of them stepped forward and unrolled a
square of pounded hide. Inside was a map. It was
green with unreadable writing on it. Wiggling lines in
brown, blue, and black crisscrossed it. Colored symbols in a variety of mysterious shapes pockmarked it.
It might have been a children's drawing, for all that
was recognizable about it.

One of the witches extended a brown finger to a
dark circle. "*Oceotl.*" She moved her finger to a

squared-off triangle a couple of inches away from Oceotl. "Monequi." The mountain where they'd entered Cemanahuatl from Kodu Riik. Reisil nodded. The witch moved her hand past and slightly left to a blue spot. "Atli Cihua." She waited for Reisil to nod understanding. The map was instantly withdrawn.

Now they lined up double-file again with Reisil just behind the two leaders. They led her out of the meeting house. Reisil carried Saljane cradled in her arms. Stars glittered above, and the moon shone full. All of the houses remained dark. No one spoke as they strode out of the village and back up the trail into the jungle. Reisil stepped carefully, too aware of the rocks biting into her feet and the unfamiliar wash of air on her exposed skin.

~*I hope this is worth it,* she grumbled. Having sorted out making wards, she wasn't terribly concerned about the dangers of the forest, or of getting wet or cold. She had Saljane to help with food and her own magic as a weapon. The waste of time, however, seemed criminal. And what if she got lost? She tried to remember the map, but found that it had already grown hazy in her mind.

When they came to the wardpost marking the boundary of the village, the two nahuallis in the lead stopped. They turned to face Reisil. One produced a clay jar. It was filled with a greasy orange substance. She dipped her fingers into it, daubing Reisil's forehead, cheeks, chin, and breasts. It felt unexpectedly cool. When she was done, the other witch raised her arm, pointing meaningfully at the moon. Reisil nodded understanding. She had until the space of the next full moon to get there.

Now the two women stepped aside, silent and severe.

~*Not fond of good-byes, are they?*

Reisil strode away, not bothering to look back. Her bladder prodded at her, and she sighed. First thing was to find a bush. Second thing, find a place to spend the night. Saljane couldn't see in the dark and carrying the goshawk would make for slow going. Third, craft wards against weather and predators. And then hurry.

But as she climbed the trail, her thoughts fled to Yohuac and silent tears slipped down her face. *Be well*, she said silently to the night.

Chapter 27

Soka leaned against a wooden tie-rail, watching the sparring practice. It was late in the morning. He glanced at the leaden sky, feeling the passing moments like blood draining from his veins. He'd been cooling his heels for two weeks, waiting for his father's decision. He dared not push. Too much was at stake. He crossed his arms, his muscles knotting. He was tense, strung tighter than a longbow. He'd kept himself busy these weeks by riding out with the Huntmaster, though Soka was an abysmal hunter. A fact that Prefiil no doubt reported to his father. Not that the Thevul would be at all surprised. He expected his son to be weak. After all, he'd had a soft upbringing.

Soka had also ridden once to Raakin, his own holding. It was tenanted by a very capable steward—a third cousin on his father's side. He'd spent the night, reviewing the logs and touring the land. And then he'd returned to Bro-heyek, where he'd spent his evenings dallying with a half dozen women, and dicing with the soldiers.

Soka's lip curled. He'd decided that he'd left his father too long alone. The Thevul found it only too easy to dismiss Soka from his mind. It was time to become a thorn in his father's buttocks. He had little doubt his mere presence would grate painfully. The Thevul found their limited conversations at dinner barely tolerable. No more so than Soka. Just sharing the same air made him furious.

Soka watched the squad of men hacking at one another with practice swords. They wore sleeveless gambesons made of heavy hide and padded inside with curly sheepskin. It had rained the evening before, and the ground was slick. Soka chuckled as one fighter ducked beneath a blow and slipped heavily onto his backside. His opponent leaped on top of him, pressing the dull point of his practice sword to the prone man's throat.

"Think you can do better?"

"I could hardly do worse," Soka said.

A younger man sidled up beside him. He was shorter than Soka by half a head. His features were fine and narrow and his chestnut hair fell thick over his forehead. His clothing was finely patterned damask in green and yellow. The hilts of his sword and dagger were showy things made of silver and gold and set with sparkling rubies in the shape of a snarling bear's head. He was Soka's cousin, by his mother's brother, and had fostered at Bro-heyek since soon after Soka's departure to Koduteel.

"I understood you didn't have permission to carry a sword, as hostage to the court," Valetama said, lifting one brow. "Boasting aside, perhaps you ought to be out there with them?"

Soka smiled maliciously as he turned to look at Valetama. "And you, cousin, do you have no need of practice?"

His cousin puffed up. "I have been trained by the best—your father. It would be cruel to pit my skills against these men."

"Perhaps you would like to teach me?" Soka drawled.

Valetama eyed him narrowly. Soka could almost read his mind. His cousin was a snide, superior sort and had viewed Soka's return like a baker finding a swarm of ants in his grain stores. He'd been suspicious and had made it his personal mission to keep a constant watch on the prodigal son. This was in no little way motivated by Valetama's young bride, who seemed to find Soka enthralling. He was equally impressed by her blond locks and buxom figure. It only spiced his enjoyment that she belonged to Valetama. He smiled, remembering the stolen half hour the afternoon before. Ah, but she was delicious.

"I would be pleased to teach you a lesson," Valetama said now, flushing.

"Very kind of you, I'm sure," Soka said, following the other man out onto the grass and flicking back his cuffs.

"You may want to put on a gambeson."

"I'll take my chances."

"As you wish," Valetama said shortly.

They took up a position away from the other men. They each drew their swords and daggers, saluting one another before settling down to spar. Valetama was quite good, Soka decided. And very predictable. He was a workhorse sort of swordsman, very good at the meat and potatoes, but not very creative when forced out of his routine.

Soka met the other man's attacks easily, feeling his muscles loosen and warm. After fifteen minutes, Valetama pulled back, wiping his forehead with his sleeve.

"You've had some training," he said.

"Some."

"Well, then. Let us push a little harder."

With that, they began to spar in earnest. Soka was forced to move more quickly. But he'd learned from Metyein, who was the best in Kodu Riik. And he'd never softened his blows, or let Soka rest. He'd drilled him unmercifully. Soka had blossomed under his tutelage. He'd practiced swordplay hour after hour. And he'd *learned*. He was better than Valetama; he knew it. And soon his cousin would too.

Slowly Soka took control of the match, moving more rapidly, stepping into patterns that had become second nature. He moved fluidly from one to the next. Their swords clanged a sharp staccato across the bailey, and the other men stopped their sparring to watch. Valetama dripped sweat. His damask clothing was scored from the touches Soka had made on him. He wheezed, stumbling and slipping on the muddy field.

Soka was more tired than he cared to admit, but he didn't allow it to show. But it was time to end this match. He stepped into a quick series of unrelenting, hammering blows. When the last swing of his sword would have chopped Valetama in two, he turned his blade, smashing the other man with the flat. His cousin dropped to the ground, gasping for breath. He held his right elbow and moaned.

There was a smattering of applause. Soka ignored it, sliding his sword home and reaching down to help Valetama to his feet, picking up his sword and handing it back to him.

"I think I am the one to have learned a lesson," Valetama said dourly.

"More surprises," Soka's father said.

Soka started. How long had his father been watching?

"Right then, back to work. Standing about goggling won't improve your skills any. Soka, with me."

Soka followed his father into the Great Hall. His muscles shook with his exertion, and his clothes and hair clung wetly to his skin. His father led the way to his office and motioned Soka inside. His father seated himself beyond the desk.

"Sit."

Soka did as ordered, perching on the edge of the chair, aware of his dampness and filth.

"Kohv?"

He nodded and his father poured them both a cup from the clay carafe on his desk. He pushed the cup across the desk.

"Interesting display down there. I'd have thought the Iisand would not have permitted you to carry a sword, much less learn how to use it," his father said, tapping the sides of his cup.

"He thought it unseemly that the heir of a noble

house lack skills in that area. He allowed me to take lessons with his arms master."

"So you learned your skills from him?"

Soka smiled bleakly, remembering the awkwardness and the rage he'd felt. "No."

"Then from whom?"

"A friend."

"A very capable friend."

"None better."

His father turned to look out the open windows at the men practicing below. "Would that I had someone of such capability to school my men."

"Valetama is able enough."

"He's quite good at what he knows. But he's unimaginative."

Soka couldn't resist. "He says he trains with you."

His father turned back around, brows arching. "Did he? Well, it is true. I suppose that makes me unimaginative too."

Soka refused to look away.

"I have given some thought to this." His father opened a drawer and pulled out the message from Emelovi and Metyein.

"Have you?"

Even as the words escaped, Soka's gut twisted. What a time to antagonize his father. Prodding him would only make him shy off.

Staring expectantly across the desk at his father's grim expression, Soka held his breath, wondering if he'd failed Metyein.

"I have decided to give you the metals you need," Thevul Bro-heyek said abruptly.

Soka's stared a moment, uncertain that he'd heard correctly. But his father wasn't through.

"And I've decided that I am too much out of the way of the goings-on in the south. I will be returning with you to Mysane Kosk. I want to see it for myself. And I want to meet this new regime and see what I can do to guarantee its success."

Soka's lips twisted. If Honor won, then his father

won. It was only good business to come help. Metyein wouldn't regret the addition of a blooded general, or new troops. If his father thought Soka would argue, he was to be surprised.

"When can we leave?"

"I've sent for the ores to be collected and sent here. It will take two weeks, and eight more to get there, if the snows hold off."

That would put them back at Honor a few weeks before Miidagi, the rebirth of the year. It left precious little time to forge weapons and train the men to use them. Soka blew out a quiet breath. He'd send Slatts and Ferro to Metyein with the news. He was about to stand and excuse himself to do just that when his father caught him off guard.

"There is another matter I wish to discuss with you."

Soka hesitated, suspicious.

"It would be wise to establish an heir for you. I have selected your bride. You can be married at Na-sadh, though the girl will not be unwilling to be bedded sooner. She understands the need."

Soka's jaw dropped. His father rolled his eyes and waved his hand dismissively.

"Close your mouth, boy. You've spread your seed here liberally enough in the last couple of weeks, but I want something on the right side of the sheets. Your brother is too young yet to marry, and you are about to go to war. Do your duty. Protect the line." His tone brooked no argument. The terms were clear: Marry now, or there would be no metal for Honor.

Soka stared in hot incredulity, biting back hard on his fury. But his father was unmoved.

"Well?"

He stood. "As you wish. Perhaps I might be permitted to bathe first?"

"Don't take overlong. Do you have any questions about the girl?"

Soka shook his head. "What do I care so long as she has a scabbard to sheathe my sword?"

His father shrugged. "Then I'll have Roomila sent to your quarters. Perhaps she can scrub your back. At any rate, Valetama will be pleased you're too busy to diddle his wife anymore."

Soka smiled derisively. "I don't know about that. I have great stamina."

His father startled him with a bark of laughter as Soka retreated to the door. He paused on the threshold.

"Have my new bride bring food. I'll need my strength. And wine. A lot of it."

Soka's wedding occurred the day before the caravan departed Bro-heyek. It had been two and a half weeks since his first night with his new bride, and to his surprise, Soka wasn't entirely pleased to be leaving her behind. Roomila had turned out to be a brash girl, with a sharp tongue and a love of erotic sport. In fact, she was exactly the sort of woman Soka might have picked for himself, if he'd ever intended to marry. As it was, Roomila made leaving Bro-heyek more difficult than he expected. And now he had a reason to return.

"Do you want to stay here or go to Raakin?" he asked her lazily, reaching for his glass of wine on the nightstand. Next to it was a pewter box, inside of which was the poison bead from his mouth. It had become too dangerous in their lovemaking. Beside him, Roomila sprawled on her stomach, her skin flushed and damp, her blond hair a glorious tangle down her pale back. The daughter of a local landholder, she was strong-willed and clever. She turned on her side, taking the glass from his hand.

"Raakin. I am your wife, now. I should have charge of it while you're away."

"Mercenary. It could be lonely."

She shrugged, turning onto her back and rubbing her plump belly. "I'll be dragged back here fast enough if I have a child. The Thevul will want to tuck the little heir under his wing. I may as well have a bit of freedom while I can."

"He may surprise you. He's not got a good history of protecting the heir."

"Then I'll do it myself at Raakin." She sounded defiant, and Soka glanced at her in surprise. She prodded his chest with her finger, her nail biting into his skin, her words fierce. "If your mother had been alive, you can bet you'd still have your eye, and you'd not have grown up at court," she said. "Your father may be surprised if he decides to take liberties with *my* child."

"You're a lion," Soka teased, rubbing his hand over her arm. But she pushed him away, sitting up with her hands on her naked hips.

"This is no joke. You're about to head off to who knows where and won't likely be back for another ten years, if ever. *You* aren't going to protect the child. Which leaves just me. And my baby isn't going to become fodder for your father's ambition. Not while I'm around."

Soka reached over and pulled her into his arms, surprised at the rush of feeling her words engendered, both guilt and admiration. He kissed her, rolling on top of her, holding her by the wrists as she struggled to be free. He raised his head.

"Don't laugh at me," she said, her chin jutting.

"I'm not. I'm delighted my bride is so brave and independent. And you will have independence in more than just your fiery spirit. Before I leave I'll make sure you have money safely hidden for whatever you need. In case of emergency. And I promise you this: If all goes well, I will return here for you."

She stared at him, her blue gaze like turbulent ocean waters. "And if all this is moot—if I'm not pregnant?"

Soka brushed his lips against hers. "Then we try again. If you want."

"I'm your wife. Do I have a choice?"

"With me? Always."

She smiled slow, her lips red and full. "Then you'd better get to work. We don't have a lot of time left. And this is our wedding night."

Chapter 28

Traveling back through the jungle was much harder than Reisil had anticipated. Her feet and hands were torn and blistered. Her skin was bruised and scraped beneath a layer of grime. There wasn't anything she could do about it. When she tried warding herself from harm, she couldn't feel the ground or the things her hands gripped. The result was that she could neither walk nor climb properly. It was like trying to scale ice. The best she could do was ward herself against weather and predators.

Saljane brought back birds and rodents for Reisil to eat. More often than not, Reisil pushed them aside. Without a knife, she had no means to skin or gut them. Even if she felt like it. Her body seemed far distant. All its pains and demands were like fading echoes. She focused feverishly on moving forward, on getting to Atli Cihua. Soon she stopped only when exhaustion crippled her.

~Eat. Now.

Reisil stared down at the creature Saljane had dropped on her bare lap. Blood dripped down her legs from punctures in the small animal's hide. Reisil poked it. It didn't move. Her fingers caught her attention and she turned her hand over and flexed, fascinated at the play of muscles beneath the filthy, scraped skin.

Losing interest, she looked up, forgetting instantly about her hand and the furry body in her lap, dreamily surveying her surroundings. Nothing looked familiar. She was sitting on a mossy log. Volcano ants swarmed the ground and log on either side of her, checked by the invisible shield of her wards. Reisil watched them curiously. They piled over one another, their legs digging for traction on the wet wood.

~Do you hear me? You must eat. Saljane's voice was stern and unrelenting.

Reisil twisted ponderously to look at the goshawk perching beside her, protected from the ants by the ward attached to her leg.

"What?"

~Eat. We are running out of time.

Reisil's head was heavy and thick, and her mouth felt dry. She licked her lips. They were rough and cracked. Her teeth felt grainy and sticky. She made a face, her mind sliding away along another gauzy thought line. Saljane caught at it.

~We must get to Atli Cihua before the next full moon or the nahuallis will not help us. Kodu Riik will be destroyed. Your strength is fading. You must eat. Saljane spoke slowly and forcefully, leaning forward to fix Reisil's attention with her brilliant crimson gaze.

Slowly the words seeped through. Kodu Riik. The nahuallis. A muted thrill of urgency flittered along Reisil's nerves. She touched the animal again.

"How?" she rasped stupidly. Her tongue felt thick and unwieldy.

Saljane bent and snatched up the limp little beast. Holding it in her beak, she slashed her talons down its ribs, ripping a wide gash. Then she dropped it back on Reisil's lap.

Reisil stared at it, repulsed. But Saljane's mind pressed against hers. She could not resist. She pressed the animal to her lips and licked.

The intense, warm flavor rocked her backwards, and she retched, dry, wrenching convulsions. But when her body quieted, Saljane pushed at her again.

~Eat.

Reisil began to gnaw obediently. Her repulsion changed swiftly to shrieking hunger. She ripped the flesh from the rodent and bolted the meat without chewing. She gnawed the bones and licked her fingers.

During the next days she began to come back to herself. A wild self, one that gulped the warm gobbets of raw flesh and hot blood with animal relish. She regained her strength. Her mind sharpened, but retained a fierce wild edge. She fashioned a makeshift gauntlet from tough vines and the uncured hides of the creatures Saljane captured for her. This way she could carry the goshawk into the night.

They came to the flat-topped Monequi mountain with less than a week to the full moon. Reisil remembered the map the nahuallis had shown her with crystal clarity. Go left around the mountain, and then out at an angle, toward the northwest. Urgency dug spurs into her.

Now she slept only a few hours at a time. Reisil sent Saljane to fly high above the jungle canopy, looking for some sign of the Atli Cihua. How would they know it? Was it a building? A mountain? A spring? Fury at not knowing made her run harder, faster. She was rabid in her determination. She would not fail.

The morning before the full moon, a drenching rain fell. The jungle floor streamed with water. Reisil tripped, falling heavily. She screamed, more with frustration than with pain. She pushed herself upright, limping. But even as she did, her mind became sharp as a silver knife honed fine.

She felt it. It *summoned*.

~It's close. Atli Cihua, Saljane called eagerly, showing Reisil the path.

It was the afternoon. The full moon would rise an hour after nightfall. Reisil began to climb again.

There was no trail. The mountain was steep and thick with vines and trees. The air quieted and the wind stilled. There was a fecund feel to the mountain—an opulent heat. Sweat ran down her skin. Reisil clawed

through the undergrowth. The air thinned and it grew
difficult to breathe. She gasped, her ribs heaving, her
head whirling, her muscles screaming.

She found herself near the top of the mountain,
facing a nearly vertical slope. She scrabbled up halfway, only to slide back down, scraping her skin raw.
It had grown dark, and the last sliver of the sun was
fading to night. There was no more time! She clutched
at the rock, gripping tiny cracks and protusions with
her fingers and toes. She inched upward, pulling herself over the top lip by sheer will. Then she staggered
up and was running. She wedged herself between the
great trees that grew so close that she had to turn
sideways to squeeze through.

Inside the trees, she found a ring of warm red tile
that matched the spell circle in Yohuac's village. Her
feet left bloody footprints as she lumbered toward the
blue-stone building. All her attention was fixed on the
black doorway. The summons of the place pulled at
her like an ocean tide.

Reisil flung herself through the rounded entry.
Shock made her gape, her ragged wheezes echoing in
the silence.

The inside was identical to the meeting hall in
Oceotl, from the blue tile floor to the fire bowl in the
center to the cushions around the wall. She might well
have gone in a circle and returned where she started.
Through the chimney hole in the roof, she could see
the silver gleam of the full moon rising. Unexpected
relief crashed over her, and her body went boneless.
She slumped to the ground. Dry sobs racked her. Saljane, who remained outside, poured a balm of love,
praise, and approval through their mental link.

At last the sobs ended, leaving Reisil more wrung
than before. She gazed around the room in dull expectation. What now?

Come.

It wasn't quite a sound, was not quite inside her
mind. The command resonated in her flesh as if she
were the plucked string of a harp.

Come.

She stood, following the call across the meeting room. She couldn't have resisted if she wanted to. She went through a narrow door that led into a dark passage. Heavy sconces shaped like fierce forest animals held lit candles. They screwed downward along a steep stair.

Reisil limped down, beginning at last to register the pain of her many wounds. Her stomach rumbled and cramped. She tried to remember when last she'd eaten. It might have been a day or more.

She didn't know how long she walked. She went slowly, her thighs and calves quivering. She missed a step and barely caught herself. Her head spun and her arms hung heavy. But the call pulled at her. She couldn't stop, if she had to crawl on her knees.

Slowly she became aware of a low rumbling sound threading up from below. It sounded like drums. The heavy beating sent shivers of trepidation through her naked flesh.

A golden glow began to lighten the gloom. The rumble sounded louder. Reisil turned a last curve. The stairwell opened up into yet another expansive cavern. It was lit with a bright green light that seemed to come from nowhere. The walls were painted with pictures of the Teotl in scenes of building, nurturing, and destruction. The roof was devoted entirely to the might of *Ilhuicatl*, in all his incarnations. There didn't seem to be any floor, only a lake of ebony that filled the cavern from wall to wall. A few steps inside, a stone path hung out over the emptiness. It was no more than eighteen inches wide. Black space yawned on either side. Reisil hesitated. It had been a long time since heights had bothered her. Flying with Saljane had cured her fear. But this . . .

Her toes curled. She winced at the shards of pain digging into her flesh. There was no choice. She firmed her jaw, feeling Saljane's strength through their bond.

She strode out onto the path, fixing her gaze just beyond her bloody, torn feet. She forced herself not to think about how narrow the path was, or what might wait below. Ten paces, twenty, thirty. Nothing happened. Reisil's shoulders and neck ached with tension. Something was going to happen. Soon. She reached for her power. It rushed to her, hard and hot. She held it ready.

Air.

The wind slammed her. Reisil's feet lifted off the ground. She tumbled upward like a leaf in a storm. Instinct saved her. She flung ropes of power at the path. They drilled into the rock. She pulled herself back, sprawling on her stomach. The wind dropped.

Reisil lunged to her feet, crouching. She panted, fear making blood thump in her veins. She drew a deep, steadying breath and released the power anchoring her. Slowly she began to walk again.

Fire.

Flames erupted, blocking the path. They roared up to the cavern roof. Heat seared her skin. Her eyes felt parched and turned gritty. She could scarcely breathe. But the task was clear: Follow the path. She pulled her power around her in a thin shield. Instantly the heat dropped. She slid her left foot forward, then her right.

She inched along, blinded by the fire. She reached out, trying to tamp down the flames. They responded by blowing more fiercely, turning blue and green. The heat inside her shield increased unbearably. Reisil ceased attacking the inferno and concentrated on shuffling ahead.

She was tiring. She'd gone weeks without real rest or food. She was reaching the end of her strength. Her muscles trembled with a palsy, and her eyes blurred. Reisil shook her head, trying to clear the muzziness.

It might have been seconds or hours, but at last she came to the other side of the wall of fire. Her legs sagged. But her relief was short-lived. She hardly had a chance to collect herself before it hit.

Water.

The icy deluge cascaded from the sky in pounding sheets. The cold was shocking after the heat. Reisil canted to the side, teetering on the edge of the path. Desperate, Reisil dropped and straddled the path. The sharp edges of the stone cut painfully into the insides of her thighs. She bowed her head, striving to keep from drowning as the flood washed over her head and down her face. The torrent beat against her back like thundering blows from a barrel stave. She gasped, inhaling water. Her lungs and throat spasmed. She gagged. More water filled her mouth and she retched, her stomach jerking. She snatched frantically at her magic, feeling it squirm away. She flailed, catching at it desperately. She caught it and knit it into tattered shields.

Better.

She caught her breath. Her body shook with uncontrollable tremors. Getting to her feet proved very difficult. Reisil had to push the shield up to create enough room, and then convince her legs and arms to hold her weight. It was nearly more than she could manage. At last she gained her feet, lurching as she tried to find balance on the slippery stone.

When at last she was upright, the water sluicing over her shields, she began to slog forward. Her magic was beginning to sear her bones, roiling against her weary control. She staggered forward. And out. But it wasn't over. She dared not relax. Grabbing the fraying edges of her shields, Reisil held on with all her might.

Earth.

The path softened. She began to sink. Instantly she realized her shields would do her little good. Clenching her fists, she drew hard on her store of magic, howling at the feel of fishhooks pulling at her nerves. She let the power pool inside her until she thought she'd explode. She released it, pouring it into the shape of a bridge. It jutted in the air before her, looking decrepit and flimsy. Reisil didn't have time to test its strength or think about where to anchor the other end. She was already knee-deep in the stone path.

She flung herself onto her bridge, wriggling and dragging herself upward. She kicked her legs free. Her bridge wobbled like stretched canvas. She crawled on all fours, concentrating on holding it steady, though the pain was excruciating. *Hurry! Hurry!* She scuttled forward like a crab. But already her bridge was sagging and there was a tear in the magic. She couldn't hold it any longer.

Reisil crashed back down to the path. She landed hard on her knees. She braced herself against a slow plummet to the bottom of the cavern. The path held. She slumped, sobbing with relief. The sound echoed in the silence.

Reisil felt raw and burnt. Her bones felt like they'd been shattered. But she couldn't remain here. Somewhere she found the strength to stand. Her head reeled. Hunger twisted her gut. She bent, bracing her hands on her knees and drawing deep, rasping breaths.

Slowly she found her equilibrium. She straightened. The path fled away before her, obdurate in its silent demand to continue. Reisil obeyed, easing forward, her legs trembling. She steeled herself for the next test. But nothing happened.

The path ended abruptly as a platform resolved itself out of the darkness. It was round and covered in copper. Shapes had been etched across the middle. *Rinda.* The edges were bordered by the blue stone favored by the nahuallis. In the middle was a pedestal topped by a round slab of gold bigger than Reisil's head. It was two inches thick, its top burnished smooth, as if awaiting an artist's touch. Above the gold disc danced a watery distortion.

Spirit.

Reisil limped forward, her brow crimping. She circled the pedestal. At last she approached closer, scrutinizing the distortion. She bent, looking for a clue to tell her what to do.

Something grabbed her head and shoulders. It picked her up and jerked her down. Into the disc. Reisil found herself floating in a miasma of gauzy yellow light. There were no smells, no sounds. The silence was perfect. Then she caught a glimpse of something moving in the mist. Reisil tried to move forward, but she was tethered in place.

Slowly a shape emerged from the mist. If she could have cried, she would have.

Elutark hovered before her. Her mentor and friend. The old woman was barely recognizable. Her body was ravaged by the plague. She stared reproachfully, blood trickling like tears from her eyes. Her arms and legs were black, and swollen so large her fingers had all but disappeared. Her eyes burned. But she had no tears. There was nothing she could do. Nothing.

And then another form emerged from the mist. Ceriba. The sight of her struck Reisil a wounding blow. Kebonsat's sister was naked. Her body was battered and spattered with blood. It was clear she'd been raped and tortured. But this wasn't the Ceriba from a year ago. These wounds were new. Reisil stared, appalled. By the Lady's grace! How could such a thing happen a second time? Pity swamped her. It was like the punch line of a horrible, horrible joke. Her eyes went to her friend's throat. It gaped like a hideous smile.

Much as she wanted the visions to be a nightmare, Reisil knew deep down that this was a true vision; both women were dead.

Sinking loss and guilt gnawed at her. Tears streamed down her cheeks. Reisil could do nothing, trapped in silence. Part of her wanted them to shout or accuse her of not protecting them—something. But they did nothing.

Reisil had no sense of time passing. Her own wounds had ceased to pain her; her exhaustion was forgotten. But urgency prodded at her. She stared at her two ravaged friends, trying to think. What was she supposed to do?

Her mind moved sluggishly. Suddenly Reisil had an idea. She lifted her arms, stretching them out. For a long moment, she thought she was wrong. Then Elutark drifted forward. Reisil embraced her lovingly, un-caring of the horrific damage to her body. Elutark's spirit burned like flame, vibrant, joyous, angry. But not at her. At the Regent, at the men who'd come, at the disease that destroyed her.

Be strong, daughter. Do what you need to do. Cling to the Lady. Believe.

And then she was gone. Reisil reached out to Ceriba.

The first thing she felt was pain, all over her body, but most excruciatingly in the intimate cleft between her legs. Dreadful, shrieking pain. Reisil spasmed, her spine twisting. But she did not let go. The pain faded, only to be replaced by a crushing surge of humiliation. Waves of it rolled over and through Reisil. It was replaced in turn by fury. A cold, determined fury that wanted justice.

Pity the ones who yet live. I had my mercy. I goaded them. They murdered me in their fury. Their master was not pleased. The Regent is evil, Reisil. His heart is black. You must stop him.

She melted into Reisil and through. Her spirit was like sunlight sparkling on the winter ice. It left Reisil feeling powerful and deflated. She felt flayed, inside and out and to the depths of her soul.

Abruptly she found herself back on the platform staring down at the golden disc. Coiled on top was the *copicatl*, its yellow eyes glowing like tiny suns. Reisil glared at it.

"What do you want?" she rasped.

It uncoiled and stood impossibly on the tip of its tail. It lengthened, stretching until it was as tall as Reisil. Then it began to twist and bend. Gradually it shaped itself into a complex, three-dimensional figure. What did it mean? What was it for? Reisil forced herself to concentrate on it, to fix it in her memory. Long before she was sure she had it, the snake unwound itself, shrinking back down until it disappeared entirely.

At the same moment, lights appeared on the other

side of the platform, revealing another path. With weary fatalism, Reisil followed it. What next?

But the path led into a tunnel, leaving the cavern behind. Crimson candles lined the walls. The floor was smooth, like polished marble. Reisil stumbled along, hardly able to lift her feet. Her body pulsed with pain and hunger.

She had not gone far when the passage turned sharply right and then left and emptied into a new room. It was small, only twenty paces across. Sheets of hammered gold covered the interior. *Rinda* made of crystal spangled the walls, ceiling, and floor. Pedestals lined the walls. On each stood a figure. Reisil didn't have to count to know they were representations of the Teotl—Cemanahuatl's fifty-two gods.

Some were beautiful, others grotesque. Most were only part human. The only one Reisil recognized was *Ilhuicatl*. He dominated the center of the room. He looked much as he had in the bathing room of Oceotl. The statue was three-sided. Three penis-spears protruded into the room, each one tipped in gold and crusted with the magical blue stone. The rest of him was made of gold set with precious stones and metals. Rubies for blood, obsidian for his eyes, diamonds for his teeth, emeralds and amethyst for the snakes . . . it was beautiful, in a garish, monstrous sort of way.

Reisil marched up in front of it, bracing her legs wide and waiting for something to happen. Nothing did. At last she grew too tired to hold herself upright. She sat, sacreligiously propping herself against *Ilhuicatl's* pedestal. She glanced up at the god.

"Well?" she said. There was no answer. She sighed and closed her eyes, unable to keep them open any longer.

Well, then, she has come. And just in time.

Too close.

Is it good enough?

She did better than most. And in a strange land.

She is brave.

She isn't much, is she?

Neither are you.

I call him puny.

Look at that. They won't like that. Strings on her soul.

Oh, but they will *like it. At least the one too attached to him. The child that would come of such blood . . . but most definitely not this other. They'll want to cut it.*

If you tell them.

I think . . . not.

They are our children. Your children. Yours especially.

No. Not this one. This one is not ours. She never was. Her mother was yours, before.

Yes. But this one is not.

She is the Hope.

Yes. And we must protect it. We must protect her. Or she will fail. She must have her strings. They are her strength. It must be so. Do not disobey. Now we must give her the gift promised.

The multitude of disembodied voices floated through Reisil's mind, distorted and rippled, as if through deep waters. One was stronger than the others, deeper and edged with fire. *Ilhuicatl.*

Warmth wrapped her in a gentle hand, swirling inside her like a spring breeze. She smelled sweet honey-thistle and pungent sage. There was a feeling like bubbles in her blood and a frisson of tickling inside her skull. The feeling passed and a wave of lassitude and comfort spread through her. As she felt herself drifting away into a deep sleep, a sudden flare of something too bright to look at flowed across her mind's eye in a slow, undulating spurt.

Sleep. Rest. When you wake, there will be much to do.

The voice paused as if debating something. At last it spoke again.

My children mean well. They live and die to serve me, and Cemanahuatl. But . . . there is more here than they can see. And they are bound by what they are. Be warned.

Then the light of *Ilhuicatl* faded and Reisil fell into a deep, dreamless sleep.

Chapter 29

Reisil woke groggily, gasping as her wounds flared and her muscles protested. Hunger made her weak. She was lying on the chilly gold floor of the sacred room. Above her, the statue of *Ilhuicatl* loomed grotesquely. She stared at him. It was difficult to equate the statue with the voice she'd heard and the elegant fire-trail in her mind.

She rolled onto her stomach and awkwardly pushed upright. She groaned, every bit of her hurting. Her stomach made a rumbling sound and she winced, rubbing her brow, trying to remember what had happened. She had been visited by the Teotl. They'd done something. . . . She frowned, trying to remember, but it all crumbled away like ash, leaving behind phantom impressions. Something about strings, something about the nahuallis.

Reisil ground her knuckles into her temples. *Ilhuicatl's* warning rose stark in her mind.

My children mean well. They live and die to serve me, and Cemanahuatl. But . . . there is more here than they can see. And they are bound by what they are. Be warned.

Gooseflesh pimpled over her arms and down her back. The nahuallis had sent Yohuac to find her. They resented that they had to depend on an outsider, but surely they would help her? Surely they wouldn't endanger themselves for pride?

Be warned.

Reisil drew a deep breath. All right, she'd be careful. There wasn't much else to do at the moment, but find Saljane and something to eat. Reisil limped back to the doorway, moving sluggishly, her body not wanting to obey. She gritted her teeth and zigzagged back through the passage and up the tunnel, wanting nothing more than to be out of the chamber and back outside. She dreaded passing back through the vast emptiness of the great cavern. But when she came to the end of the tunnel, she found herself instead at the foot of the stairs. Mystified, she turned to retrace her steps, but found only a wall behind her.

She retraced her path up to the meeting room where she'd entered, walking quietly on the balls of her feet. She paused when the silence was broken by the sounds of women talking. Not just talking. Arguing.

Reisil inched higher, straining to hear. Surprise rocked her to the soles of her feet as she picked words out of the rattling voices. She grinned triumphantly. The gift she'd been promised. Understanding.

She came to the doorway and paused, hanging back in the shadows.

"I say again. She is not one of us. No matter who her mother was."

Reisil flushed angrily. Did everyone know about her mother but her?

"It is agreed, Piketas, but we are bound to help her. That is what my foreseeing revealed. She is the one who will help us cleanse Ti'Omoru. She is the key."

"I don't like it."

"Nor any of us. But we cannot do it ourselves. We have tried all we can. I do not know why you argue."

"We have not tried *everything*," Piketas said.

There was an ominous silence.

"We must heed the vision."

"Perhaps it is false."

"Do you think *Ilhuicatl*, would send lies? Do you say you doubt me?"

"How can you be certain the vision came from him,

Ampok?" came the strident response. "Many of the Teotl would enjoy watching us suffer the indignity of sharing our secrets with this *clecha*. They are jealous of the favor *Ilhuicatl* shows us. They would enjoy such a trick, seeing us crawling on our knees. Or perhaps we misunderstand the message. How can we be certain? We must not trust her. She does not care about Cemanahuatl. She wishes only to save her own land. What does she care if we perish? If the magic dies entirely?"

Piketas's last words sounded shrill. Reisil grimaced. The air of superiority and strength the nahuallis wrapped around themselves was paper-thin and shredding. Which meant she had to work quickly. Their magic might be fading, but they were still very strong. The spell they'd cast in Oceotl was proof enough of that. And if they decided she wasn't useful, or was a threat, who knew what steps they'd take? What if they tried to destroy their version of Mysane Kosk— Ti'Omoru? She shuddered. It could only be a disaster. The end of both their worlds.

"What do you suggest?" Ampok asked. "She is here. The Teotl has welcomed her. *Ilhuicatl* has blessed her. We are bound to our word."

"Then let us watch her carefully. We must guard ourselves. She must not learn how weak we've become. We must be ready to stop her. She is strong, but she cannot stand against all of us."

"Sister, you speak true. But we must also welcome her. She is our gift. She has passed the tests of senior nahuallis. She has stood in the presence of the Teotl. She is one of us now. She will add her strength to ours, and Cemanahuatl will be saved."

"And if she does not agree?"

"She will."

A worm of fear and anger inched down Reisil's spine. There was a fanatical, relentless promise in those words. She thought of Tapit.

"She will not succumb easily," came another voice, younger than the first two.

"Nothing valuable is won without cost. She will help us save Cemanahuatl, and then she will be ours. Or her children will. Her blood will enrich us. It is enough."

Suddenly the lush scent of food came drifting into the stairwell, and Reisil's mouth watered painfully. She had to catch herself to keep from blundering into the midst of the women. Instead she retreated quietly down the stairway about twenty steps. Then she jogged upward, letting her feet slap the stone noisily. She didn't stop at the top, but strode into the meeting room, stopping abruptly in pretend surprise.

The gathered women had already turned to greet her, hearing her coming. They smiled at her, their teeth white and predatory. Reisil felt like a fish among sharks.

"We greet you, sister," said one, stepping forward. Reisil recognized her voice. It was the third speaker. She was shorter than the others, and lithe, with strong, calloused fingers. She gripped Reisil's hands in hers, pulling her forward while another offered her a loose robe to wear. "I congratulate you. You have proven yourself to be one of us."

One of us. When pigs rode horseback. But Reisil only smiled. "I am glad to be here. To at last be able to speak with you."

"We are glad as well. But come. You must be hungry. And we will see to your wounds. My name is Ilhanah."

Reisil was introduced around. Three names stuck with her. Ilhanah, Piketas and Ampok. The three she'd overheard talking.

They chattered at her and amongst themselves while she bolted her food voraciously. They asked about the ivy on her face, about Kodu Riik, whether there was the same trouble there as in Cemanahuatl. Reisil was too busy eating to answer in more than grunts.

After she finished, they dressed her wounds. The salve they smoothed over the cuts numbed her skin, giving immediate relief. There were several places

where it was necessary to stitch the gashes closed. Reisil refused anything stronger than the salve to deaden
the pain, biting on a length of green wood when the
agony was too much.

When they had finished, she found she was hungry
again. When she set aside her cup and plate, she
looked up to find Ilhanah watching her.

Ilhanah smiled. It was a feral expression, like a jungle cat stalking its prey. Unaccountably Reisil thought
of Ceriba's words: *His heart is black.* As she looked
at Ilhanah, Reisil felt a terrible qualm. The nahuallis
might not have black hearts. But certainly they were
ambitious. And scared. They trusted Reisil as much
as she trusted the wizards. Maybe less. She thought of
the ominous silence when Ampok had said they had
not tried *everything.* Reisil's chest tightened and dread
coiled around her throat. There was a spell so dire,
so awful, the nahuallis would rather trust Reisil than
try it. For now. But if they thought Reisil would fail,
or betray them, they'd risk it. And anything they were
afraid of doing made Reisil very nervous. Their hearts
didn't have to be black. Only cold and desperate.

Reisil was yanked out of her reverie by Ilhanah's
next words.

"Drink this. It is *necho.* It is the blood of *Ilhuicatl.*
In the name of the Teotl, we welcome you to Atli
Cihua and Cemanahuatl as our sister."

Ilhanah handed Reisil a blue-stone cup the size of
a thimble. Inside was a golden liquid that looked like
honey and smelled like spring. Following Ilhanah's example, Reisil tipped it back and swallowed it in one
gulp. It tasted sweet and hot. Heat ran through her in
lazy ripples that grew more powerful with every passing moment. A feeling of languor and wholeness suffused her.

"It is well?" Ilhanah asked, smiling that same, predatory smile.

"Yes. Very well."

"Good. The council will meet at moonrise to discuss

our situation with you. Until then, you should rest. Then Ampok will show you to a room. Ampok?"

Reisil didn't argue. A few hours would make little difference, and the sleep would help her think better. She rose and followed after Ampok, feeling as if she were floating.

She was a stocky woman, perhaps thirty summers old. Her face was broad and her features coarse. Her eyes were muddy-looking and her mouth was too wide.

Ampok led her into another part of the building. The corridors snaked in looping curves. Reisil soon lost all sense of direction, her head muzzy with the effects of the *necho*. At last they arrived at a plain wooden door. It was streaked red and black and had no handle. Ampok touched it, muttering something beneath her breath, and it swung open.

Reisil went inside, noticing only the bed in the center of the room. She tumbled into it. Her last coherent thought was of Saljane.

Chapter 30

Tapit sauntered across the courtyard, looking for Tillen. He'd returned to Mysane Kosk four weeks before to await Reisil's return. After he'd made known his ability to read, write, and cipher, he'd quickly been passed along into the keeping of Tillen, the Head Steward of Honor. Tillen received all newcomers, assigning them lodging and work with a blunt, cheerful disposition that brooked no argument. More important, he doled out supplies, organized work schedules, routed building materials, and gave daily reports to the Lord Marshal.

Through Tillen, Tapit learned everything that was happening in Honor, from the smallest to the largest detail. He knew more about midden waste and laundry than he ever wished to know, but he also knew a great deal about more important things, like the secret tunnels connecting the stockades, and the plans to withstand an attack.

The wizard made himself indispensible and quickly became the Head Steward's prime assistant. Soon, Tapit hoped he would be invited to the daily briefing of the Lord Marshal.

Oddly enough, Tapit found that he enjoyed the work. And Tillen. The stocky, snub-nosed man had sharp wits and did not suffer fools lightly. He was forthright and honest, something Tapit appreciated. His own brethren, while genial, tended to be secretive and somewhat morose. A natural development, having had to retreat to the stronghold with their tails between their legs.

Tapit sighed, realizing he'd made a mistake in adding a column of figures. He began again. As far as he was concerned, retreating to the stronghold had been fortuitous. The change in their habits of magic and the isolation had forced his brethren to become more inventive. With the aid of the power provided by captured *nokulas*, they were swiftly overtaking their previous feats of magic. Even with the inconvenience caused by Reisil's attack. But she had galvanized the wizards to action. They had foolishly neglected to guard the fruits of their labor—Mysane Kosk. But there was time to correct that mistake.

Tapit scratched a number at the bottom of the column, setting the pen down and rubbing his eyes. He yawned.

"Done with the weeklies?" Tillen asked, coming into the room behind him.

"Right here. Wait a moment. It's still wet."

Tillen pinched the top paper between his thick, calloused fingers, perusing the numbers with a knowing eye. "Looks well enough. We're going to need a lot more salt, though. And we'll not have as much wheat or barley as we first planned. The *nokula* battle took a heavy toll on the fields. Still, should be enough to keep everyone fed, including the horses. Maybe not as well as they like, of course." He shrugged. "We'll send harvesters out to cut hay if we can spare anyone before the snows. At any rate, the Lord Marshal will be pleased. And the Dazien," he added, flushing pinkly.

Tapit lifted an eyebrow. He hadn't bothered to disguise himself with Reisil gone from the encampment. In fact, since his return, he'd resisted any use of magic, not wanting the witch woman they called Nurema to notice him.

"I've heard some say she is too weak to take on her brother. That we can't win. Do you think so?"

One of the things that impressed Tapit about Tillen

was that the other man's loyalty was not blind. He frowned, one eye narrowing as he considered.

"She's green, that's for sure. But the Lord Marshal is sharp as any I've seen. And so's that Patversemese knight of theirs. She's doing her best to learn, and she's not a fool. As to whether we can win—" Tillen bent forward conspiratorially. "I'm not here to die. But even if I was, Reisiltark won't let it happen. She's true *ahalad-kaaslane*. She'll be back to take care of us. No need to worry about them Scallacians."

"You sound like you know her," Tapit said, straightening up. This could be useful.

"I do," Tillen said proudly. "Happened when we was living in the Fringes outside Koduteel. Family was sick, and the baby wasn't feeding. Times was getting downright hard."

Tapit snorted low. He'd been in the Fringes when spying on Koduteel. He knew well enough what life there had been like.

Tillen nodded. "Exactly so. Reisiltark was the only *ahalad-kaaslane* interested in the Fringe folk. She came down, took care of Suli and the baby. Then she healed a whole lot of others. It was like the Lady Herself came down. . . ." He trailed off, lost in the memory. Then he shook himself. "Anyhow, I learned then what Reisiltark is. She don't desert her friends, and she don't forget her duty. Now them wizards, I hear tell they'd as soon eat their children raw as not, if it meant getting ahead of the others. Scallacians ain't no better. Reisiltark would die to help Kodu Riik. More than that. She'd *suffer* for us. Not many as can say that."

Tillen's faith in Reisil was somewhat unsettling. If only because it reminded Tapit that he himself had *liked* her. She was strong and had courage. He'd been tremendously impressed at her final apprentice trial. He sighed quietly, picking up his pen and twisting it through his fingers. Hunting her down had been a stimulating challenge. He liked that about her too.

"You've been working like a donkey for weeks,"

Tillen said suddenly. "Time you took a few hours' rest."

Tapit looked up in surprise. He opened his mouth to argue, but Tillen cut him off.

"Not a word. I'm your master, remember? So off with you. I've seen you looking at the mountains. I know you weren't meant for this kind of close quarters. Go stretch your legs."

The idea sparked a sudden longing in Tapit. He stood with alacrity.

"I'll go now."

Tillen's grin did not diminish Tapit's eagerness. He fairly trotted out of the room. He did not immediately head toward the gate, but went to the stockade kitchen and collected some bread and cold meat, two hard-boiled eggs, and several carrots. He stuffed these in a sack and filled a water pouch before making his way out Eagle's main gate. He veered south around the wall, mostly to avoid the rush of people along the road. He crossed the harvested wheatfield, past Lion and up the sloping feet of the mountains.

His heart expanded as he left behind the gabble of voices, horses, hammering, and all the other sounds of too many people gathered in one place. He climbed swiftly, his legs tiring more quickly than they should have. But he'd been stuck behind a scribe's table. He hadn't had to climb.

He found himself drawn to the overlook above Mysane Kosk. He climbed up the rocky slope and out onto the overlook. It was late afternoon. There was a refreshing chill to the air. He sat cross-legged on the ground, setting aside his meal sack and water pouch. He gazed down at the mist-shrouded city below. It was magnificent. He closed his eyes, feeling the magic inside it like the sensual sweep of feathers over his skin. His body hardened. He sat for a long time, enthralled.

At last, when his body began to ache and and the sharp prod of a rock in his posterior grew too uncomfortable to ignore, he pulled himself together, shifting his seat and reaching for his food. As he munched, he considered again Tillen's words. He thought about those who'd been killed by Reisil. He'd known most of the dead wizards, some better than others. But he didn't feel any particular loss at their deaths. Mostly it had meant a setback in the council's plans. For Tapit, it had confirmed that Reisil was a worthy challenge, an opponent to test his skills. Much as he'd enjoyed hunting the *nokulas* and the coal-drake, they did not fire his blood the way pursuing Reisil did.

He leaned back, closing his eyes. The magic of Mysane Kosk washed over him in slow, caressing eddies. He sighed with pleasure. He would take Reisil alive, of course. There was no art to killing her. Maybe he'd even keep her. He smiled. He wasn't one to keep trophies, but this hunt wouldn't be over with the capture. She'd fight for her freedom. He ran the tip of his tongue around his lips in hungry anticipation. The battle would continue. She'd never give up.

The Head Steward finished his report, passing a sheaf of papers to Metyein, who rifled through them, asking some questions. Emelovi listened, trying to remember everything. Her head ached, as usual. The skin on her cheeks and forehead felt hot and tight. It was the dread of being here, of pretending she was capable of leading her people. She had never known all that must be thought of, all that must be done, in order to rule. How could any one person do it? How could *she?*

She smoothed her hair over her temples. Her fingers trembled. She dropped them back to her lap, clenching them together, a rush of anger warming her belly.

"Do you have any questions, Dazien?" Metyein asked when Tillen finished.

She shook her head. "You have been very thorough," she said to the Head Steward.

He tipped his head. "Thank you, Dazien."

"Then we will see you tomorrow, Tillen. And I will let you know when we can expect another shipment from Dannen Relvi. He's aware of our need for salt. Will the forges be ready as soon as Kaj Raakin arrives?"

"Ready as can be," the gruff Steward affirmed stoutly.

"Good then. Bright evening to you."

With that, Tillen departed, leaving Emelovi alone with Metyein. He turned to her.

"You have been quiet this evening. Is that a testament to your understanding?"

"You have taught me a great deal," Emelovi said carefully.

"A very politic statement," Metyein said dourly. "But you avoid the question."

"And what is that?" Emelovi said, rising and going to fill her wineglass. She offered the decanter to Metyein, who glared at her.

"All right. I'll play. What I want to know is, how are you doing?"

"Quite well, thank you."

His breath made a hissing noise. Once she would have blanched and yielded to the annoyed exasperation in his expression. Not today, however. She was tired of that Emelovi.

"Dazien—" He began, but she cut in before he could finish.

"Yes, I know. 'Dazien, you must behave yourself. Dazien, this is very important. Dazien, stop acting like a child. Dazien, do this, hear this, know this.' Does it never end? No, don't answer that." She paced away, her arms crossed tight over her breasts. She stopped at the window and then whirled about.

"All right. You want to know how I am doing? I am tired. My head feels like it's been stuffed fatter than a Nasadh goose. There are six more plague victims this week. That makes thirty-eight total. And that six is triple what came in last week. Is the epidemic beginning? If not this week, then next?

"And what am I to do about it? What am I to do about anything? I am absolutely useless. All I do is sit in your shadow and listen to reports on stores, supplies, weapons, horses, fighter training, tunnels, barracks, middens, and it never ends! What exactly is the point?''

She stood now with her hands on her hips, glowering at Metyein. He was smiling. Fury sent a rush of heat to her cheeks. She balled her fists, wanting to kick him. He read her desire and smiled wider.

"And there it is. If I really were any kind of a ruler, I'd have you sent to the headsman for insolence. Aare certainly would," she declared, throwing up her hands and returning to stare blindly out the window.

She heard Metyein's chair scrape and footsteps as he came to stand behind her. He settled his hands on her shoulders. She jumped at the unfamiliar touch, and then closed her eyes as he rubbed at her taut muscles. Tears welled in her eyes. It had been so long since anyone had touched her in anything but a perfunctory way. Kebonsat— But no, never again.

"You *are* learning to rule, Dazien," Metyein said softly, his fingers rubbing gently over her shoulders. "You already know a great deal. You have sat at the feet of your father. He was a great Iisand."

She gasped, feeling physical pain at the mention of her father, at the speaking of him in the past tense. Metyein's hands dropped to her arms, rubbing slowly as she collected herself. He turned her to face him, waiting until she met his somber gaze.

"But now you are to be the one who rules. And that means learning a great many details, trivial as they may seem."

Emelovi shook her head. "Anyone with eyes knows that you rule here. As it should be. They trust you to lead them well. They have no reason to believe that of me."

"They will. I don't have Varakamber blood in my veins. That counts."

"For what? Aare's a Varakamber. And he's a leader. The rightful heir to the throne."

"Yes, and he's hunting down the *ahalad-kaaslane*.

He's betrayed the Lady and his people. You said it yourself: He'd cut off a man's head for mere insolence. He'll be a very bad Iisand. And his first act will be to destroy Kodu Riik. If Nurema is right, if Reisiltark is right, then if he destroys Mysane Kosk, that will be the end of everything. You have no choice. None of us do. Your brother has to be stopped. I can lead the people against him, but only you can give them the heart to fight."

"How?"

Metyein shook his head slowly. "Only you can decide that."

With that, he let go of her and retreated to the table, scooping up the papers and stacking them together.

"I'll give you some privacy," he said. "Kebonsat asked me to review the troops." He paused, as if to say something else, then shook his head and turned to leave. Just inside the door, he stopped. He returned to the table and set the papers back down.

After he was gone, Emelovi remained still, watching the closed door, listening to the crackling of the fire in the hearth. The loud *pop!* of wood exploding startled her from stillness, and she began to pace.

He was frustrated with her. He wanted her to be more independent, to take charge. How? She didn't know anything about any of this! She made a sound of disgust. The first thing she had to do was quit pitying herself. And then she had to stop doing nothing. She wandered over to the papers, running her fingers over the edges. She sat down.

More than an hour later, she'd gone through them all. Reading them slowly gave her the chance to pause where she wanted to, to flip back and reread, to make connections she hadn't made before. There was a shortage of cloth and thread. That meant using hides for clothing and blankets, but there were too few of those ready. Which meant that someone had to make decisions about who got what.

When she sat back, she wore a thoughtful expression. Once she began to think of all the numbers and issues in terms of the people, *her* people, she began to see why the details were so important. The people *were* the details.

She stood up and stretched, her bones popping. With a satisfied smiled, she headed back to her quarters to change for dinner. She had questions for Metyein. She even had one or two for Kebonsat.

It was a start.

Chapter 31

Juhrnus slid awkwardly off Indigo. He gripped the pommel, his legs shaking. Exhaustion hung on him like heavy mail. He let go of the saddle and staggered forward. He dropped down on a rock, yanking off his hat and wiping the sweat from his forehead. He'd been riding since before dawn, not bothering to stop to eat. But he was elated. He'd left Mekelsek Keep the day before, with promises of aid to follow quickly.

Lord Mekelsek had died in the spring. He'd been gored by a bull. Juhrnus had been pleasantly surprised to find that Edel had the rule of Mekelsek, dropping the honorific -sat that had previously indicated he was the heir.

Juhrnus had arrived at dusk, not wanting to call attention to himself. He'd ridden up to the gates, Esper hidden in his sling. Saying he was a messenger with urgent news, he'd been taken into the Hall. Edel had greeted him gladly with a pounding hug. Edel was a tall, well-built man, with black hair caught at the nape of his neck, and a close-trimmed beard. His nose thrust prominently beneath his gray eyes. He pushed Juhrnus away, glancing at the other occupants of the Hall.

In a low voice, he said, "But you must not be seen. News of an *ahalad-kaaslane* in Patverseme would spread quickly indeed, with the blockade."

They'd retreated to Edel's offices. Edel sent for

food while Juhrnus released Esper to lounge on the warm hearth.

Juhrnus then began fielding a peppering of questions. He waved them aside, and told the story as he knew it. The telling went well into the night. He ended it by handing the oilskin-wrapped packet to Edel. The other man set it down, drumming his fingers on it, his expression grave.

"I had not heard about the Scallacians being involved," he said at last. "This Kedisan-Mutira sounds . . . intriguing."

Juhrnus smiled thinly, raising his glass in a salute and tossing the red wine back in a single swallow. "She is. Never let it be said I choose easy women."

Edel laughed ruefully. "What would be the adventure in that? How is Kebonsa—" He stopped, shaking his head. "It's easy to forget. Kebon. His brother wears the title of heir now. It has been a heavy blow to his father. To know his son is alive and in trouble, and have no remedy for it. And Ceriba—all that she went through, and to be in the Verit's hands. Poor girl."

"Kebonsat's been invaluable to Honor's Lord Marshal," Juhrnus said, refusing to drop the honorific at the end of his name. "Though the Dazien is none too friendly to him."

"The Iisand Samir has truly turned *nokula?*" asked Edel. "I can hardly imagine it. Any of it. But tell me, why have you risked the blockade to come here?"

Juhrnus rubbed his hands over his face. His eyes were gritty and he'd not slept for two days. "To get help. It's all in there." Juhrnus thrust his chin toward the packet. "I've been on the road for five weeks. Took longer than I thought to cross the blockade. Honor's running out of time."

Edel nodded thoughtfully, and then rose to his feet. He went to a small door nearly hidden in the rosewood paneling behind his desk. He opened it. Beyond Juhrnus could see a well-appointed apartment furnished in masculine shades of forest green and burgundy.

"You should clean up and sleep. Lock the outer door. The bath is already prepared for me. It'll be cold, but it'll have to do. We'll speak again in the morning."

Juhrnus had slept like the dead. In the morning, Edel had done all he could have asked for.

"I'll bring my men as soon as we can assemble. Probably two hundred strong, maybe a few more. I'll send word to Vadonis as well. It may be that they will send men too. It'll be two weeks before I can get started. We have to finish the harvest. There's too few of us after the war; I can't leave my people without winter stores. And I'll need to make arrangements for looking after Mekelsek."

Juhrnus nodded. As much as he wanted to push for speed, he didn't. It was a miracle that Edel was willing to help at all. To do so, he had to cross the blockade. And that meant every likelihood of losing Mekelsek and his title and everything else. Same as Kebonsat.

"I've already sent men with the messages to the Karalis and to the Wizard Guild. The latter isn't strong, you know," Edel cautioned against raised hopes. "There are few wizards left after the banishment, and of those, only a handful have any real power. If they do decide to help, they won't be able to hold back the Scallacians or the banished wizards long."

"Long enough for Reisil to fix things, I hope," Juhrnus said.

"How long before she returns?"

"Lady only knows. She doesn't even know what she's looking for, or if these nahuallis have it. She promised to return by midspring, with the answers or not."

"She does not break promises," Edel said softly.

"Sometimes you don't get a choice," Juhrnus returned flatly.

He'd stayed a few more days to rest and to regain his strength before returning home. The wounds he'd suffered in Kodu Riik had healed, but he was terribly, terribly tired. He slept a lot, spending the evenings talking with Edel. One night he asked about the spread of the plague in Patverseme.

"It's in pockets, mostly on the east slopes of the mountains and along the border of Kodu Riik. Anyone gets it, and the entire town is quarantined. When the plague finishes its course, the town is burned to the dirt. There have been only a few survivors. All are completely blinded. You have had such survivors as well?"

Juhrnus answered in the affirmative. A very few people survived the plague, and inevitably they were blind. No one knew why.

"I included word of these plague-healers in the letter I sent the Karalis. There have been rumors of *no-kulas* in some of the towns—but now I wonder if they are instead plague-healers. It would be a relief, if so. One of the towns hit was Priede, did you know? Not too long ago. Maybe three months. They'll be burning it before long, I expect. Avoid it when you go back."

"I didn't realize. I passed near there when I came across the Sadelema."

"Not too close, I hope," Edel said with a wry grin.

"Wouldn't matter if I did. I'll never get the plague. I was born to hang. Can't avoid fate."

Edel chuckled. Juhrnus quickly returned to the business at hand.

"Once you're through the blockade, you can cross at the bridge at Kallas. I spoke to Varitsema, the mayor. He will have supplies ready for you. With any luck, I'll meet you there and guide you the rest of the way. But I have to warn you, it was a close thing getting through the blockade. How are you going to bring your men through?"

"Luckily, I sent a number of troops in support of the blockade. They'll pass us through. And anyway, no one really cares about people going east; it's coming back that's going to be a problem."

A fact that Juhrnus hoped would speed his own journey home.

With a gusty sigh, he pushed himself to his feet and uncinched Indigo's saddle, dropping it heavily to the ground. He rubbed the wiry dun down with fistfuls of grass, lifting his hooves to pick out any rocks. He then picketed the animal at the edge of the meadow near the tumbling stream. Next he set about collecting wood and building a fire. He sat again, propping himself against his saddle, thinking he would rest a moment before baiting hook and catching his dinner.

~*I'm getting too old for this.*

~*You are just soft,* Esper jeered lovingly.

~*And who's been toting you around? Talk about soft.*

~*I do not dream of feather beds and rich food.*

~*No, because you're spoiled. You get waited on hand and foot. When was the last time you had to walk anywhere on your own?*

Esper answered with a hissing noise. He was tucked warmly in his sling, his tail wrapped around Juhrnus's waist.

~*That's what I thought.*

Juhrnus woke in the night, shivering. He was stiff from lying on the hard, frosted ground. Esper was curled up on his stomach. Juhrnus's head ached and his gut churned with hunger. He sat up, pushing a disgruntled Esper to the side. He dug through his pack for some hard bread and cheese that had begun to mold. He made a face at the taste, but forced himself to swallow it, and then took a swig from the brackish water in his water pouch. Grabbing his blanket, he curled up to sleep again, pillowing his head on his saddle as Esper burrowed against his chest.

The next day he was groggy and queasy. Juhrnus kicked himself for eating the moldy cheese. Later, his gut began to gurgle and he was forced to stop or mess himself. By midafternoon, he gave up and set up his camp, picketing Indigo. He quickly fell asleep, not bothering to eat, waking only to relieve himself of the cramps in his belly.

In the morning, his head ached and he felt weak. His skull felt stuffed with gauze and his entire body ached with pains that had nothing to do with exertion.

~What's wrong with me?

Esper didn't answer.

~Esper?

Still no answer.

Juhrnus struggled up into a sitting position, gazing about blearily. Esper lay at his feet, his tail thrashing slowly from side to side, his eyes wide and staring. He looked . . . Juhrnus fumbled for the word. *Scared*. He looked scared.

"Esper?" The word was raspy and weak. Juhrnus swallowed. His throat felt raw. He reached up and brushed his fingers across his forehead. His skin felt hot. *Chodha*. Not now. He remembered his joke to Edel. He was born to hang. He swallowed again, looking back to Esper. They'd better hang him fast then. Because he had the plague.

He knew what to expect. It began mildly, with a low fever, aches and pains, stomach upset, and dysentery. Then the fever would explode and the pain would be crippling. He'd become extremely sensitive to light and have dizzy spells. And then he'd get a rash and start bleeding internally. He'd find blood in his stool and his vomit. After that, things would get bad. He'd get big yellow blisters, and his arms and legs would start to rot off. He'd bleed from his ears and eyes and gums. Not that he'd see it. By then he'd be blind. The pain would be beyond bearing. All in all, sometime in the next two to three weeks, he'd be dead.

He spent that first night of horrified realization curled in a ball, hugging Esper tightly. There were no tears, just the pain of looming loss. To be without Esper . . . And then he wouldn't be able to help Reisil. He was going to let her down.

By the next morning, he'd gotten a shaky hold on himself. Esper had become stoic, refusing to let Juhrnus see his fear and pain. At least sisaliks didn't get the plague. It wasn't a lot of comfort, but it was some. Juhrnus elected to ride higher into the mountains, far off the trail. He didn't want to accidentally spread the disease to some unlucky traveler. He didn't know what to do with Indigo. The gelding was Reisil's horse. He knew she'd miss the beast. She'd miss him, too, hard as it was to believe, thinking back to when they grew up.

In the end he turned the gelding loose. And then he waited. In those short, bittersweet hours, he noosed himself tightly to Esper's mind.

On the fourth day, he began to burn. He was stricken with a dreadful pain. It made his body spasm and shake. He tied a tunic over his eyes, unable to stand the light. It pierced his head like knives of fire. He couldn't eat. He'd caught and dried some fish and filled his pack with late berries, but nothing would stay down but a few sips of water. He drank it sparingly; even the act of swallowing sent unbearable pain ripping through his body.

He lost Esper. He floated in blue flames that flayed his skin and shattered his bones. Fragments of thought ricocheted through his mind, but they were like nonsensical bits of a broken mirror, lacerating his brain as they swirled into strange, incomprehensible patterns. His flesh caught fire and charred from his bones. Steel jaws gnawed his entrails. He felt himself fracturing, crumbling into dust and nothingness.

Sound. Beautiful, clear, trumpeting fanfares. A light dancing trill of notes. A spiral, a waterfall, a single, pure tone.

He woke. He lay still. He felt . . . like wind. He frowned, wondering. That sound, like broken earth and torn sunlight. Rain falling upward and melting stone rivers. Wrong, wrong, wrong, wrong. Lightning freeze. Volcano spin. Earthquake breathe. Far away, too close, calling.

He blinked his eyes open. Everything sparkled and

shimmered with gossamer webs. So vibrant. In every color the world had ever thought of. It was glorious. But. Uneven. Stuttering. Discord.

Bites and stings and scrapes and holes.

Shiver.

Tug.

He looked down at himself.

Amazement.

There was a web inside him, intersecting through him. He was the center. The strands twisted away to *elsewhere*. Glossy, sparkling, matte, pearlescent, transclucent, opalescent. Jasper, citrine, raspberry, carrot, rhododendron, kohv. How many there were. A tree trunk, one. Unbreakable. A cable vine, two. Unbreakable. A diamond-bright thread. Unbreakable. He touched it.

Silky heat and something, *something*. It was vital. He knew it. He needed it. *Wanted* it. *Her* . . .

In the palace in Koduteel, Kedisan-Mutira felt a shock of something so intimate run through her that it seemed to stroke fingers through the fibers of her soul. She froze, caught in the moment, in the touch. "Juhrnus?" she whispered.

A feeling bloomed inside her like starshine. She gasped, tears rolling down her cheeks. She sat up in her bed, charms chiming gently together. She was whole now, her broken bones healed, her torn body knitted back together. Gone were the shackles she'd been made to wear before attaining *penakidah*. Now she no longer had to accept the commands of her brother sorcerers. She did, of course. It wasn't time yet to reveal her true abilities. But they'd failed to truly test her limits, and they would pay for that dearly. And soon. Once she decided how best to get what she wanted.

But this was something she hadn't expected.

"Something's wrong," she whispered to the presence she felt. It *must* be him. She rubbed her chest with the heel of her hand. The moment she'd seen him, something had rooted in her. Not magic. Something else. She had no explanation. But she'd *longed* for him. She'd feared for him. And much as she hated feeling bound to anyone, she could not sever the tie that had been forged between them in that first look. And now . . .

"What's happened to you? How are you here?"

She had a sense of song, uncertain and stumbling, but the notes were like struck crystal. Tears rolled down her cheeks.

"Will I see you?"

There was no answer. But she knew she would. At Mysane Kosk. Her fingernails bit deeply into her palms. Enemies.

There was a sudden swirl of green and volcanic orange, and then he was gone.

For the first time since she could remember, Kedisan-Mutira cried.

He returned to himself slowly. He turned his head with little jerks, curious now. Where was this? Billows of light and shadow and color. Song. Tapestry. He approved.

Juhrnus.

That was . . . not him.

A noise. Not song. Inside. His eyes widened with a pleasing trill of surprise. He explored. He paused when he came again to the strand of his web that resembled a tree trunk. He touched it.

It grabbed him back.

Home.

Images spun on a hurricane. Fragments without threads. They overwhelmed him, filling him up. He struggled against them. They caught in his webbing and crawled inward. Fear made a discordant sound. It resonated and echoed in the air, swelling and spreading away in rippling waves.

Wrong! No!

Panic spun the mass and everything escalated.

Here. Safe. Us.

He went still. He was held. Soft and warm. Pink and blue. He huddled into the other. Other?

~*Esper.*

Gray confusion.

~*Esper.* Ahalad-kaaslane.

~*What?*

~*We.*

The discordant sounds were smoothing, becoming harmony. He eased, but did not struggle to be free. He didn't . . . want . . . freedom.

~*What? Who?*

~*You remain, but you are different. We remain; we are not different. We are* ahalad-kaaslane.

The words were melodious. Soothing. Right.

~*Yes.*

~*Come look.*

And now there was a wriggle. Color unfurled. Sunlight and meadow grass. Dazzling. Entrancing. He followed. Esper. Sunlight and meadow grass. Trust. Bones of the earth.

They walked. Not far. Forever. It didn't matter. They stopped at the edge of a pool, an eddy in a slow-running brook. It tripped and tinkled in a gentle, right rhythm.

~*Look. See.*

Esper helped him. The wash of color and light thinned and receded, pulling away like a blanket. Reflection. The face that looked back at him was pale as mountain snow. The hair was white. The eyes were silver and opaque. A second face appeared. Memory. From Esper. Himself. Before. Curling brown hair, cheeks flat, not ridged, brown eyes circled in white, sun-browned skin.

~*Juhrnus.*

He looked at the brown-haired other. Juhrnus. Yes. He looked at himself. He cocked his head. Juhrnus?

~*You remain, but you are different. We remain; we are not different. We are* ahalad-kaaslane?

This time the last was a question.

Ahalad-kaaslane. He tested the word, listening to its

music. It circled inside his web, touching strands, striking notes that swirled together in melody. He understood.

~*Yes.*

He felt the other's relief and joy. The strands of his web suffused with gold. Yes. But as he paused to enjoy it, to listen, he heard the wrongness again. Discord. He shared it with Esper.

~*We must go there. We must sing it to harmony. Beauty.*

He must *sing.*

~*It is dangerous,* Esper cautioned, showing him images of decay and death, of others, like himself, being attacked. He watched, fascinated, as they unrolled across his mind's eye. It all had a rhythm, a pattern and a song. Beautiful in its starkness and rawness. But underneath it all was the unwinding dissonance, fraying the weaving of the concerto.

~*We must go.*

~*Yes.*

Juhrnus turned and began to walk.

~*Wait.*

He stopped.

~*What?*

~*We must bring the horse.*

~*Horse?*

Esper showed him the animal. From his mind flowed memories.

Juhrnus found the animal. It tossed up its head nervously, snorting. He sang to it and it settled, coming to nudge him. Delight filled him at the sound. Every thing, every action, every thought—these were snatches of melody in the grand symphony.

Esper showed him how to saddle and bridle the horse. His body remembered how to ride. But that was part of the music too. Esper lay across his shoulders, nearly weightless. And they rode down the mountain. To a place called Priede, where the song was broken.

Chapter 32

Reisil jerked awake, her heart thumping. Something was wrong; someone was in trouble!

Saljane remained fisted in her mind. She was safe. The relief was short-lived. Who then? Yohuac? She reached out with all her might, flinging herself farther than she thought she could. At last she brushed lightly up against Baku. He was surly, though his mental touch was surprisingly gentle.

~No harm here. He wins.

And he was gone.

Reisil let out a shaky breath and sat up, arms wrapped around her stomach. The foreboding didn't leave her. Something terrible had happened. She ground her knuckles against her eyes, swallowing her grief. Whom had she lost? And then she remembered Elutark and Ceriba. Silent sobs shook her shoulders.

Elutark had been one of the finest healers in Kodu Riik. And she was one of the strongest and wisest people Reisil knew. More than that, she'd been the closest thing Reisil had ever had to family.

"Lady keep you," Reisil whispered. "Lady keep Ceriba, too."

What a dreadful irony. That Ceriba should have escaped the fate Upsakes and Kaval had planned for her, only to fall prey to the Regent. She wondered if Kebonsat knew, and she pitied him. He would blame himself.

"The Regent will pay," she promised herself darkly. "Ceriba will have justice."

~*Yes,* came Saljane's firm reply.

~*Have I been asleep so long?*

~*It is the afternoon.*

~*But?*

~*The moon rises full again tonight.*

A chill ran down Reisil's spine. That wasn't possible.

She flung off her bedclothes and lunged to her feet. There were no windows in her room. It contained a comfortable bed, a chest of drawers and a small table. The things she'd left behind in Oceotl—her pack, gauntlet, and clothes—were neatly stacked there. The floor was covered in satiny wood that was warm to the touch. It smelled woodsy and fresh, and there was a current to the air.

Reisil started for the door and then stopped, drawing a deep breath. If Saljane said the full moon was rising again, then it was true. But how could that be? How long had she struggled in the great cavern? How long had she slept in the chamber of the Teotl?

She paced around the room, her body stiff. She scrubbed her hands through her hair and started for the door. Before she'd gone two steps, she glanced down at herself. She was still wearing the robe. Quickly she dressed and braided her hair. When she was through, she slid on the gauntlet.

Have you been all right?

Reisil caught the image of the circle of great black and red trees marching on Atli Cihua.

~*The hunting is good. I have been dry.*

Saljane sounded smug and Reisil couldn't help but smile.

~*I'll come get you as soon as I can figure my way out of this place,* she promised.

There were still no shoes, and Reisil sighed. She shrugged and went to the door. In the large meeting room—or blue room, as she thought of it—she found a handful of the elder nahuallis, including Ilhanah, Ampok, and Piketas. Reisil's entrance silenced them. Ilhanah rose, coming to grasp her in a chilly embrace.

"Welcome, sister. We greet you in the name of *Illhuicatl*. Come and sit with us."

She led Reisil back to the circle. Piketas scooted aside to make room for her. Ilhanah retreated to a nearby door for a moment and then returned to sink gracefully to her cushion.

"Food will be brought. But this may soothe your hunger until then. Xochil is an acquired taste," she warned.

She poured a rich, dark drink. Specks of red floated in the foam on the top. Reisil held it to her lips, sniffing. It smelled wonderful.

But the fragrance was deceiving. It could have used sugar. A lot of it. The taste was bitter with an intense flavor that overwhelmed her mouth. It wasn't entirely unpleasant. But long after she swallowed, her tongue and throat continued to burn with a heat that had nothing to do with temperature. Vaguely she remembered Yohuac describing xochil, that it was far better than kohv. She smiled inwardly. He could keep it.

When she'd eaten, Ilhanah stood. "Sister, the council will convene in two hours. Until then perhaps you would like to wander the grounds outside?"

Reisil bit back her frustration. More waiting. Still, she would like to see Saljane. She excused herself and did as suggested.

The goshawk leaped onto her fist with a glad cry. Reisil smiled, stroking Saljane's feathers.

"A fine animal. I wondered if you had lost her on your journey."

Reisil jumped, turning to find that Ilhanah had followed her.

"You have trained her well. I would have thought she'd have flown off without your care."

"She's in a strange land," Reisil said, realizing that Ilhanah had no idea of their real bond. Reisil planned to keep it that way. "And she's been with me some time. I would have been more surprised if she had not waited."

Ilhanah nodded, apparently satisfied. But her next question thrust deep. "And your other pet? The winged *copicatl*? What became of it?"

Reisil thought quickly. "I sent him back to Kodu Riik," she lied. "I wanted them to know I'd found you."

Ilhanah nodded, but didn't look entirely convinced.

"I borrowed him from a friend," Reisil went on, spinning out the lie. "He's a magical creature, you know. Juhrnus does not manage well without the coaldrake's power to fuel his spells. He'll need his full strength to keep things stable until my return."

The idea of Juhrnus trying to use magic was enough to make Reisil smile. But it faded at Ilhanah's frown. "He?"

And Reisil was suddenly reminded that the only accepted magic wielders in Cemanahuatl were women. "Yes."

"Do many men practice magic in Kodu Riik?"

"Not many, no." Nor many women. But Reisil didn't elaborate.

"Ah. Some men are exceptional, then."

Reisil could go along with that. Many of the men she knew were quite exceptional, in one way or another. "Yes."

"And the nahuallis accept this? They don't find it causes . . . difficulties?"

How to answer that? "Some, but they add to our strength. We need all we can get, at the moment." Which Reisil guessed was something Ilhanah understood well.

"That is true." The other woman walked silently with Reisil for a few minutes longer before retreating inside. Reisil could tell Ilhanah wanted to ask more questions, but then she might have to answer a few of Reisil's.

Reisil sat beneath one of the great trees with Sal-jane, breathing deeply of its rich, mellow scent. Reisil closed her eyes.

A scrap of memory fluttered through her mind. She came awake suddenly, scrabbling to capture the fragment. It hovered just out of reach. Tantalizingly close. Something she'd overheard . . . something Ampok had said. *If the magic dies entirely . . .*

Reisil sat up straight. Why hadn't she put it together before? The magic in Cemanahuatl was dying! Fading to nothing. And in Kodu Riik it was growing. Excitement gushed through her.

The magic was draining away from here and spilling into Kodu Riik. That's why the nahualli *rinda* was turning up in the spell-chains of the *nokulas.*

It was a key piece of the puzzle. Reisil could feel it. The wizards had told her that the spell they cast at My-sane Kosk was to seek greater power. And though it had gone terribly wrong, it had also succeeded. The power the wizards sought was flowing. But Kodu Riik wasn't meant to hold the magic of two worlds. If she didn't stop it, Kodu Riik and Cemanahuatl would be remade. Would the *nokulas* even survive? Reisil wondered. Maybe, just maybe, they wouldn't want to take that chance.

Reisil started when Ampok came for her. The nahu-alli's hair was violet. There were *rinda* painted on her forehead, arms, and legs in pale blue and yellow.

"Come. We begin."

As they went inside to join the nahualli council, tiny beads of rain began to fall, making a sizzling sound on the paving tiles. Ampok and Reisil ran to escape its stinging wrath.

The council began with all the women filing in. There were more than a hundred of them. They wore their gold and silver ornaments, with their hair hanging loose and black. They sat in concentric circles, with the senior closer to the center. Age did not determine seniority, Reisil noticed. Undoubtedly the "elders" were the most powerful. Reisil was given a position of honor in the centermost circle.

A dinner followed. Platters were carried in and passed around. There were thirteen courses in all. By the time pitchers of the bitter, spicy xochil were passed around, Reisil was stuffed to the gills and itching to get started.

At last Ilhanah set aside her cup and began a low chant. The nahuallis in each circle picked up her words and repeated them, but in a staggered fashion, so that soon the room was full of looping voices all saying something different. Not just something. They were invoking the Teotl. They were saying each of the fifty-two gods' names. Slowly the sound traveled to the outer ring and the voices at the interior fell silent. When the entire room was still, Ilhanah spoke again.

"Sisters! We gather here at our most sacred place to hold council. The Foreseeing made by Ampok has brought us a new sister. I ask her now to speak her tale so that we may learn and consider what must be done next."

Reisil took a breath and began, speaking loud enough so that everyone could hear. She began with the drought, and the plague and the *nokulas*, and of learning that they had come from Mysane Kosk. She talked about the attack of the wizards there, and the spell that had gone awry. She explained that they did not know what had gone wrong. She talked about discovering what the *nokulas* were, and about the Foreseeing by Nurema, once a nahualli from Cemanahuatl. At the mention of her, there was a jittering of voices.

"Nurema?"

"She said she went by Nixcira before she came to Kodu Riik."

There was an audible gasp from many of the women. Even Ilhanah looked startled.

"We thought she was lost. Ampok's Foreseeing spoke only of you and your mother, Kinatl."

Kinatl. These women had been her friends, even her family. Was one of them Reisil's aunt or cousin? She swallowed, feeling like she'd been punched in the stomach. She bent her head down, hiding her reaction. Ilhanah didn't notice.

"This is very good news. She has been missed."

The babble continued for a few more minutes, giving Reisil the chance to gain control. When Ilhanah had quieted the room, Reisil began again, her voice gravelly.

Now she told about Nurema's Foreseeing—that both Kodu Riik and Cemanahuatl would be unmade if Mysane Kosk could not be saved.

"She is sure of this?" The question came from an older nahualli. Though her hair remained black as coal, her face was lined with age.

Reisil nodded.

"How is it to be done?"

"I don't know. That's why I've come. But there's one other thing."

And now she told them about the Regent and his determination to destroy Mysane Kosk. "He has asked for help from the Scallacian sorcerers. But neither the wizards nor the *nokulas* will permit Mysane Kosk to be destroyed, though the wizards would attempt to do so themselves if they thought the Scallacians might gain control of it. Nurema believes the Scallacians will try to gain control. It is too great a source of magical power to just destroy it.

"No matter what happens, there will be a tremendous battle. The magic unleashed will certainly wreak havoc on Kodu Riik. It is precarious at best. And if that happens, Cemanahuatl will surely be destroyed."

"When do you expect this to happen?" Ilhanah demanded quietly.

"Within half a year. The Regent will march when the snows melt and the passes clear."

There was a sudden silence. Reisil could almost hear Piketas's thoughts. If Reisil did not succeed before then, they would take matters into their own hands and destroy Ti'Omoru in the hopes of stopping the backlash from the battle. Reisil shivered. She couldn't let them do it.

Her train of thought was interrupted by first one question, then another. They pelted at her faster and

faster, like a hail of arrows. The nahuallis were interested in the details. Nothing seemed too small. Reisil
told them everything she knew, hiding only the special
bond of the *ahalad-kaaslane,* the extent of her own
abilities, and anything about Yohuac.

At last the silence returned. Reisil was sweating as
if she'd run up the mountain again.

"I thank you, sister, for bringing us this news. We
must now retire to consider it. The council remains
open. We will meet together again at daybreak," Ilhanah said.

"I have one more question," Piketas said before
anyone could move. Reisil faced her, knowing what
the question would be. She was not disappointed.
"You have said what will happen if this Mysane Kosk
is destroyed. But what happens if we seal the rift at
Ti'Omoru? What if we cut the head off the snake
biting us?"

Before Reisil could answer, Ilhanah interrupted.

"It is a question we will consider. Let us retire."

With that, the small interior circle rose and filed
out, and then the next circle and so on. Reisil was left
to sit alone. Fear clutched her entrails and she hardly
realized the passing time. At last she stood. Ampok
stood waiting.

"I will show you to your room. It is easy to get lost
until you know the way."

Reisil thanked her, grateful for the consideration.
By the time they arrived at her door, she was thoroughly lost.

"Someone will come for you in the morning,"
Ampok said, unsmiling.

Reisil went inside, settled Saljane on the bedstead,
and stripped off her clothing. She flung herself onto
the bed. Saljane hopped down onto the pillows near
her head.

"What will I do if they decide to destroy Ti'Omoru?"

Saljane only rubbed her beak against Reisil's cheek.
There was no good answer to the question.

"Well, at least they're finally talking to me. Maybe

tomorrow I'll begin to find the answers and it won't be a problem," Reisil murmured, stroking Saljane's breast feathers.

~You will return in time. Kodu Riik will be safe, Saljane said confidently.

But Reisil remembered the feeling that had woken her that morning. Something terrible had happened to someone she cared about. Again she wondered who.

Chapter 33

The journey had been long and exhausting. Soka reined in, turning to scan the long line of wagons trundling over the rutted road. They hadn't had any trouble whatsoever with raiders or snow, but there had been a more than a dozen broken or fallen-off wheels, three shattered axles, five spills, and more lame horses than he could count. Not to mention getting stuck in the mud and losing one entire wagon and team through the ice on a river. The piled ore in the high-sided wagons made them top-heavy and difficult to safely maneuver, especially over steep terrain.

It had almost been as though someone were sabotaging them. But it was all just bad luck. And worse luck was that it meant spending a whole lot more time with his father than he wanted to. With the frustrations of the repairs and the constant urge to hurry, Soka's temper was frayed to a hair.

Soka had managed to spend most of his time dealing with the various troubles and avoiding his father's company. It was a large caravan. There were twenty heavy ore wagons, ten lighter supply and equipment wagons, and a string of ten extra draft horses and twenty cavalry horses. The whole caravan was escorted by a hundred and twenty soldiers. There was a lot that he could do that didn't require sitting across the fire from his father. Not that Thevul Bro-heyek did much sitting. The man was everywhere, and he didn't mind getting his hands dirty. Truth be told,

Soka had learned a thing or two from him about leadership and organization. But he didn't have to like it.

They'd stopped and picked up the cache of weapons and equipment hidden by Reisil. Chunks of bone still littered the killing field, with bits of dried flesh clinging to them. They crunched beneath Soka's feet, and he tried not to remember the grisly horror of that day. The men who called themselves the Rum Bluffers had deserved their fate. But the memory of the butchery churned his stomach. Soka's father paced beside him. His face grew steadily paler as they crossed the field to the copse where Reisiltark had hidden the trove of weapons.

"What happened here?"

"They were a blight," Soka said sharply, feeling the need to defend what Reisiltark had done.

His father bent and picked up a piece of skull. A portion of lower jaw dangled by a thread of sinew from a small section containing part of an eye socket. It was one of the larger bits remaining from that day.

"This is— How?" Thevul Bro-heyek sounded repulsed, and beneath it was a thread of fear.

"Magic. One thing you should not forget about Reisiltark. She's *ahalad-kaaslane*. She will protect Kodu Riik to her last breath. And she's fierce."

"Fierce?" His father's laughter was a harsh croak in the still air. "She's bloodthirsty."

"She's a mother wolf. Be glad you're one of her children."

"I'll be sure to introduce myself to mommy," his father said, tossing the broken skull aside.

Soka laughed.

Reisil had set up the wards with a "lock" hidden up in a tree. When Soka climbed up, he found a twist of silver wire. It didn't look like much. But she'd told him to cut it and the rest of the wards would stop working. He did as he'd been told, and the mound of weapons appeared. He climbed back down to find his father staring, stunned, at the heaped weapons and armor.

"How many hands died?" he grated.

Soka shrugged. "Do you count the rats or do you just kill them and be glad they aren't eating your food and spreading disease?"

His father turned to look at him, his eyes clouded. "What in the Demonlord's three hells are we about to walk into?"

Soka rubbed his hand over his mouth, feeling the rough bristles of his new-growing beard. He thought of Aare and prodded the poison bead with his tongue, conscious of the rest of the poisons secreted around his body. A slow, cruel smile curved his lips. "The rending of the world. And if we're lucky, we get to keep our swords," he said, gesturing to the pile, still stained with blood and dried gobbets of flesh.

That had been weeks ago. And now they were nearly back to Honor. Soka itched to ride ahead. He felt a sudden streak of worry for Metyein. There was a heaviness in the air, matched by the thick pewter clouds above. Something was *building*. Like steam in a teakettle.

His horse pranced and sawed at the reins. He turned as his father rode up beside him.

"Trouble?"

Soka shook his head. "If the *nokulas* or wizards wanted to stop us, they would have by now." But then, they weren't worried about swords and spears.

Thevul Bro-heyek nodded, his face a mask.

"What is it?" Soka asked.

"There ought to be more snow."

"There's been a drought."

His father shook his head. "Even so. The passes are going to clear quicker. If they are even blocked."

Fear wriggled into Soka's bowels. If that was true, then Aare was going to come much sooner. He swore softly.

They tipped the rise into Honor's valley at midday. His father's gasp of shock at the crystalline brilliance of Mysane Kosk was audible. The thickness of the air had increased. It was warmer here, too, like early spring. Soka shrugged out of his cloak and slung it over his horse's withers, foreboding crawling like spiders along his skin. He jerked his head to look over his shoulder, as if expecting an army to ride up the road behind them.

The sound of horns echoed across the valley as they trundled down the road. Gravel filled in the worst of the ruts, lending them better speed. The fields were still green, though clearly they'd been harvested in preparation for winter. Infantry and cavalry trained on the fallow turf. At the sound of the horns, they paused; then two riders came galloping. Behind him, Soka felt his father's troops snap to attention.

Metyein and Kebonsat thundered up, reaching for Soka and thumping him on the back, grinning widely.

"You lice-infested *ganyik!* All of this is ore?" Kebonsat said, his eyes scanning the wagons greedily.

He was thinner than Soka remembered. He radiated an intensity that felt dangerously volatile. Like he had little to lose. Which meant pushing the line, taking stupid risks. *Takes one to know one.* The poison bead clicked against his teeth.

"Ore and some weapons and armor. Should keep you busy for a little while."

Kebonsat was already reining around and galloping for Raven, where forges had been set up. By the time the wagons got to the valley floor, the fires would be raging.

"He's not been this happy since . . ." Metyein shook his head. "A while. It's good to see you, and—" His gaze shifted to the man riding beside Soka. Suddenly the air was frigid. "Thevul Bro-heyek," he said, tipping his head in the barest of bows.

"Lord Marshal," Soka's father returned, scanning Metyein up and down, settling on the chain of office.

The younger man didn't flinch, didn't shy from the clear challenge in the Thevul's gaze. Metyein had changed too, Soka thought proudly. Gone was his uncertainty. He wore the skin of leadership like he'd been Lord Marshal for a decade.

"Welcome to Honor." Metyein put peculiar emphasis on the last word.

Thevul Bro-heyek flicked up his brows. "Subtle." His voice was honey-smooth.

"I wouldn't want to be mistaken," Metyein said, looking pointedly at Soka's eye patch. "Did you get it back?" he asked Soka.

"No."

"Why not?" This directed back to his father. It was asked in the crisp tone of a Lord Marshal to a subject. The chill emanating from Metycin grew downright glacial.

Soka stared. This was a side of his friend he had not seen. His stomach clenched slowly as he thought of the two hundred men behind them. One word from his father and Metyein would be cut down. And they were too far from the stockades to get help. His hand crept to the pommel of his sword. But he didn't know if his pounding heart was in readiness for a fight or eagerness to hear the answer to the question. When it came, he felt flattened. It was so . . . ordinary. Why hadn't his father told him long ago?

"It is buried with his mother," came the uninflected reply. "But that is not truly the question that you are asking. You want to know if I can be trusted. After all, what kind of man will risk something as precious as his son's life and pain for mere conquest? I've got two hundred men at my back. That's a significant problem for you if we turn rogue."

"It is." Metyein pulled his horse up, turning to face Soka's father. Behind them, the wagons creaked to a halt, and there were shouted questions down the line.

Thevul Bro-heyek nodded, looking first at Metyein and then at Soka. "All right, then. I have lived on the high line of Kodu Riik all my life. Far from the court, far from the war and the strife. In many ways, those of us who live in the shadow of the Tornaat Mountains are of a different land, with different laws and customs. It is easy to forget about Koduteel and about the Iisand and to simply do as we see fit.

"I knew Geran from my youth. I had been to court; I had even fought at his side during the Fourth Guelt invasion. We were friends. And so I did not truly believe him when he told me he was taking my son, that I must stop raiding against my neighbors. I thought that he would take you under his wing, that he would teach you the lessons of the court.

"Basham Riinles held much of the land bordering Bro-heyek. He was a devious, cruel, and corrupt man, and a piss-poor warden of his lands and people."

"So you thought you'd just walk in and take over for him," Soka said, his teeth clipping together.

His father's eyes blazed with an emotion Soka couldn't read. He continued on as if he hadn't been interrupted.

"Riinles feared me. He began collecting an army. Mostly men who'd run from the war, and others who were running from the law. And he brought in Gueltians. Since I was leashed by my promise to the Iisand—guaranteed by you—Riinles felt free to expand his own borders. He stayed out of Bro-heyek—Geran would support anything I did to fend off hostility. He went after the smaller holdings, forcing the Holders to sign over their rights and become tenants.

"That was bad enough, but men who serve out of greed are quick to become restless and hungry. Soon they were beyond his control. They began to pillage and burn. They took women and girls from good families and kept them as whores, passing them around and discarding them when they became poxed or pregnant. They destroyed entire villages, killing whomever they pleased.

"At last Riinles came to me and begged for my help. I was furious with him, but the vermin had to be dealt with. I had been sitting on my hands, watching, for far too long. No man with balls should sit while that sort of thing goes on without trying to stop it. By then, only Bro-heyek had the strength to challenge them. Maybe that was Riinles's plan all along.

I was stupid. I'd forgotten I was not dealing with an honorable man."

At that, Thevul Bro-heyek flushed, but his gaze remained unwavering on his son. "It is for that stupidity that you lost your eye. I began a campaign that summer to destroy Riinles's marauders. The moment it began, Riinles sent word to Geran that I'd broken my pledge and invaded. We succeeded in putting his men down, but the damage was done. I received your eye in a box."

Soka felt like he'd been hit on the head. He hardly knew if he could believe the story. "I never knew," he said softly.

"It was a condition of keeping Bro-heyek. I'd already lost you. Riinles convinced Geran that I should not be allowed to raise my own heir. You would be tainted, taught to emulate me. Instead, you should stay at court and acquire a proper education on how to serve Kodu Riik. Any contact from me to you would be considered grounds for stripping my title and lands. There was nothing I could do. Riinles had laid his trap well, and I blundered into it like a moon-blind calf," he said, his knuckles turning white as he gripped his reins.

Metyein considered him for a moment. "Stupidity is not a persuasive argument for joining us," he said stonily.

"No, but you asked for the truth. And you can ill afford to turn down two hundred trained men. Consider as well that it is in my best interests for you to succeed. Otherwise, as Soka had pointed out to me, the Regent will undoubtedly strip my lands."

Finally Metyein nodded. "It will do."

They rode down into Honor. The Bro-heyek men were billeted in the unfinished Salamander. Its walls were up, but it had no gates or buildings. It would be completed quickly enough with the added manpower. Kebonsat took charge of overseeing the unloading of the ore and weaponry, while Soka cleaned himself up and reported to Metyein.

"It's good to see your ugly face again," Metyein said, slapping Soka on the back. "Though men across Honor are locking their wives and daughters up."

"I'll have you know I'm a happily married man," Soka said, pouring himself a mug of mulled wine. When only silence met his announcement, he turned to find Metyein gaping, his mouth opening and closing. "You look like a fish. Or a mind-blighted whore."

"Married?" Metyein at last squeezed out. "To who?"

Soka smiled, enjoying his friend's astonishment. "A pert young thing, with a razor mouth. And energetic." He waggled his eyebrows. "Her name is Roomila."

"But . . . how? You, of all people."

Soka dropped into a chair and kicked out his legs, crossing them at the ankles. "Come now. Couldn't I have been desperately smitten with a young beauty on first sight?"

"Her breasts, maybe." Metyein sloshed wine into his mug and sat opposite Soka. "So, what happened?"

"The usual. My father decided I ought to try to conceive an heir before I ran back here and got killed. The next thing I know, Roomila's in my bed, and I've got a ring through my nose." He left out the tacit threat that had gone along with it: Marry or no metal. It hadn't been a bad bargain, and it was his to make. For Honor and for his friends.

Metyein sat back, scratching his neck. "I hope she's got a steel backbone."

"I believe that she does. And sharp claws. But tell me, what has been happening here?"

Metyein began to speak, giving reports on building, supplies, and training. "Kebonsat and I have been drilling with the troops regularly. They won't break under the first attack, anyhow, and they'll likely not cut off their own hands or shoot their neighbors," Metyein said sardonically.

"Any word from Koduteel? What's Aare up to?"

Metyein reported what Juhrnus had said.

"I sent him to Patverseme for help."

"So what are you doing for supplies?"

"Some of our shipments have come through, and we got a harvest in, such as it is. Our hunters have to go fairly far afield anymore, but they've been preserving the meat, so we have stores. I've sent fishermen up the Sadelema River above Mysane Kosk and we've dried barrels of trout and grayling. We've been cutting hay for the horses in the mountain meadows. We've enough to last."

To last until Aare came? Or until Mysane Kosk swallowed up the valley? And how much time was there between the two?

"No word from Reisiltark?"

Metyein's only answer was a silent shake of his head.

"Where's Juhrnus now?"

"On his way home, with any luck. I expect him by early next month."

"How is Emelovi?"

"She's . . . coming along. My father always said that information was three-quarters of the battle. Once you know what you're working with, you can decide what to do. That's Emelovi. She started paying attention. Now she asks intelligent questions and makes useful suggestions. She's a good judge of character and potential. At least, most of the time."

"Kebonsat?" Soka asked knowingly.

"She's unbent with him. At least enough to be civil. But more than that—" He shrugged.

"What about the *nokulas* and the wizards? Any attacks?"

"Quiet. But we figure they're waiting for Reisiltark to return and Aare to get here. We aren't much of a threat until then."

"And what about the plague?"

Metyein drew a heavy breath. "We were doing well. A couple of cases here and there, nothing out of control. But then a month ago, it got worse."

Soka's mouth went dry. "How many?"

"Total since you left? Just under eighty dead. There's about forty still alive now. We lost Gamulstark, too."

Soka stared. So many . . .

Soka had seen the plague at its worst. He'd hidden in a plague wagon to escape Koduteel. He'd seen the bodies and the pyres, but somehow he hadn't thought of how many people died of it. How many could still die of it. Unexpectedly he thought of Roomila and felt a pang of something he didn't care to examine too closely.

"Any luck finding one of these plague-healers Reisiltark told us about?" he asked roughly.

Metyein shook his head. "We found a body in a village south of here. It had been hacked up with an ax. Wasn't much left. They don't look like *nokulas*, not really. Mostly it's in the eyes. But they are definitely not human. And scared folks are going to kill something like that before it can kill them. I don't know if we'll ever get to one of these plague-healers before someone slaughters it."

Soka watched his friend, seeing the lines of worry pulling his mouth and eyes down. He hesitated, not wanting to add to the burden the other man shouldered. But he had to be told.

"There's something else," he began.

Metyein stiffened. "What?"

"We had a lot of trouble with the caravan. A lot of wheel trouble and so forth. But in one thing we were lucky. The roads were absolutely clear. Hardly two inches of snow where it was deep."

It took a few moments for the information to sink in.

"No snow? But it's midwinter. I thought it was just an effect of being in the valley—" Metyein thrust himself to his feet and paced to the other side of the room and back. He stopped, his eyes meeting Soka's.

"It's going to be an early spring."

"Very early," Soka agreed.

"Reisiltark won't be back before Aare gets here."

Soka didn't answer.

Metyein tapped his thigh, thinking, as he stared at the floor.

"I'd better get Kebonsat and Emelovi. We'll have to adjust our plans. What about your father?"

Soka lifted one shoulder. "He's one of the best. You'd be a fool to not use him. As he said, it's in his best interests for us to succeed."

Metyein came to stand before him, stretching out a hand. Soka stood and took it, gripping tightly. "You did well," Metyein said soberly, putting his other hand on Soka's shoulder. "I know how much it cost you to go to Bro-heyek and beg for us. I was never so proud in my life as when I saw you riding at the head of the caravan. And beside your father, no less."

Metyein's words lit a glow in Soka. He grinned. "I told you. I won't fail you."

Chapter 34

A fist pounded on the workroom door. "Come quickly!"

Reisil set aside the spell she'd been working on, yanking open the door with a frown. But the young nahualli messenger was already knocking at another door, shouting her message. Reisil glanced over her shoulder unhappily. It contained bins of the spiky-shaped *rinda* made of stone, wood, cloth, metal, and clay. There were three low workbenches set in a triangle and a scattering of cushions for sitting. On one of the tables was the spell she'd been working on. She hated to leave in the middle of it. But the summons was imperative. With a frustrated sigh, Reisil closed her door and sealed it. She used wards of her own making. She joined the other women emerging into the corridor.

The workshops were located underground beneath the living quarters of Atli Cihua. She'd had hers for six weeks, since just after Miidagi, when the dark power of the Demonlord began to wane and the Lady's waxed golden. Before that, she'd been schooled in the meaning and history of each *rinda*. And there were a lot of them. Fifty-two of the greater *rinda*, a hundred and six of the lesser, and the thirteen moon *rinda*. After she'd demonstrated a thorough understanding of each, her teachers had given her some sense of crafting the spells. Unlike the wizards who constructed chains, the nahuallis built spell sculptures, or so Reisil had come to think of them. The pieces of *rinda* were fitted together like a three-dimensional puzzle. Figuring out which to choose and how to order them was the hard part.

When at last they'd given her a workroom, Reisil had locked herself inside nearly round the clock. She slept on her seat cushions, and came out only when her stomach wouldn't let her ignore it any longer. She'd forgotten to bathe as well, but by the end of the first week, the other women had refused to let her eat until she was clean. And *they* had scrubbed her. Now Reisil made sure to bathe more regularly, and retired to her room for at least a few hours' good sleep.

Working with the nahualli *rinda* was both easier and harder than the wizards' *rinda*. Creating the puzzle-sculptures seemed nearly effortless. But choosing the *rinda* to achieve her effect was confusing at best. There had to be balance, and some of the *rinda* fit together better than others, as if their natures called to or shunned others. The greater *rinda* were most difficult to work with, requiring a great deal of stamina and a constant flow of power. They seemed to have a mind of their own, and controlling them was grueling. As for the moon *rinda* . . .

At first Reisil had hesitated even to touch them. They were made of pure silver and they radiated something that reminded her of the *nokulas*. They felt molten, seeming to change shape to mimic other *rinda*. It took all of Reisil's concentration and magic to control them and fit them together as she wanted. And she still had no idea how to construct the spell-sculpture that the *copicatl* had shown her in the cavern.

She was beginning to understand some of what was happening at Mysane Kosk. The wizards had sought to open up a well of power. Instead they'd opened up a kind of drain. The magic of Cemanahuatl was emptying into Kodu Riik through Mysane Kosk. But the magic of Cemanahuatl wasn't merely an unformed flow to be molded as desired. It already had form: the *rinda*.

They existed already, floating in the nethersphere. The shapes Reisil used to build spells in her workshop were *rinda* that had been captured. Left alone in the nethersphere, they merged and combined naturally to create balanced, natural spells that then were too heavy, too solid for the nethersphere. Spontaneous creation. The *rinda* wanted to *be*. They wanted solid form and purpose. This natural impetus made it easier to shape them. It also accounted for the changes at Mysane Kosk, and for the *nokulas*.

Reisil remembered the spell-chains that made up the *nokulas*. The nahualli *rinda* were never meant to be chained together. But the spell the wizards cast had called them out of the nethersphere and allowed them to combine with the *rinda* in the original wizard spell. The result had been spell-chains that married the two *rinda* to create new beings, new landscapes. That was why none were the same. No combination was alike.

Reisil had begun experimenting with combining some of the wizard *rinda* with the lesser *rinda* of the nahuallis. Her first attempt had been to create a cup of hot kohv topped with nussa spice. Nothing that existed in Cemanahuatl. The first fifty attempts had gone badly. Then . . . it had worked. The *rinda* had seemed at last to understand what she wanted them to do. The right blocks seemed to jump into her hand.

She'd experimented with other spells. The greater *rinda* were much more recalcitrant to her wants, and the moon *rinda* . . . She could almost hear them *singing*, a siren song of want and power. She found her hands drifting toward them and had to concentrate every waking moment not to succumb to their call. Her dreams were filled with song that made her heart race and her body ache with endless want. She didn't sleep often.

Today she'd begun trying to merge the nahualli *rinda* with the ordinary Kodu Riikian words she'd used in creating her wards. If it worked— An idea was beginning to worm its way up into her mind. She couldn't quite reach it yet. But soon. She just needed a little bit more time.

Reisil joined the nahuallis congregating in the blue room. More and more came in, filling it to bursting. There was no space to sit. Reisil suddenly realized that there were far more now than had been at the first council. They'd been slowly drifting into Atli Cihua. Were all the nahuallis in Cemanahuatl here? She tried to count. There had to be nearly four hundred. If not all of the land's nahuallis were here, most were, Reisil guessed.

A gong sounded and quieted the buzz of voices. Then Ilhanah rose in the air, floating above so that everyone could see. Her eyes glittered with excitement.

"The *pahtia* draws to a close. The remaining champions are near Tizalan. They will ascend the Temple soon. We must go. We leave in an hour."

Reisil stood confused as the nahuallis fled to prepare. Leave? She wasn't ready. She had to stay and figure out what to do!

She waited as Ilhanah descended lightly to the floor.

"I can't leave," she said bluntly.

Ilhanah's expression tightened. She'd been one of Reisil's teachers, but their sessions had grown frostier and more wooden as the days progressed. Reisil wasn't sure why. Sharing so much with an outsider, perhaps. Or perhaps Ilhanah was starting to agree with Piketas.

"The *pahtia* ends. The nahuallis must gather. It is our way."

"Surely I can stay and work," Reisil said, but Ilhanah was already shaking her head.

"It would be a dishonor to *Ilhuicatl*."

Reisil wanted to argue more, but could see that Ilhanah was not going to change her mind.

"When will we return?" she asked, her voice sharper than she intended. Easier to catch flies with honey, she silently reminded herself.

"As soon as we may," was Ilhanah's unhelpful reply. Then she softened, seeing Reisil's dismay. "We serve *Ilhuicatl*. We must be there when his son is born to Cemanahuatl."

As Reisil returned to her quarters, she had a sickening feeling that this was the last time she'd stand in Atli Cihua. She'd learned a lot. And an idea had begun to simmer. But was it enough? It had to be.

She went first to her quarters, stuffing her few possessions inside her pack. Then she returned to her workroom, locking the door behind her. For a moment she thought about barricading herself inside and then dismissed her foolishness. The nahuallis would pry her out by whatever means necessary, and she dared not challenge them. Every day reports came in of things getting worse in Cemanahuatl: more death, more terrible storms, more news of unmaking. More and more of the nahuallis had begun to look at Reisil with a kind of fatalistic hopelessness. As if they'd given up on her. Defying them might push them to desperate measures: to destroying Ti'Omoru. Piketas wasn't the only one who argued it was their best chance of saving Cemanahuatl.

Reisil looked at the bins of *rinda*, wondering what she should take with her. She found herself staring at the thirteen moon *rinda*. Hardly knowing what she was doing, she gathered them up. Their song intensified at her touch and she shuddered with the power that streaked through her.

She turned to her pack. It seemed ludicrous to just jumble the *rinda* inside and toss it over her shoulder. Would the nahuallis even allow her to take them? No. She had to hide them.

Reisil piled the *rinda* on a table. She grabbed her stylus and the ink she'd made from charcoal, sap, and plant dye. She opened her pack and began to write on the inside. Her hand moved quickly and surely across the leather. She hurried as fast as she dared. She didn't want to force them to come for her.

At last she finished. She was sweating and breathing

hard. She scooped up the moon *rinda* and dumped them unceremoniously inside, ignoring their song. *Dear Lady, let my spell hold.*

She tied the pack closed and instantly the song muted. Reisil let out a sigh of relief. She slung it over her shoulder and left the workroom and sealed it again. If any nahuallis were left behind, they'd have to work hard to open the door. Hopefully it would be too late to stop her by the time they got it open.

The journey to Tizalan took eight days. They went overland the first two. All but Reisil had dyed their hair violet and painted their faces with *rinda*. Only the elders, Reisil noticed, were permitted to wear the greater *rinda*. None wore the moon. Saljane floated above, jumping from tree to tree. Reisil was delighted to see her. Once Reisil had begun experimenting with the *rinda*, the goshawk had decided to retreat back outside the walls of Atli Cihua to keep from distracting her *ahalad-kaaslane*.

Midmorning on the third day, they came to a great river, its sluggish waters green and murky. The opposite side was a dim, gray shadow that faded into the clouds. A flotilla of canoes carved of a strong, light wood and covered with bark were tied within the trees, protected by wards. They boarded them as the rain began again. There were ten women in each.

As she paddled along, Reisil had a chance to think. Yohuac's face haunted her. Would she see him? Would he see her? Did he even live? Baku didn't answer her when she reached out to him. The idea was nearly crippling. Her body spasmed and she dropped her oar. Ampok fished it back out of the water, handing it to her wordlessly. Reisil was very glad of the nahualli's habitual chill silence. She couldn't have borne talking at that moment.

On the the sixth day, the enormous river they followed joined another, even larger waterway, fully two leagues across and very, very deep. Enormous fish and other things swam in the swift waters. Now only six of the nahuallis in each boat rowed. The other four watched the water restlessly. Power crackled in the air as they held ready to defend the flotilla of canoes.

"Keep your hands and legs well inside," Piketas advised. Reisil didn't have to be told twice.

She continued to reach out to Baku. He never answered.

~*Can you reach him?* she asked Saljane.

~*No.*

~*Is he—?* She couldn't finish the question.

~*I don't know.* She sounded as worried at Reisil.

They came at last to Tizalan at sunset on the eighth day. Cemanahuatl's only city, Yohuac had once told her. It was glorious. It glittered like a jewel on an island in the middle of the great river. The buildings were made of yellow stone, with copper-colored roofs. The temples were shaped like tall, blocky pyramids, reminding Reisil of the *rinda* spell-sculptures. They were leafed in hammered gold and sparkled with precious stones. Rising out of the middle of it all was one that appeared to be made entirely of gold. A long stairway led to the top, its steps stained rusty brown. Reisil swallowed, knowing it was blood. Her body went cold.

Upon seeing Tizalan, the nahuallis let out a piercing cry. Inside the city, gongs began to sound, one after another until Reisil thought she'd go deaf. They guided their canoes into a shallow harbor, and a crowd of people came down to help disembark. No one spoke, but there was a rising excitement in the air.

Reisil caught Saljane on her fist as the goshawk dropped out of the sky. She lifted the bird onto her shoulder.

"What's happening?" she asked Ampok, who came to walk beside her as they paced regally into the city.

"Six days ago, those who survived the *pahtia* entered the Temple of the Sun. Five entered. Soon we will witness *Ilhuicatl's* Choosing. We go to wait."

And wait they did. The crowds around the temple parted to allow the nahuallis passage. The witches made a loose circle around the entire temple, and then sat cross-legged to wait. Three more days passed. People brought them food and drink, and some would wander away periodically to relieve their bodies and return to take up their silent watch.

Reisil found it increasingly difficult to sit still. She fidgeted, biting her nails to the quick. Her head ached. She ate little, and slept less. All she could think about was Yohuac. Was he inside? Was he alive? Where was Baku?

Suddenly, between one moment and the next, the sky went dark. Clouds streamed in like flocks of birds swarming. Reisil felt a tingle across her skin. The earth thrummed. Power pressed in on her and she found it hard to catch her breath. As one, the nahuallis stood. Reisil scrambled to join them.

The sky was black, pregnant and heavy. The wind died. The silence was absolute. Then the clouds parted. A streamer of yellow sunlight slipped through, illuminating the Temple of the Sun in a dazzling glow. There was a stirring at the top of the bloody stairway. Reisil's heart clenched. She stood on tiptoe.

~Saljane, let me see.

And suddenly she was looking out of Saljane's eyes. In the shadows of the wide archway inside, she could see three men. They were on their knees. Her heart leaped. Yohuac! He looked worn. He was naked. His skin was covered with bruises and cuts. One eye was swollen shut. Reisil skipped to the other two men. They appeared much the same.

~He said the pahtia *was dangerous. Most men do not survive,* Saljane reminded her.

But he had. Elation made her breathless. Where was Baku? She couldn't hear him at all.

She became aware of a low chant coming from the circling nahuallis. They strained upward, their song guttural and harsh. It was full of terrible longing. Foreboding rippled through Reisil.

Now another man appeared. He wore a cape made of yellow and red feathers, which fell to his feet in a brilliant sweep. On his head he wore a grotesque mask. Protruding from his genitals was an enormous gold penis tipped in the sacred blue stone. In one hand he held a burning brand, in the other a wicked knife, longer than Reisil's forearm and shining like a wedge of the moon.

Reisil's eyes flicked to the blood on the stairs and her gorge rose. Her whispered, "No!" was lost beneath the nahuallis' rising chant.

Now the Sun Priest motioned for the three men to rise and walk out onto the sunlit platform. They stopped before a blocky altar. The voices of the nahuallis grew louder, but there was no noise from the crowds jamming the avenues. The Sun Priest raised his hands. The voices of the witches cut off. Reisil bit her lip.

"Praise *Ilhuicatl*, who sends the wind, the moon, the sun, the rain, and holds us safely in his hands while the darkness spins in rage! Praise *Ilhuicatl*, who spreads his seed so the kalmut grows and the animals bow to our knives! Praise *Ilhuicatl* for the fire in our hearts, the fire in our blood, the fire that feeds Cemanahuatl!"

Rinda flared white along the platform. Moon *rinda*. His voice reverberated through the air, aided by the ancient spells set into the Temple. There was no one in Tizalan who couldn't have heard. Reisil shivered, the power in the air intensifying. Lightning crackled along the horizon and thunder grumbled. The hairs on her arms lifted.

"Praise *Ilhuicatl* for the gift of his flesh and blood, the gift of his Son! Through him, *Ilhuicatl* returns to Cemanahuatl. Through him, the flesh lives! Through him, *Ilhuicatl's* might returns to the blood!

"But we must show our gratitude for this great gift. We must not be greedy. Three men stand before you. One will be Chosen. For one golden year, he will live among us. He will bask in the warmth of *Ilhuicatl's* blessing. What he touches will flourish. And in one year, *Ilhuicatl* will call his Son home to watch over us from afar."

Call him home? A buzzing sounded in Reisil's ears. Call him home?

Now the Sun Priest turned back to face the kneeling men, tilting his head back to stare up into the streaming sunlight.

"Father of us all, our best stand humbly before you. We ask you to *Choose*."

The air imploded. Reisil couldn't see, couldn't breathe. Terror clutched her around the throat. Light flared. She jerked her head, covering her eyes. The thunder rumbled louder and louder, until the cobbles beneath her feet jumped and trembled. The air tasted like burnt peaches. Wind roared through the streets, pushing and pulling her. Raindrops stung her skin. In a moment she was drenched. She swayed and staggered forward, unable to keep her balance.

Then abruptly it was done. The lightning, thunder, and rain stopped. The wind wandered away, leaving behind absolute stillness. Reisil looked back up at the platform, her heart clenching.

Two of the men were kneeling. Between them, on his feet—Yohuac. She closed her eyes, relief and joy burbling up inside her.

–In a year he dies. Watch.

Baku's voice. The bitterness was like poison. Reisil watched through Saljane's eyes. The buzzing noise in her ears drowned out any other sounds.

The Sun Priest bent and kissed the first man's forehead. Then he reached out with his burning brand and touched it to his head. The man *burned*. Orange and yellow flames wrapped him in a flickering shroud. He did not scream. He did not move. Reisil didn't know if it was a spell or something else. The horrifying stench of crisping flesh wafted down to her. She shuddered. But she couldn't look away.

Next the Sun Priest went to the other man. He helped him to stand and led him to the altar. The man lay back on it. Reisil shook her head, sensing what was coming next. The silver knife flashed. The Sun Priest cut into his chest, pulling apart his ribs. He reached inside. The heart was still beating. Reisil's gorge rose. But she couldn't look away from the butchery.

The Sun Priest lifted the heart up to the sky and then set it in a brazier. It burst into flames that rose hundreds of feet in the air. And now he lifted the dead man's body with preternatural strength and flung it down the stairs. It tumbled and careened, landing three-quarters of the way down, the legs and arms twisted at unnatural angles.

The Sun Priest turned back to the gathered crowds, his arms uplifted, his hands red with blood.

"*Ilhuicatl* has chosen his Son. Praise him!"

Now the crowds roared and screamed in furious happiness. Reisil could only stare, eyes streaming. Yohuac looked grim, staring straight ahead.

At last the Sun Priest called for quiet. He went to Yohuac, leading him to the altar. His wounds were gone. His matted hair had turned silky, and his skin carried a sheen of gold.

"Behold, the Son of *Ilhuicatl*!"

The crowds roared. They stomped their feet and clapped. The Sun Priest raised his hands, calling for quiet. There was an excited, hungry tension to the crowd now. They pressed forward. Reisil glanced at Ilhanah who stood closest to the stairs. Her eyes gleamed and her face was a mask of triumph. Reisil looked away with a sickening feeling. Suddenly she knew what was coming next.

The Sun Priest's grotesque gold penis stuck out obscenely before him. Reisil's eyes hooked on it and she couldn't look away.

"*Ilhuicatl* sends the rains to water our fields; he sends the sun so our crops grow; he gives us the plants and animals to nourish us; he gives fire to light our spirit. And for one golden year, our flesh becomes the earth where he plants his seed. Our fallow bodies and spirits are reborn. Let the rebirth begin!"

He flung his arm out to the bottom of the stairs where Ilhanah waited, smiling. Two lines of acolytes from the Temple of the Sun appeared from the bottom of the Temple. They wore capes of white with gold codpieces on their genitals and golden masks that hid all expression. Each carried a bowl of fragrant burning oil. They circled around from opposite directions. At the stairs, they turned and marched slowly upward until they lined the steps. When they were ready, Ilhanah began her ascent. She climbed resolutely, stepping easily over the body of the sacrificed man.

Reisil could not look away, even as she began to tremble.

The Sun Priest cut away Ilhanah's clothing with slow, ritual movements. When she stood naked, he offered her a glass that was colored like living flame. She sipped and handed it back. The Sun Priest set it aside and helped her up onto the altar. Moments later Yohuac climbed on top of her.

The noises of their coupling were broadcast across the crowds, even as the Sun Priest's voice had been. Ilhanah's pleasure was loud and gurgling. Then Yohuac stepped down. The Sun Priest helped Ilhanah to stand. An acolyte led her away inside.

And so it went. One after another, into the night. All the nahuallis. Ampok. Piketas. Joyful moans and blissful cries. The crowds remained, waiting for a turn. The sun was long since gone, but the platform was illuminated by brilliant moonlight. Yohuac never tired, never ceased. He was *Ilhuicatl's* Son. Would he service all the women of Tizalan tonight?

Reisil didn't know what to do. She couldn't leave, even if she wanted to. The crowds were too thick. Her emotions were too scattered, too volatile, to use her power to safely create an escape hole through the throng.

And then she was the only nahualli left.

She was trapped. The crowd pushed her closer, herding her, until she began up the stairs. Tears streamed down her face. Her body was clenched tight. She stepped around the body of the sacrificed man.

The stomach-turning smell of charred flesh grew stronger. She climbed.

~*You must go,* she told Saljane as she neared the platform. There was enough light that she would find a perch easily enough. The goshawk didn't argue, but leaped away.

At the top, Reisil endured the ministrations of the Sun Priest as he stripped away her clothing, his fingers lingering on the gold ivy spreading over her pale skin. She hardly noticed when he cut the gauntlet from her arm. She felt cold to the depths of herself. She didn't look at Yohuac, keeping her eyes fixed on the ground. The Sun Priest handed her the flame-colored glass. She took a sip.

Glory spread through her. Inside she felt heavy and ready. Her nipples throbbed, her lower body ached. She hardly noticed the Sun Priest as he helped her onto the altar. She lay back, her legs falling open in wanton invitation. Then he was there. His eyes were like gold coins. His skin was spangled with flecks of sunlight. But his face was the same. And so dear. So very, very dear.

He kissed her, his hands running over her skin. Ecstasy. She moaned and bucked, trying to impale herself, to have the fullness she craved. He did not make her wait. He slid inside her, rocking with ancient rhythm. Reisil's mind shattered into fragments and she heard herself crying out as wave after wave of rapture swept over her.

When it was over, she could hardly move. Hands helped her down. Her legs were weak and inside she felt *something*. A memory prodded at her. *On each I would get a child. Even barren women.* Reisil stopped short. She was pregnant. Or would be. Hands gripped her elbow and hand.

"Come. We must talk. We must be alone."

Reisil turned in wonder. The man escorting her wasn't an acolyte. It was Yohuac.

Chapter 35

He paced. "I'm sorry. I am so very sorry. I didn't mean— You shouldn't have had to—"

Yohuac's face was twisted with guilt and self-recrimination. Reisil watched him from where she sat on a large bed. Yohuac's bed. He'd brought them to his quarters within the Temple. They were more than luxurious. They were fit for a god—or the son of a god.

The drug the Sun Priest had given her was starting to wear off. But instead of exhausted, she felt . . . wonderful. Energized and rested. And strangely enough, she neither regretted their very public act of love, nor the child that would come of it. She rubbed her stomach wonderingly.

Yohuac saw her and his expression darkened.

Before he could apologize again, Reisil stood. She was wearing the short robe made of a soft, delicate material that he'd given her. She went to stand before him, taking his face between her palms.

"I am not sorry. If I think about it too much, I might start to get a little embarrassed, and you can bet I'm not telling Juhrnus about tonight. But. I. Am. Not. Sorry."

He stared at her, those strange golden eyes doubting. But he read her sincerity. Suddenly he swept her up against him, his face buried against the crook of her neck.

Finally he pushed her away.

"Are you hungry?" And not waiting for an answer, he led her into another room, where a feast had been laid out.

"How much do they expect us to eat?" Reisil asked, sitting down across from him.

In fact, they were both hungry and ate far more than Reisil would have expected. Finally they pushed back. Yohuac sipped at his cup of xochil. Reisil refused the hot, peppery drink, choosing instead a glass of fruit juice.

"I am glad to see you," he said softly.

Reisil's heart thumped. But before she could answer, he changed the subject.

"Have you learned what you need to?" he asked.

"I don't know. Maybe. I have some ideas." She sat up. "My pack. Where is it?"

"I had them bring it here. It's with your clothing in the bedroom."

Reisil unfolded her legs and went to the bedroom. The pack was intact, the laces still tied. She'd walked out of Atli Cihua with the moon *rinda* and no one knew. Not yet anyhow.

She turned and found Yohuac standing close behind her.

"Everything all right?"

She nodded. "I . . . borrowed . . . something from your nahuallis. They probably aren't going to be very happy when they figure it out."

He shrugged. "It doesn't matter. You have my protection. They cannot stand against me."

"Until I leave the Temple. And then you go back to—" A hot sob stopped the words and she turned away.

Yohuac gripped her arm and pulled her around. He put his fingers under her chin.

"Until this is over."

"I don't understand. You're *Ilhuicatl's* Chosen, his Son."

He nodded. "I am. And that's why I'm going back to Mysane Kosk with you."

Reisil stared, repeating him stupidly. "Going back to Mysane Kosk?"

He nodded.

"Maybe you'd better explain," Reisil said weakly. Hope made her heart thunder. But he couldn't mean it. Could he?

He led her to the bed, settling in beside her, holding her firmly against his chest as if he were afraid to let her go.

"Five of us made it to Tizalan. Five of more than two hundred. We were brought to the Temple. The last trials of the *pahtia* are conducted by *Ilhuicatl* himself. I did not know what to expect. None of us did. We were each brought to a room. I came here. I was fed and bathed. I went to sleep—and I dreamed."

Something in the way he said it told Reisil how potent those dreams had been. How excruciating. He'd entered the Temple six days before the nahuallis arrived in Tizalan, and then they'd waited another three. He'd dreamed nine days. She remembered the bruises and welts on his body as he knelt at the top of the Temple.

"In the end, I came before *Ilhuicatl* himself. He asked me why I was worthier of being named his son than my competitors." His eyelids dropped, hooding his eyes as he remembered. "They were brave, strong men. I was bred for this by the nahuallis, but was I better than them? Would I serve my people any better? I could not truthfully say so. But I could not say nothing. I told him that the nahuallis had bred me to return the magic to Cemanahuatl's blood, and that was one way I could serve that my competitors could not."

"What did he say?"

"He asked, 'Is that all?' I had to do better if I wanted to win. But I was no braver, no stronger, no more a man than they. So I told him the truth. I told him I was no worthier, but that I needed better weapons to help you save Cemanahuatl."

"And that convinced him?" She frowned. "But you're supposed to stay here. You can't come back with me."

"When I was standing on the platform, when the light came down and *Ilhuicatl* chose me, he said I must go quickly, and hurry. Time is short."

"The nahuallis won't take your leaving well. Or mine."

"No one will. But this is far more important. I can help you." The last was not—quite—a question.

"You can," Reisil assured him. "I just didn't think . . . I don't think the nahuallis will let you go without a fight."

"I have already given them a great deal of what they wanted. In nine months they will all have children. By then I will be back to breed them again. And to spread my seed to the rest of Cemanahuatl's women. It will be enough."

Would it? Reisil doubted it. The nahuallis were very ambitious. Her hand crept down to cover her stomach. Even if all the rest were true, they would want this baby, this child of such power.

~*The witches return.*

~*What?* Reisil struggled upright, concentrating. *Are you sure?* Saljane could not see in the dark.

~*They have come. They sit as before, around the Temple. They are waiting.*

This last came from Baku. His bitterness had turned feral and so very, very black. Reisil felt his power, like a cold draft in a warm room. It was . . . vast. No wonder the wizards had wanted him so much.

"Did you hear that?" Reisil said to Yohuac.

He nodded and swung his legs over the bed.

"They're waiting for me," she said, sliding off the bed. "They won't like that you've chosen to favor me by bringing me here." She hesitated, not knowing what to do. "I don't think I can go back to them."

Yohuac's eyes narrowed and they began to glow. *Ilhuicatl's* Son. Reisil refused to be afraid of him.

"You think they will hurt you? They need you. Their own Foreseeing showed them this."

"A lot of them are beginning to wonder if it was true. Or rather, if they've interpreted it correctly. They see the magic draining from their land, and know it means the death of everything. They have a vision that says I will help them, but they've been tricked by the gods before." She remembered the overheard conversation between Piketas and Ampok. *Many of the Teotl would enjoy watching us suffer the indignity of sharing our secrets with this* clecha. *They are jealous of the favor* Ilhuicatl *shows us. They would enjoy such a trick, seeing us crawling on our knees. Or perhaps we misunderstand the message. How can we be certain?*

Reisil gripped Yohuac's hands tightly. "They can't let me go back. They think I only want to save my land. They don't believe I can do it without destroying Cemanahuatl." She paused. "And that's not all. This child that I'm carrying—the nahuallis want it. Want me." She thought of the speculative, predatory way Ilhanah always looked at her.

"I didn't expect to come here and . . . get pregnant. But the nahuallis knew I would. They made sure I would. They're farmers and they made me part of their herd. They created you to become *Ilhuicatl's* Son and return power to the blood. And you have. In nine months, their decades of careful breeding will bear fruit. Imagine the power that will run in the blood of the children you sired on the nahuallis. And in ours. They won't let me take it away with me.

"If I go back to them, they'll take me off to Ti'Omoru and insist that I fix things from there. I won't be able to. I have to go back to Mysane Kosk. But they'll try to stop me. And even if they can't, they'll try to destroy Ti'Omoru and stop the drain of magic from Cemanahuatl before I can get to Mysane Kosk. And . . ." Reisil's voice faltered. She swallowed. "If they do, then both our worlds will be unmade. I won't be able to stop it."

For a moment Reisil didn't know if Yohuac believed her. He paced away, stopping to stare at the wall. At last he turned around.

"We can leave now. But you will have little time. If what you say is true, then when they realize you've gone, they will go straight to Ti'Omoru."

Reisil's heart dropped. "Then we've lost. It will take us weeks just to get from the Melyhir Mountains back to Mysane Kosk."

"Are you sure you're done here?"

Reisil stiffened. His voice rumbled like the earth gnashing its teeth. Vases on the tables vibrated in response. Slowly she turned. The glow in his eyes had increased. If she looked close enough, Reisil thought she could see flames dancing inside. The golden flecks on his skin had grown lustrous. He was terrible. And he was beautiful.

"I've learned all I can. I know how the *rinda* work. And I have those." She pointed to her pack. "Now I have to solve the puzzle. And to do that, I need to go to where it began. I have to go inside Mysane Kosk."

"Then I will take you there."

Reisil didn't ask how or if they'd be in time. She snatched up her clothing and dressed, then slung her pack over her shoulder.

"Where to now?" Reisil asked. "We've got to get Saljane. She says the Temple Pyramid is lit well, but she cannot fly far."

Yohuac smiled. It was a strange, faraway expression. Immense power flowed out of him. The son of a god. Doubt wriggled inside Reisil. What could they do for Mysane Kosk that the gods could not? She refused to consider it. The wizards had caused the problem, and she and Yohuac would fix it. The gods had nothing to do with it.

The air around Yohuac rippled like heat on sand, and suddenly Saljane appeared, her talons clutched around his forearm. They did not break the skin. He held out his arm and the bird fluttered to Reisil's fist. She looked down in wonder. The gauntlet the Sun Priest had cut away now sheathed her arm, undamaged. She looked back at Yohuac, who smiled crookedly.

"Come to me, Baku."

The words were a golden rope. Reisil felt them unwind and wrap their prey. Then Baku shimmered into being beside them. Suddenly the expansive bedroom felt much smaller. Reisil reached out and stroked her hand down Baku's neck in a gesture of welcome. She had missed him and his surly temper. His head jerked around at her touch and she half expected him to snap at her, but he only prodded her ribs with his muzzle. She smiled. He missed her too.

Yohuac held out his hands. Reisil took one. He gripped one of Baku's neck ridges with the other.

"We go," he said, and then the world turned to flame.

Remembering their fall between Kodu Riik and Cemanahuatl, Reisil had expected that they would float upward, or climb. Instead they dropped inside a crucible. Heat enveloped them in a smothering blanket. Though Reisil sweated and Baku's tail lashed, Yohuac was unperturbed by the heat. It was almost impossible to breathe. Reisil found herself panting, her lungs crisping. Roaring filled her ears, snapping and crackling. She doubted she could have heard herself shout.

She pulled Saljane into her stomach. The goshawk trembled. Reisil didn't dare draw on her own power to shield them. Not here. She had a feeling they were traveling through the body of *Ilhuicatl* himself, through the heart of the sun. Pulling on her own power, even to protect Saljane, could be fatal.

~I am here, my heart. I am here and we are safe. Hold on just a little longer, she crooned, over and over. Saljane pressed closer.

It went on and on for what seemed like days. Thirst was at first uncomfortable, and then intolerable. But Reisil didn't have free hands to open her water pouch. She grew dizzy and found herself slumping. Only Yohuac's grip kept her from falling.

And then as suddenly as they began, the flames and heat disappeared.

Reisil sat down hard as her sweat-slicked hand slipped free from Yohuac's. She gasped, drawing deep, soothing breaths of the cedar-scented air. Cedar. She looked around. She was sitting in a meadow surrounded by tall cedar, spruce, and pine. There was a great traveler's pine opposite them, its limbs sweeping the ground. It was familiar.

She stood, turning in a circle. Yes, she remembered. This was where Sodur had met her when she and Yohuac had fled from Tapit. She looked at Yohuac. His eyes had ceased to glow, but they still shone like golden coins.

"Why here?"

"It was a place I remembered," he explained. "And close to Mysane Kosk. I couldn't risk stepping between worlds any closer. I don't know what might happen."

Stepping between worlds. Easy as that, for the Sun God's Son. Reisil turned away. *In one year, Ilhuicatl will call his Son home.* She couldn't worry about that now. Now they had to sort out Mysane Kosk.

"We'd better hurry. They will have felt our arrival. They will come looking for us," Yohuac said.

He meant the *nokulas* and wizards. The Scallacians too, if they'd arrived. Once again, they'd become prey.

Chapter 36

As feared, the lack of snow had brought Aare's army to Honor's doorstep far sooner than originally anticipated. But they were as prepared as could be. The stockades were finished and every man bore metal arms. And now there was nothing to do but sit snug inside the stockades and wait for the battle to begin in earnest.

Metyein paced the top of the wall at Eagle, gazing out into the predawn gloom. Aare's army was camped along the eastern end of the valley and in the hills around. Honor was completely surrounded. No surprises there. But Aare had amassed fully six thousand men, all mounted. Honor had less than half of that. Edel's arrival had added five hundred battle-hardened men to their rolls. Two-thirds of them had come from Vadonis. With the newly forged weapons, plenty of food and water, and the advantage of Reisil's wards on the walls, Honor could easily hold off the greater force for months.

Metyein's lips pulled into a humorless smile. Aare couldn't afford to let this drag out. He couldn't feed his men and horses off the land, and Metyein doubted he had supplies to last more than a month.

But then, Aare didn't intend to have to be there more than a month. He had his pet sorcerers. He planned to raze the valley in a matter of days, destroy Mysane Kosk and be on his way back to Kodu Riik within a week. Or had planned. Once the sorcerers figured out that Mysane Kosk fueled the wards, they'd attack there in order to break them. If Aare was thinking clearly, he'd attack there first anyhow. After all, the *nokulas* and plague were far greater threats to Kodu Riik than a handful of rebels.

But Aare was an arrogant *ganyik*. He wasn't going to let Honor's defiance pass unaddressed. So he'd push his pet sorcerers at the rebellion first. At least Honor wasn't without magical defenses. They had the wards, Nurema, and the three young members of the Whieche who'd come from Patverseme to help.

Metyein started at the sound of boots thumping up the stairs. From the covered guardhouse emerged Kebonsat and Soka.

"Anything?" Kebonsat asked, peering over the wall.

He'd lost weight. There was an edginess to him, like bowstring pulled too tight. But there was no way to release the tension. Emelovi remained distant and frosty, and who knew what Aare was doing to Ceriba. Luckily, Soka had tactfully chosen not to speculate. Now that they were trapped inside the stockades, Kebonsat's temper was fraying. When it snapped— Metyein's lips tightened. He was going to have to talk to Emelovi. Honor couldn't afford for that to happen. She was the only one who could help.

"Nothing yet," Metyein replied.

But it was coming. Even he had felt the surge of *something* the day before. It had quaked through him, leaving him staggering like a drunk and burning with an unaccountable fever. He still felt tattered and wrung from the experience.

"What did Nurema say?"

"She had no idea. She thinks maybe the wizards are up to something."

Kebonsat swore. "Just what we need."

"I don't know," Soka said flippantly. "It probably made the Scallacians nervous. Not to mention the *nokulas*."

Yes, let's not mention the nokulas, thought Metyein acidly. But ignoring them didn't make them go away.

"If the sorcerers believe the wizards are coming, they'll speed up their attack. They don't want to be fighting on two fronts."

Metyein gazed back over the wall. If only he could talk to his father, convince him to stand down. His father didn't know what destroying Mysane Kosk would do to Kodu Riik. If he did, he'd hold his men. That would slow Aare down.

"We have to hold them back until Reisiltark gets here," he muttered. But she wasn't due for at least a month, and probably not for two. Would anything be left of Honor and Mysane Kosk when she did finally arrive?

Aarc launched his attack before the sun had cleared the mountains. It was little more than a feint to test their strength. Five hundred men created a horseshoe around Bear, staying out of the cross-fire fields created by nearby Raven and Salamander. Bear contained men from Bro-heyek and Honor with Thevul Bro-heyek in command. Edel and his men had gone to Salamander. The two stockades protruded into the valley like prongs and would take the brunt of the initial fighting.

When Aare's men had arranged themselves, they launched boulders from trebuchets. The rocks bounced away, leaving no damage, thanks to the wards. Next they tried flinging burning bundles of brush and wood. As soon as they struck, the flames went out and the bundles slid to the ground. This went on much of the day at various points around the perimeter, until finally they realized the futility and gave up. Then one of the sorcerers marched onto the field. Metyein was too far away to recognize him. He fumed, itching to go through the tunnels and join Bear. Kebonsat wouldn't permit it. Instead he watched and waited. Soka stood beside him.

The sorcerer flung his hands up. Metyein felt a *gathering* in the air behind him. The hairs on his neck stood on end. He spun around. The mist covering Mysane Kosk sparkled and swirled. He swallowed. Something inside was answering the sorcerer.

"I don't like this."

"That's only because you don't like getting burned alive in a magical conflagration," Soka said.

"You do?"

"Better than enjoying Aare's hospitality."

"You ever going to tell me about it?"

"Find your own nightmares," Soka snapped. End of conversation.

A gray gauzy fog began to gather above the sorcerer. It built, piling in great billows like a thunderhead. It darkened, turning first pewter and then purple-black, like bruises. Wind gusted, butting hard. The feeling of something looming behind them grew. Metyein kept peering over his shoulder, expectantly, but the mist shrouding Mysane Kosk didn't vary. *What's happening beneath the rainbow veil?*

The great cloud suddenly drifted forward until it hovered directly over Bear. Metyein's throat tightened and his hands gripping the wall were white-knuckled. The cloud dropped. Bear disappeared.

"Hag's tits," Soka murmured.

Metyein could only stare in rigid silence. The sorcerer didn't move, his arms extended straight out before him. Ruby sparks flashed around his hands. A stream of red power spurted out to lick at the shadow-cloud.

It exploded.

The sound was deafening. Metyein fell backwards as if struck by an invisible hand. He sprawled on his back, his breath ripping out of his lungs. He lay there, black shards splintering his vision. He blinked, dazed. Then fear snatched him by the throat. He rolled to his stomach, wiping away the blood running from his nose. He pushed himself up. He staggered back to the wall. By the Lady, what could survive being in the middle of that?

Dust filled the air. Metyein coughed. His ears rang

with the noise of the blast. Horses screamed and men yelled. There was nothing to see but a curtain of brown. Grass and dirt pelted down around them. He reached out to help Soka to his feet. His eye patch had been knocked askew and blood ran from where splinters had lodged in his cheek. His face was gray.

"Soka! You didn't . . . the poison bead . . ." Metyein said weakly, clutching Soka's shoulders and giving him a shake.

"I'm fine." He dusted himself off, his mouth pinched.

Metyein heard the click of the bead and felt a wash of relief. It died a moment later.

"Take a head count. Find out what the damage was. Find Tillen. He'll help you. I want to hear from all the stockades within an hour. See if the tunnel is still open to Bear."

Soka nodded and stumbled away, shaking his head to clear it. Metyein went back to keeping watch.

The dust settled slowly. Minutes ticked past, each one longer than an hour. The outlines of Raven and Fox appeared first. Then slowly Bear emerged from the haze. His heart nearly stopped. Intact.

The sorcerer still stood, arms slack at his sides. Aare's men were in disarray. Horses had bolted in every direction, some straying within reach of Honor's arrows. Forty or fifty bodies littered the valley floor.

A horn blew the retreat and Aare's people fell back to their camp. Cheering sounded from the stockades.

Then suddenly Metyein went cold. That force looming within Mysane Kosk seemed to crouch. It felt angry. No, that was too tame a word. It raged.

He waited, certain it was about to spring. Nothing happened. Metyein's chest tightened with the tension. And still nothing. He turned to descend the stairs. Soon enough. And when the *nokulas* went after the sorcerers, they were going to plow through the middle of Honor. He didn't know what would survive. If anything.

*　　*　　*

"Lord Marshal! Lord Marshal! Come quick! They say it be an emergency!"

The messenger was hardly more than a boy. He was covered in dust and dirt. His eyes were wide and his hands were shaking.

"They says you gotta come now!"

The panic in his voice galvanized Metyein. He followed the man back to the trapdoor tunnel entrance. The messenger swung over the edge and scrambled jerkily down the ladder. Metyein followed swiftly on his heels. At the bottom he snatched up an unlit torch and touched it to the brand held by the tunnel guard. He wanted to ask for more information, but the man was already trotting ahead. Toward Fox.

Metyein hurried to catch up. In one place, the wall had collapsed, blocking half the passage. Loose rock and dirt sifted down, pattering his head and shoulders. Metyein ducked his head and squeezed through, wondering if any of Honor's other tunnels had been blocked. Another blast like that last and they might all collapse. He grasped the messenger's sleeve.

"What's happened? Fox is quarantined."

The man paused, his feet shifting nervously in the dirt. "I know, sir. I'm one of the tunnel guards. Remuntark said you must come. Right away. He said it can't wait or everyone will die." His voice shook. "*Everyone.*"

Fear made Metyein's voice rough. "Let's go."

They scuttled through the tunnel, choking on the dust thickening the air. At the end of the tunnel another guard waited. He looked scared.

Metyein ignored him and reached for the ladder, climbing up to slide open the bars locking it in place. He pushed the trapdoor open. Hands reached down to lift him out. He was surrounded by a dozen tarks.

"Welcome to Fox, Lord Marshal," Remuntark said in a shaky voice. "I wasn't sure you'd come."

"It didn't sound like I had a choice."

"You need to see something. This way, please."

To Metyein's surprise, they went up onto the wall. A haggard Remuntark led the way and the other tarks trailed behind. They curved around to the western side overlooking Mysane Kosk.

Fox was the closest stockade to Mysane Kosk. The perimeter of the mist circle had been expanding for years, more swiftly in the last two. But it shouldn't have been a problem. Not for another year. Only when he came to the allure, Metyein found himself standing an arm's length away from the mist. It overlapped the wall and cut across the walkway.

"How? When?" he asked in a sharp, businesslike voice that didn't seem to be his own.

"After the blast, when the haze cleared. One moment it was a quarter of a league away; the next it was . . . here."

He'd gotten it wrong. The sorcerers didn't need to attack Mysane Kosk. With the protective wards anchored to the power of Mysane Kosk, magical attacks on the stockades would force the *nokulas* to respond. But he'd never imagined this. One more attack would swallow Fox. Maybe the whole valley.

His face was a graven mask when he turned to look at Remuntark. "The tunnel's half-blocked. We couldn't move your patients even if we had time or a place to take them. They'll have to stay. The rest of you evacuate to the other stockades. Don't argue. These people will have to trust the Lady. But we can't risk losing any of you. Honor will need your skills very soon. Leave them water and food. I'll give you an hour before I send guards."

With that he strode back to the tunnel. He told the guards to allow the evacuation of the tarks and then hurried along to find Nurema. She had to take the wards down. All of them. And now.

Snatches of song. Echoes. Memories.

Pain.

Juhrnus came to the place that had lured him across mountains. It smelled of breaking and undoing.

Silence.

He wandered and paused, sat and listened. Here. There.

Silence.

The discord was gone. The song was gone.

~*They burned it. Edel said they would.*

~*Edel?*

An image in his mind's eye. Yes. He remembered. A bit of melody twirled in his mind. Deep notes. Brassy. Edel.

He let the music fill his mind and his body. Other memories, other harmonies. He sat, enraptured, while the memories returned.

And then in the distance, he felt a hard twang, like ruptured strings on a harp.

Pain rent his soul. He shuddered.

Wrongness. It was deeper, more profound than this one that had called him here. It *hurt*.

He stood and went to the horse.

The dissonance gnawed at him and he cringed from the slow agony building inside him. Beneath the shattering sound was an ocean of Silence. So vast. So total.

~*A Song begins with a single note. You must sing back the Silence. Others will sing too.*

Juhrnus hesitated. Could he?

But he must sing. He must coax the harmony.

He mounted Indigo and began his journey to the heart of the Silence.

Tapit retreated to his room. The siege had barely started and already he was at his tether's end. He couldn't stand the unending noise, the constant stench of so many people living on top of one another. It wore on him until he wanted to lash out with his magic. Even within the sanctuary of his tiny living space, the noise and smells permeated. He dragged his fingers through his hair. By the Demonlord's sacred Darkness, he wanted free of this anthill!

He could leave. It would be a small matter to get past the guards and into the tunnels. Lion was on the south edge of the valley. He could be free in the mountains in a matter of hours. His heart leaped hungrily at the idea, but he brutally snuffed the temptation. He could have his reward later. This was no time to lose his focus and abandon the hunt.

He sat on the edge of his bed, staring at the floor between his feet.

But these last months lying in wait would be for nothing if he couldn't keep the Scallacians from attacking Mysane Kosk. Or if he couldn't keep his own brethren from drawing on its power. Thanks to Tillen, Tapit had finally gained entrance to the Lord Marshal's quarters and discovered where Reisil had gone and why. She'd gone to find a way to stop the uncontrolled wash of power from Mysane Kosk, while still preserving it. She hadn't gone to find a weapon, as he'd thought. She'd gone to *become* it.

He licked his lips, his hands going suddenly damp. He had to have her. He'd do whatever it took, even if it meant remaining in this demon-blighted anthill for another year. He closed his eyes. He'd make the cage himself. She'd never break free.

But first, he had to stop the Scallacians and his fellow wizards from destroying Mysane Kosk and, if the witch woman was correct, the entire world.

Tapit knew his brethren were on their way. They would have come hunting the moment they felt the massive burst of power set off by the Scallacians. Tapit had little time to devise a plan. During the summer, a large contingent of wizards had established a camp not far from here. The spreading magic of Mysane Kosk disguised their presence. The witch was the only one besides Reisil with the power to detect their nest, but she never left the valley. Even Tapit had had to work to find them. And that was his special talent.

He stood, pacing absently back and forth. They'd be here within a day or two. With the witch taking down the wards, the wizards would be able to stroll right in and do whatever they pleased. With their backs to Mysane Kosk and drawing on its power, the wizards would be invincible. The Scallacians would be ground underfoot. Unless someone stopped them.

And not even Tapit could do that. Even if he wanted to. He paused, the idea persisting. Did he?

There was no way to get word to them, to warn them to abandon the attack. And if they did, everything would be destroyed. He'd never get Reisil then. But if he helped the witch woman . . . Tapit rubbed his long fingers over his jaw thoughtfully. His brethren would go after the Scallacians. Even without Mysane Kosk, the wizards would overwhelm the sorcerers. All he had to do was keep Mysane Kosk safe. Until Reisil came. He'd let her stabilize the spell. And then he'd take her. He smiled. Yes.

Tapit began to go to the door when something stopped him. He halted midstride. A lightning touch brushed electrically across his innermost senses. A taste, a smell. He dropped to his knees, straining. He focused on the touch, trying to catch it again. His tongue slid out between his lips. Yes, there. He'd never forget that musky flavor, that rich, honeyed bite of magic. Reisil. There was a deeper intensity to her now, the difference between a promise and fulfillment, between a spark and a flame.

He didn't know how long he remained on the floor, savoring the essence of her that was his special talent to sense. At last he tore himself away and stood up. His body felt stiff and heavy. He shook his head to clear it.

The witch was taking the wards down. His brother wizards were coming to fight the Scallacian sorcerers for their prize. Reisil was back.

The hunt was on again.

Chapter 37

The burst of power from Mysane Kosk took Reisil's breath away. With her spellsight, she could see waves of rippling magic spreading into the sky. They feathered outward, flickering and pulsing.

"What was that?" Yohuac asked.

The Scallacians? The wizards? Reisil had hoped they'd return long before Honor was under attack. Her stomach twisted.

"We've got to hurry."

They were close now, only a league away. They set off at a jog, scrabbling up the steep slopes and sliding down the other side.

~Wait.

Baku's voice sounded thick and fuzzy. He was only a few yards away. Reisil and Yohuac stopped, panting.

~There are sentries.

Sentries? That meant—

~Show me, she said to Saljane, flicking a worried glance at the tendrils of magic unfurling in the air like stranglevines. *Be careful.*

The goshawk leaped from her perch in a birch tree and winged away toward Honor. Reisil and Yohuac hunkered down between two boulders, waiting. They drank from Reisil's water sac, the water warm and stale.

~See.

Saljane pulled Reisil into her mind.

"By the Lady," she whispered.

"What's happened? What do you see?"

"The Regent has come. Honor is surrounded. There are so many men!"

Saljane circled and swooped lower. Bloody bodies littered the shorn fields. "There's been fighting. There's a fire at Bear. I don't understand. The wards—" She broke off suddenly, her hands knotting. "Oh, my Lady . . ."

Yohuac's hands closed around hers. "What is it?"

Reisil pulled out of Saljane's mind and stared into his golden eyes. "Mysane Kosk is twice the size it was when we left. All that—" She waved her hand at the lights flaming above. "There's going to be a rupture soon. If the sorcerers or wizards attack one more time, it'll release the destruction Nurema saw in her visions."

"What do we do?"

As if she knew. His faith in her was childlike in its absolute totality. Reisil rubbed her forehead with a shaking hand. The trouble was, she had only the beginnings of a plan. But to get even that far, so much depended on everything going *right*. And if it did, what did she do next? She pushed the thought away. She'd figure that out when she got there. First things first.

She drew a deep breath, squeezing Yohuac's hand. It was strong and comforting, like holding sunlight. She stood, pulling her pack over her shoulder. Inside were the moon *rinda*. And floating in her mind was the shape the *copicatl* had shown her in Atli Cihua.

"We go inside Mysane Kosk now. Everything began there. That's where it has to end."

End without destroying it and the *nokulas*. She thought about the wizards, the sorcerers, and the na-huallis. Another attack might rip open the hole between Cemanahuatl and Kodu Riik. The resulting torrent of magic would be impossible to halt. Reisil rested her hand on Baku's neck.

~Baku, I want you to go to Honor. *Find Nurema. Tell her she has to keep the wizards and the sorcerers from attacking Mysane Kosk. Whatever it takes, she*

must hold. And hurry. We are going to need you. We'll meet you in the valley.

Reisil felt a finger-brush of pleasure at her trust before the coal-drake launched himself upward. Twigs and pebbles spun into the air as his powerful wings pumped. Reisil watched him go.

And now to do something very difficult.

~Saljane.

But Reisil didn't have to say the thing she dreaded. After her atavistic journey across the jungle to Atli Cihua, her tie with Saljane had become so instinctive and intimate that speaking had become more habit than necessity.

~Go. I'll wait. She sounded both reluctant and fierce.

~I love you. Fly strong.

~Be careful.

Then she felt Saljane dig hard talons into her mind. For a moment the sensation was agonizing. Her entire body twitched with the effect. The pain faded as quickly as it had come. But the sense of someone holding tight to her remained. And there was something else. She felt the wind on her wings, the rush of the air, the taste of the sun. Saljane was Reisil's link to Kodu Riik. She was the anchor to guide them back out of Mysane Kosk. If their bond was strong enough. If they weren't killed in the effort. If she could heal the damage caused by the wizards.

But first she had to convince the *nokulas* to help.

Kebonsal galloped across the field that separated Lion from Eagle, leaping over scattered bodies. All of them were Regent's men, sent to test Honor's defenses. There had been a collapse and he didn't have time to work his way through the alternate tunnel routes, even if they were still open. The yellow pennant he carried showed a red gryphon inside a green ring. It signaled that he belonged to Honor.

He heard shouts from the top of the wall as he approached. The gate swung wide enough to allow

him entrance and slammed shut behind. Kebonsat was
already swinging off the horse. He ran to the building
that housed both Metyein and Emelovi. The heart of
the new Kodu Riik.

He burst into the meeting room, not bothering to
knock. Inside, Metyein was poring over maps and lists.
At Kebonsat's clattering entrance, he lunged to his
feet, his face hard with concern.

"What's happened?"

"I've a message. From Baku."

For a moment there was shocked silence.

"She's back?" Metyein's eyes flashed with hope.

Kebonsat nodded. "Baku said we need to keep the
sorcerers and the wizards from attacking Mysane
Kosk. He was very clear. Whatever it takes, we have
to hold them back until Reisil can do whatever she's
going to do."

Metyein sank slowly back down in his chair.
"Chodha." He sat for a moment, gazing at the tabletop. Then he visibly gathered himself. "All right. Send
for the others. Soka, Thevul Bro-heyek, Edel, Emelovi, and Nurema. And better bring those wizards the
Guild sent. Tillen, too. Have them here in an hour.
Did Baku say what Reisil was going to do? Or when?"

Kebonsat shook his head. "It'll be soon. He was in
a hurry."

"All right then. Get going. I'll draft a plan."

A kind of fatalistic foreboding closed around Kebonsat as he retreated. Any plan Metyein devised
would mean the devastation of Honor.

The meeting was already under way when Kebonsat
returned. Everyone had gathered except Nurema and
the Guild wizards from Patverseme. They were making their own preparations. When he'd located her,
Nurema had looked at him with an odd, knowing look
as he argued with her to obey Metyein's orders and
attend the meeting.

"Ain't nothin' he's gonna say that's gonna change
what we'll do. We're gonna try to shield Mysane Kosk.
We won't be able to hold long against what they'll

throw at us, so you toddle off and tell his Lord Marshalship that we're his last line of defense. He's gotta keep that attack from coming. Now leave us be so we can get ready."

Kebonsat slid inside the door, remaining standing. The only open chair was next to Emelovi. She tolerated him now, but he couldn't bear the way she pulled herself away when he was too close, the way she carefully avoided touching him, the way her voice turned to sandpaper when she spoke to him.

But it was almost over. Reisil had returned, and for good or for bad, soon he'd no longer be tied to this place, to Emelovi. The knowledge sliced his soul. He didn't know where he'd go, what he'd do. He'd find Ceriba, of course. He'd send her home. Or Metyein or Emelovi would take care of her. After that? He no longer had a name or a country.

Pain flailed inside him. He grappled it, wrapping it tightly inside a cocoon of control. Not yet not yet not yet. But soon. He would let it go. There would be no more pain.

"Nurema's not coming. She and the Guild wizards are working on shielding Mysane Kosk," Kebonsat said when Metyein asked. "She says they won't be able to hold long, so we'd better keep them distracted."

"All right then." Metyein took a breath and gazed around the table, locking with each pair of eyes for a measuring moment. "Here's the situation. Reisiltark has returned. That's the good news. However, she has asked us to keep the wizards and Scallacians from attacking Mysane Kosk so that she can do what she has to. So we will. We've taken the wards down. Honor no longer has any magical protections. It may be that the most we can do is throw bodies at them until they get too tired to fight. If so, that's what we'll do," he said grimly.

"I've got a plan sketched out, but before I tell you what I have in mind, there are some things you need to know. A few of you know most of this already. But everyone here should know the whole of what we're fighting for. And what we're fighting against.

"When the wizards cast their spell here during the war, it created a powerful well of magic that has been spilling unchecked into Kodu Riik. This magic is the source of the drought, the plague, and the *nokulas*. Every one of the *nokulas* was once either a man or a woman or who knows what else. Each one wandered through the blight-circle and was changed." He paused. "Iisand Samir is a *nokula*. The *ahalad-kaaslane* Sodur is a *nokula*. There are many more."

Thevul Bro-heyek, the Head Steward, and his assistant looked shocked. Without giving them time to ask questions, Metyein continued tersely.

"Left alone, eventually the spill of magic would rip apart Kodu Riik and the rest of the world. But destroying Mysane Kosk is no answer. That would just speed up the process. You've all seen the blight-circle and how it expanded after a single sorcerer attacked. But the Regent is determined to destroy Mysane Kosk. That's what he's come for. But he may be surprised. Mysane Kosk is an enormous source of magical power. Now that they have seen it, the Scallacians may not be so willing to cooperate. But the wizards aren't going to just stand by and let them have it. Neither side will let it fall into the other's hands. That means they'll try to destroy Mysane Kosk if they can't keep the other from having it, which brings us back to the original danger. And then one last problem. The *nokulas* aren't going to sit idly while their home is attacked. Honor is going to be the killing field in the battle between the Scallacians, the wizards, the *nokulas*, Aare's army, and us."

"But the wizards aren't here," Tillen broke in nervously.

"They will be," Edel said darkly. "Don't doubt it."

"So what do you have in mind?" asked Thevul Bro-heyek.

Right to the point. Good man, Kebonsat thought.

"Reisiltark went to try to find a cure to our problem. We need to buy her some time. And let me say again, the fate of not just Kodu Riik but the *entire world* rests on whether we succeed or fail. If it takes every last one of us, then the price is not too high. Do you understand?" There were nods all around.

Metyein unrolled a parchment that contained a map of Honor.

"First, Emelovi and Kebonsat. I want you to leave. You'll go out through Hawk's northern tunnel. You'll be on foot. You won't get far, but that doesn't matter."

Kebonsat's eyes narrowed, and Emelovi looked ready to spit.

"I'll not run away and hide," she said hotly. "I'm here and I'm not going to have you rolling me up in cotton wool."

Kebonsat's icy voice sheared across hers and her lips snapped shut in fury. "You're going to use us for bait."

Metyein nodded. "Aare wants Emelovi. And he wants you. The idea of his sister running off with a Patversemcsc *ganyik* is the only thing that might distract him. He'll be after you as soon as he finds out. With luck, it will delay his attack on Mysane Kosk."

"When will you tell him?"

"I'll send a man out to get captured. Nurema will spell him. He'll talk, eventually."

And buy them more time. Kebonsat nodded.

"Aare will kill him," Emelovi said, her voice high and thin. "He'll torture him. We cannot do that. I won't allow it."

Metyein turned to her, his face grave. "We all must sacrifice, if this is going to work. My man knows what he's facing. He volunteered, anyway."

Tears slipped down Emelovi's cheeks, but she did not object again. Kebonsat's heart swelled with fierce pride for her. She looked frightened, but the fear didn't dominate her. She lifted her chin resolutely. She'd grown since she'd been here, shed her timid subservience. She would rule Kodu Riik well, he thought. And no matter whom she married, *she* would rule. Emelovi had chosen, now. Not to stand up to Aare, but to protect her people and her land. In the end, it came down to the same thing. Kebonsat meant to see she had the chance.

"In the meantime, I am going to visit my father," Metyein declared.

"What?" Soka lunged to his feet, his chair clattering over backwards.

"I am going to see my father," Metyein repeated. "He doesn't know what danger we're in. If I can convince him, then he might help us. I have to try."

"Then I'm going with you."

"I wouldn't have anyone else."

Soka made a guttural sound, but made no reply.

"What about the rest of us?" Thevul Bro-heyek said.

"You and Edel are going to coordinate our defense," Metyein said. "Tillen, I want you and your assistant to make people understand what we're fighting for. Spread the word. Tell them Reisil has returned; tell them what's at stake. Make them believe."

He turned back to Thevul Bro-heyek and Edel. "Tillen has been indispensible. If you have questions about anything, he'll know. And his assistant—" He looked at the gray-eyed man apologetically. "I don't recall your name."

There was the barest pause.

"Tapit."

Metyein nodded, turning back to Edel and Thevul Bro-heyek. He opened his mouth and froze. Kebonsat caught it the same moment. He yanked his sword free as Metyein and Soka did the same. Soka grabbed Emelovi and shoved her into a corner, shielding her with his body. The gray-eyed wizard stood up. Tillen looked confused, but he moved against the wall and out of the way of the swords now pointed at the wizard's lean form.

"Reisil has told you about me, I see," the wizard drawled.

"I don't know what your game is, but we aren't playing."

"Aren't you?" Tapit smiled. His expression turned Kebonsat's marrow to ice.

Suddenly Kebonsat's sword felt very, very heavy. He struggled to keep it steady, but the weight only increased. His hand grew slippery with sweat, but he could not let go. His hand would not unclench. Fear mixed with fury as the tip of his sword clanged to the ground. The other men were like contorted reflections of himself.

"Stop it!" Emelovi stepped around Soka and stomped across to Tapit. She stabbed her finger into his chest. "Stop it. Now. You could have walked out. We never had to know. So you must want to be here, to talk to us. So do it. But stop this or I will find a way to kill you myself."

She spoke so fiercely that Kebonsat could imagine her snatching up a knife and driving it into the wizard's heart. He grinned, despite himself. Yes, Emelovi had come out of her shell. She had strength and courage, everything needed to rule. If she could stand up to a wizard then she could stand up to her son-of-a-whore brother.

"As you wish, Dazien," Tapit said, with a slight bow. Suddenly the weight of the sword released and Kebonsat could stand. He wanted to leap forward and drag Emelovi away from the wizard, but he resisted.

"I merely thought it prudent to demonstrate what you have correctly stated. I *could* have walked out without any of you knowing who I am. I chose not to. I could also have killed each of you long ago."

"So why didn't you? What do you want?" demanded Metyein.

"I've been waiting for Reisil's return," he said bluntly. "I've come to take her back."

"You can't have her," Kebonsat said through tight lips. Emelovi was standing too close to the *sharmuta*. It was taking everything he had not to step between them. But she wouldn't forgive him for it. Maybe Metyein, but never him.

"We'll see," came Tapit's unruffled reply. "But that will have to wait until this business of Mysane Kosk is laid to rest. I have decided to help you."

"Into our graves, maybe," Soka muttered.

"Why?" asked Metyein.

He smiled again. "I have my reasons."

"And you expect us to just let you walk in here and do what you want?" Soka said contemptuously.

"I expect that you may try to stop me. I expect you will fail. Fatally. I will do as I wish here. It serves my purposes."

Tense silence met his declaration. He was right. There wasn't anything any of them could do.

"So what help did you have in mind?" Metyein said grudgingly at last.

Tapit smiled. "I will bolster the shields of your witch and the Guild wizards. We will attempt to deflect the sorcerers and my brethren when they arrive. Be assured, they *are* on their way. And you are entirely correct. They will not willingly give up."

Metyein nodded grudgingly. "All right then. Since we cannot stop you. But know this: If you betray us, you will be killed. One way or another, if I have to hunt you down myself."

"It will be my pleasure. I always enjoy a good hunt," Tapit said, his smile widening. It was an unpleasant expression. "I will leave you to your work then."

Much to Kebonsat's fury, the wizard reached out and lifted Emelovi's hand. He bowed and kissed it and then departed, closing the door sharply behind.

Kebonsat wasn't the only one who started swearing. Then they remembered Emelovi and broke off. Kebonsat glared at her. What was she thinking to stand so close to the wizard? He could have killed her. When reason reminded him that the wizard could have killed her from across the room, or at any time in the last weeks, he remembered the kiss to her hand

and his fury waxed hotter. He sheathed his sword. He didn't have a right to be angry. He didn't have a right to feel anything at all for her. She'd made that more than clear.

"Well," Metyein said, and coughed. "It seems we have some unexpected help. I hope. But there's nothing we can do about it except pray to the Lady he doesn't destroy us all.

"Let's get to what we can do. Dazien and Kebonsat, I want you to leave within the hour. Find someplace safe. Take a dozen of your best men, Kebonsat. Soka and I will also be on our way." He looked at Edel. "Our people have become accustomed to Kebonsat. They don't—quite—think of him as Patversemese. And they haven't had much time to think about you at all. That will change when you take up command. I suggest you wear this." He handed him a strip of green material. "Tie it around your arm. Make it conspicious. And mention you're friends with Reisiltark. They'll walk through fire for her if need be."

Edel took the proffered material and Kebonsat helped him tie it on.

"And now, if there's nothing else?"

"Still no word from Juhrnus?" Edel asked.

Metyein shook his head and he answered heavily. "No. And I wish he were here. I'd send him in to try to talk to his sorceress. Anything else? Good, then let's go. And may the Lady smile on us all."

There was a moment's pause as they each looked at one another. Then Kebonsat stretched out his hand to Metyein. One by one, the men said farewell, and then kissed Emelovi's hand. When it was Kebonsat's turn for the latter, he moved aside, not looking at her.

As they trooped out of the room, he fell in beside her. "I'll come for you as soon as I gather supplies and organize our escort. Dress warmly in sturdy clothing."

He didn't wait for her to answer, but spun on his heel and strode away. It would all be over soon. And then he would be free of her, one way or another.

Chapter 38

Reisil gazed awestruck at the mist-filled circle surrounding Mysane Kosk. She couldn't bring herself to call it a blight-circle, as Metyein and the others did. If the *nokulas* were hers to protect, they could not be a blight. It swirled and danced with lights and crystals. And it was *enormous*. Getting safely across it into the city where the wizards had cast the spell was going to take a lot longer than she thought. And if the *nokulas* fought them the whole way—they might not make it at all.

She rolled her head on her shoulders, wishing there had been time to sleep before making this attempt. But who knew when the wizards or Scallacians would attack again? Soon the continuing rupture between Kodu Riik and Cemanahuatl would be so large that she wouldn't be able to stop this at all. It was now or never.

She turned to look at Yohuac and Baku behind her. The coal-drake sat hunched on the ground, his neck and tail turned in a protective half circle around Yohuac, who stroked his black hide absently.

"Are you ready?"

"Yes."

~Yes.

~Are you ready? she asked Saljane.

~Yes.

Reisil had a sense of sharp, cold air and clean, pungent forest.

~Hold tight.

~I will.

Reisil had the urge to say something else, to continue the interaction, but there was no more time. She drew a deep breath to steady herself, clutching her pack under her arm. She raised her mental walls so that only Saljane could reach through, and blinked into spellsight.

"Then let's begin."

It was difficult to do nothing. But she had to rely on Baku and Yohuac to insulate them from the warping magic of Mysane Kosk and get them all the way into the city, where the wizards had cast their spell. Reisil had to hold herself in reserve so she'd have the strength to heal what the wizards had damaged.

But the *nokulas* had to let them pass. The *nokulas* had an endless supply of magic available to them. They would quickly overwhelm the shields Yohuac and Baku produced, like a tidal wave to snuff a candle. She had to convince them. And the best way to do that was from the inside.

She felt a *gathering* as Yohuac began. Instantly, she felt an answering *push* from the mist. She glanced over her shoulder and blanched. There was a swelling at the edge of the mist-circle, as if something were shoving against it, trying to get out. Her mouth went dry. She felt horribly exposed, and suddenly realized she'd made a terrible mistake. She was too close to the mist. There was little to stop the *nokulas* from leaping out and dragging her inside. She might whip together a fast shield to protect herself from the warping effects of the magic, but it would not last long.

Reisil inched away up the slope, watching the bulge warily. She'd hardly begun to move when several things happened at once.

There was a sound of galloping hoofbeats and a scrolling, high-pitched sound, almost like song. At the same moment, Yohuac's gathering of magic tightened into a tight ball. In that instant, the bulge erupted. Inside, Reisil saw silver teeth and maws, spines and claws. And eyes that looked like a pirate's treasure in jewels. She snatched her own power and it stormed over her, fed by the waters of Mysane Kosk. Reisil wrapped her magic around herself, turning to face the *nokula* pack.

But they weren't attacking anymore. They hung suspended in mideruption. The edges of the mist fluttered like tattered rags around them. Their eyes glittered and their teeth clicked together as their mouths gaped open and shut. Their claws flexed and curled in dawdling rhythm. Their muscles rolled and twitched sluggishly. Saliva dripped from their mouths in long, slow strings. They were caught fast, as if in a crystal paperweight.

As she felt the danger ease, the roar of Reisil's own pounding heart faded. She released her spellsight, then tensed. The high-pitched sound continued. It unwound in an uncomfortable, spiraling melody that scraped her nerves and set her teeth on edge. It seemed unfinished, somehow, as if it were part of a larger harmony. Alone it was unsettling, but woven together with another, it might be beautiful. Reisil shook herself and looked over her shoulder at Yohuac and Baku, careful not to turn her back on the *nokulas*. They stood in an attitude of frozen shock, staring past her shoulder up the slope. Reisil shifted around to follow their gaze.

She forgot about the *nokulas*; she forgot about Mysane Kosk. The entire world disappeared in a black wash. Her knees buckled and she crashed heavily to the ground, catching herself on her hands, unable to look away.

It was Juhrnus. Or what was left of him.

He looked just like the plague-healers Reisil had rescued from the wizards. His skin was pale as milk, his forehead broad, his cheeks ridged beneath slanted eyes that were silvered from corner to corner. His hair was still curly and long, but it had turned white. He wore the same clothes as before, but they hung on him oddly. His head was tipped slightly and he watched her sideways, like a crow. His mouth was pursed. He was the source of that eerie song.

For a moment Reisil tried to convince herself that this creature was not Juhrnus. It was someone else, an impostor made to resemble him as a plague-healer. But as much as she wanted to believe it, she could find no logic that would explain why anybody but Juhrnus would carry an enormous sisalik draped over his shoulders. Combined with the fact that he was riding Indigo, there was no possibility that it wasn't Juhrnus.

Tears ran down Reisil's cheeks as she silently stood.

Juhrnus dismounted, his movements fluid and sleek, like a *nokula*. Indigo sawed his head against Juhrnus's shoulder, shoving him sideways. He staggered and Esper made a disgruntled sound. It was such an absolutely *normal* scene that it made Reisil laugh. The sound tore her throat.

He did not stop his singing. He eyed Reisil with that sideways look and walked past to where the *nokulas* hung in the air. Tatters of the mist floated in the air like motes of dust, drifting slowly to the ground. He watched them, his head tilting one way, then another. The music changed. Now the mist began to melt away around the beasts. It pulled back into itself, so that the sparkling dome returned to being smooth and whole. The half dozen *nokulas* inched down to settle on the winter-killed grass.

The plague-healer who was Juhrnus glanced at Reisil. She understood. He was going to let them go. She wrapped herself in a magical shield, sinking it deep in the earth. The *nokulas* would not be able to move her. Behind her, she felt the gathering of magic as Yohuac and Baku did the same.

The song ended.

The *nokulas* yowled and leaped to their feet. They spread out in front of Reisil and Juhrnus in a crouching semicircle, separating them from Mysane Kosk.

"Juhrnus? What's happening?"

"Song is broken. Silence rises. Must sing back the harmony. Else Silence."

His words seemed meaningless, and yet Reisil knew exactly what he meant. And more than that, what he could do with his song. He'd tamed the mist. He could help her with the wizards' spell. If they could get through the mist-circle. And the *nokulas*.

"I want to talk to Sodur," Reisil said to the slavering beasts.

Their only response was to yowl and snap. She had a sense of hammering thuds against her mental walls. She shook her head as if bothered by flies.

"Let me talk to Sodur."

Juhrnus added a snatch of song to her request. At the sound, the *nokulas* sank to their bellies, whining. Suddenly Sodur's hulking shape emerged out of the mist, followed by Lume and another, slightly smaller form. Reisil recognized it from the dungeons under Koduteel. It was the Iisand. She nodded to him. Reisil had a feeling that hundreds more lurked inside the opalescent curtain just out of sight.

She felt a questioning poke against her mental barrier. She lowered it slightly, holding tight to Saljane.

~*You should have run.*

Sodur's voice had changed. There was a vibrant quality to it, like echoes of many voices.

"And I told you I couldn't do that." Reisil spoke aloud so that her friends could hear. "I told you I was going to figure out a way to save Kodu Riik and Mysane Kosk. That's what we've come to do. And there isn't much time left. On the other side of the spell in Cemanahuatl, the nahualli witches are preparing to attack. And the wizards and the Scallacian sorcerers. And when they do . . . we won't be able to stop what happens. So we have to come in, and you have to let us."

As one the *nokulas* bared their teeth in a snarl. Or perhaps it was a bestial smile. Reisil couldn't tell.

~*You have come to try to destroy us. We will fight.*

Reisil gritted her teeth, anger crackling up through her.

"Don't be more stupid than you have to be," she snapped, her eyes raking the gathered *nokulas*. "Those of you who used to be *ahalad-kaaslane* should know better." She paused, a thought striking her. "Actually, just because you've become *nokula* doesn't mean you've quit being *ahalad-kaaslane*. You still serve the Lady; you still serve Kodu Riik. I'm telling you now that this is the only way to save us all. Including yourselves. So you need to decide. Are you still *ahalad-kaaslane*?"

There was a shifting among the *nokulas*. Sodur crouched down to the ground, propping his head on his forelegs in an oddly doglike manner. He stared at Reisil intently, saying nothing. Reisil was glad he didn't ask what she intended to do. She didn't know what she'd have said. She wasn't sure herself. All she knew was that she had to get inside and see the spell itself. Only then would she know what to do. And she would. She had to.

When it didn't appear that Sodur was going to reply, Reisil knelt down, staring into his opaque silver eyes. She wasn't just talking to him; all of the *nokulas* were listening. "You know that the wizards and the Scallacians are definitely going to try to hurt you. The wizards have been taking *nokulas* prisoner and stealing their power. The Scallacians are just as greedy. If they don't try to steal your power and your lives, they'll try to destroy you. And then there's me. Some of you know me. A long time ago, the Lady told me to heal Her land and Her people. She was very clear. She said *all Her people*—and She was talking about you. You have to know that you're in dreadful danger. Let me try to stabilize the spell. I promise you, I'll die before I do anything to destroy you or your home."

Sodur only blinked; then his eyes drifted shut. Startled at the drowsy reaction, Reisil straightened, chewing the inside of her cheek. She glanced at the other *nokulas*. They remained equally still. She had the feeling of an enormous discussion going on. She remembered what Sodur had told her about the way the *nokulas* tended to swarm like fish under the lash of wind and tide. Which way would they swim this time?

Suddenly Sodur's eyes flicked open and he rolled to his feet.

~*You may try. We will not stop you.*

The sudden wash of relief made her dizzy.

"Thank you."

~*We wish you good luck. In the meantime, we will go hunting. It is time the wizards answered for what they have done to us.*

~*Good,* Reisil said savagely. *And when this is over, we'll go together and rescue whoever's left in the stronghold.* It was a sore spot that she'd had to leave anybody behind at all.

Sodur's lips curled into a frightening snarl. But this time Reisil was sure it was a smile.

~*We will enjoy that.*

With that he edged closer to her, stopping at the edge of her shield. Reisil hesitated a second, and then dropped it. Trust created trust. He extended his snout, the teeth like daggers. His nose brushed against hers. She felt the puff of his breath against her mouth. A moist swipe of his tongue on her lips. And then he was gone, bounding away up the slope. A stream of *nokulas* leaped from the mist, following him. There were hundreds.

Reisil watched them until they disappeared over the ridge. She turned back to her friends.

"Let's go. Juhrnus, Yohuac and Baku are going to build a shield around us. You'll have to stand close."

He tipped his head and then smiled. It was a sly, merry expression. Reisil could almost see the Juhrnus she knew in it. Then he whistled a trill of notes and wandered down to the edge of the mist. He stuck his hand in and pulled it out, waggling the fingers. Then he stood and waited.

Reisil stared, her heart clenched. He could go inside

without being warped by the magic. She didn't know why, but the knowledge made her want to cry. Swallowing hard, she looked at Yohuac.

"It's just us, then."

Once again, Yohuac gathered his magic. Reisil watched as a gold bubble formed around him. His eyes glowed as if lit from within, and the sun flecks on his skin seemed to flicker like flame. The golden bubble pushed outward, encircling Baku and then Reisil. As it pushed through and around her, Reisil felt a flash of heat that reminded her of the return from Cemanahuatl. They'd traveled through *Ilhuicatl's* heart, Yohuac had told her. Through the sun. The bubble firmed. Blue-tipped flames continued to dance along its surface.

A moment later Baku began his shield. White sparks spiraled down his black length, like fireflies. The bubble he made was silvery blue, like the North Star. As Yohuac had done, Baku pushed the shield out. When it passed through Reisil, she shivered. It swelled until it melded against Yohuac's gold shield. There was a crack like thawing river ice.

It was done.

"Walk slowly. Stay on one side of Baku, and I will be on the other. Hold tight to him. We must not separate."

Reisil nodded, gripping one of Baku's neck ridges with her right hand. Yohuac's hand settled on top of hers, his fingers wrapping hers tightly.

Lady, help us if you can, she prayed. And then they inched down into the mist, Juhrnus pacing alongside.

Chapter 39

Tapit opened the door without knocking. The room was lit only by a crackling fire. The witch woman, Nurema, sat talking with three members of the Whieche. Demonlord, but they were young. And scared. They started and turned, eyes wide. He could smell their fear. He looked appraisingly at the witch woman. She had gray hair that was scraped back into a tight bun. Her skin was dark and made leathery by the sun. She had snapping black eyes and a taste— His eyes widened and he nodded respectfully. There was more to her than he had thought.

"Well, now, Tapit, yer finally here. And none too soon," she said caustically.

"You were expecting me?" he asked, startled. He had only just left the others. Who had warned her?

She laughed, the sound reminding him of a donkey's bray. "I've known you was coming for years." She laughed again at his shock and waved him toward a chair. "I'm a seer, boy. But ye don't need me to say we're about to have troubles. Now sit yerself down and ye can tell me about yer wizard friends. They're gonna be here by daylight. We have to be ready."

Soka and Metyein crawled up out of the tunnel into a carefully planted thicket of pine and huckleberry bushes. It screened the entry entirely. Soka lowered the trapdoor cover. It was covered with rocks and debris held in place by wire and glue. Metyein brushed the ground to wipe away the evidence of their passing, and the two slid out into the night.

They were in the hills due south of Lion. The command tents for Aare's army were at the eastern end of the valley, in the middle of the enormous camp. It was going to take most of the night to work past the sentries and join the camp. Then they had to work their way through to the command tents. Metyein hoped to reach his father before dawn, while he was still alone. Otherwise, he'd have to wait until the evening to get their chance. By then it might be too late.

Neither man spoke to the other as they began to ease through the darkness. Metyein winced with every snapped twig. Suddenly, from Honor, came shouts and the blowing of horns. It was a diversion. Metyein touched Soka's shoulder and they hurried faster.

They ran over the rocky ground, slinking from tree to boulder to bush. The first of the sentries was caught up in the commotion below. He never noticed the knife that severed his vocal cords and arteries in one vicious thrust.

"Can't do much more of that or they'll notice we're here. Drag him over there," Soka whispered, motioning to a gully shrouded in bushes.

Metyein wiped his dagger on a handful of leaves and obeyed. His mind felt clear and alert, as if it weren't quite attached to his body. He was grateful for that. He'd killed men before, but never from behind, never when they were helpless.

They threaded through the sentry perimeter. Most soldiers were distracted and not very worried about intruders. A few were more diligent. They killed two more men before reaching the edge of the bustling camp. They hid the bodies as best as they could. But when daylight came and the watch changed, the dead men would certainly be found.

Soka and Metyein stripped the last two of their tunics. They'd knocked in their skulls, and the clothing, while greasy and stained with food and grime, was not bloody.

"Are you ready?" asked Soka, a peculiar light glinting in his eye.

"As I'll ever be."

They came out of the shadows, striding purposefully toward the interior command area as if they belonged. They nodded to the other men but did not stop to talk, except to say they had a message for the captain. No one asked which one. It was enough to silence suspicion. Better soldiers might have prodded them, but these weren't much better than street rabble. They served because it paid and gave them regular meals. And because they'd be killed otherwise. Most were sleeping or dicing or telling lewd stories as the fires burned low. There were a few camp followers with whom the men enthusiastically romped while their friends watched and leered, waiting for their turn.

Closer to the command tents the security tightened. These men were regulars. Metyein and Soka straightened, marching more determinedly.

"Hold up, there. What do you want?" A man stepped in front of them, his thumbs hooked in his sword belt.

"Message for the Lord Marshal," Metyein said, meeting the sergeant's glare with a steady gaze.

"Give it here, then." The other man thrust out a meaty slab of a hand.

"No, sir. We were ordered to take it to the Lord Marshal's aide-de-camp." Metyein spoke crisply.

The sergeant scanned them up and down, his lip curling at their filthy tunics. His gaze snagged on the black rag tied over Soka's eye.

"What happened to him?"

"A disagreement," Soka replied.

"Stirring up trouble?" the sergeant said, rolling forward on the balls of his feet, his eyes narrowing.

"No, sir. Ending it."

The sergeant stared a moment, considering, and then nodded. "Follow me."

Metyein breathed out in relief. They followed the

sergeant, threading through the maze of tents and campfires.

It was still an hour before dawn when the sergeant brought them to the Lord Marshal's pavilion. It was made of heavy canvas and was fully a quarter acre in size. A pennant near the door indicated the Lord Marshal was within. On the hill behind, Metyein saw Aarc's extravagant pavilion. It was made of midnight silk with golden gryphons gamboling around the bottom and top edges. His pennant flapped in the breeze above the doorway. Metyein's heart pounded. To be this close . . .

The aide-de-camp was sent for. His name was Samles. He'd been with Metyein's father for eight years. At last he emerged, straightening his clothing, his narrow face hard with annoyance.

"What is it?" he barked at the sergeant who snapped to attention and saluted.

"Message for the Lord Marshal, sir."

"Well? Give it here."

The sergeant turned sharply around with military precision. "Present your message," he ordered Metyein.

Now the aide-de-camp fixed his attention on the two grubby men. Recognition flickered in his eyes, but his expression did not vary.

"It's not written, sir," Metyein said, standing at attention.

"Hmph. All right. Inside. I'll have my kohv and breakfast while you spit it out. This had better be worth it, or you'll have full-time duty digging latrines. Try not to drop any of your filth on the carpet. Don't touch anything." He hardly paused as he turned his attention to the sergeant.

"Master Sergeant Vicker, I confess myself disappointed in the poor personal grooming exhibited by these men. I think the Kodu Riikian army should have higher standards. I want inspections. I want to see a little order and pride. See to it personally. I'll have my clerk write the orders. Anyone who gives you lip can take latrine duty. Understood?"

"Yes, sir!" the sergeant saluted again.

Samles led the way inside, pausing to relay his orders to a groggy clerk sitting at a low table just within. He then led them farther inside to a small sitting room.

"Wait here, please. I'll call the Lord Marshal."

Neither man sat. Soka prowled restlessly while Metyein stood still. He went over his arguments in his mind and prayed for his father to see reason.

Five minutes later, the curtained door behind which Samles had disappeared was pushed aside and his father entered, with Samles close on his heels.

For a moment father and son stared at each other. Metyein noted that his father was thinner and looked haggard. Then the other man opened his arms. Metyein stepped into his grasp, hugging him back hard. Emotion flooded him and he blinked away hot tears.

After a moment, Metyein pulled away. "There's not much time."

His father's expression tightened. He nodded and turned to Samles. "Tighten the guard. I don't want any visitors. Make sure they're *ours*."

Samles nodded and withdrew, his gaze lingering on Metyein. Metyein gave a half-smile, thanking the Lady that it was Samles who still served as his father's aide-de-camp and not someone new.

"Why are you here?" his father demanded as soon as Samles was gone. "This is beyond dangerous. It's downright stupid. If Aare found out—" He broke off, his face turning to stone.

"I came to ask for your help," Metyein said simply.

"Help? You chose another side. You're a traitor. There's no help I can give you."

Metyein studied his father. Did Aare even know what he had in Derros cas Vare?

"I have some things to tell you. And then you can decide what you will do. But first I'll remind you of what I told you before. I do what honor and duty require. I serve the Lady and I serve Kodu Riik.

"Now I'll be as quick as I can for the rest of it. The first thing that you don't know is that if the Scallacians or the wizards attack Mysane Kosk again, then Kodu Riik will be destroyed. Honor's wards were tied into the power of Mysane Kosk. When the sorcerer hit Bear yesterday, you saw what happened. The blight-circle doubled. And it isn't just Kodu Riik that will be obliterated. It's everywhere. The world will be re-made; and nothing will survive.

"Reisiltark is going into Mysane Kosk to try to fix the problem. But an attack will destroy her. If she dies, then there is no hope at all. I can't allow that to happen. And since I know you don't trust her, let me tell you this. Aare arranged to have me kidnapped so that either I could spy on you, or else he could hold me hostage as a lever to keep you in line. But things went wrong. I was gut-shot and Soka was taken instead. I should have died. Reisiltark healed me. If she hadn't, I'd be napping in a dirt bed right now. Later, he set Soka free to spy on me and you. After he tortured him. That's the man you serve."

Metyein didn't give his father a chance to speak, but hurried on, searching for the words that would convince him.

"You know he's gone after the *ahalad-kaaslane*. You know he's not loyal to the Lady. He is a traitor to his land and his people. You owe him nothing. Dazien Emelovi is her father's daughter. She's the one you ought to be serving.

"So here's what I came to ask you. I need you to keep the sorcerers from attacking Mysane Kosk. Nothing else matters."

He stopped, breathing fast, feeling like he'd been running uphill. His father's expression had not changed. Metyein wasn't even sure the other man had heard. *Skraa!* How could his father continue to be loyal to Aare?

"I'm sure you believe what you've told me," his father said finally. "But what proof can you offer?"

Metyein pulled up his tunic, exposing the scar on his stomach. "Courtesy of the Regent," he snarled softly.

His father's gaze flicked to the rippled, twisted flesh. He shrugged. "You were shot. Reisiltark healed you. But what proof have you that the Iisand was behind it? What proof have you that it wasn't one of her plots to gain your loyalty and use you? If she can heal that, then why not the plague? Why not Geran?"

Metyein stared, his stomach flipping. The Iisand? Aare had gained the throne? He looked away. This was futile. His father was what he was. Metyein might have convinced him while Aare was still Regent, but not now.

"I've said what I came to say. I don't have any other proof for you. If you don't recognize the truth when you hear it, if you want to serve that *ganyik*, then so be it. We'll go now—unless you want to arrest us?" he asked coldly.

"If he doesn't, I certainly do," a cruel voice purred, and Aare stepped out from behind the curtains. His gaze raked over Metyein and then to Soka, who looked feral. "What have we here? Traitors both." He licked his lips and smiled. "I will have to welcome you properly."

Metyein glanced at his father. He'd gone gray, but his expression remained stoic.

"Daz Aare. What brings you to my quarters at this hour?"

"I understood you had visitors," he said mildly. But no one could mistake the threat in his voice.

"Oh?" There was a wealth of resentment and distrust in that question.

"Yes. Thanks to our Scallacian friends, I know when anyone who doesn't belong to me enters the camp."

Fury flashed in Derros cas Vare's eyes and his nostrils flared. "I am responsible for safeguarding this camp. Why wasn't I informed?"

Aare waved the question away. "Oh, it wasn't necessary. I daresay I'm entitled to a few secrets, am I not?" he asked silkily. "Now, what to do with these two?"

He walked around, scanning both Metyein and Soka up and down. Metyein gritted his teeth. Soka merely stared straight ahead and looked bored. No doubt the poison bead was safely ensconced in his cheek. He'd not be tortured by Aare again. Metyein was glad for him.

"We'll have to make a lesson of them," Aare murmured. "Something to demoralize the rebels. Something to remind the men of the price to be paid for betraying their country and rightful leader. Something to remind Emelovi of her place." This last was said in a vicious whisper. Metyein glanced at his father, who looked sick.

Quick as an adder he whipped his sword from his scabbard and drove it at Aare's chest.

His arm wrenched as the sword stuck fast in thin air, inches from Aare's chest. The new Iisand chortled delightedly. Metyein struggled to pull it away or let go, to no avail. He cursed himself. Of course Aare would have magical protection. He had the sorcerers in his pocket. Suddenly something crawled up over his hand. He tried to wrench himself away again. The sensation continued, tickling, like centipedes crawling onto his flesh. And then . . . they *burrowed*.

Metyein screamed as voracious jaws chewed into his flesh and under his skin. They gnawed a slow, winding path to his bone. His flesh split open as more and more of the invisible creatures devoured his skin and muscle. There was no blood. They crept toward his elbow. Soon his hand and forearm were nothing but pale bone, not even a scrap of flesh remaining. The pain was beyond anything Metyein had experienced. He heard himself scream, jerking his arm so that his shoulder came loose from the socket. Still he was trapped.

Soka and his father drew their swords. The two

male sorcerers emerged from behind the curtain to counter them.

"I wouldn't move," Aare said conversationally. "You don't want to share his fate, do you? If you're good and quiet, I will let him die sooner rather than later. Now, sheath your swords and watch what happens to traitors. And, dear Derros, take careful note. He is not your only son."

Lord Marshal Vare slowly lowered his sword. His face was white. Metyein turned to look at Soka, pleading. The creatures had burrowed up to his armpit and he dangled helplessly by his ruined arm, unable to stand, unable to let go of the sword. Agony screamed along his nerves and he began to retch convulsively. His body spasmed and vomit splattered the floor. Aare pulled his robe aside and stepped back in distaste.

And then with a strangled sound, Soka leaped forward. His mouth was pulled in a rictus of hate and anguish. His sword flashed. Metyein felt the clean bite of steel against his neck. And then everything went black.

"Here, Dazien, let me help you."

Emelovi smiled at Ledus and let him take her hand to steady her as she half slid down the steep bank. Kebonsat waited below with Dumen. Both Ledus and Dumen were Patversemese knights who had accompanied Kebonsat on his ambassadorial mission to woo her. Like him, they'd been declared dead by their country and families when the blockade had gone up and Aare had taken them hostage. And they'd joined Honor to help fight against Aare's despotism.

Emelovi winced as Kebonsat reached up to catch her if she fell. But it was reflexive. In fact, she was startled to realize she no longer felt the hot wash of bitterness that usually accompanied thinking about Kebonsat. She frowned. When had she stopped being so angry with him?

She reached the bottom of the gully without incident. Kebonsat stepped away without touching her, his expression remote. Emelovi frowned at the irrational irritation she felt, stepping aside while the rest of their escort scrabbled down. Pebbles bounced around them. One struck her a stinging blow on the back of her hand. She stifled her cry of pain and rubbed the sore spot.

When all the men had descended, Kebonsat waved them forward. He led the way with four men behind him. Then came Emelovi with Dumen and Ledus flanking her. The rest of their escort fanned out behind. The group went slowly and silently, following the twisting path of the gully. The ground turned muddy and it was difficult to walk. The dark made finding her footing even worse. Emelovi struggled to pull her feet free of the sticky mud. She slipped, and the two men at her side caught her arms, lifting her back up. Her legs began to burn as they climbed higher out of the valley. She quickly grew hot and wished she could remove her cloak. She panted, her chest beginning to hurt.

At last Kebonsat whispered an order to rest. Dumen and Ledus remained by her side as she settled on a rock. Black-haired Ledus offered her a piece of journeybread. He smiled encouragingly as she took it and ate, glad to have something to fill her stomach. He then offered her his water bag. She drank gratefully.

Kebonsat came and squatted beside her. He held himself stiffly apart, not meeting her eyes. His voice was terse, lacking any emotion. Emelovi frowned again, surprised at her reaction. This was the way she'd wanted it, wasn't it? Certainly she missed him, missed his friendship and the way he made her feel when he looked at her, as if she were the only one in the room. *But he'd betrayed her*. She found herself shushing the shrill protest. What was betrayal? He'd wanted her safe. Yes, he'd lied. And no, she wouldn't have come if he had told her the truth. But if she were honest, that fact wasn't anything she was proud of. In the last months, she'd come to understand her duty to Kodu Riik, to her people. If not for Kebonsat, she would have let Aare continue on, knowing he'd turned from the Lady, knowing he was hunting the *ahalad-kaaslane* and betraying his people. Worse, she would have let him prostitute her to the sorcerers, to whomever he wanted. The thought made her cringe hotly from herself. Much as she wanted to deny it, she couldn't, and the knowledge repulsed her.

The only reason she was here was Kebonsat. She still didn't like that he'd lied to her. But because of him, she'd shaken off the habit of helplessness she'd cultivated under Aare's dominion. Because of Kebonsat, she'd found courage and purpose.

"The next bit is going to be hard. Are you ready?" he asked in a low voice.

"When you are," she said softly, wanting to say more. But this was not the time. She didn't know when would be. Or when he'd be willing to listen, if ever.

She examined him closely in the gloom, not liking what she saw. He'd changed. There was a recklessness about him, an edginess that reminded her of Soka. As if he were constantly dancing on the edge of a cliff. As if he no longer cared about his own safety. It worried her. The lack of information about Ceriba only made things worse. The agony of knowing Aare had her, but being unable to rescue his sister was driving Kebonsat mad. Emelovi could see it. Her own frigid anger had not helped settle him down. She wanted to offer him comfort. But between them was a fence of thorns. One of her own making. And she didn't know how to tear it down. She drew a breath. Later. There would be time later when this was all over. She contented herself with the promise that she would put things right then.

"We'll find a place to hole up before dawn," he said. "But it's going to be a hard climb. Can you make it?"

"Of course."

He nodded and rose, making his way to the front again. Emelovi watched him go, her heart tight.

Kebonsat was right. The climb became steeper, the ground more slippery. Soon Emelovi was covered with mud, her fingers scraped and bruised from scrabbling for handholds. The night sky began to lighten as dawn approached. Kebonsat turned around a massive boulder and up a narrow path out of the gully. There was only room to go single-file. Emelovi gripped the rocks on either side, pulling herself up on the craggy path. At least it wasn't muddy, she told herself.

Suddenly the *twang* of an arrow string shattered the silence. She heard the clunk of arrows battering the rocks, and the sodden thump of those that found their targets. Ledus grabbed her, shoving her down into a crevice and shielding her with his body. There were shouts. The clang of swords. More twangs, more clunks and thuds.

Emelovi trembled. A few feet away, between the rock and Ledus's arm, she could see Dumen's wide, staring eyes, an arrow protruding from his neck. He looked startled. Bile rose in Emelovi's throat and she retched.

"Hear that, boys?" a voice shouted close by on the rocks above.

Emelovi froze.

"Someone's off his feed. Now which of you done that to th' poor sod?" Mocking laughter echoed in the gray air. "C'mon out, now. Don't be shy. We'll be gentle. I promise." More laughter and then the sounds of booted feet on the trail. Emelovi wriggled backwards. Ledus thrust his dagger at her.

"Take it," he ordered. "I'll hold 'em best I can."

And then he stepped away, around the corner. Swords clanged. Shouting. Emelovi pulled the dagger from its sheath and held it in both hands. They shook. Nothing she could do would make them stop.

"Cowards!"

Emelovi's breath caught. It was Kebonsat.

"Come on out and fight like men. Or do you do all your killing from behind in the dark?"

"Brave words from a man hidin' in them rocks. But

then all your friends is dead. Say! I got an idea! Why don't you save us a bit o' trouble. Come out and let us give you a chance to dance for your freedom. No arrows. Just steel."

No! Don't do it! Emelovi cried silently.

"All right then," Kebonsat said, and Emelovi heard the scrape of his boots on the path. "Here I am. Let's see what kind of men you are."

Emelovi knew he was giving her a diversion and buying her time to get away. Reason told her there was no way Aare's men could have known they were going to be here, that she was among them. It was just bad luck. They'd probably walked into a patrol.

The sound of swords clashing rang in the morning air. Emelovi started. Then she crawled out of the crevice. She stepped carefully around Dumen's body and inched up the path. Ledus lay across it, a gaping wound in his chest, his intestines spilling out onto the ground. Emelovi's gorge rose again and she pressed a hand to her mouth, swallowing hard. The other four men who'd been between her and Kebonsat were crumpled dark heaps, arrows sticking out of them like porcupine quills. Tears rolled down her cheeks and she hurried past, toward the sounds of fighting.

She rounded a corner and then ducked back into the shadows. Kebonsat stood in the middle of half a dozen men. His sword whirred in the air, faster than she could see. He ducked under a blade and drove his own deep into a man's stomach. The man toppled as Kebonsat smoothly pulled free to block another man's feint.

It was a dance. An awful, macabre dance. Emelovi watched in terror as one after another of Aare's men fell with horrible wounds. It never occurred to her to flee, to abandon him.

Kebonsat kept swinging in silent fury. Crimson streaks appeared on his arms and legs, on his chest. Blood ran from a slice across his cheek. But his energy seemed boundless. He leaped and swung, ducked and rolled. He slammed the pommel of his sword into one man's jaw and rolled off him as a blade cut through the air where he'd been standing and chopped through the man he'd punched.

No one spoke. There was only the clang of metal, grunts of pain, the rasping pant of effort, and the whimpering of death. Soon there were three men facing Kebonsat, then two, then one. This last had more skill than his brethren. He parried and feinted, his sword flashing with deadly intent.

The fight ended so quickly that Emelovi didn't understand what her eyes told her. Kebonsat tripped and Aare's soldier drove down in a powerful, hammering thrust, the edge of his sword shining in the moonlight. Kebonsat rammed himself at the man's legs. The soldier's blade slammed into his back. Emelovi screamed. There was a crunch of bone and both men fell, with Kebonsat landing on top of the other. He lifted his arm and drove his dagger into the soldier's chest.

No one moved. Kebonsat remained as he'd fallen. Emelovi heard the sound of stricken breathing and smelled the foul stench of blood and body waste. She hesitated a bare second and then stumbled across the muddy battleground, dropping to her knees beside Kebonsat. Blood flowed from the horrible wound in his back. Emelovi could see the gleam of bone peering through from his shoulder to his hip. She gripped his shoulder.

"Kebonsat? Can you hear me?"

There was a guttural moan and then nothing more. She pulled her hand away. It was sticky with blood. She stared down at her hand and then back at Kebonsat's limp body, fear turning her to stone. The wound on his back was a fatal one. She knew it. She could see it.

Suddenly a noise erupted from her, like a wolf snarling. She lunged to her feet, looking for something to bind him, to stop the bleeding. Reisiltark had returned. She could heal him. All Emelovi had to do was keep him from dying before Reisiltark could save him.

She'd lost her father. She wasn't going to lose Kebonsat too.

Chapter 40

Kedisan-Mutira watched from behind the curtain wall as Metyein's decapitated head spun and hit the floor with a sodden thud. For a moment, no one made a sound. Then Menegal-Hakar made a sweep of his hand and muttered something. The headless body dropped to the floor, blood spurting from his neck. The Lord Marshal staggered back to sit stricken on the edge of his desk. Aare swore furiously.

"You're going to pay for that insolence," he declared to Soka, red blotches blooming on his cheeks.

Soka wiped his sword clean on a tablecloth and sheathed it deliberately. He turned. "Do your worst," he said, a queer light shining in his eyes.

He looked . . . insane. And murderous. Kedisan-Mutira knew that look, knew the fatalism and recklessness that drove it. It was the mirror of her own soul. Her fingers curled into her palm. Neither Menegal-Hakar nor Waiyhu-Waris could touch her anymore. They'd failed to make her reveal her true power. And now it was too late for them. They didn't know it yet, of course. She'd bided her time. But now . . .

For weeks since the visit of that *presence* had woken her, she'd been on edge. The thread that bound her to Juhrnus had changed. He was still there, but not the same. He was elusive and yet constantly with her. She dreamed of him. She smelled his scent in empty corridors and felt his touch when she was alone.

When she'd come to Kodu Riik, she'd hoped to make an alliance, to begin establishing her base of power so that she would be a dominant force in Scallas. And then she'd met *him*. And now none of the rest seemed to matter. Her eyes swung back to the Lord Marshal's dead son. She frowned. Metyein had been Juhrnus's friend. She looked at Soka, at the newly crowned Iisand and the two sorcerers flanking him, their expressions gloating.

Something snapped inside her.

She stepped into the room, the charms on her chain robe chiming. Beneath it she wore a thin shift. She was not cold.

She didn't speak. She didn't use grand theatrics. She didn't need them. She looked at Menegal-Hakar and with a thought she invoked the charm she'd hung on the hem of his robe when she'd risen from her bed after passing her *penakidah*. He burst into flame. The fire burned only him, not even scorching the carpet.

Kedisan-Mutira ignored his screams, ignored the stench of his charring flesh. She looked at Waiyhu-Waris. He was muttering, working his fingers together. She curled her lip. He was weak. So very weak. Another charm, another thought, another invocation. His body erupted in a second column of flames. Kedisan-Mutira watched the two sorcerers burn with silent satisfaction. She did not hate them for the things they'd done to her—for the things they'd made her do—in the course of the *penakidah*. That was only what was expected. She hated them for failing to see her. For their weakness and for not realizing they were weak.

She turned, suddenly realizing that the Iisand was speaking.

"Yes?" she said absently.

"You did this?" He sounded loud and scared.

"Of course."

The Iisand made a strangled noise and Kedisan-Mutira focused on him, stroking the place between her breasts where the thread connecting her to Juhrnus was anchored.

"What are you doing? I have promises, assurances from your Kilmet. You are here to serve me."

"I serve Dahre-Sniwan, who rules the heavens with a frigid hand and curses his enemies with unrelenting heat. He is all-knowing and all-powerful. He is the light and the wind and the water. He is ice and lightning," she said evenly. Then her voice dropped, and smoke the color of blackberries coiled around her fingers. "I *do not* serve *you*."

As she spoke, she approached so that she brushed up against him. She called in the cold, dropping the temperature of the air so her breath frosted on his cheek. "If Menegal-Hakar or Waiyhu-Waris or the Kilmet made you promises, then you can take it up with them. But here is *my* promise, puny man," she said, resting her fingertips lightly on his chest and pushing him back to sit in a chair. She detached a charm from her chain robe and set it on his knee. The silver wire was shaped like a snowflake. She ran her finger over the surface, binding and invoking the spell in the space of a heartbeat. She knelt so that she could look directly into his eyes. "When that falls, then your protection spells will turn on you and you will die, just like the Lord Marshal's son. No one else will be able to move it for you. No one can touch you. Just like Menegal-Hakar promised."

She pushed to her feet, turning to Soka. "Well enough?"

He nodded. "Nothing will ever be enough. But it will do."

"Then let us go. I feel others coming. Wizards." She spat the word. "Your people will need help."

"We need a wagon," the Lord Marshal grated suddenly, pushing himself to his feet. Soka caught his arm and steadied him. The older man was still gray and his hands shook. "I won't leave Metyein here." His voice broke on the last. He caught himself with an effort. "Samles will arrange it."

Kedisan-Mutira nodded. "Tell him to hurry."

* * *

Reisil could feel the press of the magic against the shields like the weight of an ocean. It made her teeth ache and the marrow of her bones shudder. With every step they took, the feeling grew worse. And this without the *nokulas* trying to stop them. She shuddered. They had a long way to go.

"Please, Lady, help us if you can," she murmured.

Yohuac squeezed her hand, but said nothing. He couldn't, she realized. Not and maintain the concentration he needed for holding the shield. Sweat dampened his skin and beaded on his upper lip.

The crystalline landscape shimmered beyond the shield walls. Juhrnus kept pace with them, striding along easily. Reisil blinked into spellsight and gasped. As before, when she'd gazed down on Mysane Kosk from the overlook months before, the landscape and air were full of *rinda* chains, some floating, some gnarled into beautiful shapes. And Juhrnus –he was like lace, the *rinda* that wove him together was fine and tight and balanced. There was a polished quality to him that the *nokulas* lacked. And somehow, Reisil knew the difference was terribly important.

As they drew closer to the core of the spell, the landscape inside Mysane Kosk became more and more fantastical. It was as if faeries had constructed a world entirely of rainbow ice. Some of the shapes were beautifully ethereal, while others were grotesquely twisted.

They came to the outer edge of the city. It was like walking through sculptures of cobwebs, ice, and spun sugar. The road was opalescent and its power hummed through Reisil's bones. The pressure of magic pushing against them was increasing. It came from the unwinding spell in the core.

They remained on the road, guided by the strengthening tide. Yohuac and Baku were slowing. Their strength was waning. They bulled their way forward, fueled by stubborness alone. Even Juhrnus was beginning to struggle. Reisil found herself scratching at her skin, scraping away bloody strips. It did not assuage the furious gnawing inside her muscles, like voracious ants.

Almost there.

Strands of broken *rinda* chains flowed past Reisil, intermixed with half-formed spells made from nahualli *rinda*. Sometimes the chains looped around the broken structures, as if the nahualli *rinda* had summoned them, seeking a way to wholeness. But even as she watched, many of those couplings broke apart. Understanding hit Reisil like a bolt of lightning. Of course. That was why the *nokulas* had begun as human or animal. They had to. The *rinda* needed the wholeness of the living body to provide a stable foundation for becoming.

The current of magic was becoming violent. It sheared around them in a tightening circle. They were almost on top of the place where the original spell was cast—like walking into the eye of a cyclone. Reisil cast a nervous glance at the layered shield. It was beginning to falter. It flickered and shrank, becoming more a skin than a bubble around the three. Yohuac's face was haggard and Baku's hide had lost its luster.

It wouldn't do any good to lose the shield. She pulled up her magic and let her strength flow through her hand into Yohuac and Baku. The shield firmed. They pushed forward, between two towering structures made of amethyst crystal and covered with spikes. The ends burned brilliantly.

They emerged into what must have been the town square. The air turned cloudy white and opaque, like milk. It was suddenly quiet here, the currents of magic disappearing. But the pressure of the magic was very tight, making it difficult to even breathe. Every step was like pushing through mud.

They struggled forward, Reisil guiding them. She felt an *intensity* drawing her like a flame in the dark. She followed it, nervousness balling in her stomach. What if she couldn't do it? What if the wizards attacked before she was through? What if the nahuallis struck from the other side? She tried to hurry faster, fighting against the sticky density.

They emerged from the milky fog into a narrow open circle no more than twenty feet across. The ground was cobbled. The wizards had inscribed *rinda* on the stones in the shape of a spiral. But much of those had been eaten away, from the inside out. Magic spurted up from the center of it in a twisting geyser. It reminded her of the spell cast by the nahuallis when she'd first arrived in Oceotl. A maelstrom pinned in place by magic.

The problem, Reisil realized, was that the magic from Cemanahuatl was filled with *rinda* that were constantly joining and shifting, searching for wholeness. They spewed violently from the well and knocked against the containment boundaries set by the wizards in the original spell. But the wizards hadn't anticipated the nahualli *rinda*. Instead of bouncing harmlessly away, the nahualli *rinda* fastened onto the wizard *rinda* and tore the spell-chains free. Now nonsensical bits and snatches of mixed *rinda* spun and shattered against one another in a wild tempest, at the same time the containment shields were being eaten away. The boundary no longer contained the magic, and it flooded outward through the gap like spilled kohv. Except it didn't entirely run away. The *rinda* pushing out of the well into Cemanahuatl called it back. The maelstrom formed. And it was steadily growing larger, fed by Cemanahuatl's magic.

Reisil frowned. She understood what was happening, but the boundary should have been chewed up and destroyed a long time ago, limiting the number of wizard *rinda*, feeding the spell. But there were far more here than there should have been. She scanned the open space, looking for answers. She found them in the cobbles. Etched into the stone were row after row of tiny *rinda*. They glowed with a dim fire. The symbols were ancient, like the spells in the prison chamber beneath Kodu Riik. Years of dirt and wear must have obscured them until the wizards cast their

spell. With the Lady's presence suppressing magic i
Kodu Riik, there wouldn't have been any way to tell
they were there until it was too late.

~*He wants to know what you wish to do*, Baku said.

Reisil started and looked at Yohuac. He opened his
mouth and spoke, but she heard nothing. Nothing at
all. Not even her own fast breathing. There was only
silence.

Silence. She looked at Juhrnus. *Silence rises.* She
looked back at the unraveling spell, her fingers clenching on her pack. She was supposed to be here, with
the moon *rinda*, with Juhrnus and Yohuac and Baku.
All together, they were supposed to fix this. Each had
something important to contribute. She knew it. Each
in their own way was a melding of two worlds: Reisil
born of nahualli and *ahalad-kaaslane* blood; Juhrnus
transformed; Yohuac and Baku united.

Yohuac and Baku had gotten her here safely.
They'd done their part. So it was up to her and Juhrnus. The spell had to be stabilized. Not only did they
have to find a way to stop the magic from flowing out
of Cemanahuatl; they had to turn the flow back so
that there was a balance. And she had to protect what
she did from the nahuallis, who might even now be
trying to destroy it.

She knew what part of the answer had to be. If only
she could create it. If only she had enough time. She
pulled her pack from her shoulder. Somehow she had
to form the thirteen moon *rinda* into the shape the
copicatl had shown her after her trial.

Chapter 41

Soka stumbled and fell, hardly noticing the pain shooting through his knee. He lunged to his feet and strode after the wagon. Samles drove with Metyein's father sitting beside him. He looked like he'd aged twenty years. Soka had no pity for him.

Beside him, Kedisan-Mutira was a ghostly presence. He knew she was there, but his eyes refused to settle on her, sliding away and forgetting. Metyein's death replayed again and again in his mind. And his screams . . . Soka's eyes burned, but he shed no tears. The poison bead clicked against his teeth and he caught it, biting, feeling the hard shell give with the pressure.

"Don't. He would not wish it."

The sorceress's voice was soft, but it contained no pity. If it had . . . He didn't hit women. But today he'd murdered his best friend, the brother of his heart. His fists bunched.

"What do you know about him?" Soka rasped.

She said nothing for several moments. "Some choose power. Some choose pain. Some choose to hide. A few choose sacrifice. I know that much."

Sacrifice.

"Why are you helping?" he asked at last. If she'd stepped in sooner— Rage roared inside him, and it took all his strength to hold it in, to wait for an answer. But if it was the wrong answer . . .

"Because of Juhrnus," she said simply.

"Juhrnus?"

She stopped and he turned to face her. Her shape solidified so that he could see her clearly. She put her hand out, settling it over his heart. He flinched from the touch, but did not pull away.

"You killed your heart to save his suffering. The sacrifice should not be wasted. Nobody's should."

Soka grappled at the puzzle of her words. How did Juhrnus fit? "Juhrnus has sacrificed," he said slowly, understanding seeping in. "What has happened to him? Is he—?" He couldn't bring himself to say *dead*.

"He is coming. He is close. But he is . . . different."

"Different? What does that mean?"

She shook her head, pulling her hand away and rubbing her fingers gently between her breasts. "I do not know. But he will not have to sacrifice any more."

Her last words were menacing and cold. She walked away, catching up to the rumbling wagon. Within two steps she'd faded to ghostliness again. Soka pressed his palm to his chest where she'd touched. Sudden horror gripped him. Beneath his thumb he felt the lump of the protective ward Reisil had made for him. He hooked his fingers under the string and ripped it off his head. It dangled from his hand, glinting in the bright morning sunshine. Just a coin. *It could have saved Metyein.* If Soka had thought to give it to him, Metyein would still be alive.

Pain and guilt tore through him. His soul was bleeding to death. He stood there, waiting to die. How could he not? But such wounds were not fatal.

Aare's soldiers were beginning to notice him. They began to gather, eyeing him suspiciously. He had to move. He had to keep going. Metyein would want him to defend Honor. To see this through. Jerkily Soka began to walk again, twisting the necklace cord through his fingers. *A few choose sacrifice. Some choose betrayal.* He'd betrayed Metyein to Aare, the thing he'd fought so hard not to do. If only he'd thought to give him the ward, if he'd remembered . . .

He would make sure Metyein's sacrifice had not

en for nothing, Soka promised himself. And when
was over . . . His lips twisted and he spat the poison
bead to the ground. When it was over, he would go
on. Because he owed Metyein that much justice. To
suffer for his murder.

Alone in the Lord Marshal's tent, the Iisand sat
very still. He'd forced the coronation in the last day
before marching north. No one had objected. No one
had dared.

His eyes were fixed on the silver snowflake perched
on his knee. It burned with unrelenting cold. He resisted the urge to twitch and knock it away. Sweat
from the effort trickled down his temples and dripped
from his nose. He wasn't going to let them get away
with it for free. They would pay, and pay dearly. He
didn't need magic to raze the stockades and butcher
those *sharmutas*.

A rustle caught his attention. A scribe stuck his
head through the curtain and then blanched at seeing
Aare, the pool of spilled blood, and the piles of ash
on the rug. He began to pull back hastily with a muttered apology.

"Boy! Attend me!" Aare ordered sharply, careful
to keep his body very still.

The boy nodded and inched back, his face pale
with fear.

"Fetch Commander Salives. Bring him here
quickly."

The boy hesitated and then scrambled away. Aare
smiled grimly. Yes, they would pay. He looked at the
snowflake, and fear made his bladder swell urgently.
He couldn't hold it in. Warmth flooded his crotch and
trickled down his legs. His teeth ground together,
smelling the stink of piss filling the curtained room.
He'd have them all slaughtered. They would feel the
horror of his death as acutely as he did.

"Good. You are here," the witch woman said, greeting Kedisan-Mutira as if she'd been expecting her.

They stood inside the abandoned Fox. There was
stench of decay, of bodies rotting. Above them th
crystal-mist dome of Mysane Kosk loomed like a
mountain.

"We must combine our strength to create a shield
around Mysane Kosk. This will keep the wizards from
drawing on its power, and it will keep them from making things worse."

She gestured for them to sit, putting Kedisan-Mutira
on one side of her and the gray-eyed wizard on the
other. The other three wizards closed the circle. They
were white as snow-flowers, and they trembled.
Kedisan-Mutira watched them with amazement. These
were the infamous Patversemese wizards who'd always
been so hard to defeat in the wars? How was it
possible?

"Join hands," the witch woman ordered. "We will
layer our shields, one inside another. You three will
form the outer shields," she said to the nervous wizards. "Next will be me, then Tapit, and last you," she
said to Kedisan-Mutira. "You must not hold back or
give up. If we fail, then Reisiltark will fail. Do you
understand?"

A few choose sacrifice.

They each nodded.

"Then let's begin."

Soka paced by the window while his father and Edel
grilled Lord Marshal Vare on the strengths of Aare's
army. Metyein lay on the bed in Soka's quarters,
wrapped in the rug from the Lord Marshal's pavillion.
The sorceress had helped transport him through the
tunnels before congregating with Nurema and the wizards. Metyein's father had regained some of his color,
but there was still a quake to his voice that wouldn't
go away. Soka liked him better for it.

"He knows your wards are down. We should have
killed him and been done with it," Lord Marshal Vare
said harshly.

"It wouldn't have made much difference. That's an army out there, and they're primed to attack. They've come for the loot and the women and they aren't going to just walk away empty-handed. With or without the Scallacians, with or without the Iisand, they'd have come again," Soka's father said.

"Besides, a quick kill wouldn't have been nearly enough," Soka added darkly. "He's getting what he deserves."

Suddenly warning horns sounded their piercing cry. "They're coming," Soka said, running to the door and out. The other men followed close on his heels. Up to the battlements.

"Hag's tits," Soka murmured.

Aare's army had pooled at the far end of the valley and was advancing. They pushed siege towers and trebuchets out in front of them. Within an hour, they established a position out of bow range and began lobbing boulders at Bear and Salamander. They struck the walls with great booming *cracks*. The walls shuddered under the thundering hail.

"I'm going back to Salamander. I'll be more help there right now," Edel declared, and strode away. Soka's father hesitated and then he glanced at Lord Marshal Vare. "I too should go. But only if you'll take command of the rest. We need a Lord Marshal." Metyein's father gave a reluctant nod. There wasn't anyone else.

"I'll go with you," Soka declared. His father gave a sharp glance, but did not object.

They emerged into Bear twenty minutes later. The men greeted Soka's father with a certain amount of relief, but they'd done well. They hadn't panicked, and the walls still held. Soka's lips tightened with smug pride. Metyein had insisted that the walls be sunk deep and braced by boxes of buried timbers. The buildings lining the walls only added to their strength. They didn't fear rocks. But soon Aare's men would get around to fire. There were barrels of water and rags stationed every few feet at the base of the walls and up on the battlements. All they could do now was sit and wait for Aare's army to come within range.

"We need to drive them up between the stockades," Soka's father said as they stood together, staring at the waiting army. "Their rabble. They don't have much discipline and they'll be getting bored. Wouldn't take much to get them moving." He rubbed his hand thoughtfully over his mouth.

A coil of brutality uncurled in Soka. "I've got an idea," he said, starting to walk away. He halted, pulling the ward that Reisil had made him from his pocket. He looked at it, his lip curling, and turned back to his father. He held the necklace out. His father took it, curious. "Wear it in good health," Soka said, and walked away, ignoring the questions his father called after him.

He gathered a team of men he trusted: Clano, Temles, Ferro, and Slatts. They joined him without hesitation. Soka stopped at the stables, ordering each to collect a thick bundle of straw and a pair of hatchets apiece. Soka also picked up a roll of heavy twine. They dropped down into the escape tunnel. There were torches at the bottom. Each took a half dozen. Soka lit one of his and jogged ahead, lighting the way. He was numb. He didn't feel the bite of his overworked muscles or the ache in his lungs.

They clambered out of the tunnel, screened by boulders and bushes.

"The wind's blowing from the east. We've got to hurry before it changes. We're going to build fires to drive the *ganyiks* into the killing field. Clano and Slatts, you're with me. We'll skirt around to the far side and work our way back. We'll take the high line and stay above your fire line," he said to Ferro and Temles. "Set them quick and make sure they are burning well before you move on. One of you should stay and nurse the first while the other sets the second. Then leapfrog back. We'll check yours on our return. This will help," he said, handing them each a heavy x from the pack he bore on his back. "It's pitch. Keep an eye out for sweep patrols. I doubt they'll use them. They think we're hemmed in."

It took Soka, Clano, and Slatts nearly two hours to work around to the other side of the valley carrying the bulky straw bundles.

"I'll start. You two backtrack and get fires going. I'll leapfrog back when this one is blazing," Soka ordered tersely.

The others nodded and hurried off. Soka hacked wood from a rotting log and piled it around the base of a snag. He added straw and handfuls of twigs. Lastly, he rubbed pitch on the dead tree's trunk. He struck a flint to a torch and jabbed it into his kindling pile. It flared with quick heat, ringing the tree in flames. Soka hacked out more rotting wood and added it to the fire. Soon the flames were crackling high above his head, catching on the spreading limbs of the snag. For a moment he remembered the burning figures of the Scallacian sorcerers and he grinned. The expression faded instantly as he remembered Metyein's head lolling on the floor.

He couldn't contain the primitive scream of fury that burst from him. It tore his throat and lungs. A blood vessel burst in his eye. He came back to himself when he ran out of breath and began to cough. The tree continued to burn well. Satisfied, Soka took out the roll of twine and wrapped it tightly around a wad of straw. He lit it on fire and then dragged it over the ground in the direction Clano and Slatts had taken, going slowly. With any luck, the straw bundle would strike a few more fires and add to the conflagration they were trying to set ablaze.

Slowly the three of them worked back toward the tunnel. Smoke began to billow on the slopes below as Temles's and Ferro's fires caught. A pall drifted over the valley, hiding Aare's army and the stockades.

Soka's team reunited at the tunnel entrance. All of them were streaked with soot. Slatts had singed his eyebrows and hair, and Ferro's hands were blistered and raw. But all five of them grinned fiercely at one another. A full-fledged forest fire raged along the ridge, driving into the valley.

"That ought to get them moving," Soka murmured.

Then suddenly the air exploded. He felt as if he were being turned inside out. He collapsed to the ground, gasping, as invisible hands jammed him against the hillside. White light burned across the sky. He jerked his head away from it, flinging up his arm and shutting his eye. He felt the ground trembling under him and heard screams and shouts from the valley below.

After a moment, he struggled upright.

The explosions continued, shattering the air and rattling the earth, but they seemed oddly far away, behind the fire. They did not seem to be focused on Honor at all.

"What's happening?" Temles whispered. He clutched his arms around himself, gazing nervously upward.

"I think the wizards have arrived," Soka said, coughing. He spat to clear his mouth and rolled to his feet. "Let's get back."

They ran for the tunnel entrance, dropping inside. The ground shook again. Dirt sifted from the tunnel roof.

"Run for it," Soka advised, pushing Clano ahead of him and motioning for the others to follow. He brought up the rear. Sound was muffled underground. He could hear only faint sounds of shouting and the whumping thumps that could have been the wizards' magic, or the thunder of rocks flung from siege engines. Their own heavy breathing and shuffling steps made it difficult to hear anything else.

They were halfway along when Soka heard the ominous creaking of the support timbers. Then there was a screeching *crack*. Soka looked up as the tunnel roof slowly began to sink.

"Run!"

He thrust himself forward. Behind him, dirt clogged

...he passage and clouds of dust exploded around them. He sucked in a breath and then began to gag. He struggled along, tripping over Ferro, who'd collapsed. Blood ran from a gash in his forehead. Soka lifted him up and helped him along. They careened off the walls as they stumbled forward. Slatts came back and grabbed Ferro's other arm. Together, he and Soka pulled the injured man away from the collapse.

Temles and Clano waited at the bottom of the ladder. They helped push Ferro up and out and then followed behind. Soka was last up. He crawled over the edge and rolled onto his back, panting. He blinked. Something was wrong. Through the smoke, the sky was . . . red. The color of blood. He rubbed his eye. It remained.

Suddenly he became aware of screaming and men running. He staggered to his feet, swaying. Aare's men were coming over the walls. The defenders hacked and slashed, and blood ran in rivers across the battlements and dripped in pools onto the ground. But the men coming over the walls were white-eyed with fear and fury. They swarmed like ants, hardly seeming to care about the carnage. Soon the bodies would be piled so deep on the battlements that the men of Bear would have no place to stand. They'd be forced to retreat down the stairs to the bailey.

Soka pulled his sword and ran at a man in a royal tunic who'd slipped through and was going for the gate. His sword clanged against the soldier's with satisfying violence. He beat him back, ducking under his overhand swing and thrusting through his stomach. He shoved the soldier off his blade and met the next intruder with ruthless efficiency. Metyein had taught him very well.

But there was no holding back that endless tide of men. Driven by fire and fear of the attacking wizards, they scrabbled over one another like ants. They overran the defenders with sheer numbers. For every man of Bear who fell, four of Aare's soldiers dropped. But they kept coming.

Soka's strength began to fla_ His sword windmille_ and seemed to strike flesh v_ _ ery cut. He slipped in churning red mud. Some_ _ked him, flipping him over. He heard bones_ _ feeling the pain only dimly. He rolled bef_ _ _ blade split him in two. He fetched up agains_ _ base of the tower and leaped to his feet. His ribs shrilled with agony. It was hard to catch his breath. The pain cut through the haze clouding his senses. He clung to it. It felt right. Deserved.

His attacker crouched. The soldier was grinning, the tip of his sword winding slowly back and forth like a cobra.

"Can't run, *ganyik*. Ain't nowhere to hide. Are you ready to dance with Cateel?"

Something appeared over Cateel's shoulder. A glimmer, a flash, like moonlight on the ocean. Soka froze, his eyes narrowing. Cateel chose that moment to lunge. Something caught him around the head. He jerked like a rag doll, his neck snapping as gouges erupted on his forehead. He was tossed aside, landing in a broken heap. Soka straightened, captured by the silver eyes boring into him. The rest of the *nokula* rippled into view. Soka gulped hard, his eyes wandering over the thick slab shoulders, spined back, and six-inch claws dripping blood.

It thrust its head forward on its sinewy neck, its jaws gaping wide. Hot breath brushed across Soka's cheeks. He drew back, pressing against the wooden tower. The beast's tongue unfurled slowly, a flat, tapered streak of white. It whispered across Soka's lips, tasting. Soka watched the dagger teeth hovering only an inch from his eye. Then abruptly the *nokula* drew away. Its muzzle opened wider in what Soka could have sworn was a grin. Then it whirled and bounded away with a flick of its stumpy tail.

Soka stared after it, fear clamping around his bowels. What was happening? He shook his head and straightened. He staggered in a circle, astonished. Aare's soldiers continued to fling themselves over the all. But fewer made it into the bailey. Many were being torn limb from limb by invisible claws, gutted with a single swipe of a powerful paw. By the Lady's Light—the *nokulas* were . . . helping.

Soka smiled. And then his mind went blank and pain was forgotten as another of Aare's soldiers swung at him. He blocked the cut, stepping under it and letting the other man's sword slide down his to stick in the ground. He thrust his palm against the man's throat. The soldier wobbled backwards, choking. Soka yanked his dagger free and drove it into the soldier's chest. He crowed triumph at the way the man slid to the ground, the primitive beast inside clawing free. And then there were more men and he was killing them and killing them. . . . Every one wore the face of Aare. Every scream he heard was Metyein's agonized last cry. Every blow he struck was for vengeance.

Chapter 42

Something was wrong. Reisil stared at the spell taking shape in her hands. It was nearly there. Near to becoming the spell that the *copicatl* had shown her. Something was wrong with it. She could feel it. But what? And what role did Juhrnus play in healing Mysane Kosk? He crouched outside the shields, watching her with that birdlike curiosity that seemed neither frightened nor urgent. Esper remained perched on his shoulders, untainted by the warping magic of Mysane Kosk. How was that possible? She had no idea. And no time to sort it out.

Reisil tore her gaze away from him and examined her creation. She ran her fingers over it, feeling the connections between the *rinda*, feeling the way the magic in them wove together. What was wrong with it?

Slow realization seeped through her anxiety and exhaustion. The spell-shape had been given to her by *Ilhuicatl*. It was supposed to save Cemanahuatl. He didn't care about the *nokulas*. He didn't care about Mysane Kosk or even Kodu Riik. They weren't his responsibility. For whatever reason, the nahuallis couldn't create the spell, or they couldn't deliver it. Reisil jerked her head in an angry refusal. Neither would she. She'd *promised*.

She closed her eyes, drawing a calming breath. Her hands were shaking from the effort of molding the oon *rinda*. Though they had bent more easily to her will than she expected, still it had taken an enormous flow of energy to meld them. Time was running out. If she failed, if she was too late . . . She looked at Yohuac and Baku. They stood still as statues. Yohuac's feet were braced wide and Baku's tail curled tightly around the small of the straining man's back. Yohuac gripped Baku's neck ridges. The tendons stood out on his hands. His face was a mask of concentration.

They were stretched tight. Nearly past their limits. If she used *Ilhuicatl's* spell, it might very well save Kodu Riik. But the *nokulas* would die. She was certain of it. If she tried something else and it failed or she wasn't ready in time, then Cemanahuatl and Kodu Riik would be lost too.

She didn't have to consider. She was supposed to protect them. She had told them she would. Her fingers began to work, pulling apart the spell. It took nearly as much energy as building it.

She set the *rinda* before her, her brows furrowing. *Hurry . . . hurry . . . hurry!* Fear twisted her mind. Her thoughts whirled, unable to settle on anything. *Stop it. Get hold of yourself. Think.*

She picked up one of the moon *rinda*, feeling the power coursing through them, the way they called to each other. They were malleable in a way. They wanted a shape, a purpose. Reisil caught her breath and stiffened. An idea slid through the depths of her mind. She snatched at it. It flittered away. She took a breath, relaxing her shoulders. Another breath. Deep in, deep out. *Yes!*

They were malleable. Their shape could be bent. And it could be added to. The *nokulas* and Mysane Kosk were proof that the nahualli *rinda* could be combined with something else. She thought of the wards she'd made by infusing her will into common words. All she had to do was decide what she wanted and bend the *rinda* to do it, adding what she needed in

common language. A part of her snorted sardonically—
all she had to do. Easy as climbing a mountain without
clothing or shoes. But she'd done that too.

There was no time to waste. There was no time to
be careful. She was about to reach for her magic when
she glanced at Juhrnus. She froze. He had a role here
too. She thought of the way the mist responded to his
song, and the balanced structure of the *rinda* inside
him. And the way Esper remained unchanged. And
she remembered the Silence.

"Help me," she said. "Sing."

He nodded as if he'd been waiting for her signal,
and began. The song was not the same as before. It
rode the range from high to low. The melody did not
repeat, but wound on, ever changing.

It wasn't merely sound. Reisil could feel a power in
the song, like *rinda*. It was tangible. It spun through
the shields protecting Reisil. She reached out and
touched it, held it. She smiled. She pulled her magic
into herself, dropping all her barriers. It blasted into
her with a shocking force, amplified by Juhrnus's song.
She rocked backwards. Her head banged against the
shield. Then she convulsed forward, her muscles
spasming. She shuddered and quaked. Her hair waved
in the air on an invisible wind. It crackled and
sparked.

She didn't wait to gain control. She grabbed up the
first of the moon *rinda* and fitted it with another. She
knew their essences. They each contained an elemental fragment of life: fire of love for a child, passion for
a lover, hatred, want, hope, fear, pain, need, rage, joy,
bliss, quiet, guilt, greed, isolation, grief, home, and triumph. These were the seeds. Now she had to grow
the vines to make the sculpture.

She wrapped her hand in the web of the song, letting
it course through her fingers. She fed her power into
each joining, muttering all the while. *Keep the* nokulas
*safe . . . bind the wizards' spell . . . circulate the magic
back to Cemanahuatl . . . find a balance. . . .* The words
slurred together. Images of her friends, of Kodu Riik

nd Cemanahuatl, collected in her mind like drifting leaves. So many memories. So many wonders and losses. So much joy. So much sadness. Tears dripped down her cheeks and onto her fingers. She didn't dare brush them away. The torrent poured through her.

She felt the attack on Mysane Kosk. It was muffled and far away, but the maelstrom around them sped up, burgeoning hotly, pushing outward. Reisil sucked in a gasping breath. Almost done. Almost—

Done.

She stared down into her lap, at the sculpture she'd created. It didn't look like anything. It was knobby and sharp, smooth and silken. There was a wildness to it, and a liquid quality, as if it were moving. Reisil bent close. There were words etched into the silver surface. *Keep the* nokulas *safe . . . bind the wizards' spell . . . circulate the magic back to Cemanahuatl . . . find a balance. . . .* They scrolled over the skin, like the spells written into the cages that had held Baku and the plague-healers. She smoothed her fingers over the surface, feeling a fluidity, like the sound of the song. And she felt the *rightness* of it. She looked up at Juhrnus. He was watching her. He had stopped singing, and the silence was complete.

She pushed herself upright, her legs stiff and aching. She limped to the edge of the shield, looking through at the hole in the center of the *rinda* spiral from which gushed the lifeblood of Cemanahuatl. To insert it, she would need to leave the shield. Juhrnus could put it in, but it was going to take more than that. She'd realized it only in creating the sculpture. All those emotions came from life. The nahualli *rinda* were drawn to life. It was going to take life to unlock the spell. Which was not going to make anyone else happy.

She looked at Baku and Yohuac. They were watching her intently. Yohuac's face was gaunt, but hopeful. Reisil steeled herself. This was not going to be easy. They'd fight hard.

~*It's time for you to go now. All of you. The rest I have to do alone.*

She wasn't prepared for Baku's reaction. He snarled
and snapped at her. At the same moment, a wave of
crashing fury swamped her mind. It drove her to her
knees. Then as suddenly he attacked, he pulled back.
Reisil staggered up, trembling and swaying. She had
a sense of the two of them talking together. Yohuac's
face darkened and his gold eyes flared brilliantly.

~*He says we will not go until you are safe*, Baku
declared defiantly, the tip of his tail flicking back
and forth.

~*I'm not going to be safe*, Reisil said bluntly.

This time she was ready for Baku's reaction. The
surge of his anger was deeper than the ocean and
bleaker than a winter night in the icy north. And inside it was Yohuac, his love, his fear, his anguish. Reisil squeezed her eyes shut, holding firm to her walls.
She daren't let them in; she daren't feel their hunger.

~*You must go. I must stay. There is no time to
debate.*

~*We will not leave you.*

There was no arguing with that unyielding stubborness. She didn't know what would happen when she
set the spell, but she could not wait any longer.

~*All right. Do what you have to. But don't get in
my way.*

She snatched up the spell-sculpture and strode
toward the shield. Before she got there, Baku's tail
snaked around her. She stopped and looked at him.

~*Let me go. This must be done.*

~*You cannot. Kodu Riik needs you. For healing, for
the* nokulas. *They will need you if they are to be accepted in Kodu Riik. I have done what the Lady called
me to do. Once he is gone . . . Let me be the one.*

Reisil hesitated. She did not want to die. But she
was ready to do so for Kodu Riik and Cemanahuatl.
That was what being *ahalad-kaaslane* meant—sacrifice.
Baku was *ahalad-kaaslane*. But could she send him to
his death? It seemed so much harder than going
herself.

~*I am the wiser choice.*

Reisil nodded at last, aware of the speeding time. The nahuallis would be trying to destroy Ti'Omoru. He took the spell-sculpture delicately in his mouth. Reisil showed him what he had to do. It wasn't much. She could speak the necessary words.

~*Let us move near the hole*.

She waited for Baku to pass the message to Yohuac, who nodded understanding. His expression was stoic. Under the mask he wore, his heart had to be breaking. She settled her hand over his again.

~*Are you ready?* Baku asked.

Reisil didn't let herself think. She called up her magic to take up the burden of holding the shields. She nodded. Baku withdrew and she let her magic go. It flowed like water rushing from a broken dam. She didn't have the strength to temper it. The shields blazed. Reisil blinked and squinted, hardly able to see. She felt Baku scooting forward and she shuffled along beside him, letting him guide the way.

She knew when they stood beside the hole. It was like being continuously struck by lightning. She wanted to melt into it. She looked down into the shining darkness: the heart of the magical well. It pulled at her. Mesmerizing. She leaned her forehead and hands against the shields, starting to pull in her magic. She wanted—she *needed*—to touch it.

Suddenly Baku's tail whipped around, knocking her to the side. At the same moment, Yohuac reached for her, yanking her over Baku's back. She lay there a second, her ribs bellowing as she drank in air. The flow of her power faltered. The shields flickered and shrank. Quickly she bolstered them, sliding to her feet and settling her hand on Baku's neck.

~*Go quickly*.

She curled her fingers, pressing hard against Baku's neck. In the flash of a moment, she dropped her barriers, letting him know how much he'd come to mean to her. She felt the warm rush of his gratitude and the deep reservoir of emotion he held for her. She caught her breath. Her throat knotted.

~Farewell.

With that, Baku suddenly glowed incandescent
and slid out of the shields as if they weren't even
there. Reisil squinted against the flare of light as nahualli *rinda* clustered around him like flies on spilled
honey. Baku began to move arthritically, as if he'd
aged. His hide glistened white and silver beneath the
gathering *rinda*. He lowered his head, gently setting
the spell-sculpture in the hole. It revolved and floated,
as if it were looking for the proper fit. Reisil sighed.
Almost there.

Suddenly, she became aware of an odd feeling. Like
a puff of hot air in a cold room. She frowned. The
feeling . . . it was like a wave growing far out on the
ocean. What . . . ? And then she knew.

She watched frantically as the spell-sculpture bob-
bled and rose and then settled slowly, oh, so slowly,
down into the well. Reisil held her breath, her heart
thundering. *Hurry! Hurry!* She silently urged the spell.
Lower and lower. Almost there. Almost—

There was a soft *snick!* like a key turning in a lock.
At that moment, Baku limped heavily over the hole,
hiding the well and the spell-sculpture from view.

Quickly Reisil spoke the words to activate the spell.

"Let life guard life. Let the flood rise and fall. Let
the wheel turn. Let balance find a way."

The words were mute in the smothering silence. For
a moment Reisil thought they'd failed.

Suddenly Baku shattered like glass. Nahualli *rinda*
clung to the fragments as they rose on a stuttering
whirlwind. The spell-sculpture began to turn, slowly at
first, then spinning faster until it looked like a silver
flame. There was a pulling sensation, like the turn of
tide.

And the hole . . . widened.

Reisil stared in horrified shock. By the Lady! She'd
made it worse! She pressed her fists against her mouth.
Her stomach clenched and she fought the urge to
retch.

But as she watched, the magic spilling out of the

hole began to turn in a spiral instead of gushing like a volcano. And inside it . . . Reisil clapped and grinned so hard her face hurt. Inside a new spiral began. But this one was upside down. It sank down through the first one until its pointed tip was centered around the spinning silver spell that Reisil had made. The spiral above it remained steady.

Now the clusters of *rinda* and the fragments of Baku began to fall, funneling downward. They glimmered with a blue light that seemed to coalesce as it descended. Reisil felt a wash of silk over her inner senses. *Baku*. The clot of blue light and *rinda* spun downward through the spell-sculpture and disappeared. Reisil watched, waiting. That feeling of something rising was growing stronger.

Then something hit from below. The ground jumped. Reisil clutched Yohuac for balance. The nahuallis had tried to destroy Ti'Omoru. But they'd failed. The sculpture continued to spin.

It was working! Reisil put her arm around Yohuac, hugging him hard. It was going to work. The *nokulas* would be safe, and Cemanahuatl would get the return of its magic.

Already she could feel the change. She could see the milky-white fog surrounding them begin to shred. And she could hear. Juhrnus was singing. It sounded like a dirge. Reisil swallowed, looking up at Yohuac. Tears streaked his face. She looked away.

"May the Lady bless him. May She hold him in Her heart."

A strange feeling of warm hands on her shoulders made Reisil start. She glanced sharply over her shoulder, but there was nothing there. She frowned, shifting uneasily. The feeling did not leave.

~*You have done well*, ahalad-kaaslane. *I wish I could reward you as you deserve, but the gift you crave is not mine to give. But know I am proud. And if you have need, come to this place and I will hear. Though I may not return to Kodu Riik, I will always watch. I will always guard.*

Then the pressure of the invisible hands was suddenly gone. But as the Lady's voice faded, the talisman Reisil wore around her neck flared warmly, sending a joyous glow through her. She pressed her hand over it in wonder. The Lady was not gone. Kodu Riik was not abandoned.

She glanced at Yohuac. He wore a blank expression, as if poleaxed. Reisil knew the Lady had spoken to him. She turned to look at Juhrnus. He stood still, staring upward at nothing. There was a blissful expression on his face. He stroked Esper and the sisalik crooned.

"It's really going to work," she murmured, still hardly able to believe they'd done it, and before the nahuallis or the wizards or the Scallacians could stop them.

Soon a magical balance would be established. Magic would circulate between Kodu Riik and Cemanahuatl, bringing *rinda* to the *nokulas* to feed them. The *nokulas* would always have a home. The wizards would still covet it, but the *nokulas* could defend themselves. She'd help them.

She sighed, sagging with exhaustion.

"Let's go. We're done."

Before the Lady had touched her, she'd felt raw and blistered, the way she had when she'd rescued Yohuac from the wizards. But now she felt strong. The flow of magic fueling the shields was nearly effortless.

As they walked away, Reisil became aware of a song unwinding through the mist. It came from the spell they'd cast, and it swelled, layering over itself in a complex symphony the farther they went. The sound cast a net over the crystalline landscape, and though Reisil could see few changes, she had a sense of a push here, a settling there, a shake, a twist, a straightening. It was as if everything had been just slightly off, and now it was clicking into the right pattern. She looked at Juhrnus.

"What's going on?"

"Harmony. Right."

Oh. And suddenly Reisil became aware of all she'd lost, and that there was still more to come. There was a battle raging in Honor. People were dying. Her friends were dying. Her body tensed and her lungs contracted painfully. Her heart ached. She began to hurry.

It was still daylight. Reisil could hear the sounds of fighting from up the valley. Saljane swooped out of the sky in a long dive. She snapped her wings wide and dropped onto Reisil's uplifted fist. Reisil brought her close and stroked her *ahalad-kaaslane*'s breast feathers, smiling as Saljane nipped her fingers affectionately.

~*The Lady won't ever be able to return, will She?* Reisil asked. *Not really.*

~*Her presence smothers the magic. She cannot, if the* nokulas *are to live.*

~*How can She speak to us inside Mysane Kosk, then?*
~*I do not know.*

Not that Reisil was truly interested. She was only trying to stave off the inevitable moment when she had to say good-bye to Yohuac. Her heart was bleeding. It felt like a mortal wound.

~*What will we do?* She wasn't really asking about the Lady. But then, Saljane knew that only too well.

~*She will still send the* ahalad-kaaslane. *She will still watch over Kodu Riik.* Saljane's voice was gentle and pitying. She flitted to Reisil's shoulder and tucked herself against Reisil's neck.

She turned to face Yohuac. He was looking at her with those golden eyes, the stoic mask gone. He looked agonized. Haunted.

"It's time, isn't it?" Reisil whispered.

He nodded. "*Ilhuicatl* calls. I must answer."

He reached out for her. His hands cupped her hips as he pulled her close. His mouth trembled. He kissed her softly.

"I do not know how to say good-bye," he murmured.

"I don't either," Reisil said, smoothing her fingers over his shoulders and resting her forehead against his chest. She breathed in his smell, trying to inscribe it in her memory. She stepped away, curling her fingers together behind her back. Tears blurred her vision.

"I will not forget you," she said, her voice cracking.

"Nor I you."

The air around him began to flicker and glow like flames. Reisil couldn't help herself. She reached out her hand, wanting to touch him one last time. But he vanished like a blown candle. She stared at the spot where he'd been.

Tears slipped down Reisil's cheeks.

She looked down, startled, as Juhrnus clasped her hand. He was warm. She'd almost thought he'd be cold. She glanced up at him. For a moment, the sideways, birdlike expression dropped away. He looked at her full on. In his eyes she could see him, the boy she'd grown up with, the man she called friend. She squeezed his hand. His head tilted, the mask of difference returning. But her Juhrnus was in there too.

She didn't let go of him as she turned back toward Honor. She was needed. He was needed.

Chapter 43

The wind gusted, driving stinging pellets of snow into
Reisil's cheeks. She adjusted her hood and ducked her
head. The wind scoured the snow from the road and
drifted it against the hedgerow.

Lady, but she wanted a hot kohv and a fire!

~I see you.

Reisil looked up, peering through the swirling snowflakes.

~Where are you?

Saljane dropped out of the sky to land on Reisil's
upraised fist. She shook her feathers and mantled. Reisil lifted the goshawk up to her shoulder with a smile.
The wards she'd created for the rains in Cemanahuatl
worked just as well against the snow in Kodu Riik.

"How far?" a woman's voice called.

Reisil pulled up, waiting. Felias rode up beside her.
Her *ahalad-kaaslane*, a weirmart, flopped happily
across her lap, as undaunted by the weather as Saljane, thanks to another of Reisil's wards. Felias looked
far older than her twenty-five summers. She was pale
and drawn and her eyes had a wide, harried look.
Felias had been captured by the wizards and held in
the stronghold. Reisil had met her once in Kallas, before Saljane had come to claim her.

"A quarter of a league," Reisil said.

"Good. I can't wait for a hot bath. I'll tell the
others."

Felias loped back to the caravan. She rarely sat still,

always fidgeting and moving. A consequence of being caged, Reisil guessed.

The caravan that followed consisted of two dozen wagons, a full regiment of soldiers, and forty-two travelers. They were accompanied by thirty *nokulas,* who were invisible to all but those with spellsight. They ranged through the hills, not bothered by the cold. Like the people in the caravan, they were coming for the coronation and wedding.

Reisil sighed, nudging Indigo into a swinging walk. She hadn't been back to Koduteel in nearly two years. She wasn't sure she wanted to return now. But there wasn't much choice. She was needed there, and then too, she wanted to be there for Kebonsat and Emelovi.

A sudden wriggle beneath her cloak and a querelous cry told her that her son was awake. She pushed aside the folds of green material and peered in at him. He was cradled in a sling around her shoulders. His gold eyes seemed luminescent in the gloom beneath her cloak. He saw her and gurgled happily, struggling to free his hands from the blanket she'd wrapped him in.

"We'll be there soon, sweetling," she crooned. "You can eat and have a warm bath."

Hilis was two months old. She'd had him in Honor. It was turning into a bustling town. The *nokulas* had rooted out the remaining wizards, killing most and sending the rest fleeing. Thanks to Juhrnus, the plague had been eradicated. Lately he'd been acting as a go-between for the *nokulas* and the rest of Kodu Riik. The fact that he resembled the *nokulas* and could walk without shields in Mysane Kosk made them trust him.

He'd been there when Hilis was born. His song had made the birth easy. Juhrnus had spent much of his time with her and Hilis in the last two months. He said he liked their harmony. Reisil was trying hard to get to know him again. Most of the Juhrnus she knew was gone, transformed. She still caught glimpses of the man he used to be, but she knew she would never get him back. She needed to become acquainted with who he was now. But the bond he'd formed with Kedisan-Mutira had grown stronger, despite his transformation. Or maybe because of it. The two were inseparable. Three, Reisil corrected herself. Esper was as attached to Kedisan-Mutira as was Juhrnus.

She sighed. She was going to miss them. Juhrnus had decided to travel to Scallas with his sorceress. They'd left Honor when Reisil and Sodur did, deciding not to attend the coronation and wedding. Too many people stared at him, at his silver eyes and strange face. She smiled. They would stare plenty at the *nokulas,* if they decided to show themselves.

Suddenly the snow thinned. Up ahead, Reisil could see the walls of Koduteel. Banners and flags fluttered from the towers and walls. The Lady's Gate was wide open. People and wagons trundled briskly in and out, despite the cold weather and snow.

Felias trotted up beside her. The other woman was spinning a blue ball of light around the fingers of her right hand. Like many of the *ahalad-kaaslane,* she'd discovered she had a talent for magic. Which, no doubt, was the reason the wizards had kept her alive. Like food in the larder. She might be useful.

Feeling Reisil's gaze on her, Felias looked up and flushed. Her hand closed and the magical ball disappeared. She laughed shakily.

"I thought it would be easier to come back," she said.

"You've been a prisoner of the wizards for almost two years," Reisil said. "But you will be welcomed. The *ahalad-kaaslane* have begun to gather again at the Lady's Temple. It will be good for you to be among them again."

"I'm not so sure," Felias said meaningfully. The blue ball of light reappeared.

"You aren't the only *ahalad-kaaslane* to discover a talent for magic," Reisil said. "I'm going to stay for a

while and teach them. That's something—since I've
been teaching you, you'll be far ahead of them. They'll
be begging you for help."

Felias smiled and looked a bit less apprehensive.

At the gates, the guards waved them through with
enthusiastic greetings. As they did, Reisil became
aware of a presence. She blinked into spellsight. Sodur
and Lume had joined them. The two *nokulas* paced
along, invisible. The crowd parted for them to pass.

~*Neat trick*, Reisil said dryly.

She'd been learning to be friends with Sodur again,
too. Like Juhrnus, he'd changed. And so had she.
She'd lost too many friends to hold on to grudges.
And this Sodur still had a keen sense of humor and
a sharp intelligence.

~*They would not like to see us*, he replied with a
mental shrug.

~*They'll have to get used to you. You're* ahalad-
kaaslane, *and you're part of Kodu Riik.*

~*It will take time. But I have a feeling I will live a
very long time. I can learn patience.*

Reisil chuckled.

They wandered through the brown district toward
the Lady's Temple. Much of the city had been burned
during the Regent's reign. There was clearly a vigorous effort at rebuilding, but it would take years. Still
there was a sense of happiness and hope permeating
the city. The streets bustled with people who whistled
and chattered and laughed. It was a far cry from the
Koduteel she'd escaped from less than two years
before.

Reisil half feared that Emelovi's brother would have
destroyed the Lady's Temple, but it looked the same.
She turned Indigo into the spacious courtyard that was
contained between two sweeping wings of the Temple.
It was four stories tall and was constructed of green
stone in every shade known to nature. Felias and Reisil handed their mounts over to the waiting grooms
and went inside, followed by Sodur and Lume. The
two women stamped their feet, glad of the warmth.

"I'm hungry," Felias declared.

"So am I. But I want to feed Hilis and have a bath first."

"Oh, all right. But if I have to wait too long, I'm going to eat the furniture."

They checked in with the housekeeper, who became flustered when she realized who Reisil was. Her agitation grew worse when Sodur and Lume resolved out of thin air. She stared, her face paling.

~You couldn't have let me warn her?

"Glerona, you remember Sodur and Lume? Well, perhaps not. But nevertheless, this really *is* Sodur and this really *is* Lume. They will also need lodging."

Glerona marshaled herself, two red spots blotching her cheeks, her lips scrunched tightly together.

~Won't be long before everyone knows you're here.

~Saves trouble, doesn't it? Glerona always was a busybody. Better than a broadside for spreading news.

Reisil frowned at Sodur. Had he winked?

The housekeeper stationed them in expansive suites with plush carpets and velvet coverlets. She ordered baths to be brought for both women, as well as a tray of snacks and mulled wine.

"You'll want something to tide you over until dinner," she said.

"I doubt I'd have merited such treatment if I hadn't tagged along with you," Felias said when the housekeeper had left. She scooped up a slice of potato that had been topped with cheese and bacon. "Mmmm. This is heavenly. I wonder what she sent up to Sodur and Lume?"

Reisil nibbled on the snacks as she nursed Hilis. Afterwards, she build a nest for him on the bed, leaving Saljane to watch while she bathed.

When they entered the dining room, they were met with cheers and applause. They were ushered in with eager hands and settled in comfortably. Many eyed the corners and empty spaces with suspicion, but Sodur and Lume were absent. Reisil wondered where they'd gone off to. But then, Sodur had lived much of his life in Koduteel. No doubt he had visits to make. She smiled and sipped her wine. She hoped his unsuspecting hosts had strong hearts.

The night passed in a pleasant blur. This was what Reisil had dreamed of when she'd first come to Koduteel. She'd dreamed of having a family. But then Sodur had poisoned them against her. She glanced down at her son sleeping in her arms. Sodur had done what he thought was best. And in the end, now that Kodu Riik was safe, who was to say he hadn't done right?

The next day she spent fielding all sorts of inquiries. The other *ahalad-kaaslane* came to her for advice, for direction. They wanted to know what to do. Some had been bonded since the Battle of Mysane Kosk. They were uncertain of what to do and how to do it. Many were frightened by their newly discovered magical talents. Reisil found herself being pushed into the role of their leader.

~It won't stop, you know. Sodur told her. *They trust you. They believe in you. Even the old ones.*

~The ahalad-kaaslane aren't supposed to be led by anyone, Reisil protested. *They are supposed to be independent.*

"Someone has always led. If only by example. And they are right. They need you. Better get used to it."

Three days before the coronation and wedding, Reisil tucked Hilis into his sling, lifted Saljane up on her shoulder, and wandered out into the city. She found herself stopping to heal someone, to lend a magical help in building a wall, or settle an argument between neighbors. Everywhere she was welcomed. Everywhere people wore a bit of green. There was an air of jauntiness and celebration in the air. They adored Emelovi, and they oddly didn't seem to resent the fact that Kebonsat was Patversemese.

"They're in love, doncha know," one plump old baker woman told Reisil, passing her a crumb cake. "They say he nearly killed himself protecting her.

That's the kind of man who should sit at our Emelovi's side. That's the kind of man Kodu Riik needs.''

Reisil only smiled. She was happy for Kebonsat. He deserved this happiness. So did Emelovi. They had fought hard to find each other. For a moment Reisil returned to the day they'd saved Kodu Riik. By the time she and Juhrnus had walked to the stockades, the battle was nearly over. The Regent's army had been decimated—Reisil still couldn't think of him as Iisand. Between the *nokulas*, the fire, and the hail of arrows from the walls, the invading army had had little chance. They'd been slaughtered. Reisil regretted that. Many had been good men. She sighed. There was no profit in regrets.

It had been hours before anyone had found Emelovi. Even now Reisil believed she'd held Kebonsat to this world by sheer will. And love. He'd lived for her because she asked him to. And not even death would make him fail her again. Reisil had healed the terrible wound in his back, and he and Emelovi had been inseparable ever since. The baker woman was right: Together, Emelovi and Kebonsat would be very good for Kodu Riik.

Reisil found herself wandering down to the salt quarter and out the Sea Gate. She walked out to the bluff and up the icy steps of the lighthouse she had once called home. She stood out on the deck, enjoying the spray of the ocean. Thanks to her wards, neither the cold nor the wet bothered her. After a while, she grew tired and went inside. The furniture Juhrnus and Sodur had hauled up for her remained. There was still a pile of firewood by the fireplace. Reisil stacked it on the hearth and lit it with a touch of her finger. It crackled merrily.

She settled Saljane on the back of a chair and nursed Hilis. He fell asleep and she wrapped him in her cloak and settled him down near the fire. She wandered around the room, feeling edgy and restless.

She sat down on the bed, remembering the night

she'd found Metyein wounded in it. She wiped away the tears that rose at his memory. They'd buried him at Honor. The next day Soka had disappeared. No one had heard from him since. He and Metyein had been close, like brothers. He needed time to lick his wounds and heal.

Nurema had died too. And the three young Whieche. And Tapit. It saved her the trouble of killing him herself. Like the other wizards of the stronghold, he was vermin and needed eradicating. And at least he'd done something good with his life before he died, despite himself.

The Regent had been found mutilated. No one knew who had done it to him. Reisil suspected it had something to do with Metyein, but no one said. His body had been tossed unceremoniously onto the pyres. He was better off forgotten. Lord Marshal Vare had declared that he would retire after the coronation and wedding. He was done with war. He wanted to go home.

Reisil found those memories too dark to bear. She stood and resumed her pacing. So much death. So much change. The problem was, she didn't really know what she wanted to do with herself. She knew she needed to stay in Koduteel and mentor the young *ahalad-kaaslane*. But she couldn't seem to want to settle down in one spot. Restlessness drove her. Like she was searching for something. Something she couldn't have. Not in this world. Not even in Cemanahuatl.

Silent tears ran down her cheeks. She hadn't let herself think about Yohuac, or mourn for him. She'd lost him a year ago, but today he would die. A year ago he'd stood on top of the Temple of the Sun in Tizalan and been chosen *Ilhuicatl*'s Son. And today, he would be sacrificed. The Sun Priest would cut open his chest and take out his heart.

Reisil slid down the wall, burying her head in her knees. When the storm of weeping had passed, she opened the pouch Glerona had given her and ate. There was cold meat and bread slathered with honey-butter, and a flask of milk. Reisil smiled. Glerona was determined that Reisil should gain weight and pestered her constantly about eating.

Tiredness began to weigh on her, and Reisil retrieved Hilis, wrapping them both in her cloak and lying on the bed, pillowing her head on her arm.

When she woke, it was dark. The coals of the fire gleamed red. Her eyes were gritty and her mouth dry and sticky. Hilis wriggled and began to cry.

"In a moment, little man. Let me stir up the fire and see if I can find a candle."

She piled more wood in the hearth and set it alight. On the corner of a shelf, she found a candle. She lit it and went to pick up Hilis.

Shock glued her feet to the floor. She dropped the candle and it rolled away. Now only the light of the fire lit the room.

"This is a dream," she said.

The man standing by the window walked slowly forward, as if afraid to frighten her.

"It's not a dream," Yohuac said softly. His eyes were molten gold, just like his son's. His skin glowed faintly. He lifted a hand to brush his knuckles against her cheek, but stopped before he touched her.

"You're dead. They were going to sacrifice you today."

Yohuac smiled lopsidedly. "They did."

"Then . . . how? Are you even real?" she whispered, her fingers lacing together as she stepped back.

He shrugged, his expression wary. "Yes and no. I am not what I was."

He held out his hand. Reisil slowly reached out to take it. Her hand closed on heat. There was no feel of flesh. But neither was he shadow. It was akin to holding the moon *rinda*.

She frowned, looking questioningly at him.

"When the sacrifice was complete, *Ilhuicatl* called me to his throne. I was to stand by his side through eternity, like his chosen sons who have come before. But I could find no joy in that. He saw my unhappiness and asked why I grieved. I told him I longed to come home. To you. He was not surprised. He said the strings that bound us together in life had not severed with my death. They remained as strong as ever."

The mention of the word *strings* triggered a memory for Reisil. Of dreaming in Atli Cihua, of listening to the gods speak in the dark. What had they said? *Strings on her soul.* One binding her to Saljane, the other to Yohuac—in life, and in death.

"*Ilhuicatl* granted me my desire, as a reward for saving Cemanahuatl. But he could not bring me back; he could not make me whole. I am no longer a man. This is all I am, all I ever will be. It is the best I can offer you. It is not what you deserve. I will go if you choose." His voice went hoarse with the last.

Reisil stared, chewing her lips. He sounded so normal, so alive. Just like himself. But he was dead. A ghost. Or something like it. Did she still want him this way? But she already knew the answer. Not a night went by that her dreams weren't haunted by his face, when she didn't wake up with his name on her lips. Since losing him, she had come to feel like a ghost herself, only half-alive.

He was watching her. Reisil stepped forward, pressing her hand to his chest, allowing herself to believe at last. There was no heartbeat. Only the fire of power and spirit. It was enough. It was more than she dreamed.

"Welcome home."

One woman's choice will save a kingdom.

PATH OF FATE

by
DIANA PHARAOH FRANCIS

In the land of Kodu Riik, it is an honor to be selected by the Lady to become an ahalad-kaaslane—to have your soul bonded with one of Her blessed animals, and roam the land serving Her will. But Riesil refuses to bow to fate—a decision that may have repercussions across the realm.

"[FRANCIS] SWEPT ME AWAY WITH HER MASTERFUL FEEL FOR THE NATURAL WORLD."
—CAROL BERG

"A STUBBORN, LIKEABLE HEROINE."
—KRISTEN BRITAIN

0-451-45950-4

Available wherever books are sold or at
penguin.com

r013

The stunning sequel to *Path of Fate*

PATH OF HONOR

by

DIANA PHARAOH FRANCIS

A year has passed since Reisil's arrival in Koduteel, and her hopes of a happy life in her rightful home are being dashed. Kodu Riik is decimated by plague, famine, and war, and its enemies are beginning to move. And Reisil's power to heal has been lost, replaced with a surging new ability—to destroy.

"A STUBBORN, LIKABLE HEROINE THRUST INTO EVENTS FRAUGHT WITH DANGER, WIZARDS, AND GODS. I LOOK FORWARD TO MORE OF THE ADVENTURES OF REISIL."
—KRISTEN BRITAIN

0-451-45991-1

Available wherever books are sold or at penguin.com